IN CHAMBERS

CONSTITUTIONALISM AND DEMOCRACY

Gregg Ivers and Kevin T. McGuire, Editors

IN

Stories of Supreme Court
Law Clerks and Their Justices

CHAMBERS

Edited by Todd C. Peppers and Artemus Ward

University of Virginia Press | Charlottesville and London

University of Virginia Press

© 2012 by the Rector and Visitors of the University of Virginia

All rights reserved

Printed in the United States of America on acid-free paper

First published 2012

9 8 7 6 5 4 3 2

Library of Congress Cataloging-in-Publication Data

In chambers : stories of Supreme Court law clerks and their

justices / edited by Todd C. Peppers and Artemus Ward.

p. cm. — (Constitutionalism and democracy)

Includes bibliographical references and index.

ISBN 978-0-8139-3265-1 (cloth : alk. paper)

ISBN 978-0-8139-3266-8 (e-book)

   1. Judges—United States—Biography.   2. United

States. Supreme Court—Employees—Biography.

3. Law clerks—United States—Biography.   4. United

States. Supreme Court—History.   I. Peppers, Todd C.

II. Ward, Artemus, 1971–

KF8744.B44 2012

347.73'2636—dc23

[B]   2011030215

CONTENTS

PART III

The Modern Clerkship Institution

Illustrations follow page 108

CLARE CUSHMAN

Foreword

The Supreme Court operates as nine separate little law firms. Each justice has traditionally hired his or her own staff, consisting of a messenger, secretaries, and clerks. The relationship between justice and law clerk is complex, intense, and a perennial subject of fascination to the public. Young men and women not long out of law school provide an array of services that allows the justices to produce opinions that instantly become the law of the land. Without the clerks, the workload would not be manageable. How individual justices have deployed the brains, energy, and talent of their clerks is an intriguing subject that gives us a historical glimpse at how the justices have operated in chambers over the course of time.

The first law clerk, Thomas Russell, was hired by Horace Gray in 1882. A Harvard Law School graduate, he performed various tasks for the justice, including chauffeuring him to the Court. Gray paid him out of his own pocket. Congress provided funds in 1886 for a "stenographic clerk" for each justice to help copy out opinions in the days before mimeographs or photocopiers. As the justices did their work from home offices, these clerks, who were either law school graduates or professional stenographers, had little contact with the Court or each other. They also tended to stay with the justice for many years.

The modern clerkship developed in the 1920s as the justices' workload expanded. Clerks acted less as personal secretaries and takers of dictation and started being asked to do more legal research. In 1922 Congress appropriated funds allowing each justice to employ one law clerk, a perquisite that became permanent in 1924. After the Supreme Court got its own building in 1932 and the justices started working in chambers instead of at home, the clerks became more integrated into the institution. Yet they were now usually expected to stay for one only term.

For many decades clerks were selected in an ad hoc fashion. Nepotism was occasionally a factor in the nineteenth century: both William Rufus Day and John Marshall Harlan hired their sons to clerk for them. Justice Gray's half-brother, John Chipman Gray, selected the best graduates from Harvard Law School, where he taught, and sent them for one-year stints to Gray and his successor, Oliver Wendell Holmes Jr. Before being appointed to the Court in 1939, Felix Frankfurter, a distinguished Harvard Law School professor, also liked to recruit his most promising students and send them to the justices he admired. Other justices chose clerks from their own alma maters. For example, Harlan Fiske Stone, as Bennett Boskey can attest in these pages, always chose clerks from Columbia Law School. The first female clerk was hired in 1944 by William O. Douglas, who was stymied by a shortage of stellar male candidates due to the war effort.

An increasing number of petitions for certiorari—petitions asking the Supreme Court to take up a case for review—prompted the justices to hire more clerks and to delegate more responsibility to them. In 1941, they were authorized to hire two clerks apiece. Now each justice is allowed four law clerks (until the 2002 term former justice John Paul Stevens preferred only three; the chief justice gets a fifth to help with administrative tasks). Most of them have graduated at the top of their class from prestigious law schools—where a justice will often have a close relationship with the dean who preselects candidates. Justices may also seek out candidates from their home state or who have clerked for particular lower court judges whose recommendations they trust. To ease the transition to the Court, a freshman justice will sometimes hire the clerk of his predecessor to show him or her the ropes.

Despite these extra pairs of hands (and eyes and legs), in the 1960s the justices felt increasingly burdened by the rising number of petitions—now numbering in the thousands—that each chamber had to read and summarize each year. In 1972 the justices decided to collectively pool their clerks and divvy up the incoming cases. Clerks in the "cert pool" began writing summary memoranda that were shared among all the justices, who then decided in conference which cases to review that term.

What are the other key duties of a Supreme Court law clerk? Once the justices have selected a list of cases to be argued that term, it is up to the clerks to research and analyze them so they can help prepare their justices for hearing oral arguments. To accomplish this, the clerks review the lower court records, research relevant precedents, and summarize the essential information. Unlike the cert pool memoranda, these "bench memoranda" are written specifically for a clerk's own justice and are tailored to suit his or her particular interests and needs.

The next important function a clerk performs occurs in the spring, once cases have been argued. That is when the clerks assist their justices in writing opinions, be they majority, concurring, or dissenting. Clerks are deployed to help with the negotiating that goes on among chambers as a draft majority opinion circulates and undergoes revisions until at least four other justices sign on to it. According to the clerks whose memoirs make up this collection, each justice has had a unique way of using the services of the bright, extremely hard-working men and women who devote a year of their life to the Supreme Court.

Over the course of the term law clerks have usually developed intense bonds with their justices. As the following reminiscences demonstrate, clerks become a kind of extended family, meeting annually for reunions and serving as a support network for the justices long after their clerkships have ended. This intimacy is particularly strong with justices who enjoyed engaging with their clerks in extrajudicial activities. For example, Justice Hugo Black liked to recruit tennis players, John Marshall Harlan II preferred golfers, and Sandra Day O'Connor took her clerks whitewater rafting.

In the pages that follow, Todd Peppers and Artemus Ward have assembled a fascinating collection of firsthand accounts that illuminate how work has been accomplished in chambers under the auspices of different justices. Because each member of the Court has displayed a distinctive approach to tackling the workload, these memoirs are valuable to understanding the modus operandi of individual justices. From a historical perspective, these accounts also provide useful snapshots of the work of a Supreme Court justice at different periods in the Court's history and illustrate how the nature and format of the workload have evolved over time.

IN CHAMBERS

Introduction

Approximately ten years ago, we each decided to study what we believed to be an important but misunderstood institutional practice of the United States Supreme Court, to wit, the hiring and utilization of law clerks. While law clerks had been featured prominently in a few newspaper articles and non-academic studies of the Supreme Court, much of what the legal academy knew about law clerks was limited to the practices of a few justices or to a specific time period and was based on rumor, unverifiable sources, and the puffery of former law clerks (who wanted to either burnish their justices' reputation or exaggerate their own role at the Court).[1]

We did not know each other at the time we began our separate studies of the elusive law clerk, nor were we aware of the other's choice of research topic. Convinced that we (individually) would write the definitive work that would educate future generations of Court scholars on the historic role of the law clerk at the Supreme Court, we began to feverishly read the universe of existing literature on Supreme Court law clerks, review the personal papers of former Supreme Court justices at the Library of Congress, and interview past and present law clerks. Ironically, these two completely separate research projects crossed the finish line at virtually the same time, with Ward's book (*Sorcerers' Apprentices,* coauthored with David L. Weiden) being published two weeks before Peppers's (*Courtiers of the Marble Palace*).[2]

While the two books diverged slightly in the range of topics discussed, both provided a theoretical framework by which to understand the evolution of the formal and informal rules and norms that governed the hiring and utilization of Supreme Court law clerks. Additionally, both books addressed the question of whether law clerks wield inappropriate levels of influence over judicial decision making (Peppers was a bit more tentative in his finding of undue influence than was Ward).[3] All in all, the books offered the reader a comprehensive picture of the various roles that law clerks have played over the last 125 years at the Court and theoretical lenses through which to understand the evolution of the clerkship institution.

In the months after the publication of the two books, we continued to research and lecture on law clerks. We chatted about working on a joint project that would further our understanding of the law clerk institution. Since completing *Courtiers of the Marble Palace*, Peppers started publishing a series of articles in the *Journal of Supreme Court History* that took a closer look at the personal bonds that formed between law clerks and their justices. We were enthusiastic about these articles and agreed that there were some remarkable stories left to tell about this less-known aspect of the clerkship institution.

In point of fact, much of the feedback we received since our books were published pointed us in this direction. As noted above, our individual books focused on the rules and norms governing the hiring and utilization of law clerks. As part of that story, we spent some time discussing individual justices and their unique relationships with their clerks—but our focus was on institutional development, and we necessarily underemphasized personal relationships. Yet it was the tales we told about individuals—both justices and clerks—that most intrigued and captivated our readers.

While we eagerly embraced a new project that highlighted the personal side of the clerkship institution, we quickly appreciated that we could not analyze individual justices and clerks without an eye toward the larger institutional working relationship. By emphasizing the personal, we hope that these essays will build on our earlier works and help us understand how the private bonds between selected justices and clerks impact the clerkship institution and the Supreme Court in general. The influence of a Supreme Court law clerk does not turn solely on the job duties assigned, but on the trust placed in that clerk by the justice; alternatively, whether a law clerk follows a justice's instructions turns, in part, on a sense of loyalty and duty. And the justices' maturation process, their changing jurisprudential and political attitudes, and the degree to which they rely on clerks are affected by the relationships they form with their law clerks. Thus the private and the professional are two sides of the same coin, and both give us invaluable insight into how the Supreme Court operates.

Throughout *In Chambers: Stories of Supreme Court Law Clerks and Their Justices*, we have endeavored to pull back the thick red curtains that hang behind the Supreme Court bench and provide a rare glimpse of the bonds—some positive and enduring, some negative and fleeting—that form between justices and clerks as well as the institutional rules and norms that define these relationships. Our essayists are former law clerks, judicial biographers, practicing attorneys, and political scientists. We have asked our contributors to go beyond the standard "warm and fuzzy" tribute pieces that have routinely appeared in law reviews and instead provide a more critical—and hopefully more balanced and objective—picture of the clerkship experience.

The book consists almost exclusively of new, unpublished essays on important justices and clerks. However, a few previously published articles are also included, as we feel that these already excellent, and arguably "hidden," pieces will take on new life in a structured, edited volume. In general, this volume provides single essays on individual justices and their relationship with their clerks. Our goal was to have more depth than breadth. Instead of attempting to be comprehensive in terms of including every justice or even most justices—which would necessarily lead to an unwieldy volume, relatively short essays, or both—we selected a smaller number of justices so that each author could go into greater detail about the justice-clerk relationship. And because we include a range of justices over the life of the clerkship institution, readers will be able to get a comprehensive view of how the role of clerks has changed over time.

In some instances we deviate from our general structure of one essay per justice and include additional essays from a clerk who had a unique relationship with his or her justice (such as Professor Charles Reich's essay on living and working with Hugo Black) or essays on individual clerks because of their importance to the development of the institution (for example, the essays on the first female law clerk, Lucile Lomen, and the first black law clerk, William T. Coleman Jr.). While many of the essays cast the clerkship experience in a positive light, not all law clerks found a mentor and lifelong friend in their particular justice. Nowhere are the negative aspects of a clerkship more keenly described than in essays by Dr. Bruce Allen Murphy, who analyzes the tumultuous relationship between William O. Douglas and his clerks, and by Dr. Craig Smith, who chronicles the tensions and difficulties of clerking for Charles Evans Whittaker.

We readily concede that our collection of essays are time bound. The only essays that feature justices who have served on the Supreme Court in the last ten years are Ward's essay on Chief Justice William H. Rehnquist and his clerks and Peppers's piece on Justice Ruth Bader Ginsburg and her clerks. Simply put, it is nearly impossible to coax either sitting justices or their clerks to talk about the clerkship institution; most of the present justices are disinterested in (or perhaps wary of) discussing their staffing practices, and the former law clerks themselves feel constrained by confidentiality concerns.

In short, we hope that this volume will help fill a gap in Supreme Court studies generally and research on law clerks specifically. While there are numerous empirical studies of the Court, many of them important and widely read, there are very few that provide the kind of "thick description" or narrative format that delves more deeply into the institution and its actors. To be sure, traditional judicial biographies are steadily produced. But these more historical or qualitative narratives focus on one justice at the expense of their colleagues and the institution as a whole. This book helps to fill a niche between the empirical and biographical approaches by analyzing multiple justices and their clerks over time. In this sense, the essays demonstrate how the Court, and specifically a Supreme Court clerkship, has been fundamentally transformed. By delving into the personal as well as the working relationships between justices and clerks, the volume paints a highly readable and accessible portrait of the institution that we hope will be of interest to both scholars and lay readers alike.

In order to assist the reader in placing the essays about individual justices and their law clerks in the appropriate historical and institutional context, a brief tutorial on the history of the clerkship institution is necessary. We begin by charting how the clerkship institution developed. We then turn to how clerks have been selected and detail how their job duties have dramatically expanded over time. No longer simply the personal assistants of the justices, "modern" law clerks have become the engine without which the Court could not function. They review certiorari petitions, write bench memoranda, make recommendations on pending cases, draft opinions, and negotiate across chambers, and we briefly discuss the clerks' role in each of these processes. Finally we say a word about the secrecy surrounding clerk-justice interactions and how the contributions in this volume shed new light on what is largely a hidden relationship.

Historical Development

Throughout their early history, Supreme Court justices were assisted by a small number of support personnel—including the clerk of the Supreme Court, the official court reporter, the marshal of the Court, and personal messengers. The Court's workload grew dramatically in the decades following the Civil War, however, and by the 1880s the justices were begging Congress for money to hire judicial assistants. One justice, however, didn't wait for Congress to act. When he began his tenure on the U.S. Supreme Court in 1882, Justice Horace Gray started the practice of employing law clerks by hiring Harvard Law School graduate Thomas Russell and paying his young assistant out of his own pocket.

Gray first hired clerks in his previous position as chief judge of the Massachusetts Supreme Judicial Court from 1873 to 1882 (one of his law clerks on the state court was future Supreme Court justice Louis D. Brandeis), and he simply continued the employment practice upon his elevation to the Supreme Court. Gray's half-brother, Harvard Law School Professor John Chipman Gray, selected the law students—thus beginning the dual traditions of the justices (1) relying on a few elite law schools for talented law clerks, and (2) depending on law professors and deans to make the selections.

In 1886 Congress authorized funds for the hiring of a "stenographic clerk" for each of the justices, and soon all nine justices had hired clerks. In the first decades of the clerkship institution, the justices varied in the types of substantive and nonsubstantive job duties assigned to the clerks; some assistants performed legal research, while others were literally stenographers. Moreover, the tenure of the clerkship varied in these early years. Though Gray's clerks served for only one or two years, some justices employed long-term clerks. For example, Frederick J. Haig clerked for Justice David J. Brewer from 1893 to 1909, while Detroit College of Law graduate S. Edward Widdifield clerked for four different justices over a span of twenty-one years. Long-serving clerks were relatively rare, however, and the single-term clerkships—before departing for positions in academia, government, and private practice—soon became the norm.

Though clerkships were born out—at least in part—of the apprentice model of legal education, the expansion of clerks at all levels of courts has largely been due to workload pressures: as courts have handled a greater number of cases, the numbers of both judges and clerks have expanded over time. Yet their responsibilities have not always developed purely as a result of workload, and seemingly nonrelated institutional changes in the way that courts conduct their business have given rise to increasing clerk responsibility and influence. Within fifty years the position had evolved into what we recognize as the modern law clerk, and today each associate Supreme Court justice is permitted to hire four clerks (the chief justice can hire five clerks) to assist with the Court's voluminous work.

Selection of Law Clerks

As a general rule, the most desirable and prestigious clerkships have been held by the top graduates of such elite law schools as Harvard, Yale, Chicago, Columbia, Stanford, Virginia, and Michigan. Historically, clerkships have been the province of white males from upper socioeconomic classes. Yet women and minorities have made inroads into this institution, just as they have increasingly populated law schools and the legal profession as a whole. Lucile Lomen was the first female law clerk to serve at the Supreme Court, working for Justice William O. Douglas in 1944. Yet it was not until two decades later that another female clerk was selected, when Margaret Corcoran was picked by Justice Hugo Black in 1966. The number of female law clerks started to slowly increase in the 1970s and 1980s, and today women routinely comprise 40 percent of the High Court's clerking corps. African Americans and other minorities have also had some success at obtaining clerkships, beginning with William T. Coleman Jr.'s selection by Justice Felix Frankfurter in 1948. Still, fifty years later there had been a total of fewer than two dozen African American Supreme Court law clerks.

In the 1940s and 1950s, it was rare for a Supreme Court law clerk to have previous clerkship experience. Today it is a de facto job requirement, and clerks spend one year clerking at the U.S. Court of Appeals for a handful of judges (so-called feeder-court judges) who routinely place their clerks at the high court. For example, Court of Appeals Judges J. Michael Luttig, Laurence Silverman, and James Skelly Wright have placed over thirty of their clerks with Supreme Court justices. Social scientists have argued that the justices rely on these feeder-court judges not merely as a source of experienced clerks but also as a means of providing law clerks who are ideologically compatible with the individual justices.[4]

Agenda Setting

Initially, Supreme Court law clerks only studied and briefed the petitions for certiorari that came to the Court as a way of learning the law. The exercise rarely if ever helped their justices, who met in regular private conferences with each other to discuss each petition.

As the number of petitions grew, Chief Justice Charles Evans Hughes decided to end the practice of the justices discussing each petition. Instead, it was up to the individual justices to decide for themselves which cases should be formally considered in the justices' conference. As a result, more and more justices began turning to their clerks for help in analyzing the petitions and asked for their recommendations of whether each case ought to be heard by the Supreme Court.

In the early 1970s, a number of the justices decided to pool their clerks to reduce what they felt was a duplication of effort. Prior to the creation of the "cert pool" each of the nine justices had one of their clerks write a memo on each case. Today, every justice—save Samuel Alito—is a member of the cert pool. The eight justices in the cert pool share the pool memo written by one of the clerks from the eight different justices, thereby reducing duplicated effort and freeing up clerks for other work (namely, opinion writing).

The cert pool has generated a fair amount of controversy, with critics suggesting that it has led to greater clerk influence.[5] Overall, 90 percent of clerks told Ward and Weiden that they were able to change their justices' mind. Specifically, of those who were able to change their justices' minds, 38 percent of past clerks said that it was in the decision whether or not to grant a case compared with 32 percent on opinion content, 22 percent on opinion style, and 4 percent on case outcome. Over time, clerks have been more likely to agree with their justices on whether particular cases should or should not be granted. This increase is likely due to the fact that modern clerks personally review fewer petitions than their predecessors—particularly before the cert pool was created and expanded.[6]

Decision Making

Clerks make recommendations and even attempt to change their justices' minds in a number of ways. Ward and Weiden asked clerks how frequently they were able to change their justices' minds about particular cases or issues before the Court.[7] Twenty-five percent of former Supreme Court clerks answered that they were "sometimes" able to do so, with more recent clerks responding that they were able to change their justices' minds more often than claimed clerks from the past. When asked to name the most likely occurrence of changing their justices' minds, 29 percent of past clerks said that it was in the legal or substantive content of an opinion while 20 percent said that it was in an opinion's stylistic content. Only 3 percent said that it was in the outcome of the case, that is, who wins and who loses. Therefore, while clerks may have relatively minimal influence on decisions on the merits, they have far more of an effect on the other decisions that justices routinely make.

An almost completely hidden yet crucial part of the clerks' job is the ambassadorial role played out through the clerk network: the informal process of information gathering, lobbying, and negotiation that goes on among clerks from different justices. Prior to the creation of the Supreme Court building in 1935, every Supreme Court clerk worked at the home of their justices and rarely if ever saw the other clerks. By the time all of the justices and their staffs moved into their own suite of offices at the new building in 1941, the clerks knew each other, routinely lunched together, and began discussing the cases on which they were working. The justices quickly recognized that the clerk network could be used to gain information on what was happening in other chambers, which in turn helped them make decisions and form coalitions.

The justices became so reliant on the clerk network that they eventually established a separate, enclosed eating space in the Court cafeteria reserved specifically for the clerks so that they could speak with each other undisturbed and without fear of eavesdropping tourists, attorneys, and members of the press corps. For example, a memo to Justice Blackmun from one of his clerks demonstrates how important the clerk network is to the decision-making process: "Last week . . . the Chief circulated a memo to Justice White. . . . This is sure to stir up trouble. . . . Justice O'Connor has sent Justice White a memo asking for several changes [to the opinion] . . . According to [O'Connor's clerk] . . . Justice O'Connor is still inclined to wait and has no plans to join [the opinion] anytime soon. . . . I understand from Justice White's clerk that Justice White has no intention of removing the references . . . in his [opinion] draft. . . . I will keep you posted."[8]

Opinion Writing

Perhaps the most controversial part of a clerk's job is drafting the opinions that are issued in the names of their justices. As with the agenda-setting process, initially Supreme Court clerks drafted the occasional opinion as an exercise in learning the law. Justices rarely if ever used any of these clerk-written drafts in their own work. Early clerks, however, did conduct legal research, edit draft opinions, and complete footnotes. Today, it is rare for justices to draft their own opinions and routine for clerks to write the initial opinion draft.

One cause of this dramatic change was arguably the decision by Chief Justice Fred Vinson, later continued by Chief Justice Earl Warren and all subsequent chief justices, of distributing opinion writing evenly among all nine justices. Prior to Vinson's 1950 shift to opinion equalization, opinions were assigned according to the speed at which they were completed. Therefore, speedy writers such as Justices William O. Douglas and Hugo Black wrote far more opinions of the Court than did their more deliberate colleagues such as Felix Frankfurter and Frank Murphy. When Vinson and later Warren practiced the equality principle in assigning opinions, the slower writers were forced to rely on their clerks to keep up the pace. Over time, a norm of clerk-written opinions developed, which continues to this day.

Though practices can vary from one justice to another, evidence shows that some justices routinely issue opinions wholly written by their clerks with little or no changes. When Ward and Weiden surveyed former clerks and asked how often their justices revised or modified their draft opinions, 70 percent said that their justices did in all cases. However, 30 percent of clerks responded that they had their drafts issued without modification at least some of the time.[9]

To be sure, clerks cannot write whatever they please, and justices generally provide direction and carefully read, edit, and rewrite the drafts written by their clerks. Still, judicial opinions are far different from speeches or op-ed pieces that are regularly ghostwritten for public officials. In the law, word choices and phrases are often crucial, so that a seemingly harmless phrase such as "exceedingly persuasive justification" can be placed into an opinion by a clerk at one time and years later become a crucial test in sex discrimination law. Furthermore, the more that it is understood that clerks are doing the drafting, the greater the possibility exists that the words and phrases used will lose authority with litigators, lower court judges, and government officials responsible for implementing the decisions.

Secrecy

Given the weighty responsibilities that clerks have taken on, one might not be surprised at the lengths to which they go to remain in the shadows of their justices' robes. Unlike their counterparts in the White House and on Capitol Hill, the selection and utilization of law clerks is a topic that current and retired Supreme Court justices are generally loath to discuss. No longer do modern justices follow the practice of such eminent jurists as Oliver Wendell Holmes Jr., who stood at his grandfather's writing desk and drafted his opinions in longhand while puffing on a cigar, or Louis D. Brandeis, who refused to permit his law clerks to prepare memoranda on cert petitions or cases set for oral argument because, as former Brandeis law clerk Dean Acheson once explained, the justice wanted to present the parties before the Supreme Court "with a judicial mind unscratched by the scribblings of clerks." As detailed above, today's justices routinely require their clerks to do a substantial amount of judicial work.

Not only is the Supreme Court reluctant to discuss the heavy responsibilities imposed on their clerks, but the Court has consistently denied the public access to the written code of conduct governing the behavior of its clerks.

Titled the *Code of Conduct for Law Clerks of the Supreme Court of the United States,* it dictates that the law clerk owes both the individual justice and the Court "complete confidentiality, accuracy, and loyalty." The *Code of Conduct* applies from the start of the clerkship and is intended to survive after the clerkship is completed. Law clerks are required to sign the code. If a law clerk violates the code, the range of punishments includes termination.

Many justices and law clerks have interpreted the *Code of Conduct* to apply not only to discussions about specific cases and issues of constitutional law but also to the very job duties and responsibilities given to the law clerks; in other words, current and former law clerks are forbidden to reveal whether they prepared the first draft of opinions or recommended that cert petitions be granted or denied. If we assume that this is a correct interpretation of the *Code of Conduct,* then we believe that such a lack of transparency is problematic, and that the refusal of the Supreme Court to release a copy of a conduct of ethical behavior applicable to public servants is frankly mystifying.

Perhaps no example is more instructive of both the increasing institutionalization of the clerkship institution and the related issue of secrecy than the 1994 proposal by Jack Mason (Rehnquist, October term 1975) and Bill D'Zurilla (White, October term 1982) to establish a formal alumni "Association of Supreme Court Law Clerks" (see Appendix A). Mason and D'Zurilla surveyed former clerks at a cocktail party of the annual meeting of the American Bar Association in New Orleans and sent a copy of the proposal to Chief Justice Rehnquist. While exploratory, the proposed organization would hold annual meetings, publish a newsletter with all manner of Court happenings including employment listings, compile a directory of former clerks, and offer education and public outreach. In response to the solicitation, Lowell Gordon Harriss (Rehnquist, October term 1972) expressed his support but also added this concern:

> Although I commend many of your ideas concerning what the activities of such an association might be, I believe one of the major, if indeed the major issue, not directly addressed in your distribution is the extent to which members of such an association could or would be encouraged to share experiences, war stories, insights, and evaluations to which they were privy or at which they arrived, and if so with whom. I believe that the implicit oath of confidentiality—whether derived from respect for the particular justice for whom one clerked, the institution, or the legal process—would be seriously tested, and perhaps implicitly unobserved on occasion, in some of the activities you referred to in your

communication. This development would, I believe, be a serious step in a new and uncertain direction. For example, during the O.T. '72 I tried to keep a running diary of some of the matters which I was privileged to witness. I have never shown it to or discussed those matters with anyone; I do not know if I ever will, but I certainly would not even think of doing so until long, long after WHR has left the Court. This is not limited to WHR and the respect and feelings which evolved over that Term; he is the only Justice currently sitting who was a Justice then. If he were no longer on the Court but others from that Term were, I believe I would apply the same test.

I raise these issues directly because, although I agree that such an association could have benefits for the members and others, there has to be some discussion of ground rules both among those who are involved in organizing such an endeavor and with, I respectfully submit, input from the current membership of the Court as well as retired Justices. Absent some such discussion of ground rules, or taboos, I fear that the creation of such an organization would inexorably lead to the impulse "to disclose" (whether phrased in that manner or as "to discuss" history, process, legal evolution, or even "characters I've met"). This impulse will, I fear, be more likely to surface from a member of an "organization" or an "association" (perhaps for a variety of motives and perhaps even with the purest of hearts) than from an "unorganized" or "unassociated" individual. Such impulses could have individual and institutional consequences that are not fully discernible now. It is one thing to have an occasional article by a clerk for Hand or Frankfurter, discussing matters a half century old, and another to establish an organization (hopefully not located in D.C.) of former Supreme Court clerks, including those who participated in the most recent or "newsworthy" decisions. The types of questions raised by the "publication" of Justice Marshall's (Thurgood) papers surely would surface.[10]

Harriss sent a copy of his reply to Rehnquist with a covering note: "My concern, expressed in the letter, is that once one establishes an institution, then that institution begins to have institutional objectives. Indeed, Washington, D.C. is Exhibit A in the proof of that proposition. My gut tells me that, over time, an institution such as Jack proposes will probably develop goals not perfectly aligned with those of the institution of the Supreme Court."[11] Rehnquist replied: "Until I received your letter . . . I had not realized that there was an effort under way to form an association of former law clerks. I think I share some of your reservations about the idea, but don't plan to volunteer any observations unless they are requested."[12] While it is impossible to say whether concerns over confidentiality served to sink the proposed alumni association, this episode makes plain that the clerkship institution is an important one that carries not only great responsibility but also increasing concern over secrecy.

Justice Thurgood Marshall famously told a law clerk who suggested a change in a draft opinion that "you're missing two things. . . . Nomination by the President and confirmation by the Senate." In other words, law clerks who wield influence over the decision-making process—as well as the crafting of constitutional doctrine used to reach a result predetermined by a justice—impermissibly encroach on the judicial power granted to the justices under Article III of the Constitution. If, however, clerks do not influence judicial decision making, then why all the fuss and secrecy over the job duties of law clerks? If the justices do not heavily depend on their clerks, then why did Justice Antonin Scalia recently make headlines when he told an American University law student that he selected his clerks from only the top law schools because "[t]hey admit the best and the brightest, and they may not teach very well, but you can't make a sow's ear out of a silk purse."[13] Such unnecessary secrecy, not to mention paradoxical statements about law clerks, can only erode the public's confidence in its government institutions.

Justice Brandeis once observed that "[t]he reason why the public thinks so much of the Justices is that they are almost the only people in Washington who do their own work." What this book plainly demonstrates is that while this was arguably once true, it is not the case today. Yet given the general silence that results from the law clerk *Code of Conduct,* the largely reputation-crafting approach to the few clerks who have previously spoken out, and the complicity of Congress during confirmation hearings in failing to ask pointed questions about law clerks, it is no surprise that the myth of justices doing their own work continues to persist. While it is likely that the myth helps strengthen the Court's legitimacy in the eyes of the public, we submit that there is a need for more scrutiny of the clerkship institution and clerk-justice relationships.

Conclusion

In all, the law clerk institution has undergone dramatic transformations over time. What began as an apprenticeship in learning the law has become a crucial part of the judicial process. Clerkships are highly competitive, coveted positions that lead to prestigious careers in academia, government, and private law fields. As the responsibility and influence of clerks has grown over time, a concomitant danger of unelected, unaccountable clerks overstepping their bounds has also escalated. For the first hundred years of the Supreme Court, there were only nine justices conducting the Court's business. In the one hundred years since, the justices have added three dozen clerks and ceded much of the Court's work to them.

Our hope is that these essays, taken as a whole, will provide a heretofore unseen glimpse into the hidden world of the Supreme Court law clerk. Simply put, a Supreme Court clerkship is more than a fabulous legal apprenticeship. And it is more than the ultimate "golden ticket" that guarantees a position in a top law firm, on the faculty of an elite law school, or in the upper echelons of the federal government. A Supreme Court clerkship offers the rare opportunity to form lifelong relationships with arguably the most cloistered, most colorful (with some exceptions), and brightest members of our government. In short, to borrow a phrase from federal appeals court judge Patricia M. Wald, a judge-clerk relationship is "the most intense and mutually dependent one I know of outside of marriage, parenthood, or a love affair."[14] But with these "intense and mutually dependent" relationships come substantive job duties and responsibilities, powers that raise concerns about political legitimacy and undue influence. Because of this institutional change, it has become increasingly important, not only for the justices and clerks themselves, but also for social scientists and legal scholars to ask whether "apprentices" and "courtiers" have been tempted to put on the robes of the master and try their hand at legal sorcery. The answer to this question has profound implications for the legitimacy of the judicial process.

Notes

1. In the late 1990s, journalist Tony Mauro triggered a firestorm of controversy with a series of articles discussing the lack of diversity among law clerks. See Tony Mauro, "Corps of Clerks Lacking in Diversity," *USA Today*, March 13, 1998; "Only 1 New High Court Clerk Is a Minority," *USA Today*, September 10, 1998. Prior to the Mauro pieces, it had been almost forty years since the popular press had fixated on law clerks. This earlier controversy was started when former law clerk William H. Rehnquist publically suggested that liberal law clerks were influencing the types of cases being heard by the Supreme Court. See William H. Rehnquist, "Who Writes the Decisions of the Supreme Court," *U.S. News and World Report*, December 13, 1957; Alexander M. Bickel, "The Court: An Indictment Analyzed," *New York Times*,

April 27, 1958; William D. Rogers, "Do Law Clerks Wield Power in Supreme Court Cases?" *U.S. News and World Report,* February 21, 1958; William H. Rehnquist, "Another View: Clerks Might 'Influence' Some Actions," *U.S. News and World Report,* February 21, 1958. Non-academic studies include Edward Lazarus, *Closed Chambers: The First Eyewitness Account of the Epic Struggles inside the Supreme Court* (New York: Times Books, 1998); Bob Woodward and Scott Armstrong, *The Brethren: Inside the Supreme Court* (New York: Simon and Schuster, 1979). One of the few purely academic articles on Supreme Court law clerks was an older piece written by political scientist Chester A. Newland. See "Personal Assistants to Supreme Court Justices: The Law Clerks," *Oregon Law Review* 40, no. 4 (June 1961): 299–317.

2. Artemus Ward and David L. Weiden, *Sorcerers' Apprentices: 100 Years of Law Clerks at the Supreme Court* (New York: New York University Press, 2006); Todd C. Peppers, *Courtiers of the Marble Palace: The Rise and Influence of the Supreme Court Law Clerk* (Stanford, Calif.: Stanford University Press, 2006).

3. Peppers was skeptical that law clerks wielded substantive influence when he wrote *Courtiers of the Marble Palace.* Since then, his views have changed slightly. See Todd C. Peppers and Christopher Zorn, "Law Clerk Influence on Supreme Court Decision Making: An Empirical Analysis," *DePaul University Law Review* 57, no. 1 (2008): 51–77.

4. William E. Nelson, Harvey Rishikof, I. Scott Messinger, and Michael Jo, "The Liberal Tradition of the Supreme Court Clerkship: Its Rise, Fall, and Reincarnation?," *Vanderbilt Law Review* 62, no. 6 (2009): 1749–1814; Corey A. Ditslear and Lawrence Baum, "Selection of Law Clerks and Polarization in the U.S. Supreme Court," *Journal of Politics* 63, no. 3 (2001): 869–85.

5. See, e.g., Rehnquist, "Another View"; Lazarus, *Closed Chambers.*

6. Ward and Weiden, *Sorcerers' Apprentices,* 109–49.

7. Ibid., 187–89.

8. *United States v. Fordice,* 505 U.S. 717 (1992); Andrea Ward to Harry A. Blackmun, March 23, 1992, Blackmun Papers, Box 590.

9. Ward and Weiden, *Sorcerers' Apprentices,* 225.

10. Lowell Gordon Harriss to Jack Mason, November 14, 1994, Rehnquist Papers, Box 144.

11. Lowell Gordon Harriss to William H. Rehnquist, November 14, 1994, Rehnquist Papers, Box 144.

12. William H. Rehnquist to Lowell Gordon Harriss, November 18, 1994, Rehnquist Papers, Box 144.

13. Debra Cassens Weiss, "Justice Scalia Tells Law Student Why She Probably Won't Be His Clerk," *America Bar Association Journal,* May 12, 2009.

14. Patricia M. Wald, "Selecting Law Clerks," *University of Michigan Law Review* 89 (October 1990): 152, 153.

The Origins of the
Clerkship Institution

TODD C. PEPPERS

Birth of an Institution

Horace Gray and the Lost Law Clerks

In a vault hidden away in a downtown Boston bank rests a large silver loving cup. The cup was presented to Associate Justice Horace Gray on March 22, 1902, by his law clerks, and engraved on its tarnished surface are the names of the nineteen Harvard Law School graduates who served as Justice Gray's law clerks.[1] While the details surrounding the presentation of the cup have been lost to history, the gift was likely prompted by the failing health of Justice Gray and his future departure from the Supreme Court. The loving cup is still held by the Gray family, passing to the heirs of Professor John Chipman Gray (the famous Harvard Law School professor and half-brother of Horace Gray) upon the death of the childless Horace Gray.

The loving cup, however, is more than a mere historical curiosity, for it contains information previously unknown to students of Supreme Court history, namely, a complete list of the men who clerked for Justice Gray. While government records contain the names of Gray's later law clerks, the identity of Gray's first three clerks—Thomas Russell, William Schofield, and Henry Eldridge Warner—are not contained in Supreme Court records. The reason why Russell, Schofield, and Warner have not been previously acknowledged for their role in the creation of the clerkship institution is not due to conspiracy and cover up. Since Horace Gray personally paid the salaries of the three men, they did not receive a paycheck from the federal government, and their names were not recorded on government rolls. When the justices were authorized in 1886 to hire stenographic clerks, governmental bureaucrats began recording the names of these new judicial assistants—and thereby created the false impression that law clerks had not arrived at the Supreme Court until 1886. Given this historical confusion about the identities of the first law clerks, this loving cup is arguably the "holy grail" for Supreme Court historians who study the origins of the clerkship institution.

The main purpose of this essay is to acknowledge Horace Gray's primary role in the creation of an enduring institution at the United States Supreme Court and, moreover, to restore Thomas Russell, William Schofield, and Henry Eldridge Warner to their rightful place as the first law clerks. I conclude by briefly discussing the other Harvard Law School graduates who clerked for Justice Gray, an impressive collection of young men who went on to careers in the law, the legal academy, and politics.[2]

A Brief History of the Supreme Court and Support Staff

As discussed in the book's introduction, Supreme Court justices have not always had the services of law clerks. Throughout most of the nineteenth century, the Supreme Court justices were assisted only by a small handful of support personnel. The Court's original support staff consisted of the clerk of the Supreme Court, the official Court reporter, and the marshal of the Court. In subsequent decades, the staff of the Supreme Court was supplemented with what Chief Justice Roger Taney called "servants about the Court," to wit, messengers.[3] Political scientist Chester A. Newland writes that although Congress first appropriated funds for the hiring of messengers in 1867, individual justices employed messengers before that date.[4] Newland states that messengers were given a number of different job responsibilities, including serving as barbers, waiters, and chauffeurs.

In the years following the Civil War, the Supreme Court's workload grew sharply, and the justices began to publicly call for reform and assistance. Attorney General Augustus H. Garland provided the justices with some relief, recommending in the *Annual Report of the Attorney General of the United States for the Year 1885* that each justice be provided "by law with a secretary or law clerk, to be a stenographer . . . whose duties shall be to assist in such clerical work as might be assigned to him." In support of the recommendation, Attorney General Garland argued that the "immense" work of the justices demanded additional staff support, noting that "while the heads of Departments and Senators have this assistance, I do not think there is any good reason that the judges of this court should not also have it."[5]

Congress swiftly acted upon Attorney General Garland's recommendation, and in 1886 it authorized funds for the hiring of a "stenographic clerk for the Chief Justice and for each associate justice of the Supreme Court, at not exceeding one thousand six hundred dollars each."[6] While the justices differed in who they hired to serve as their stenographic clerk—some justices hired lawyers or law students, while a few hired professionally trained stenographers—within fifty years the position had evolved into what we recognize as the modern law clerk.

Horace Gray and the Creation of the Supreme Court Clerkship

When Horace Gray was appointed to the United States Supreme Court in 1882, he began hiring Harvard Law School graduates to serve one- or two-year appointments as his assistants. Gray had previously been the chief judge of the Massachusetts Supreme Judicial Court from 1873 to 1882, and in this role he first started employing clerks. The clerks were selected by Horace Gray's half-brother, the aforementioned Professor John Chipman Gray. From the very beginning Professor Gray evidenced a keen eye for legal talent, and the clerks that he sent to the Massachusetts Supreme Judicial Court included future Supreme Court justice Louis D. Brandeis.

Justice Gray never publicly discussed his motivation for hiring law clerks, but the most likely explanation for Gray's decision to employ assistants was related to workload considerations. As a jurist, Gray "delighted to go to the fountains of the law and trace its growth from the beginning," for he "believed that an exhaustive collection of authorities should be the foundation of every judicial opinion on an important question."[7] Gray's indefatigability in legal research might well explain his motivation in seeking out legal assistance.

So who was this creator of the Supreme Court law clerk? Horace Gray was a large, balding man with "mutton chop" whiskers and a stern countenance. Former Gray law clerk Samuel Williston vividly describes Justice Gray:

> In appearance Judge Gray was one of the most striking men of his time. He was six feet and four inches tall in his stockings. Unlike most very tall men, all the proportions of his body were on the same large scale. His massive head, his large but finely shaped hands, and the great bulk of his frame, all seemed to mark him as one of a larger race than his fellows.[8]

Gray's contemporaries viewed him as a man "possessed of great physical as well as great mental vigor," an individual blessed with "abounding vitality and a delightful flow of animal spirits," a jurist endowed with an "extraordinary" memory, a strong work ethic, and heightened awareness of "the dignity of the court and the position of judge."[9] Attorney Jack B. Warner painted a picture of a man who was more deity than mortal. "His great stature and commanding figure heightened the impression of a presence never to be trifled with, and suggested the classic demi-god walking on the earth with his head reaching among the clouds."[10] On the bench, Gray displayed a grim, cold demeanor, and his judicial energies extended not only to cases before the court but "to the color of the clothes worn by some members of the bar in court."[11] Given Gray's status as the creator of the modern law clerk, perhaps it is only fitting to describe him in biblical terms.

Once on the Supreme Court, Gray treated his young assistants as more than mere scriveners. Former law clerk Samuel Williston writes that "[t]he secretary was asked to do the highest work demanded of a member of the legal profession—that is the same work which a judge of the Supreme Court is called upon to perform." After oral argument, Gray would give his young clerks the applicable briefs and legal pleadings and would ask them to review the "novelettes" and report back to the justice with their independent thoughts. Gray did not share his own opinion of the case with his secretary, but "[i]t was then the duty of the secretary to study the papers submitted to him and to form such opinion as he could." Since Gray "liked best to do his thinking aloud and to develop his own views by discussion," Gray and his secretary would then sit down before the Court's Saturday conference and discuss the pending cases—first Gray would ask his secretary to "state the points of the case as best he could," with Gray closely examining and challenging the secretary's "conclusions."[12] "When I made them [the reports]," Williston writes, "the Judge would question me to bring out the essential points, and I rarely learned what he thought of a case until I had been thoroughly cross-examined."[13]

Former law clerk Langdon Parker Marvin also recalled these oral examinations by Justice Gray, and he provides a vivid description of these sessions:

> After he had settled himself in front of the fire with his black skullcap on his head and a five-cent Virginia cheroot in his mouth, he would say to me, "Well, Mr. Marvin, what have you got for me today?" So then I would tell him, having fortified myself with a little bluebook in which I had made notes of the various cases. Of course, I couldn't read all of the records, or even all of the briefs, but I made an analysis of the cases and I would tell him what the facts in each case were, where it started, how it had been decided in the lower courts, how it got to the Supreme Court of the United States, and what the arguments on either side were.[14]

Throughout his tenure on the Supreme Court, Gray permitted his clerks to offer opinions as well as case recitations. Williston writes that Gray "invited the frankest expression of any fresh idea of his secretary . . . and welcomed any doubt or criticism of his own views," while Marvin confesses that "he rather astonished me early in the year by saying 'How do you think it ought to be decided?'"[15] Former Supreme Court law clerk Ezra Thayer echoes Williston and Marvin's comments about the intellectual give-and-take between Gray and his young charges. Thayer writes that Gray "liked best to do his thinking aloud, and develop his own views by discussion." During these discussions Gray "would patiently and courteously listen to the crudest deliverances of youth fresh from the Law School."[16] In his memoirs, Williston is careful not to create the appearance of undue influence. "I do not wish, however, to give the impression that my work served for more than a stimulus for the judge's mind . . . my work served only as a suggestion."[17]

Gray then adjourned to the Saturday conference. Williston writes:

> When . . . the Judge returned, he would tell the conclusions reached and what cases had been assigned to him for opinions. *Often he would ask his secretary to write opinions in these cases,* and though the ultimate destiny of such opinions was the waste-paper basket, the chance that some suggestion in them might be approved by the master and adopted by him, was sufficient to incite the secretary to his best endeavor.[18]

Marvin also recalls assisting with the drafting of opinions, but only to a limited extent. "When the Court went into recess, Mr. Justice Gray would begin his work on the opinions allotted to him. I would help him on that, looking up law, and sometimes preparing statements of fact which appeared in the Court records—but, of course, he wrote the opinions himself—in long-hand, with a stub pencil."[19]

In short, the secretaries took part in all aspects of the decision-making process. They not only culled through the records and briefs in order to distill the relevant facts and legal arguments for Justice Gray, but they then debated and argued their conclusions and suggested holding with the justice. Once Gray was assigned an opinion, the secretaries often prepared the first draft of an opinion—while that draft may have landed in the trash can, it provided the secretaries with the critical chance to frame the issues and shape the legal analysis necessary to reach the Court's position.

Finally, the free rein extended to the clerk's opinions of the work product of other justices. For example, Gray asked Williston to review the opinions written by the other chambers. Williston recalls that "I tried to induce Justice Gray to dissent [to a majority opinion written by Chief Justice Fuller], but while he did not much combat my arguments, he was prevented from complying with my wish, if by nothing else, by the indisposition, that he and other members of the Court then had, to express dissent except on extremely vital questions, lest they should weaken the influence and credit of the Court."[20] Interestingly, Gray, Marvin, and Thayer do not mention reviewing cert petitions or preparing bench memoranda—a duty that has become the staple of the modern law clerk's existence.

It is unclear whether the law clerks shouldered more responsibilities in Gray's final years on the Court, when age and poor health began to affect the justice. Former law clerk Langdon Parker Marvin recalls that "my job with Judge Gray was an extremely busy one, because he was getting rather old and he expected me to do a good deal of the spade work and to educate him so that he could take his part in the deliberations of the court."[21] Marvin's description of his job duties, however, tracks the descriptions provided by earlier clerks Williston and Thayer.

Gray and his clerks worked in the library of Gray's home on the corner of 16th and I Streets in Washington, beginning their one-year clerkship in the early summer before the next term of Court. Williston describes the second-floor library as composed of two rooms. "The walls of the library rooms were entirely covered with law books, except the spaces for windows and those over the mantel pieces. In the larger room, a portrait of [Chief Justice John] Marshall by [John Wesley] Jarvis had the place of honor, surrounded by quite small portraits of all the other chief-justices of the United States. In [the] connecting room, the portrait over the mantel was a replica of Stuart's well-known representation of [George] Washington."[22] A desk for the law clerk was placed in the larger of the two library rooms, a spot from which the law clerks observed social calls by the other Supreme Court justices. Williston adds that Gray's bedroom was on the third floor of the home. He wryly observes that Gray "was unmarried at the time, and the house seemed designed for a bachelor. He had some antipathy to closets."[23]

As for Gray's personal relationships with his law clerks, Williston remarked that Gray "was of most genial disposition" and was "a patient man" who "invited the frankest expression of any fresh idea of his secretary."[24] Marvin commented that Gray was a "delightful person" who regaled his law clerks with stories of hunting buffalo in his youth. Marvin would often have lunch or coffee with Justice Gray, and in the afternoon he took drives with Justice Gray in his brougham ("I had to huddle in the corner, as he took up most of the seat") to the local zoo.[25]

Justice Gray shared not only stories of big game hunting with his clerks but also his observations on the Court and his love life. Williston recalls that Gray freely discussed his impressions of his fellow justices with the young man, such as referring to Justice Samuel Miller as the "little tycoon" for his empathetic but misplaced belief in the correctness of his legal positions.[26] Gray's closest friend on the Court was Justice Stanley Matthews, whose daughter, Jane, Gray was courting. Williston recounts: "One morning Gray approached me with a rather sheepish smile and exhibited a beautiful ring—a sapphire with a diamond on each side of it. He said 'You being, if I may say so, *in consimili casu* can perhaps tell me whether this would be likely to please a young lady.' I assured him that the probabilities were great that it would afford pleasure. Thus, I saw the engagement ring before the recipient of it."[27]

Horace Gray died in his summer home in Nahant, Massachusetts, on the morning of September 15, 1902. His funeral was held on September 18 at the Emmanuel Church in Boston. While there were no pallbearers at Gray's funeral service, former law clerks Roland Gray, Joseph Warren, Ezra Thayer, and Jeremiah Smith Jr. served as ushers.[28]

Justice Gray's clerkship model would serve as a template for future justices on the Supreme Court. While some justices employed stenographic clerks for extended periods of time, a core group of future justices—including Oliver Wendell Holmes Jr. and Louis Brandeis—followed Gray's lead of selecting Harvard Law School graduates to serve as their law clerks for a single term of Court. The justices began to mirror Gray's practice of having the assistants perform substantive legal work, and the justices (some more than others) also adopted Gray's habit of serving as mentors to their young charges. Over the next fifty years, Gray's clerkship model would be adopted by all the justices on the Court; while the justices varied in the types of job duties assigned to their clerks, by the 1940s all justices were hiring recent law school graduates (most from Harvard, but others from Yale) as their assistants.

A Collective Portrait of the Gray Law Clerks

From 1882 to 1902, Horace Gray hired nineteen Harvard Law School graduates to serve as his law clerks at the United States Supreme Court. The early Gray law clerks were plucked from a Harvard Law School that was just becoming a modern institution of legal education, a school at which Christopher Columbus Langdell presided as dean, giants like John Chipman Gray, James Bradley Thayer, and James Barr Ames lectured, and the *Harvard Law Review* was in its infancy. Like modern clerkships, the clerks began working at the Court shortly after graduation and—with two unusual exceptions—remained with the justice for a single term of Court. Future federal judge William Schofield clerked for Gray for two years (for reasons unknown), while Moses Day Kimball died of pneumonia approximately nine months into his clerkship.

In terms of background, the law clerks were a fairly homogenous group. Fourteen of the nineteen law clerks were born in Massachusetts, and all but one clerk—Blewett Lee—hailed from well north of the Mason-Dixon line. With the exception of the aforementioned Lee, all law clerks attended Harvard College prior to enrolling in law school. Most of the clerks first attended prestigious preparatory institutions—such as the Boston Latin School and Roxbury Latin School.

As with modern law clerks, membership on law reviews appeared to be an important credential. While the *Harvard Law Review* was not founded until 1887, thirteen of the fourteen law clerks hired after the founding of the *Law Review* served on its editorial board. Finally, the high quality of Gray's law clerks is reflected in the fact that five of the clerks—Francis Richard Jones, Moses Day Kimball, John Gorham Palfrey, William Schofield, and Samuel Williston—were accorded the honor of serving as commencement speakers at the Harvard Law School's graduation ceremonies. Ezra Ripley Thayer, another Gray law clerk, managed the impressive feat of being the first in his class at both Harvard College and Harvard Law School.

The First Three Law Clerks at the United States Supreme Court

Thomas Russell was born in Boston, Massachusetts, on June 17, 1858.[29] His father, William Goodwin Russell, who was a descendent of Mayflower passengers John Alden and Miles Standish, attended both Harvard College (enrolling at age fifteen and graduating at the top of his class) and Harvard Law School and later served as an overseer of Harvard College.[30] William Goodwin Russell became a prominent member of the Suffolk Bar, first as a member of the law firm Whiting & Russell (named partner William Whiting later served as solicitor of the War Department in the Lincoln administration) and then as a member of the firm Russell & Putnam. William Goodwin Russell's biographer claims that "avoidance of all public office was a marked feature in Mr. Russell," and that his "love for private practice and a singular distaste for public station" caused Russell to turn down offered appointments to both the federal circuit court and the state supreme court.[31] Thomas Russell's namesake was his grandfather, a Plymouth merchant, and his uncle, a prominent state court judge and a classmate of Horace Gray at Harvard College.

While in law school, Russell was a member of both the Ames and Gray law clubs. He graduated from Harvard Law School in 1882 and spent the winter of 1882 and the spring of 1883 clerking for Justice Gray. Regrettably, I have not discovered any information about either Russell's experiences as the first Supreme Court law clerk or the reaction of the other justices to Justice Gray's bold decision to hire a law clerk. Russell himself never publically wrote of the clerkship; Justice Gray's meager personal papers at the Library of Congress contain no mention of Russell; and the few biographies of Gray's contemporaries make no mention of Gray's unusual experiment.

Unlike many of Gray's later clerks, Russell did not climb to the top of his profession. From 1883 to 1896 he worked at his father's law firm, Russell & Putnam, and from approximately 1896 to 1900 he worked as a solo practitioner. Russell briefly flirted with state politics as a young man—serving for two terms in the Massachusetts House of Representatives in 1893 and 1894 while simultaneously holding the position of treasurer of the Republican City Committee of Boston—and he remained active in the Massachusetts Republican Party.

I have been unable to uncover any evidence that Russell was a prominent member of the bar during his short career. Russell himself wrote little of his own legal career, observing in 1900 that "[m]y summers are spent in a small place in Plymouth, Massachusetts, where I am philanthropically engaged in feeding a large number of bugs of various kinds in my attempt to cultivate a small garden." He added that his only civic responsibility was serving as a trustee of the Worcester Insane Hospital. Russell had the financial resources to retire from the practice of law in 1909 at the relatively young age of fifty-one.

According to his granddaughter Star Myles, Russell spent most of his post-retirement days at the Brookline Country Club or the Union Club in Boston, golfing and, when a heart condition caused him to stop golfing, curling, lawn bowling, and playing "cowboy pool." Perhaps Russell himself felt reticent about his early retirement, commenting in 1929, "I retired from the law some twenty years ago and, have, I am sorry to say, done nothing of interest to anyone since." Curling was the post-retirement activity that he took most seriously. In 1927, the *Boston Herald* ran a picture of Russell and his curling teammates, an image bearing the headline "A Veteran Quartet of County Club Curlers" and the caption "although none of these four curlers is young any more, each can furnish plenty of entertainment for his more youthful opponents."[32]

Russell is remembered by Myles as a "gentleman of the old school" a tall and distinguished man who was devoted to his wife, never touched alcohol or liquor, threw elegant dinner parties, had a practiced eye for finding good antiques and oriental rugs, believed that President Franklin Delano Roosevelt was a "traitor to his class," and shared his granddaughter's love of movies involving "historical adventure tales."[33] Russell died in his Boston home on April 8, 1938.

Justice Gray's second law clerk was William Schofield, who was born on February 14, 1857, in Dudley, Massachusetts. Unlike many of his fellow clerks, the historical record suggests that Schofield came from a more modest socioeconomic background. He was forced to balance his college studies with work as a printer, and a former classmate wrote that Schofield "came from a small town, was prepared for college in one of the less known academies, which so often bring forward boys of unusual character and promise who would otherwise never go to college." While the classmate reported that Schofield arrived at Harvard College with an "inadequate" education that limited his early academic success, "his persistence and unremitting industry and his great natural ability made him a leader." This work ethic, however, came at a price. "He was always a man of serious and earnest purpose, with perhaps too little thought or care for the lighter side of life."

Schofield graduated from Harvard College with a Phi Beta Kappa key, gave a commencement address entitled "The Commercial Agitation in England," and spent a year pursing the study of Roman law in graduate school before enrolling at Harvard Law School in the fall of 1880. After his graduation in 1883 (a graduation that saw Schofield give a commencement address on "the Codification of the Common Law"), Schofield spent two years clerking for Justice Gray. After his clerkship, Schofield returned to Cambridge, practiced law, and taught at both Harvard Law School from 1886 to 1889 (torts) and Harvard College from 1890 to 1892 (Roman law). He managed to supplement his teaching (which he referred to as "only incidental work") and law practice with the publication of several articles in the *Harvard Law Review*.[34] Schofield expressed disappointment at what he perceived to be only a modest academic output, explaining to his classmates that "[t]he briefs which we lawyers write do not seem to count either as literary or as legal work, but they cost hard labor none the less."

Like Thomas Russell, William Schofield served several years in the Massachusetts legislature. As a legislator, Schofield held key committee assignments and "won fame as an impassionate orator, a resourceful debater, and keen parliamentarian and a rapid thinker" whose speeches "commanded the entire attention of the House."[35] He was noted by the local press to be a loyal supporter and friend of Republican governor of Massachusetts Winthrop Murray Crane, support that was repaid when Crane appointed Schofield to the Massachusetts

Superior Court in 1902. At the time, Schofield's appointment to the state bench was universally hailed. The *Boston Evening Journal* remarked that Schofield was "one of the best known attorneys in the State" and that "[h]is nomination is met with favor by all who know him," while the *Springfield Republican* concluded that Schofield's "personal qualities are so attractive and reliable that men have forecast for him a successful career in politics, where his adaptation for useful public service has been well proved."[36]

I have been unable to find any information on Schofield's tenure on the Superior Court. Approximately eight years later Crane would again serve as Schofield's political mentor, submitting his name to President William Howard Taft for a vacancy on the First Circuit Court of Appeals. Schofield originally declined to be nominated for the position, but later he "has at last been persuaded to change his mind by Senator Crane, who appointed him to the superior court."[37] While Schofield was subsequently confirmed as a federal appeals court judge, his federal judicial career was short-lived. The March 23, 1912, edition of the *Boston Daily Globe* reported that Schofield was slowly recovering from a "nervous breakdown" suffered earlier in the year (a vague diagnosis used to describe myriad ailments), and within three months Judge Schofield would be dead of "spinal trouble in the form of paralysis."[38] His death was viewed as "an irreparable loss to the community" by the *Boston Herald,* and over one thousand judges, attorneys, politicians, and family members attended Judge Schofield's funeral on June 12, 1912.

Of the first three law clerks, the historical record is the most sparse when we come to Justice Gray's third law clerk, Henry Eldridge Warner. He was born in Cambridge, Massachusetts, on October 27, 1860, graduating from Harvard College in 1882 and Harvard Law School in 1885 before clerking for Justice Gray during October term 1885. In an 1899 newspaper article, Warner was described as "an aristocratic appearing young man and is very democratic. He is tall and has a straight, athletic figure. His hair and moustache are black."[39] It is unclear whether the descriptive phrase "very democratic" referred to Warner's politics or a general sense of equality and fair play.

Warner immediately entered private practice upon the conclusion of his clerkship with Justice Gray, ultimately becoming senior partner in the Boston law firm Warner, Stackpole, Bradlee & Cabot. Warner's foray into politics was more modest than either Russell's or Schofield's, serving for one year on both the Cambridge Board of Health and the Cambridge City Council. He also served as a bankruptcy referee in Middlesex County, Massachusetts, in approximately 1899.[40]

In his later years, Warner moved to Lincoln, Massachusetts, to a property that he humorously referred to as "his farm." At the age of forty-five, he wrote to his Harvard College classmates that "I seem to have no unusual experiences to relate, and I fancy that my case is like that of the rest of the class, a continued endeavor to 'lead the simple life' and keep up with the procession." Like Thomas Russell, Warner was a member of both the Brookline County Club and the Union Club of Boston, and one cannot resist wondering whether the two men exchanged gossipy stories about Justice Gray and the Supreme Court over drinks. Warner died on June 22, 1954, at the age of ninety-three. His death merited several newspaper articles—not because of his legal accomplishments, but due to his advanced age. At the time of his death Warner was the oldest living graduate of Harvard Law School.[41]

Warner would be the last Supreme Court law clerk to lead a solitary and unique existence. With Congress's authorization of stenographic clerks, the other justices quickly moved to hire their own assistants. Not all justices immediately adopted the clerkship model created by Horace Gray—namely, hiring a newly graduated law student for a one-year clerkship and assigning him substantive legal work—but the die was cast. Before retiring from the bench, Justice Gray would hire sixteen additional law clerks. While the historical record is sparse for some of these men, the accomplishments and personalities of a few Gray clerks have survived the passage of time and deserve a brief mention.

Horace Gray's Subsequent Law Clerks

Today a Supreme Court clerkship is practically a prerequisite to securing a teaching position at an elite law school. The origins of this hiring norm may well be traced to Justice Gray and the alumni of his nascent internship program. Three of Gray's former law clerks—Ezra Thayer, Joseph Warren, and Samuel Williston—all returned to Harvard Law School and became full-time members of the faculty, while former clerks Roland Gray, William Schofield, and Jeremiah Smith Jr. occasionally lectured at the law school. Another Gray law clerk, Blewett Lee, would serve on the law faculties of both Northwestern University and the University of Chicago.

Of the three Gray law clerks who were permanent members of the Harvard Law School faculty, Samuel Williston achieved the most enduring fame. Born on September 24, 1861, in Cambridge, Massachusetts, Williston graduated from Harvard College in 1882 and taught at a boarding school before attending Harvard Law School. Williston served on the editorial board of the

Harvard Law Review during its first year of existence and was awarded a prize by the Harvard Law School Association for an essay entitled "History of the Law of Business Corporations before 1800." After his clerkship, Williston both practiced at the Boston law firm of Hyde, Dickinson & Howe and accepted an appointment to teach at Harvard Law School.

As his class notes obliquely observe, "[t]he strain of the double work proved to be too much, and in 1895, soon after being appointed to full professor, he was forced to take a three years' vacation." Ultimately, Williston's absence from Harvard Law School would stretch over much of the next five years and would turn out to be more than physical fatigue. Writes Hofstra Law School professor Mark Movsesian:

> It soon became apparent that he needed more than a vacation. Neurasthenia, or nervous exhaustion, was a common diagnosis during the Gilded Age, particularly for 'brain toilers' like Williston who were thought to be particularly susceptible to the strains that modernity placed on the nervous system. The catchall term covered various mental disturbances, including what we would call depression and anxiety disorder. People understood the condition to be chronic, debilitating, and potentially incurable.[42]

Williston would ultimately seek help at a sanitarium in Bethel, Maine (Movsesian observes that "[s]o many of Harvard's faculty were among the patients that the sanitarium was known as the University's 'resting place'"), where he was treated with a combination of sedatives and talk therapy.

Movsesian writes that the treatment appeared successful, and Williston resumed teaching at Harvard law School in 1900. "Although he suffered periodic relapses that sent him back to Bethel and sanitariums over the years, and never weaned himself entirely off sedatives, he was able to work steadily . . . teaching into his eighties and doing research into his nineties."[43] Williston had the courage to discuss frankly the events surrounding his periodic breakdowns, and Movsesian notes that Williston "hoped his recovery might show those with similar problems that 'some achievement may still be possible after years of incapacity.'" Writes Movsesian: "Williston himself liked to tell people that his own career had been like the path of a wobbling planet: he was proof that, however far off course one went, one could 'wobble back.'"[44]

One can only speculate whether fellow faculty member Ezra Ripley Thayer took any comfort in Williston's recovery as Thayer also battled severe depression. Thayer was born on February 21, 1866, to James Bradley Thayer (who himself would begin a teaching career at Harvard Law School in 1873) and Sophia Bradford Ripley Thayer. Thayer's college preparation included a year studying classical texts in Athens, and in 1888 he graduated first in his class at Harvard College. While in law school Thayer was a member of the *Harvard Law Review* and received the highest grades of any law student in the previous thirty-five years. Of Thayer, his classmates observed that his success "did not come from the laborious toil of one striving merely for high rank. He had extraordinary intellectual powers and capacity, a brain that absorbed easily, and a tenacious memory."

Upon Thayer's graduation, Harvard Law School promptly offered him a teaching position. He declined and clerked for Justice Gray during October term 1891. Thayer subsequently spent eighteen years in private practice, first at the law firm Brandeis, Dunbar, and Nutter and later at Storey, Thorndike, Palmer and Thayer. Thayer was described as "a good trial lawyer, but was even better known for his ability to deal with questions of law and had taken his place in the foremost rank of those who argued cases before the full court."[45] Thayer's native intelligence could be intimidating to lawyers who matched wits with him; attorney and long-time friend Charles E. Shattack once confessed that "Thayer's mental processes were so thorough and at the same time so swift that often those of us less gifted were almost appalled by them."[46] While in private practice, Thayer also lectured at both Harvard Law School and Harvard Medical School. Thayer was appointed dean of the Harvard Law School in 1910, after initially and repeatedly expressing disinterest in the position.

While biographer John Sheesley writes that Thayer did not have the time to stamp his own unique mark upon the law school, he made a number of important decisions—including appointing Felix Frankfurter and Roscoe Pound to the faculty, raising the applicant admission standards, increasing course load requirements, encouraging stricter grading, and tweaking the curriculum—while initially struggling in the classroom. As dean of Harvard Law School, Thayer made one other minor contribution—not to the law, but to popular culture. During Cole Porter's first year at Harvard Law School, Thayer gave the young man the following advice:

> I want to tell you something that may injure your self-esteem . . . but I think it is best for you. Frankly, Cole, your marks are abominable. You will never be a lawyer. But your music is very good, indeed. I suggest that you switch over to the excellent music school we have here . . . they will be gaining a talented student and we will be losing a wretched one.[47]

While it is a stretch to argue that Thayer's comments caused Porter to abandon the law for a career as a composer (Porter was a mediocre law student), one wonders whether the unvarnished advice of Dean Thayer accelerated Porter's decision to leave law school—a decision that Porter "never regretted."[48]

As with Samuel Williston, Thayer's colleagues described his struggles with mental illness in terms of strain and overwork. One colleague remarked, "Though athletic, simple and abstemious in his habits . . . the high standard which he had set for himself made too great draughts on his physical and nervous resources." Sheesley writes that "[w]hat went wrong with Thayer's body is hard to discern from contemporary accounts, owing to his era's lesser medical abilities to diagnose a patient and greater taboos about publicizing that patient's diagnosis."[49] He states that Thayer was originally stricken with "bladder disease" in approximately March of 1915, a painful condition that came and went throughout the summer of 1915. The illness pushed Thayer farther behind in his law school work, and Sheesley hypothesizes that the pain of the medical condition, combined with the work load, led to severe depression and anxiety. "A newspaper account at the time of Thayer's death stated that he was 'despondent' over this pain, and that he 'sometimes said he did not find life worth the living and would be glad when it all ended.'"[50]

Although there is some ambiguity as to the exact timing of events, most evidence points to Thayer committing suicide in the Charles River in late afternoon or early evening of September 15, 1915. His body was found in the river the next day, floating approximately five hundred feet away from his home. "The medical examiner concluded that the cause of death was drowning and pronounced it a suicide because the body's facial expression was peaceful and there were no signs of violence." Sheesley writes that many friends and colleagues connected Thayer's suicide with the pressures of his deanship, quoting William Harrison Dunbar's claims that Thayer gave "his whole power and his whole strength to the good of the [law] school . . . and to that task he finally made the supreme sacrifice of his life."[51]

"Ezra Ripley Thayer is one of the least celebrated of the men who have served as Dean of the Harvard Law School," writes Sheesley. "No building bears his name. His portrait is tucked away in a far corner of the Library reading room." While Sheesley offers a number of explanations for this, including Thayer's short tenure as dean (five years) or his lack of legal scholarship, he suggests that "there may also be an element of shame that adds to Thayer's invisibility; the Law School may be embarrassed to recall that it was guided by a mentally unstable man, or even worse, that it contributed to his death."[52]

Regardless of the reasons for "the invisibility of the Thayer period" at Harvard Law School, he must be considered one of Horace Gray's most accomplished law clerks—and his story one of the most tragic.

Joseph Warren was the second-to-last Harvard Law School graduate to clerk for Horace Gray. After his clerkship during October term 1900, Warren returned to Boston, briefly worked at Brandeis, Dunbar, and Nutter, spent a year as both counsel for the Boston Police Department and secretary to the U.S. ambassador to Rome, and then worked two years as a patent law attorney at the firm of Richardson, Herrick & Neave. In 1907, Warren returned to Harvard. After a stint in the president's office and as a part-time lecturer, he joined the Harvard Law School faculty in 1913. He was appointed the Bussey Professor of Law in 1919 and the Weld Professor of Law in 1929. Warren also served as acting dean of the law school on two different occasions, and he published two influential legal treatises (*Cases on Wills and Administration* in 1917 and *Cases on Conveyances* in 1922) as well as a half dozen articles in the *Harvard Law Review*.

To the faculty and students of Harvard Law School, Warren was "Gentleman Joe." Harvard Law School professor Edmund M. Morgan Jr. explained: "[T]his term has always been applied with genuine affection and respect. It has had no reference to manner or outward trappings; it has expressed appreciation of inward qualities, the character of the man." Morgan recounted an incident at the end of the final class Warren taught at Harvard Law School, where a representative of the class stood up, thanked Warren for his service, and then said to his fellow students, "[s]o rise and start your cheering: a gentleman departs."[53]

Several of Justice Gray's former law clerks—including Charles Lowell Barlow, William Harrison Dunbar, Roland Gray, Robert Homans, Gordon T. Hughes, Landgon Parker Marvin, James Montgomery Newell, John Gorham Palfrey, and Jeremiah Smith Jr.—achieved varying degrees of professional success as attorneys in Boston and New York. Dunbar would become a named partner in the law firm of Brandeis, Dunbar and Nutter, while Marvin practiced with future president Franklin Roosevelt. Roland Gray, the son of John Chipman Gray, followed his clerkship by serving as the personal secretary to Chief Justice Melville Fuller (who was attending the Anglo-Venezuelan Arbitration Tribunal) before joining his father's firm of Ropes, Gray and Gorham. Roland Gray would also devote much time to revising his father's famous textbook, *Rule against Perpetuities*. Palfrey balanced his law practice with his duties as Justice Oliver Wendell Holmes Jr.'s literary executor and with watching tennis matches (he was the father of Sarah Palfrey Fayban Cooke Danzig, an international tennis star who won eighteen Grand Slam titles, as well as four other daughters who also won national tennis championships).[54]

Of all these attorneys, Jeremiah Smith Jr. would have the most lasting impact on international affairs. Smith was born in Dover, New Hampshire, on January 14, 1870, to Jeremiah and Hannah Webster Smith. Like many law clerks, his ancestral roots ran deep into the early history of America. His grandfather attended Harvard College, was wounded while fighting in the American Revolution, knew George Washington, and served in the U.S. House of Representatives, as the chief justice of the New Hampshire Supreme Court, and as governor of New Hampshire. His father (also Jeremiah Smith), was on the Harvard Law School faculty for over three decades.

Jeremiah Smith Jr. attended Phillips Exeter Academy before enrolling in Harvard College in 1888 and Harvard Law School in 1892. He served as editor-in-chief of the *Harvard Law Review* and clerked for Horace Gray during October term 1895. After his clerkship, Smith would spend the next twenty years in private practice in Boston before serving as a captain in the U.S. Army during the First World War. At the end of hostilities, Smith was appointed by President Woodrow Wilson to the American Commission to Negotiate Peace. Despite the rarified air of Paris and his role at the negotiation table, Smith remained unaffected. A former classmate writes:

> Let me set down an example of the way in which he [Smith] hated sham or anything that savored of it: When the time came for the signing of the Versailles Treaty it was evidently going to be a great spectacle at the Palace, with everybody within miles of Paris anxious to attend. Jerry's official position entitled him to a seat; but he shook his head and declined to go. "No," said he, "it is a poor treaty. I don't want any part of it. Nobody will ever know whether I attend or not, but I shall know and I can't justify my presence there."

"Jerry was no prig," concludes the classmate, "but he had clear-cut conceptions of right and wrong." The same classmate described Smith as a man of "extraordinary integrity and straightforwardness" who possessed "a quaint, infectious humor in which the shrewdest knowledge of men and their foibles . . . mingled and was one with a pervasive joy in human nature and life as we all live it."

Smith subsequently returned to Boston and his legal practice, only to be again tapped for government service. In 1924, the League of Nations appointed Smith to supervise the distribution of a fifty-million-dollar loan to Hungary. According to Smith's obituary in the *New York Times,* his role was much more than that of a mere financial advisor. "Rather than 'advisor,' Mr. Smith was for a time virtually dictator of Hungary, as he controlled all governmental expenditures. His task was made doubly hard as besides being a foreigner in a foreign country, he was also dealing with the proudest race in Europe."[55] During his time in Hungary, Smith gained international admiration—not only for his financial skill in completing in twenty-four months a job predicted to take thirty years, but also for his refusal to live in a Hungarian palace and accept a $100,000 bonus.

Upon the discharge of his advising duties in 1926, Smith would spend the next ten years practicing law, serving as a director of AT&T and a member of the Harvard Corporation, and sitting on the boards of various international political organizations. Despite his wide range of duties, the *Washington Post* claimed that Smith had "turned down more offers than most men receive, including the post of Treasury Secretary, offered him by President Roosevelt in 1933."[56] Smith died on March 13, 1935, in Cambridge, Massachusetts.

Two of Justice Gray's law clerks would be denied the opportunity to leave their mark on the legal profession, dying at a young age. Moses Day Kimball was born in Boston on February 16, 1868, and graduated from Harvard College in 1889. While at Harvard College, Kimball was a member of several clubs and organizations—including the Hasty Pudding Club, the Cricket Club, the Art Club, St. Paul's Society, and the Pierian Sodality. Although Kimball evidenced an early interest in becoming a minister, he began Harvard Law School in the fall of 1889. A classmate summarized Kimball's law studies as "a splendid example of what can be one by one who adds to a good mind the untiring and conscientious will to achieve the best." The same classmate, however, implied that it was Kimball's will and work habits that resulted in his early death. "This devotion to his profession blinded him . . . to the proper measure of his physical strength, and deprived the State of his most promising life and service." Kimball died during his clerkship in Washington, D.C., on March 31, 1893, of pneumonia. Little information exists regarding Kimball's clerkship and fatal illness, and we can only speculate as to the impact that Kimball's death had on Justice Gray.

Edward Twisleton Cabot also fell victim to a premature death. Cabot was born in Brookline, Massachusetts, on September 13, 1861, graduated from Harvard Law School in 1887, and clerked for Horace Gray during October term 1887. Fellow Harvard College student James F. Moors wrote a moving tribute to Cabot after his death, extolling his intellectual and athletic virtues. "When

Ted Cabot entered college, he was best known as the most indomitable football player of the Class. 'Lay for Cabot,' had been a well-known cry from opposing school elevens." Cabot was the senior captain of both the Harvard College football and crew teams.

Describing Cabot as sometimes studious, moody, and disposed to "austerity towards frivolity and meanness and truth deformed," Moors portrayed Cabot as possessing "an impressive moral force," which caused another classmate to remark that "[n]o true friend of his [Cabot's] can ever consciously do wrong." Cabot must have suffered from a long decline leading to death, for Moor writes that "all his life after graduation was passed in the shadow of approaching death," yet he adds that even though "inexorable death was pressing upon him," Cabot "was living among us so calm and fearless that very little of the conflict between young life and inevitable dissolution was apparent even to his friends." Cabot practiced law in Boston until his death on November 10, 1893.

Finally, we come to Blewett Lee—perhaps the law clerk with the most unique family history of all Horace Gray's young assistants. Born on March 1, 1867, in Moxubee County, Mississippi, to Stephen Dill Lee and Regina Lily Harrison Lee, Lee was a member of the first graduating class of Mississippi Agricultural and Mechanical College (later Mississippi State University). Thus, Lee was the only Gray law clerk not to attend Harvard College. Lee subsequently enrolled in classes at the University of Virginia before attending Harvard Law School. Harvard classmate Samuel Williston wrote of Lee: "His brilliant mind, geniality, simplicity, and an outlook somewhat colored by his Southern training made him an attractive companion."[57] Upon Lee's graduation, he traveled to Germany and studied at the University of Leipriz and the University of Freiburg before taking a clerkship with Horace Gray.

After his Supreme Court clerkship, Lee moved to Atlanta, Georgia, and struggled to find work as a lawyer. In an unpublished history of the Lee family, the following story is recounted:

> One day a man came into the office and asked BL to establish a company for him. He said he wanted to manufacture a nonintoxicating drink. He said also that he didn't have very much money so he could only offer BL a block of stock in the new company or $25.00. BL took a drink of the stuff, thought it was awful, and took the $25.00. The man's name was [Asa Griggs] Candler and the company he started was the Coca Cola Company.[58]

Lee would eventually move to Chicago in 1893, enticed there by a professorship at Northwestern University and a salary that Lee claimed was "more than the Chief Justice of the State of Georgia was making at the time."[59] It was in Chicago that Lee met and married Francis Glessner, the daughter of International Harvester founder John J. Glessner. The marriage would produce three children but would end in divorce in 1914. Francis Glessner, described by a biographer as a "brilliant, witty, shy, intimidating, and, by some accounts, impossible woman," later achieved an unusual fame by parlaying the art of creating miniatures of murder scenes into becoming a leading expert in crime scene investigation.[60]

Lee is one of two law clerks (the other being Charles Lowell Barlow, the son of "boy general" Francis Channing Barlow) to have a famous Civil War general as a father. Stephen Dill Lee was born in Charleston, South Carolina, and attended West Point during Robert E. Lee's tenure as superintendent. At the start of the Civil War, Stephen D. Lee resigned his commission in the U.S. Army and enlisted in the Confederate Army, and it was Captain Lee—as a member of General P.G.T. Beauregard's staff—that delivered a written note of surrender to Major Robert Anderson at Fort Sumter. Upon Major Anderson's refusal to hand over the fort, Captain Lee ordered the artillery to fire upon Fort Sumter—thus firing the first shot in the Civil War. Lee survived both injury and capture during the war and rose to the rank of lieutenant general; he would later become the first president of Mississippi A&M and the president of the United Confederate Veterans. A life-sized statue of General Stephen Dill Lee, resplendent in full military uniform and his saber at the ready, resides at the Vicksburg National Military Park.[61]

After teaching at both Northwestern University Law School from 1893 to 1902 and the University of Chicago Law School in 1902 (as one of the first faculty members hired by the new law school), Blewett Lee would leave the legal academy in 1902 and eventually became the general counsel for the Illinois Central Railroad. Despite the fact that he was no longer a law professor, Lee remained intellectually curious and continued to write articles that appeared in the *Columbia Law Review*, the *Harvard Law Review*, and the *Virginia Law Review*.[62] He returned to a college campus at the advanced age of eighty years old, nearly blind, and enrolled in classes at Emory University and Agnes Scott College in Atlanta. In a March 1949 article in the *Atlanta Journal*, Lee explained his decision to return to school: "A man reaches the place where he must admit that young legs are better than old brains. He retires. But that shouldn't mean it's time to fold his hand. There is the world of philosophy, of history . . . a world of books . . . all the things he's never had a chance to study before or read before."

Lee's family describes him as a "courtly southern gentlemen in every sense of the word. He was deeply and sentimentally attached to his southern inheritance and had all the graces and charm which came from such a background . . . [a] more cultivated, intellectually gifted man it would be to find."[63] As an example of Lee's sentimental nature, grandson John Lee recounts the following story:

> My grandfather told us stories about his father's (Stephen D. Lee) experiences along the Mexican border of Texas where he was stationed in the Army before the Civil War. In his soft, southern drawl Blewett Lee describe how an alligator had eaten the company's little pet dog. The company set out to find and kill the offending beast which they did quite quickly. This was told as if it was the most important thing, and maybe the only thing, the Army had to do. When he described catching the alligator and finding the dog dead inside, tears ran down my grandfather's face. I thought this must embarrass him, so I insisted that my friend and I leave much against the wishes on my friend. Later, when I asked about his father's tears, my dad explained that this was not unusual as his father was a very sentimental person.[64]

For John Lee, his grandfather was "a kindly gentleman, the sort of grandfather everyone should have."[65] Lee died on April 18, 1951, in Atlanta and was buried with his parents in the family plot at the Friendship Cemetery in Columbus, Mississippi.

Conclusion

No major biography has been written about Horace Gray, and law professors have mixed opinions as to his place in the hierarchy of great justices. Nevertheless, Justice Gray deserves to be given his due as the creator of a new institution at the Supreme Court—the law clerk—that has helped generations of jurists efficiently and skillfully wade through stacks of petitions for writs of certiorari, prepare for oral argument, and draft legal opinions that have reshaped our political and legal landscape. And after 125 years of anonymity, Thomas Russell, William Schofield, and Henry Eldridge Warner merit at least a footnote in the history of the United States Supreme Court as the first law clerks.

Notes

Portions reprinted with permission from Todd C. Peppers, "Birth of an Institution: Horace Gray and the Lost Law Clerks," *Journal of Supreme Court History* 32, no. 3 (2007): 229–48.

1. Throughout the article, I refer to Gray's young charges as law clerks—despite the fact that in the late nineteenth and early twentieth centuries Supreme Court law clerks were also referred to as stenographic clerks, private secretaries, or legal secretaries.

2. For an early account of nineteenth-century justices and their law clerks, see Chester A. Newland, "Personal Assistants to Supreme Court Justices: The Law Clerks," *Oregon Law Review* 40, no. 4 (June 1961): 299–317.

3. Carl B. Swisher, *History of the Supreme Court of the United States: The Taney Period, 1836–1864* (New York: Macmillan, 1974) 5:296.

4. Newland, "Personal Assistants," 300.

5. *Annual Report of the Attorney General of the United States for the Year 1885* (Washington, D.C.: Government Printing Office, 1885): 43.

6. 24 Stat. 254 (1886).

7. *Proceedings of the Bar and of the Supreme Judicial Court of Massachusetts in Memory of Horace Gray, January 17, 1903* (Boston: Boston Bar Association, 1903), 11.

8. Samuel Williston, *Life and Law: An Autobiography* (Boston: Little, Brown, 1940): 92.

9. *Proceedings of the Bar and of the Supreme Judicial Court of Massachusetts in Memory of Horace Gray,* 12, 50.

10. Ibid., 30.

11. George F. Hoar, "Mr. Justice Horace Gray," *Massachusetts Historical Society Proceedings* (Boston: Massachusetts Historical Society, 1904): 21.

12. Samuel Williston, "Horace Gray," in *Great American Lawyers: A History of the Legal Profession in America,* ed. William Draper Lewis (Philadelphia: J. C. Vinson, 1909), 158–59.

13. Williston, *Life and Law,* 92.

14. "Oral History Project: The Reminiscences of Mary V. and Langdon P. Marvin," Columbia University.

15. Williston, *Life and Law,* 93; "Reminiscences of Mary V. and Langdon P. Marvin."

16. "Massachusetts Historical Society Proceedings," 36, 38.

17. Williston, *Life and Law,* 92.

18. Williston, "Horace Gray," 159 (emphasis added).

19. "Reminiscences of Mary V. and Langdon P. Marvin."

20. Williston, *Life and Law,* 257.

21. "Reminiscences of Mary V. and Langdon P. Marvin."

22. Williston, *Life and Law,* 91.

23. Ibid.

24. Ibid., 93.

25. "Reminiscences of Mary V. and Langdon P. Marvin."

26. Williston, *Life and Law,* 95.

27. Ibid., 97.

28. "Of Simplest Character: Funeral of Judge Horace Gray, Formerly of the U.S. Supreme Court, at Emmanuel Church," *Boston Daily Globe,* September 19, 1902.

29. The majority of the information that I present on the lives and careers of Gray's law clerks come from Harvard College class reports. In order to keep footnotes to a minimum, I only cite to other sources of information, such as law review articles, newspaper stories, and obituaries.

30. Winslow Warren, *Memoir of William G. Russell, LL.D.* (Cambridge, U.K.: John Wilson and Son, 1900).

31. Ibid., 7.

32. "A Veteran Quartet of Country Club Curlers," *Boston Herald,* January 9, 1927.

33. Star Myles, correspondence with Peppers.

34. William Schofield, "The Principle of Lumley v. Gye, and Its Application, *Harvard Law Review* 2 (April 1888): 19–27; Schofield, "Davies v. Mann: Theory of Contributory Negligence," *Harvard Law Review* 3 (January 1890): 263–77; Schofield, "Hamlyn & Co. v. Talisker Distillery: A Study in the Conflict of Laws," *Harvard Law Review* 9 (January 1896): 371–85; Schofield, "Uniformity of Law in the Several States as an American Ideal, I. Case Law," *Harvard Law Review* 21 (April 1908): 416–30; Schofield, "Uniformity of Law in the Several States as an American Ideal, II. Statute Law," *Harvard Law Review* 21 (May 1908): 510–26; Schofield, "Uniformity of Law in the Several States as an American Ideal, IV. State Courts versus Federal Courts," *Harvard Law Review* 21 (June 1908): 583–94.

35. "Judge Schofield Was Close to Crane," *Pittsfield (Mass.) Journal,* May 26, 1912; *Sandwich (Mass.) Independent,* April 25, 1902.

36. "Appointment as Superior Court Justice Pleases Especially Members of General Court Associated with Him for Four Years," *Boston Evening Journal,* December 25, 1902; "Two Judicial Appointments," *Springfield (Mass.) Republican,* December 23, 1902.

37. John Lorance, "Crane Persuaded Schofield to Accept," *Boston Record,* May 23, 1911.

38. "Judge William Schofield Dies in Malden Home," *Boston Herald,* June 11, 1912.

39. "To Succeed Manchester: Henry E. Warner Has Been Appointed Referee in Bankruptcy for Middlesex County," *Boston Journal,* December 5, 1899.

40. Ibid.

41. "H. E. Warner, Oldest Harvard Law Alumnus," *Boston Herald,* June 24, 1954; "Henry E. Warner," *Boston Traveler,* June 24, 1954.

42. Mark L. Movsesian, "Samuel Williston: Brief Life of a Resilient Legal Scholar: 1861–1963," *Harvard Magazine* (January–February 2006).

43. Ibid.

44. Ibid.

45. Moorfield Storey et al., *Proceedings at the Meeting of the Bar in the Supreme Judicial Court of Massachusetts in Memory of Ezra Ripley Thayer, July 7, 1916* (Boston: Riverside Press, 1916), 3.

46. Charles E. Shattack, *Proceedings at the Meeting of the Bar in the Supreme Judicial Court of Massachusetts in Memory of Ezra Ripley Thayer, July 7, 1916* (Boston: Riverside Press, 1916), 23.

47. Richard G. Hulber, *The Cole Porter Story* (Cleveland: World, 1965): 12.

48. Ibid. See, also, William McBrien, *Cole Porter: A Biography* (New York: Alfred A. Knopf, 1998): 50–51.

49. John P. Sheesley, "Ezra Ripley Thayer: Dean of the Harvard Law School 1910–1915," Harvard Law School third year writing requirement.

50. Ibid., 72 (quoting "Harvard Law School Dean a Suicide," *Boston Journal*, September 17, 1915).

51. Ibid., 77, 80 (citing William Harrison Dunbar's comments contained in *Proceedings at the Bar of the Supreme Judicial Court of Massachusetts in Memory of Ezra Ripley Thayer, July 7, 1916*).

52. Ibid., 1.

53. E. M. Morgan, "Joseph Warren: A Gentleman Departs," *Harvard Law Review* 56 (October 1942): 171–72.

54. Robin Finn, "Sarah Palfrey Danzig, Stylish Tennis Champion, Dies at 83," *New York Times*, February 28, 1996.

55. "Jeremiah Smith, Financier, Dead: Lawyer and Banker Was Called Financial 'Savior' of Post-War Hungary," *New York Times*, March 13, 1935.

56. "Jeremiah Smith: International "Refuser,'" *Washington Post*, March 17, 1935.

57. Williston, *Life and Law*, 80.

58. Percy Maxim Lee and John Glessner Lee, *Family Reunion: An Incomplete Account of the Maxim-Lee Family* (Farmington, Conn.: privately printed, 1971), 255.

59. Ibid.

60. Corinne May Botz, *The Nutshell Studies of Unexplained Death* (New York: Monacelli, 2004), 17.

61. Harold Cross, *They Sleep Beneath the Mockingbird: Mississippi Burial Sites and Biographies of Confederate Generals* (Murfreesboro, Tenn.: Southern Heritage Press, 1994); Herman Hattaway, *General Stephen D. Lee* (Jackson: University Press of Mississippi, 1976).

62. Blewett Lee, "Spiritualism and Crime," *Columbia Law Review* 22 (May 1922): 439–49; Lee, "Railroad War Bonds," *Harvard Law Review* 32 (April 1919): 709–11; Lee, "Psychic Phenomena and the Law," *Harvard Law Review* 34 (April 1921): 625–38; Lee, "The Thirteenth Amendment and the General Railway Strike," *Virginia Law Review* 4 (March 1917): 437–56; Lee, "The Conjurer," *Virginia Law Review* 7 (February 1921): 370–77; Lee, "The Rule against Perpetuities in Mississippi," *Virginia Law Review* 10 (May 1924): 533–45; Lee, "An Establishment of Religion," *Virginia Law Review* 14 (December 1927): 100–111; Lee, "Copyright of Automatic Writing," *Virginia Law Review*

13 (November 1926): 22–26; Lee, "What Cannot Be Sold Cannot Be Mortgaged," *Virginia Law Review* 15 (January 1929): 234–37; Lee, "Abolishing the Senate by Amendment," *Virginia Law Review* 16 (February 1930): 364–69.

63. Lee and Lee, 261.

64. Author's correspondence with John Lee.

65. Ibid.

The Judge as Mentor

Oliver Wendell Holmes Jr. and His Law Clerks

The pioneering legal realist Jerome Frank once characterized Justice Oliver Wendell Holmes Jr., as "The Completely Adult Jurist."[1] By this he meant that Holmes had progressed beyond the "childish" search for absolutes in the law to the recognition that experience, rather than logic, was the proper lodestar for a judge to follow. There is another sense, though, in which Holmes demonstrated his maturity. As an associate justice of the Supreme Court from 1902 through 1932, and as a retired justice until his death in 1935, he served as mentor to a series of young Harvard Law School graduates who were paid by the U.S. government to serve as his legal assistants, or to use today's term, his "law clerks." As a group, these men achieved extraordinary levels of professional success, particularly in the fields of legal academia and government service, and clerking for Holmes played a large part in that success. This fact was not lost on the clerks. Alger Hiss, Holmes's clerk for the October term 1929, remarked that "[i]t was probably the greatest emotional [and] intellectual experience any of us ever had. . . . I think Holmes was the single greatest influence on me."[2]

While Hiss's career is hardly representative of the careers of his fellow clerks, his clerkship experience was similar to theirs in important ways, not the least of which was the veneration for Holmes that it instilled in him. He would have certainly agreed with Charles K. Poe, the very first of Holmes's protégés, who wrote to the justice on the occasion of his ninetieth birthday and thanked him for "upset[ting] the notion that 'no man is a hero to his valet.'"[3] In reality, Poe and his successors were much more than "valets" for Holmes. They were his social and intellectual companions.

It is this fact that makes Holmes a key figure in the transformation of law clerking from the primarily administrative institution it had been prior to the beginning of the twentieth century into what can be termed a "noble nursery of humanity," wherein a young lawyer's intellectual curiosities could be awakened and valuable social and professional skills could be acquired.[4] Broadly speaking, the experience can be characterized as an intergenerational bargain in which wisdom, advice, and a certain amount of social capital are exchanged by an elderly judge for the companionship and affection of an ambitious young lawyer. In the particular case of Holmes and his clerks, this bargain fostered intense bonds of loyalty between young men at the start of promising legal careers in the Progressive Era and an aging icon of the late-Victorian period who was concerned about the future of the legal profession and about his own reputation as a judicial figure. By adopting the posture of mentor toward his young apprentices, Holmes instilled in them a particular view—best described as anti-materialistic—of the lawyer's role in society and a vision of himself as a heroic American whom his apprentices would one day project to the public and to posterity.

For an understanding of precisely how Holmes succeeded in establishing himself as a mentor to his law clerks—during an age when the personal apprenticeship was giving way to more institutional forms of legal education, such as the three-year law school—we are fortunate to have the diary of Chauncey Belknap, Holmes's tenth law clerk.[5] Belknap served with the justice in Washington from October 1915 to April 1916, before embarking upon a successful career as a partner in a New York City law firm and as president of the New York State Bar Association. While he is not the most well known of Holmes's ex-clerks, he profited from his association with the justice as much as they did. Although at least one other Holmes clerk kept a diary during his term of service with the justice, Belknap's chronicle is particularly illuminating because it depicts the Holmes clerkship in midpassage, at a moment when its contours had been fully developed by the justice and his nine previous law clerks and when the regime of work and learning had not yet been compromised by Holmes's advancing age.[6]

Unlike the diary kept by Mark DeWolfe Howe, Holmes's clerk in 1933–34 (after the justice had retired from the bench), Belknap's journal captures Holmes in his prime (if one can say this about a seventy-four-year-old man), and was recorded at the height of the justice's capacity to function as a mentor.[7] For this reason, the diary stands as a unique source of information about how a very bright young man and a very wise old one came to fashion a middle ground between youth and experience in Holmes's noble nursery.[8]

By examining this 140–page document as well as the correspondence that Holmes and his clerks exchanged throughout the last three decades of his life, this essay explores how the Holmes model of judicial clerking developed and how it functioned as a form of institutionalized mentorship with very tangible benefits for both mentor and protégé. Supplementing this material with a careful reading of the testimonials written by Holmes's clerks later in their lives, I argue that Holmes deployed mentorship as a weapon in his campaign to enhance his judicial reputation and in so doing inspired other American judges at the state and federal levels to do the same. By inviting his law clerks into his noble nursery of humanity rather than the stale, bureaucratic environment in which nineteenth-century legal assistants such as Melville's fictitious but representative character, Bartleby the Scrivener, "preferred not" to work, Holmes secured the loyalty of his protégés and imbued the institution of law clerking with a cultural power that has been overlooked by historians of the institution to date.[9]

I begin my examination of the judicial mentor-in-action in the next section of this essay, with a detailed description of the Holmes model of law clerking and a discussion of the historical context in which that model developed. I pay particular attention in this section to two related cultural developments that were profoundly disconcerting to men of Holmes's class and generation: what historians of the late nineteenth and early twentieth centuries have depicted as a crisis of masculinity, and what sociologists and legal historians have characterized as a crisis of the legal profession. Both of these crises, I maintain, influenced Holmes's interactions with his protégés and had long-lasting implications for the nature of law clerking as an institution.

In the third part of the essay, I shift from a general discussion of Holmes's approach to mentoring to a look at one law clerk's experience with the Yankee from Olympus. The portrait that emerges is one that might not be familiar to those who have observed and commented on the law clerk's function in the modern American judiciary, but it will make sense in light of the various factors influencing relations among legal elites earlier in the century, which are discussed in the second part.

In the fourth section, the essay shifts back from the particular to the general, with a discussion of how Holmes's clerks repaid their mentor for the valuable education and social capital he bequeathed them. A brief survey of the published articles, speeches, and books about Holmes written by his former "law secretaries" demonstrates that these men used their public and not-so-public positions to construct an exalted image of a jurist whose reputation was, at times, in need of rehabilitation.

In the final section of the essay, I suggest that the type of reputation crafting described in the fourth section has not been a practice unique to Holmes's protégés or to Supreme Court law clerks in general, for that matter. In fact, I argue that the practice has been ubiquitous among law clerks at every level of the American judiciary. I conclude with some thoughts about the implications of this underexamined aspect of the law clerk's function.

The Holmes Model of Clerking

It is impossible to make sense of Chauncey Belknap's diary without understanding several things about the Holmes clerkship experienced by all thirty of its alumni. First, the justice did not refer to them as "law clerks," as those who became judicial assistants later in the twentieth century would come to be called, or as "stenographers," as they were referred to in the federal legislation of 1886 that appropriated funding for each Supreme Court justice to hire an assistant.[10] Rather, he called them his "law secretaries," a term that might confuse the modern reader who has a particular notion of what it is that secretaries do.

This was more than a matter of nomenclature. It was a reflection of Holmes's view that the primary function of a judicial assistant was not to dispense advice on legal matters or to help draft opinions, as today's law clerks are expected to do. Nor was it simply to take dictation, as the term "stenographer" implies. Rather, it was to serve as the justice's confidant and to minister to his needs in a wide variety of private and professional matters.[11] Such duties might be as pedestrian as helping Holmes to balance his checkbook, but they could also be as interesting as providing him with a live audience for his opinions about his fellow justices or about the politics of the day—opinions that the cloistered nature of the judicial profession prohibited him from voicing elsewhere.[12]

As opposed to a mere stenographic assistant, moreover, a law secretary in the Holmesian mold was someone familiar with recent cultural and intellectual developments, at least such developments as were discussed in Cambridge. As he wrote to Frederick Pollock in 1923, Holmes liked the "young chaps from the Law School" because they helped him to "know the fashions."[13] He also enjoyed being the object of hero worship, as he often was to the younger men with whom he surrounded himself.[14] Yet the secretaries were more to Holmes than a pipeline to the new ideas floating around at Harvard Law School and more than a doting chorus of praise. The justice relished what Francis Biddle described as "the sense of resistance that youth sometimes gives to age."[15] By this he meant that Holmes enjoyed the gentle prodding his secretaries gave

him about the assumptions underlying his philosophies and the daily conversations in which he could test his long-held views on a variety of subjects
against the fresh ideas of the younger generation.[16]

A second general characteristic of the Holmes clerkship is that it took place
in the justice's home at 1720 I Street in Washington and not, as today's Supreme
Court clerkships do, at the Supreme Court Building. Actually, there was no Supreme Court building at all until 1935; prior to this, the justices had convened
in the Senate chamber in the south wing of the Capitol. Since there were no
chambers for the individual justices at this location, each of them maintained
an office in his home for himself and his assistant.[17] For a Holmes secretary,
this meant spending work days in an office adjoining the justice's on the second
floor of his home, with a large sliding door (always kept open) between them.
Besides muting the hierarchy implicit in a relationship between a member
of the Supreme Court and a recent law school graduate, the domestic space
in which Holmes and his secretaries interacted fostered an atmosphere that
blurred the lines between the personal and the professional. As such, Holmes's
private affairs became his secretaries' "business," and two distinct generations
of legal actors came to share an intimacy foreign to today's justices and clerks,
who work in the lavish, but hardly domestic, chambers of the "marble palace."[18]

It was much more than the domestic surroundings, however, that produced
the kind of affection captured by Alger Hiss's proclamation that he "had a
love affair with this great man," and by Holmes's own assertion that he had
"become deeply attached [to Mark DeWolfe Howe] during their daily intimacy" in 1934.[19] In fact, Holmes took a conscious step toward engendering
this intimacy by instituting a "no-marriage" rule when it came to selecting his
secretaries. In requiring his young assistants to be bachelors during their term
of service, Holmes sought to create, and did in fact create, a homosocial world
in which his protégés would devote themselves to him completely and would
experience no conflict of loyalties while they were under his tutelage. Holmes
offered the following explanation for his stipulation against marriage in a letter to Felix Frankfurter written in 1915, the very year that Frankfurter replaced
John Chipman Gray as the professor at Harvard Law School to whom Holmes
delegated the task of selecting his secretaries: "I put the case of the married
man to my wife. She reinforced my unwillingness as it means a major interest
outside his work. It is true that the work is not very much but if baby has the
megrims, papa won't have the freedom of mind and spirit that I like to find."[20]

Yet this explanation is incomplete given that Holmes stipulated against
marriage and not simply fatherhood when it came to hiring his secretaries. It

was not simply "babies with megrims" that Holmes feared would distract his secretaries from their intellectual engagement with him, but the specter of a domestic life that might compete with the one he had fashioned in his "noble nursery." As Holmes was certainly aware, a new conception of masculinity had been emerging since the end of the nineteenth century that was leading middle-class men away from the fraternal rituals that had previously monopolized their leisure time and toward more companionate family relations.[21] As another letter to Frankfurter indicates, Holmes did not want his boys' education to be compromised by the lure of what historians have referred to as "masculine domesticity."[22]

While, in Holmes's view, married men were less likely to make a contribution to society, masculine domesticity was only one aspect of a broader, gender-based crisis that elite male professionals like Holmes were experiencing at the turn of the century. As a leading historian of American masculinity has argued, "the real threat to the male culture of the public world . . . came from aspiring female professionals who sought to open male enclaves like law and medicine to both sexes."[23] This was more than a matter of a few women taking jobs that otherwise would have gone to men. It was a challenge to the traditionally male culture of the middle-class workplace, one that produced a vigorous male defense of gender turf across a broad spectrum of occupations.[24] The threat that women allegedly posed to male culture and authority was particularly acute in the legal profession, which had been a masculine preserve throughout most of the Victorian era, but which was reluctantly opening its doors to women by century's end.[25]

Just as homosociality was one key component of the Holmesian model of law clerking, so was the requirement that his protégés be recent graduates with little or no experience as practicing lawyers. While more seasoned attorneys would have been indisputably more useful to Holmes as legal resources, it is equally clear that the justice wanted to surround himself with neophytes precisely because they were more susceptible to his influence and more likely to embrace the kind of mentoring he offered. Indeed, there was an explicit understanding on the part of each secretary that he was choosing to forego the opportunity to get started in his career in exchange for an extra year of education. Holmes's embrace of boyishness and his favoring of an extended education for promising young men were rooted in a deeper concern than his preferences regarding the personality of his companions or the development of his protégés. He was profoundly concerned about the state of the legal profession, and his approach to mentoring reflects this concern. As historian Richard

L. Abel has shown, entry barriers that had formerly restricted the practice of the law to "gentlemen" had by the turn of the century been progressively lowered, a shift that continued to alarm Holmes and other members of the legal aristocracy for several decades thereafter.[26] Holmes bemoaned both the crass materialism that he felt accompanied this development and the degradation of the scholar-thinker produced by the increasing stratification of the bar along axes of specialty and ethnicity.[27] The justice went to great lengths to instill in his Harvard protégés a sense of the nonmaterial rewards that a life in the law could offer.

We shall see precisely how Holmes imparted his "nonmaterialist" message to his clerks when we examine Belknap's diary in the next section, but that such a message was received by Belknap's fellow clerks is clear. One must be careful, however, to distinguish between the content of Holmes's anti-materialistic message and its actual effect on his protégés.

Portrait of the Law Clerk as a Young Man

On October 8, 1915, Chauncey Belknap presented himself at the house of Justice Holmes for the first time, was ushered into the study by a "negro messenger," and was greeted by the man about whom he had heard so much at Harvard. The justice was wearing a purple velvet jacket and smoking a long cigar. To the star-struck twenty-four-year-old recently arrived in Washington for his clerkship, Holmes "look[ed] more like a cavalry captain than the popular conception of a jurist."[28] This was clearly an image that Holmes sought to project, for, as we shall see, he was more interested in leading Belknap in an assault on the mysteries of life than in subjecting him to the intricacies of legal doctrine. Setting the tone for the year to come, Holmes did not burden his new companion with work or with an orientation about his duties on his first day. Instead, Belknap received a tour of Holmes's personal library, an introduction to his wife, and a casual lecture on Holmes's theory of economics.[29]

Four days later, after thirty-six holes of golf with a friend from his undergraduate days at Princeton, dinner with Holmes and his wife at The Willard (a Washington tavern), and a leisurely Monday spent observing a case argued before the Supreme Court, Belknap discovers a pile of records and briefs on his desk and concludes that "work had begun." He describes his job at this point as "submit[ting] report[s] of the facts and arguments to the Justice who thus avoids the necessity of wading through a chaotic mass of words to get at the essence of the dispute."[30] This rather dull task remained Belknap's primary responsibility for the balance of the year. If he had any illusions about having a greater impact on the judicial process, they were quickly dispelled. Reflecting on the first month and a half of his clerkship, he writes, "I read over a couple of unimportant opinions of the Justice's. This duty has been a pure formality so far. Even if there were doubts in my mind, I should have to get myself into the state of mind of a court overruling a jury before venturing to differ."[31]

According to his diary, Belknap never did "venture to differ" with the justice, but this is not to suggest that he was too timorous for the job. Whatever one's position on the current controversy about the extent and propriety of law clerks "ghosting" for judges, it is clear that Holmes never considered delegating his Article III functions to a young man who was neither appointed by the president nor confirmed by the Senate.[32] This reticence does not reflect a distrust on Holmes's part of the intelligence or abilities of his secretaries, for as Belknap was pleased to report, "he is wonderful, [he] talks over his decisions as if I were on an equal plane of learning and powers."[33] Yet these discussions were not meant to assist the justice in disposing of his caseload but to give him a live audience before which he could hammer out his own ideas. Belknap illustrates this distinction, noting that "[t]he Justice had just finished his opinion when I reached his house. . . . [He] insisted that I sit down while he stood at his desk reading. . . . I told him I had not realized how strong the side could be made and he seemed pleased."[34]

Occasionally, Holmes would share his thoughts with Belknap before he had actually finished an opinion. He might even ask for the secretary's view on how he should handle a particular matter. Invariably, though, the justice had already made up his mind. The diary entry for December 13 reflects this reality:

> The Justice is puzzled over a case in which the Court was asked to issue a mandamus to a Mass[achusetts] Circuit Court judge who refused to [grant?] access to depositions sealed from a previous suit. He sent me to work on examining the authorities. . . . He is determined to give an order and read me a vigorous opinion covering all but the procedural point. "Do you think there is anything discourteous or uncivil to the judge below" he said. "He will know he made a mistake," I replied. "Well, I think I'll lay it on the boys and see if they swallow it," he said with a twinkle.[35]

Holmes's "determination" to issue the mandamus in this case did not deter him from soliciting Belknap's opinion, but his secretary's concern about the propriety of that course of action did not dissuade the justice from taking that course. It is clear that unlike today's law clerks, whose legal and political instincts are often a valuable resource for the justices to use in deciding cases, Belknap was not viewed this way by Holmes.[36]

Only once in the entire diary does the young clerk suggest that Holmes actually took his advice to heart. That moment came on February 3, 1916, when the justice allegedly "accept[ed] some of my modifications of his first draft." The fact that Belknap describes Holmes as "generous" to do so, however, highlights the degree to which this was an isolated incident.[37]

While court watchers a decade or so later were noting with alarm the docket crisis that seemed to imperil the ability of the understaffed Supreme Court to dispense justice, Holmes seemingly had no problem handling his workload without the direct assistance of his clerk.[38] This does not mean that he did not need his secretaries for other reasons, however, for if the Belknap diary has little to say about the legal functions its author performed, it is long on his extralegal functions. Foremost among these was the young man's duty to simply "be there" when Holmes wished to try out an idea, a philosophy, or even a clever phrase, before he communicated it to a wider or a more mature audience.

Holmes was quite conscious of using Belknap in this fashion. On New Year's Eve, 1915, at the height of the European conflict, the justice wrote to Frankfurter, expressing his view that the men "in the trenches . . . might find gaiety in the miasmatic mist of misery."[39] Whatever he meant by this bit of alliterative philosophy, Holmes admits that Frankfurter was not the first person with whom he shared it, noting in the same letter that "I repeat what I said to my secretary [Belknap], as it rather pleased me."

There was plenty of time for "song and tall talk" during Belknap's clerkship. Indeed, at one time he notes, "I am the master of a magnificent leisure."[40] It is unfathomable that a law clerk for one of the current justices would make such a comment, given the hectic work schedules that they endure. Yet the disparity in the lifestyles of law clerks early in the century and now is not simply a product of rising caseloads as one might expect. If it were, the fact that today's justices have four law clerks, while in Holmes's era they had only one, would negate the effect of that development on those clerks. In fact, Belknap's "magnificent leisure" was a product of Holmes's view of how a bright young lawyer could best serve him, and of how that lawyer could best prepare himself for a successful career. The justice actually encouraged Belknap to spend his time golfing, attending the theater, socializing with friends, and, most importantly, reading.[41]

One of Holmes's prized possessions was his "black book," the 162–page notebook in which he recorded the titles of all the books he read from 1881 until 1935.[42] As books were so crucial a part of Holmes's life that they received this sacramental treatment, it is little wonder that his secretaries were encouraged to consume them as voraciously as he did. Belknap read well over thirty books during the six months he spent with Holmes. The scope of his readings was vast, ranging from Shakespeare's *King Lear* to Oscar Wilde's *Lady Windemere's Fan* to Lester Frank Ward's *Dynamic Sociology* to Holmes's own masterpiece, *The Common Law*. He also found the time to teach himself French, to delve into the history of philosophy, and to keep up-to-date with the political theorizing of Graham Wallas and Herbert Croly. Belknap discussed many of these books with Holmes, and these discussions became one of the primary vehicles by which Holmes imparted wisdom to his protégé.

A good example of how literature functioned as a heuristic device for Holmes appears in Belknap's diary entry for October 16, in which he recounts a discussion of Plato's *Symposium* that he had that afternoon with the justice. Apparently, Holmes told the diarist that "the dominant factor in [the book's] greatness is that here Plato, first of all men, points out the interest of a life of ideas rather than of action."[43] Given Holmes's contempt for the way early twentieth-century legal culture privileged business over intellectual pursuits, it is clear that this comment was as much a lesson for Belknap about how lawyers should behave as it was an attempt to interpret Plato. Yet what was not explicitly discussed by Holmes and Belknap about this famous Greek dialogue, or at least not recorded, is important to an understanding of Holmes's role as a mentor.

The Symposium, one will recall, is the philosopher's depiction of a series of speeches given by Socrates and several of his friends on the subject of Eros, or Love. Of course, the kind of love of which Plato's cast of characters speak is that *between men* in a society that did not marginalize homosexuality. It is not my intention to suggest that a homosexual framework contributes to an understanding of the relationship between Holmes and his law clerks. What is relevant to a discussion of Holmes as a mentor, however, is the way the Greeks depicted in *The Symposium* conceived of love as the consideration for a bargain struck between ethical and intellectual teachers and young men or boys in the role of students, and the way this same bargain fostered and defined the all-male relationships that developed inside Holmes's noble nursery.[44] The nature of this bargain is most clear in the speech given by Pausanias, in which he delivers a message that Holmes may have intended Belknap to receive:

When the lover realizes that he is justified in doing anything for a loved one who *grants him favors,* and when the young man understands that he is justified in *performing any service* for a lover who can make him wise and virtuous—and when the lover is able to help the young man become wiser and better [then] the young man is eager to be taught and improved by his lover.[45]

Substituting the term "mentor" for "lover" and the term "protégé" for "loved one" in this passage, leaves us, I believe, with a perfect description of the kind of relationships Holmes sought to cultivate with his young clerks. By reading and discussing Plato with Chauncey Belknap (and it is likely that he did so with his other secretaries as well), Holmes established the terms of the bargain that defined his clerkship model.[46] That is, he promised to make his youthful companions wise and virtuous, and they, in turn, agreed to "grant him favors" and to "perform any service" for him.[47] Turning to the rest of Belknap's diary, it is possible to explore the particular notions of wisdom and virtue that Holmes bequeathed to his secretaries and to see what kinds of favors and services he expected in return.

The advice that Belknap received from his mentor was generally of a broad, philosophical nature, although Holmes was not beyond giving him more practical advice, as he did when he warned the young lawyer about the perils facing an unprepared advocate in court, or when he gave him instructions on how "to fish in the pond of judicial language."[48] Perhaps the most interesting part of Belknap's diary, however, at least in terms of understanding how Holmes conducted himself as a mentor, is his response to Belknap's "introduc[ing] the subject of beginning practice" on November 20. According to Belknap, the justice responded to this request for vocational advice with a plea that the young man worry about ideas rather than business, telling him "I can't believe the place a man starts or the position he attains has much to do with his happiness in life if he philosophizes well."[49] Perhaps Holmes was aware that this was idealistic advice to be giving a young man like Chauncey Belknap, but, as I argue, Holmes was at least as interested in being seen and portrayed as a man uninfluenced by the sordid world of business as he was in guiding his protégés away from that world.

This was not the only image that Holmes sought to project, moreover, for as the testimony of Belknap and other clerks suggests, he was also interested in portraying himself to them as a Civil War hero. Typically, this portrayal would take place in the course of the leisurely strolls through the streets of

Washington that Holmes and his secretaries shared. Belknap refers specifically to more than a dozen of these walks in his diary, and invariably they became vehicles for the justice to reminisce about his role in the Civil War.

Holmes's preaching to his secretaries about the virtues of conducting oneself with honor and grace, and of adopting a philosophical outlook toward the legal profession, was of the same sort as his effort to glorify his role in the Civil War. Both should be seen as the means by which an aging lawyer sought to endear himself to a rising generation of legal elites. So was his pristine "code of conduct," summarized by Alger Hiss in 1988 as "spartan devotion to duty," "high-mindedness in personal relations," "moral and physical courage," "fierce independence of spirit," and "a lively feeling for community and country."[50] While Holmes may or may not have abided by this code in his own life, he certainly wanted the young men whom he invited into his nursery to believe that he did. Moreover, to the extent that Holmes's clerks internalized his code, they embarked upon their careers with tools that virtually guaranteed success to men of their pedigree. Belknap acknowledged how bright his future looked about ten years after his clerkship had ended, telling the justice about his "increased appreciation of what my year as secretary meant, and is going to mean."[51]

Like most of his fellow clerks, Chauncey Belknap enjoyed a great deal of professional success in the years following his apprenticeship with Justice Holmes. After serving in the infantry during World War I, and becoming an aide to General Pershing, Belknap returned to civilian life in New York City, where in 1921 he helped to found a law firm—the successor to which survives to this day. As a lawyer, he represented a host of wealthy clients, including John D. Rockefeller, and became such a well-known figure within legal circles that he was elected president of the New York State Bar Association in 1960.[52]

Law Clerks and the Crafting of Judicial Reputation

Judging from their ubiquity in the pages of Who's Who in America, the law secretaries to Oliver Wendell Holmes Jr. formed an extraordinarily accomplished group. Over two-thirds of them appeared repeatedly in that publication, a remarkable figure when one considers that none of the first five secretaries were so honored—a likely consequence of the fact that it took a few years for the Holmes clerkship to acquire its career-enhancing prestige.[53] What is striking about Holmes's secretaries is not so much the overall success that they enjoyed, however, but the wide range of careers and disciplines in which that success occurred. Of the justice's thirty secretaries, eleven became founders or partners of prestigious law firms,[54] nine achieved some prominence in the world of politics,[55] five garnered lofty perches in the academy,[56] and four became influential businessmen.[57] (One, Shelton Hale, died three years after his clerkship.)

As one might guess, the degree to which fame accompanied success for Holmes's secretaries varied as well. Yet while some of them carved out careers that landed them regularly in the pages of the nation's newspapers, such as Francis Biddle (attorney general), Tommy Corcoran (key draftsman of New Deal legislation), and Irving Olds (president of the United States Steel Corporation), the others were equally accomplished, if not quite as recognizable. Harvey H. Bundy, for example, served as assistant secretary of state from 1931 to 1933, while Laurence Curtis served as a Republican congressman from Massachusetts from 1952 to 1962. Others, like Mark DeWolfe Howe, who became a Harvard law professor and one of America's leading authorities on constitutional law and legal history, distinguished themselves within the academic community.

No matter the arena in which they prospered, or the amount of prosperity that they enjoyed, Holmes's secretaries attributed their success to their mentor. Sometimes this attribution came early in an ex-clerk's career, as when Corcoran, only two years after leaving the clerkship, came to realize "the pricelessness of the education" Holmes had given him, or when Biddle proclaimed, "I know that my career will be more valuable because on its threshold I had the privilege of a year under you."[58] More often, however, the acknowledgments of gratitude came later in life, after the benefits of a youthful association with Holmes had become more clear.

Whether the rewards were personal or professional, whether they flowed directly from the lessons that the justice imparted or from the ex-clerk network that functioned as a large and supportive family, Holmes's secretaries had every reason to be grateful to their mentor.[59] Grateful they were, and Holmes capitalized on this sentiment in important ways. He not only basked in the immediate glow of his secretaries' admiration and affection, but he deployed them as a battalion of reputation crafters in a campaign to enhance his stature as a judicial figure. While it is not quite the case that Holmes directed his law clerks to construct a particular image of himself, he was certainly aware that this was a function they could, and would, perform.

If the published and unpublished writings of Holmes's secretaries provide insight into the nature of their experiences as law clerks, the writings also reflect the part these experiences played in constructing an exalted image of the justice both during and after his lifetime. The published works are particularly worth exploring in this regard, for they were the primary vehicles by which a salutary image of Holmes was projected.[60] It is not surprising that "authorized biographer" Mark DeWolfe Howe, the secretary to whom the justice's executor gave his papers, was at the forefront of the campaign to venerate his mentor. His two-volume biography depicts the justice's past in almost mythical terms, especially when it comes to Holmes's role in the Civil War.[61] While Howe never finished the third and final volume of this biography, which would have dealt with Holmes's life on the bench, he did publish a host of articles in both scholarly and nonscholarly forums that cast Holmes as a heroic judge. Howe's efforts in this regard are most discernible in the 1940s and 1950s, when Holmes's reputation was suffering at the hands of certain critics who had been linking his pragmatic jurisprudence to the moral relativism of the Nazi regime.[62]

While Howe was clearly the most active of Holmes's secretaries when it came to projecting judicial and nonjudicial images of the justice to the lay and scholarly publics, other law clerks who became academics joined in on the act. Arthur E. Sutherland, for example, who taught law at Cornell from 1945 to 1950 and at Harvard from 1950 to 1970, wrote that "much of the greatness of Justice Holmes was a detachment from prejudice, an aloofness from vulgar passion, an aristocracy so complete that it disdained ordinary emotional partisanship."[63]

It was not solely those ex-clerks who became academics who participated in campaigns to resolve the crisis that threatened Holmes's standing in the pantheon of American judges. While the lay audience was perhaps not quite as attuned to debates about the virtues and pitfalls of Holmesian legal positivism as were those who read law review articles, Frances Biddle was aware that the American public expected its judges to read the public's morality into the Constitution rather than their own. Thus, as early as 1932, Biddle's review of a recently published collection of Holmes's opinions was intended to help "laymen and lawyers" understand that "Holmes cannot be classified . . . in terms of his personal convictions."[64] While this attempt to extol the virtues of his mentor cannot be viewed as an attempt to rescue the justice from association with the still nascent totalitarian movements of Europe, later comments by Biddle, such as those made almost thirty years later, can be seen as such. "Because Holmes rejected static and revealed concepts," Biddle wrote in his autobiography, "this did not mean that he did not cherish his own set of moral values."[65]

While the writings of Howe, Sutherland, and Biddle represent only a fraction of the literature on Holmes written by his ex-clerks, they do convey the basic thrust of the larger body of work: that Holmes was a heroic American whose jurisprudence was both morally defensible and properly restrained. To the extent that Holmes is widely viewed as one of the great American judges, and that his detached, dispassionate approach to deciding cases remains the model by which the public and scholarly communities rate American judges, it can be said that his law clerks did a great deal to mediate the conflicts inherent in the judicial role. This contribution, in turn, is arguably the product of Holmes's efforts as a mentor. He not only gave a personal demonstration to his protégés that judges could be both human and Olympian, but he instilled a sense of loyalty in them that assured their complicity in broadcasting that message.

Conclusion

Writing to Holmes in 1926, Chauncey Belknap thanked the justice for the clerkship experience that he chronicled so carefully in his diary, and expressed his hope that "youth and gaiety are still the companions of wisdom and insight."[66] Had he asked Thomas Corcoran, who became Holmes's secretary seven months later, he would certainly have been reassured, for Corcoran described his own experience with the justice as that of a "boy, plugging through the thicket blindly . . . lifted by gentle hands to the tops of high mountains and shown the far off end of the way."[67] The alliance between youth and experience that defined the clerkship model established by Holmes proved to be a rewarding one not only for the Yankee from Olympus and his protégés but also for other judges and clerks who adopted that model.

In light of the reputation-crafting function of law clerks that this essay has sought to expose, it may be useful to apply some of the theoretical work of literary critics and others who have studied reputation more generally and to reconceptualize the nature and function of law clerking as an institution. Charlotte Templin, for example, has argued that reputation is "a contingent phenomenon, emergent from social relations and related to particular historical and institutional contexts." Her work shows how the reputations of various authors were constructed by what she calls "evaluative communities," that is, "a group of agents who, to an important degree . . . share determinate meanings of a cultural object and value the object similarly."[68] What this suggests is that it is possible to conceive of a judge's law clerks as just such a community, and to see their function as more than simply "legal" or "administrative."[69]

Just as the literary canon has been shaped by the explicit marketing efforts of the friends, mentors, and protégés of various authors, so, it seems, has the pantheon of American judges been constructed, in part, by former law clerks functioning as evaluative communities.[70] Given his intense effort to mentor and secure the loyalty of the young men who would one day help to forge his reputation, it is little wonder that the place of Oliver Wendell Holmes Jr. in that pantheon is secure. While future studies should reveal the degree to which other American judges have benefited from the bargain-based model of law clerking that Holmes popularized, it is important to realize that such a model has potential benefits that extend beyond the interests of individual judges.

Since judges at every level of the federal judiciary employ ambitious law school graduates for terms of one or two years, and since most state court judges now do so as well, it may not be claiming too much to assert that the institution of law clerking has emerged as an internal mechanism by which the American court system can maintain its integrity and defend itself from attack. In a nation whose judiciary has suffered periodically from the wrath of angry critics and has occasionally been the target of intense reform efforts ranging from jurisdiction stripping to judicial recall, the existence of an in-house public relations firm composed of loyal ex-clerks is an important, if overlooked, weapon in the arsenal of the "least dangerous branch." Of course, given the intergenerational bargain between judges and law clerks that this essay describes, the weapon is useful only if enough judges uphold their end of the bargain by conscientiously mentoring the bright law school graduates who agree to spend a year or two in their chambers.

The prospects for the survival of this kind of mentoring in the chambers of American judges are not good, however, given what scholars have referred to as the "bureaucratization of the federal judiciary."[71] One aspect of this bureaucratization is the appropriation of money by Congress so that federal judges can hire more and more clerks to assist with what is perceived to be an overwhelming volume of litigation. Coupled with the trend toward hiring full-time staff attorneys in federal courts to do more and more of the work that judges once performed with the assistance of a single law clerk, there is a real possibility that the Holmes model of law clerking, along with its extralegal benefits, will disappear from the judicial landscape. But given that the "caseload explosion" responsible for the bureaucratization of the judiciary is overstated (at least according to Stanford law professor Gerald Gunther, who clerked for both Learned Hand and Earl Warren in the late 1950s), it may still be possible to preserve the model in something close to the form that has emerged over the course of a century.[72]

For those who appreciate the role that law clerks have played in shaping the reputation of American judicial figures, and who value their role in buttressing the integrity of the American judicial system, the threat to the survival of the Holmes model of law clerking, based on the hiring and mentoring of a small number of bright, young law students for a finite period of time, is unsettling and calls for efforts to preserve the essential components of that model. There is, however, at least one survival of Holmes's model that can, and should, be jettisoned: the continued practice by judges, and particularly by Supreme Court justices, of hiring white males from elite law schools in numbers that are vastly disproportionate to their percentage of the population and to their percentage in law schools.[73] In a world where equality of opportunity has become a widely accepted goal, if not a reality, it is no longer tolerable for members of the judiciary, the individuals most responsible historically for ensuring that equality, to reserve their choicest bit of extralegal largesse—the clerkship experience—for the most privileged members of our society.

Notes

1. Jerome Frank, *Law and the Modern Mind* (New York: Bretano's, 1930): 253.

2. Katie Loucheim, *The Making of the New Deal: The Insiders Speak* (Cambridge, Mass.: Harvard University Press, 1983): 25, 31 (quoting Alger Hiss).

3. Letter from Charles K. Poe to Oliver Wendell Holmes Jr., March 4, 1931, in Oliver Wendell Holmes Jr. Papers. Harvard University Law Library, microfilm ed., reel 42 (hereinafter Holmes Papers).

4. "Noble nursery of humanity" is a term that Ben Jonson used to describe the Inns of Court in sixteenth- and seventeenth-century England. See Anton Hermann-Chroust, "The Beginning, Flourishing and Decline of the Inns of Court: The Consolidation of the English Legal Profession after 1400," *Vanderbilt Law Review* 10 (1956): 79, 100.

5. Chauncey Belknap's diary was obtained from the law library of Patterson, Belknap, Webb, and Tyler, successor in interest to the firm that Belknap cofounded in 1921 (hereinafter Belknap Diary). Not only is the diary physically inaccessible to the public at this point, but it is written in Pitman shorthand, a method of transcription no longer in widespread use.

6. While the image we have of Holmes as an octogenarian is that of an energetic man seemingly impervious to the ravages of age, some of Holmes's later clerks expressed concern about the impact of his age on their own experience. Reflecting on the justice's diminishing capacities, H. Chapman Rose, his secretary for October term 1931, complained of a "residual feeling that the year has little to offer a prospective lawyer." Letter from H. Chapman Rose to Felix Frankfurter, March 31, 1932, in Felix Frankfurter Papers, Manuscript Division, Library of Congress, microfilm ed.,

container 145, reel 91 (hereinafter Frankfurter Papers). Holmes expressed a similar concern to Frankfurter a day earlier, confessing, "I feel as if I ought not let a young lawyer waste his time in being my intelligent valet." Letter from Oliver Wendell Holmes Jr. to Felix Frankfurter, March 30, 1932, in Oliver Wendell Holmes, *Holmes and Frankfurter: Their Correspondence, 1912–1934*, ed. Robert M. Mennel and Christine L. Compston (Hanover, N.H.: University Press of New England, 1996) (hereinafter *Holmes-Frankfurter Correspondence*), 283.

7. The Howe Diary is available to the public as part of the Mark DeWolfe Howe Papers at the Harvard Law School Library.

8. What we presently know about Holmes and his law clerks comes largely from memoirs and recollections published by clerks many years after their service with him. For examples of this genre, see Francis Biddle, *Mr. Justice Holmes* (New York: Scribner's, 1942), written thirty years after Biddle's clerkship; and Alger Hiss, *Recollections of a Life* (New York: Seaver Books, 1988), published after twice as much time had elapsed. It is not only the passage of time that dilutes the value of these reminiscences for the historian, but the fact that they were written for public consumption and hence are concerned more with dramatizing the clerkship experience than with precisely reconstructing it. Biddle's book was so dramatic in tone that it became the basis of a Broadway play about Holmes's life entitled *The Magnificent Yankee*. The play, in turn, was adapted for cinema in 1950 and for television in 1964. For information on the play and its connection to Biddle's biography, see I. Scott Messinger, "Legitimating Liberalism: The New Deal Image Makers and Oliver Wendell Holmes, Jr.", *Journal of Supreme Court History* (1995): 57.

9. There has been a spate of law review articles in recent years (as well as one full-length book) that discuss the institution of law clerking from historical and current perspectives. For a collection of the most recent articles on this subject, see "Law Clerks: The Transformation of the Judiciary," *Long Term View: A Journal of Informed Opinion* 3 (1995). This volume contains articles by fifteen prominent judges, academics, politicians, and journalists. For a book-length work, see John B. Oakley and Robert S. Thompson, *Law Clerks and the Judicial Process: Perceptions of the Qualities and Functions of Law Clerks in America Courts* (Berkeley: University of California Press, 1980). Unfortunately, these efforts have all focused on the relatively narrow question of the impact law clerks have on the judicial process. Without exception, the existing literature on the subject consists either of attacks on the alleged delegation of decision-making responsibility from judges to law clerks or explicit denials of such allegations—usually written by judges and former clerks. For typical attacks on the development of the institution of law clerking for its alleged usurpation of Article III functions, see Richard A. Posner, *The Federal Courts: Crisis and Reform* (Cambridge, Mass.: Harvard University Press, 1985): 102–19; Wade H. McCree Jr., "Bureaucratic Justice: An Early Warning," *University of Pennsylvania Law Review* 129 (1981): 777; and William H. Rehnquist, "Who Writes Decisions of the Supreme Court?," *U.S. News and World Report,* December 13, 1957, 74–75. For defenses of the institution, see Alex

Kozinski, "Making the Case for Law Clerks," *Long Term View* 3 (1995): 55; "Critical Discourse in Chambers: An Interview with Judge Patricia M. Wald," *Long Term View* 3 (1995), 45; and Alexander M. Bickel, "The Court: An Indictment Analyzed," *New York Times,* April 27, 1958, VI.16.

10. Act of August 4, 1886, ch. 902, 24 Stat. 222. Unlike the elite Harvard graduates who would come to occupy Holmes's "noble nursery," the early "stenographic assistants" were typically drawn from the law schools and bar of the District of Columbia or obtained by the justices through friends and relatives. See Oakley and Thompson, *Law Clerks,* 15–16.

11. Unlike his brethren, Holmes wrote each of his judicial opinions in longhand and thus had no use for the stenographic help provided for in the 1886 legislation. He was free, therefore, to innovate with his use of assistants and to redefine the position so that it became more attractive to the graduates of elite law schools. While Justice Brandeis imitated Holmes's practice of using his "stenographic assistants" for non-stenographic purposes as soon as he joined the Court in 1916, the other justices could not afford to do so until 1920, when Congress made an additional appropriation so that each justice could hire both a "stenographic clerk" and a more highly paid "law clerk." Act of May 20, 1920, ch. 214, 41 Stat. 631, 686–87. An exception was Chief Justice Edward Douglass White, who hired a law clerk and paid him out of his own pocket until the 1920 legislation went into effect. See Alexander M. Bickel, *The Judiciary and Responsible Government, 1910–1921* (New York: Macmillan, 1984): 82, n. 323.

12. For a sense of some of the more mundane chores handled by Holmes's assistants, including "fill[ing] out the checks for household bills and keep[ing] a running account in his checkbook," see Hiss, *Recollections of a Life,* 40. Augustin Derby, the justice's secretary for the 1906–07 term, described the sounding-board function of a Holmes clerk as follows: "[Holmes] took his secretaries into his confidence. Not that he revealed any secrets of the court, but he expressed his opinions freely about persons and events, and with a great deal of color." Augustin Derby, "Recollections of Mr. Justice Holmes," *New York University Law Quarterly Review* 12 (1935): 345, 351.

13. Letter from Oliver Wendell Holmes Jr. to Frederick Pollock, January 25, 1923, in Oliver Wendell Holmes Jr., *The Holmes-Pollock Letters: The Correspondence of Mr. Justice Holmes and Sir Frederick Pollock 1874–1932,* ed. Mark DeWolfe Howe (Cambridge, Mass.: Harvard University Press, 1941) 2: 110.

14. Holmes was straightforward about what it meant to him to be admired by the younger generation. In a letter to Irving Dillard in 1928 he wrote: "Old age has its discouragements but also its encouragements. And none is greater among the latter than to be told by young men that one's life has not been in vain." Letter from Oliver Wendell Holmes Jr. to Irving Dillard, October 9, 1928, in Frankfurter Papers, container 145, reel 91.

15. Biddle, *Mr. Justice Holmes,* 148.

16. As to the personal qualities Holmes liked in his clerks, Alger Hiss fit the bill. Holmes described him as "a very pleasant companion, doing his work well and having

just enough of modernist aesthetics to add interest to his talk." Letter from Oliver Wendell Holmes Jr. to Felix Frankfurter, November 5, 1929, *Holmes-Frankfurter Correspondence*, 243.

17. See Bickel, *Judiciary and Responsible Government*, 81–82.

18. The secretaries' office is described by Belknap in his diary entry of October 8, 1915. The spatial dynamics were unchanged as of 1929, when Hiss described them in the same way. See Louchheim, *Making of the New Deal*, 27.

19. Ibid., 25 (quoting Alger Hiss); letter from Oliver Wendell Holmes Jr. to Arthur Hill, October 27, 1934, in Frankfurter Papers, container 145, reel 91.

20. Letter from Oliver Wendell Holmes Jr. to Felix Frankfurter, December 19, 1915, *Holmes-Frankfurter Correspondence*, 40.

21. See Robert L. Griswold, *Fatherhood in America: A History* (New York: Basic Books, 1993: 88–89.

22. See Margaret Marsh, "Suburban Men and Masculine Domesticity, 1870–1915," *American Quarterly* 40, no. 2 (1988): 165.

23. E. Anthony Rotunda, *American Manhood: Transformations in Masculinity from the Revolution to the Modern Era* (New York: Basic Books, 1993), 212.

24. See ibid., 209.

25. Despite decisions by the U.S. Supreme Court and state supreme courts in the 1870s denying women the right to practice law, most states had guaranteed women access to the bar before the end of the century. See ibid., 213. Nevertheless, as late as 1910, the proportion of women in the bar as a whole had barely reached 1 percent. See Cynthia Fuchs Epstein, *Women in Law* (New York: Basic Books, 1982), 4.

26. See Richard L. Abel, *American Lawyers* (New York: Oxford University Press, 1989), 85–90. Abel pays particular attention to how the composition of the bar was altered, albeit temporarily, by an influx of foreign-born lawyers in the early decades of the twentieth century.

27. Holmes was no leveler when it came to his chosen profession. In a speech he gave in 1886, for example, he criticized "the passion for equality [in the law]" when it "attacks the lines of Nature which establish orders and degrees among the souls of men." Oliver Wendell Holmes Jr., "The Use of the Law Schools, Address before Harvard Law School Association" (November 5, 1886), in *The Collected Works of Justice Holmes*, ed. Sheldon Novick (Chicago: University of Chicago Press, 1995), 3:474 (hereinafter *Holmes Collected Works*).

28. Belknap Diary (entry of October 8, 1915).

29. As paraphrased by Belknap, Holmes's theory included the following critique of capitalism: "My first doubts about the regime of private property were experienced when I read of Andrew Carnegie's endowment of a public library. By affecting his property to a nonproductive enterprise of this sort, he was failing to fulfill his public function." Belknap Diary (entry of October 8, 1915). In light of this view, one wonders what Holmes would have thought about the use to which his highly publicized bequest of $250,000 to the U.S. government was put. (It was used to fund the Oliver

Wendell Holmes Devise History of the Supreme Court of the United States book series.)

30. Belknap Diary (entry of October 12, 1915).

31. Ibid. (entry of November 19, 1915).

32. There has been a steady stream of criticism about the alleged assumption of judicial decision-making and opinion-writing responsibilities by law clerks since the mid-1950s. See, e.g., John G. Kester, "The Law Clerk Explosion," *Litigation* 9 (1983): 20; Rehnquist, "Who Writes Decisions of the Supreme Court?," 74.

33. Belknap Diary (entry of October 13, 1915).

34. Ibid. (entry of October 19, 1915).

35. Ibid. (entry of December 19, 1915).

36. For a look at how the justices of the current Supreme Court rely, to a disturbing degree, upon the judgment of their law clerks in deciding cases, see Edward Lazarus, *Closed Chambers: The First Eyewitness Account of the Epic Struggles inside the Supreme Court* (New York: Times Books, 1998).

37. The testimony of other Holmes clerks confirms that the justice always wrote his own opinions. See, for example, the comment by W. Barton Leach that "[Holmes] had a great pride in his highly individual literary style and any measure of ghost writing would have been abhorrent to him. However, when he finished an opinion it was his habit to hand it to me with the direction, 'please embellish this with citations from my favorite author.' Meaning, of course, his own opinions." W. Barton Leach, "Recollections of a Holmes Secretary (1940) (unpublished manuscript, on file with the Harvard Law School Library," W. Barton Leach File, Miscellaneous, vol. 2).

38. See, e.g., Felix Frankfurter and James Landis, *The Business of the United States Supreme Court: A Study in the Federal Judicial System* (New York: Macmillan, 1927).

39. Letter from Oliver Wendell Holmes Jr. to Felix Frankfurter, December 31, 1915, in *Holmes-Frankfurter Correspondence*, 42.

40. Belknap Diary (entry of November 9, 1915).

41. By my count, Belknap attended seven theater productions during his six months with Holmes, played four rounds of golf, took four day-long hikes in Maryland and Virginia, and spent several days observing Congress in session. He also was a frequent guest of the Holmeses as they entertained celebrities from the world of politics and academia, as well as a guest of several families in the D.C. area with whom he had family connections.

42. According to Alger Hiss, the black book was "the nearest thing to a diary" that Justice Holmes kept. See Hiss, *Recollections of a Life*, 32.

43. Belknap Diary (entry of October 16, 1915).

44. See Plato, *The Symposium*, trans. and ed. Alexander Nehemas and Paul Woodruff (Indianapolis: Hackett, 1989), xv. For a discussion of the historically differential shapes of male and female homosociality from Plato's day through the early twentieth century, see Eve Kosofsky Sedgwick, *Between Men: English Literature and Male Homosocial Desire* (New York: Columbia University Press, 1985). Sedgwick makes explicit

reference to *The Symposium* as a model of same-sex mentoring that fostered enduring inequalities of power between men and women (4–5).

45. Plato, *The Symposium,* 18 (emphasis added).

46. According to Francis Biddle, Holmes read the *Symposium* in its original Greek sometime between 1910 and 1911. See Francis Biddle, *Justice Holmes, Natural Law, and the Supreme Court* (New York: Macmillan, 1961), 5–6. Since he was still discussing it with Belknap five years later, it is reasonable to infer that the book resonated powerfully with the justice.

47. Holmes was not alone among his contemporaries in adopting this exchange-based model of mentorship based on the Greek example. Charles W. Eliot, the president of Harvard College from 1869 to 1908 and the man who convinced Holmes to join the Harvard Law School faculty in 1882, was such a firm believer that the younger generation owed a debt to their mentors for the education they received that he made this point explicitly in his inaugural address as president, exhorting his young audience to "[c]herish the natural sentiment of personal devotion to the teacher who calls out your better powers. It is a great delight to serve an intellectual master. . . . If ever in after years you come to smile at the youthful reverence you paid, believe me, it will be with tears in your eyes." Kim Townsend, *Manhood at Harvard: William James and Others* (New York: W. W. Norton, 1996), 132 (quoting Eliot).

48. Belknap Diary (entries of October 20, 1915, March 25, 1916).

49. Ibid. (entry of November 20, 1915).

50. Hiss, *Recollections of a Life,* 48–49.

51. Letter from Chauncey Belknap to Oliver Wendell Holmes Jr., March 6, 1926, in Holmes Papers, reel 15.

52. See "Rockefeller Gift Waits on Report: Lawyer Is Returning from Cairo with Information on the Negotiations," *New York Times,* February 16, 1926, 25:1. See also "Chauncey Belknap Gets State Bar Nomination," *New York Times,* January 8, 1960, 17:2.

53. Of the twenty-one ex-clerks who do have entries in *Who's Who,* all but one are described specifically in those entries as having been a law secretary to Justice Holmes. The lone exception is Charles Denby, secretary for the 1925–26 term. It is interesting to note that whereas all of Holmes's other secretaries appear in every volume of *Who's Who* from the date of their first appearance until the year of their death, Alger Hiss has entries in the 1948–49 and 1950–51 editions, but he never appears again. His purging from these annals of fame coincides exactly with his exposure as an alleged communist spy by Whittaker Chambers.

54. Charles K. Poe (Poe, Falknor & Emory in Seattle); Howard Stockton (Warren, Garfield, Whiteside & Lamson in Boston); Leland Duer (Duer & Taylor in New York); Chauncey Belknap (Patterson, Belknap & Webb in New York); Vaughn Miller (Miller, Martin, Hitching & Tipton in Chattanooga); Lloyd Landau (Root, Clark, Bruckner, & Ballantine in New York); Robert Benjamin (Parker, Duryee, Benjamin, Zunino & Malone in New York); John E. Lockwood (Milbank, Tweed, Hadley &

McCloy in New York); Robert Wales (Miller, Gorham, Wescott & Adams in Chicago); Horace Chapman Rose (Jones, Day, Reavis & Pogue in Washington, D.C.); and Donald Hiss (Alger's brother) (Covington & Burling in Washington, D.C.).

55. Erland F. Fish (president of Massachusetts State Senate); Frances B. Biddle (U.S. attorney general, 1941–45); Harvey H. Bundy (assistant secretary of state, 1931–33); Day Kimball (justice, Supreme Court of Bermuda); Laurence Curtis (U. S. congressman from Massachusetts, 1952–62); Charles Denby Jr. (assistant administrator, Lend Lease Administration (World War II)); Thomas Corcoran (key draftsman for Federal Housing Act of 1933, Securities Exchange Act of 1934, Utility Holding Company Act of 1935, and Fair Labor Standards Act of 1938); Alger Hiss (Department of State official, 1936–46); James Henry Rowe (U.S. assistant attorney general, 1941–43).

56. Augustin Derby (professor of law, Harvard); Stanley Morrison (lecturer in law, Stanford, 1924–55); W. Barton Leach (professor of law, Harvard, 1929–69); Arthur E. Sutherland (professor of law, Harvard, 1950–70); Mark DeWolfe Howe (professor of law, Harvard, 1945–67).

57. Irving S. Olds (president, U.S. Steel Corp.); Stanley Clarke (trustee, Assoc. Gas & Electric Co.); George L. Harrison (president, chairman of the board, RCA, 1941–54); James M. Nicely (vice president, First National City Bank, 1948–59).

58. Letter from Thomas Corcoran to Oliver Wendell Holmes Jr., March 6, 1928, in Holmes Papers, reel 31; letter from Francis Biddle to Oliver Wendell Holmes Jr., June 29, 1912, in Holmes Papers, reel 28.

59. The career of James H. Rowe, secretary for the October term 1934, provides a good example of how this network functioned. In 1939 he was chosen to be an executive assistant to President Roosevelt at the recommendation of Thomas Corcoran, and later he was hired by Francis Biddle to be assistant to the attorney general. See "Roosevelt Names Three New Aides," *New York Times,* July 13, 1939, 3:7; "J. H. Rowe to Be Biddle Aide," *New York Times,* November 18, 1941, 14:6.

60. According to the research done by one bibliographer, there were at least thirty-one books, articles, and reviews about Holmes published by his ex-clerks as of 1976. See Harry C. Shriver, *What Justice Holmes Wrote and What Has Been Written about Him: A Bibliography, 1866–1976* (Potomac, Md.: Fox Hill Press, 1978). I suspect that there are even more.

61. See Mark Dewolfe Howe, *Justice Oliver Wendell Holmes,* vol. 1: *The Shaping Years: 1841–1870* (Cambridge, Mass.: Harvard University Press, 1957); Howe, *Justice Oliver Wendell Holmes,* vol. 2: *The Proving Years: 1870–1882* (Cambridge, Mass.: Harvard University Press, 1963). Despite some evidence that it was actually General Horatio Wright who shouted at Abraham Lincoln to "get down you damn fool, before you get shot" during the president's visit to Fort Stevens in 1864, Howe's biography tends to corroborate Holmes's own account of the event—that it was the future justice who blurted out the impetuous order—referring to that account as "the most reliable version." See Howe, *Proving Years,* 168.

62. Mark DeWolfe Howe, Mr. Justice Holmes, Address before the Thursday Club

(March 13, 1941), in *Holmes Papers*, Reel 56, 9; Howe, "The Positivism of Mr. Justice Holmes," *Harvard Law Review* 64 (1951): 539.

63. Arthur E. Sutherland, review of *Touched with Fire: Civil War Letters and Diary of Oliver Wendell Holmes, Jr., 1861–1864*, ed. Mark DeWolfe Howe, *Cornell Law Quarterly* 32 (1947): 617 (1946).

64. Francis Biddle, "Mr. Justice Holmes" (review of *The Representative Opinions of Mr. Justice Holmes*, ed. Alfred Lief), *New Republic*, September 7, 1932, 105.

65. Biddle, *Casual Past*, 286.

66. Letter from Chauncey Belknap to Oliver Wendell Holmes Jr., March 6, 1926, Holmes Papers, reel 15.

67. Letter from Thomas Corcoran to Oliver Wendell Holmes Jr., March 6, 1928, Holmes Papers, reel 31.

68. Charlotte Templin, *Feminism and the Politics of Literary Reputation: The Example of Erica Jong* (Lawrence: University of Kansas Press, 1995), ix, 36.

69. Critical Legal Historians have been arguing for some time that law has "symbolic" as well as "instrumental" uses, in an effort to drive home their larger point about how law structures consciousness, but they have adopted a surprisingly narrow definition of law and legal forms in doing so. See, e.g., Robert W. Gordon, "Critical Legal Histories," *Stanford Law Review* 36 (1984): 57, 111. As the foregoing examination of one particular aspect of the American judiciary indicates, it is not just statutes and judicial opinions that are constitutive of social relations and cultural meanings, but legal institutions as well.

70. For works that discuss the forging of authorial reputation by such communities, see John Rodden, *The Politics of Literary Reputation: The Making and Claiming of "St. George" Orwell* (New York: Oxford University Press, 1989); Lawrence H. Schwartz, *Creating Faulkner's Reputation* (Knoxville: University of Tennessee Press, 1988); and Gladys Engel Lang and Kurt Lang, "Recognition and Renown: The Survival of Artistic Reputation," *American Journal of Sociology* 94 (1988): 79. Those who have studied judicial reputation have, on the whole, neglected the role played by reputation crafters and have focused instead on such factors as a particular judge's longevity of service, intellectual ability, ideology, impact on legal development, personal characteristics, and writing style. See, e.g., Richard A. Posner, *Cardozo: A Study in Reputation* (Chicago: University of Chicago Press, 1990); William G. Ross, "The Ratings Game: Factors That Influence Judicial Reputation," *Marquette Law Review* 79 (1996): 401.

71. Gerald Gunther has critiqued the "personnel explosion" in federal courts, emphasizing particularly how the increasing number of judicial assistants has severed the traditionally close relationships between judges and their law clerks. See Gerald Gunther, "Judge Learned Hand: The Man and the Judge," address before the California State Bar Association (October 12, 1998, C-SPAN television broadcast on January 25, 1997). For an attack on the increasing use of staff attorneys in federal courts, see McCree, "Bureaucratic Justice," 777, 787–88.

72. Gunther, "Judge Learned Hand."

73. Seventy-six percent of Supreme Court law clerks who served between 1990 and 1995 are white men, a number that is actually an improvement on the figures for the decade of the 1960s, in which 99 percent of these prestigious positions were held by white men. See Gwen Daye Richardson, "Court's Clerk Tally Is Not Race Based; It's School Based," *USA Today,* October 5, 1998, 15A. Of course, there are those, like Richardson, who maintain that these figures reflect nothing so much as the biased admission policies of the elite law schools from whom the pool of Supreme Court law clerks has traditionally been drawn, but others have blamed the justices for refusing to expand this pool by hiring clerks who attended law schools other than Harvard and Yale. See, e.g., Sam Fullwood III, "For Supreme Court Clerks, the Majority Rules," *Los Angeles Times,* October 4, 1998, A18.

TODD C. PEPPERS

Isaiah and His Young Disciples

Justice Louis Brandeis and His Law Clerks

I t cannot be said that Louis Dembitz Brandeis has suffered from a lack of scholarly attention. Considered to be one of the most influential justices in the history of the United States Supreme Court, scores of books and law review articles have been written about Brandeis the lawyer, the political insider, the Zionist, and the justice. A case can be made, however, that history has not fully recognized the important and lasting contribution that Brandeis made to the development of the institutional rules and norms surrounding the Supreme Court law clerk, an oversight that this essay seeks to rectify.

Brandeis was not the first Supreme Court justice to hire law clerks. Nor was Brandeis responsible for much of the early mythology surrounding the relationship between justice and law clerk. As discussed in I. Scott Messinger's wonderful essay on Oliver Wendell Holmes Jr., it was the "Magnificent Yankee" who summoned a generation of Harvard Law School graduates to serve as private secretaries, social companions, surrogate sons, and caretakers to "God's grandfather." It would be Brandeis's clerkship model, however, that led to the professionalization of the clerkship institution. From the hiring of his first law clerk, Brandeis demanded that each law clerk have a strong work ethic, have superior legal writing and research skills, and abide by the fiduciary relationship between justice and law clerk. While future justices have differed from Brandeis in the type of substantive job duties assigned to their law clerks (and Brandeis would likely be aghast at the job responsibilities given to modern law clerks), the expectations about the duties of confidentiality and loyalty as well as the skills to be possessed by law clerks remain unchanged. This essay explores the Brandeis clerkship model, arguing that Brandeis's rules for, and expectations of, his law clerks not only were unique for their time but forever shaped the clerkship models adopted by future generations of justices.

The Selection of Justice Brandeis's Law Clerks

The selection of law clerks by the justices on the White, Taft, and Hughes Courts varied dramatically from the selection practices of the modern Court. While today's justices pour through hundreds of applications, often assisted by a screening committee, in the early years of the clerkship institution law students at Harvard, Yale, and Columbia found themselves tapped by faculty members to work at the Supreme Court for such justices as Holmes, William Howard Taft, and Harlan Fiske Stone. Upon arriving at the Supreme Court, Brandeis began following Holmes's practice of having Harvard Law School professor Felix Frankfurter select his clerks. In a December 1, 1916, letter to Frankfurter, Brandeis writes that Frankfurter's selection of Calvert Magruder as his first law clerk strengthened the justice's confidence in Frankfurter, and two years later Brandeis states that Frankfurter now has unlimited discretion to select his clerks—while adding that "[w]ealth, ancestry, and marriage, of course, create presumptions; but they may be overcome."[1] Brandeis later supplemented his list of nonbinding hiring preferences, telling Frankfurter that "other things being equal, it is always preferable to take some one whom there is reason to believe will become a law teacher."[2]

The twenty-one men selected by Frankfurter had a few common characteristics. Of course, they were all Harvard Law School men. Eighteen of the twenty-one clerks were members of the *Harvard Law Review,* many had worked—either during their third year of law school or during a subsequent year of graduate school—as Professor Frankfurter's research assistants, and a few had prior clerkship experience with such appellate court judges as Learned Hand and Julian Mack (prior appellate clerkship experience would not become the norm for Supreme Court law clerks until the 1960s).

Another characteristic that many of the law clerks shared was religion. Brandeis biographer Philippa Strum states that the "overwhelming majority" of Brandeis's clerks in the 1920s and 1930s were Jewish. Strum writes that Brandeis's selection practices stemmed from the fact that (1) he preferred clerks who had the potential to be law professors, and (2), as Brandeis stated, he believed that "a great service could be done generally to American law and to the Jews by placing desirable ones in the law school faculties," given the fact that "in the Jew [there is] a certain potential spirituality and sense of public service which can be more easily aroused and directed, than at present is discernible in American non-Jews."[3]

Typically, Brandeis never interviewed—or even met with—potential law clerks prior to their selection by Frankfurter. At least one law clerk found Brandeis's habit of not interviewing prospective law clerks to be odd. Adrian S. Fisher (who clerked during October term 1938) asked then-professor Felix Frankfurter "if I could meet the Justice before, just to make sure he didn't think he was getting a pig in the poke or anything, but Felix looked at me like that was a real strange request, and so I never met Brandeis before my clerkship began."[4] David Riesman (October term 1935) would be one of the few clerks to meet with Brandeis prior to his clerkship.[5] After traveling to Washington, D.C., and meeting with Justices Brandeis, Cardozo, and Holmes in 1934, Riesman returned to Cambridge and immediately contacted Frankfurter. "I wrote to Felix that I would much prefer to clerk for Cardozo instead of someone who reminds me of my stern father [to wit, Brandeis]. Felix Frankfurter rejected this in a very stern letter to me. He said it was precisely for those reasons that it would be good for me."[6] The idea of somebody declining an offer to clerk for Justice Brandeis is a bit astonishing, and as discussed below, Riesman's entire clerkship experience can be viewed as the exception to the norm.

Perhaps because the law clerks did not interview prior to their clerkship, they found their first encounter with the legendary jurist to be daunting. Former law clerk H. Thomas Austern (October term 1930) describes Brandeis as a combination of "Jesus Christ and a Hebrew prophet," confessing that "in the first few months I was scared to death of him."[7] Austern's description was echoed by Fisher, who recalls that his first impression was that Justice Brandeis "seemed to be a combination of Isaiah the prophet and Abraham Lincoln. A raw bone characteristic. He had a rough hewn look, [and] a grave, almost diffident courtesy."[8] Even former law clerk Dean Acheson (October terms 1919 and 1920), writing his memoirs after a career on the international stage, remained struck by Brandeis's appearance:

> The Justice was an arresting figure; his head of Lincolnian cast and grandeur, the same boldness and ruggedness of features, the same untamed hair, the eyes of infinite depth under bushy eyebrows, which in moments of emotion seemed to jut out. As he grew older, he carried a prophetic, if not intimidating aura. It was not in jest that later law clerks referred to him as Isaiah.[9]

Given such a description of Justice Brandeis, it is hardly surprising to learn that it would take months before the clerks felt entirely comfortable in the presence of such a biblical figure.

The law clerks received little, if any, advice or instruction from Frankfurter. "He [Frankfurter] did say you were expected to work very hard, meaning mornings, afternoons and evenings, and you would have to cut down on your social life," recalls former law clerk Adrian S. Fisher. "[It] was also implied that you should not be married. Nothing explicit, but it seemed clear."[10] Through Frankfurter, Brandeis issued warnings and assigned homework to his future law clerks. Brandeis instructed Frankfurter to inform incoming law clerk J. Willard Hurst (October term 1936) "that he will be expected to be familiar with all my opinions by Sept. 15th and that the pass mark is 99¼ percent. Also say that he should otherwise familiarize himself with the tools of the trade," lamenting the fact that an earlier law clerk did not fully appreciate the scope of Shepard's Citations.[11] Brandeis subsequently added to the reading list, writing later, "[w]ould it not be well to have Hurst read, before the Autumn, 'Business of the USSC,' and Charles Warren's 'S.C. in U.S. History' so as to get in the background."[12]

The Brandeis Clerkship Model

The Brandeis law clerks reported for duty at Justice and Mrs. Brandeis's private residence—originally at their Stoneleigh Court apartment on Connecticut Avenue and later at a second apartment building at 2205 California Street Northwest. At both locations, Justice Brandeis used a smaller, second apartment to house offices for himself and his clerk. Regarding the California Street apartment, Brandeis biographer Philippa Strum writes: "Willard Hurst found the office apartment overflowing with papers and books. The bathtub was filled with folders of clippings and references to bits of irrelevant information Brandeis came across while doing research, information that interested him as well as data that might provide useful some day . . . [t]he kitchenette was piled with manuscripts and corrected proofs."[13]

Even after the construction of the Supreme Court building, Justice Brandeis and his law clerk worked at the apartment.[14] In 1920 Congress authorized the justices to employ both a law clerk and a stenographic assistant, but Brandeis did not hire either a secretary or a second law clerk. "Why Brandeis dispensed with secretarial aid was never explained, but I surmise that he was loath to share the confidences of the office more widely than the absolute minimum," writes former law clerk Paul A. Freund (October term 1932). "That, and perhaps his general avoidance of belongings."[15] Justice Brandeis's official court staff was rounded out by a series of aging messengers.

The law clerks typically reported to duty in late September, often overlapping with the outgoing clerk for several days of "breaking in." The clerks' primary job duties were assisting in the preparation of opinions and related legal research. Brandeis alone began the process by drafting the statement of facts. "This was a chore that Brandeis took upon himself," comments Freund. "[I]t seemed to me . . . that this was a token, a mark of his intellectual scruple, that before either he or his law clerk should set to work expounding the law, the facts of the case should have been thoroughly assimilated, understood and made part of himself as an earnest that his work would be grounded in an appreciation of the true nature of the controversy before him."[16] The statement of facts in the cases assigned to Brandeis can be found in his personal papers, written in his distinctive hand on lined paper "with a large black fountain pen that might have been a relic of the iron age."[17]

Brandeis did not always produce a complete first draft. "He would most frequently write out a few pages, have them printed, revise them, add a few more pages, and the whole printed again, and so forth."[18] At some point the printed pages would be handed off to the clerk for comment and revision. Brandeis did not want either himself or his clerk to treat the other's work as gospel. Writes Acheson: "My instructions regarding his work were to look with suspicion on every statement of fact until it was proved from the record of the case, and on every statement of law until I had exhausted the authorities. If additional points should be made, I was to develop them thoroughly. Sometimes my work took the form of a revision of his; sometimes of a memorandum of suggestions to him."[19]

Conversely, Acheson adds that Brandeis might use portions of his clerk's original draft opinion or instead begin anew.[20] "On occasion some sentences in the law clerk's memoranda would find their way into the opinion," writes Freund. "[M]ore often they suffered the fate of the Justice's own first drafts— radical revision, transposition, strengthening and polishing."[21] Freund's description of this laborious drafting process is reflected in the Louis Brandeis Papers at Harvard Law School, where multiple opinion drafts—some covered with the justice's handwritten edits, others with typed insertions of questions or proposed changes by the law clerks—can be found in a single case file.

It is apparent that Brandeis considered his clerk a partner (although not an equal one) in a joint task.[22] This partnership extended through the opinion-drafting process. Freund writes that both Justice Brandeis and his law clerk received copies of revised opinions from the Supreme Court printing office.[23] In describing the final editing process, Acheson comments: "A touching part of our relationship was the Justice's insistence that nothing should go out unless we were *both* satisfied with the product. His patience and generosity were inexhaustible."[24] Hurst recalls that Justice Brandeis himself referred to the relationship between law clerk and justice as a partnership, albeit with the law clerk in a more junior role. "[Y]ou were expected to have the responsibilities of a partner. He expected me to pull no punches and read everything with a critical eye. He didn't want any petitions for rehearing because of any error on his part. I was not to stand in awe of him but was to tell him frankly what I thought."[25]

Of course, this "partnership" placed tremendous stress upon the clerk. "The illusion was carefully fostered that the Justice was relying, indeed depending, on the criticism and collaboration of his law clerk," writes Freund. "How could one fail to miss the moral implications of responsibility?"[26] These implications were forever seared into the collective memory of the Brandeis law clerks as the result of a blunder committed by the young Dean Acheson, who served as Brandeis's law clerk during October terms 1919 and 1920. After discovering that there were two incorrect legal cites in an opinion he was preparing to announce from the bench, Brandeis returned to his home office and sternly announced to Acheson: "Please remember that your function is to correct my errors, not to introduce errors of your own."[27] William A. Sutherland (October terms 1917 and 1918), who himself suffered the embarrassment of letting an incorrect legal cite remain in a draft opinion, recalls that Brandeis was not angry when his young clerk committed such an error, "but he made you feel that you certainly didn't want to have something like that happen again."[28]

Law clerks did not prepare bench memoranda, and if they did review the occasional cert petition, it was at the start of the term when the pace was slow. Writes Acheson:

> In two respects my work with Justice Brandeis was different from the current work of many law clerks with their chiefs. This is sometimes closely concerned with the function of deciding. The Justice wanted no help or suggestions in making up his mind. So I had nothing to do with petitions for certiorari.... the Justice was inflexible in holding that the duty of decision must be performed by him unaided.... He was equally emphatic in refusing to permit what many of the Justices today require, a bench memorandum or précis of the case from their law clerks to give them the gist of the matter before the argument. To Justice Brandeis ... this was a profanation of advocacy. He owed it to counsel—who he always

hoped . . . would be advocates to—to present them with a judicial mind unscratched by the scribblings of clerks.[29]

Freund suggests another, more practical reason for why the clerks did not discuss the cases with Brandeis prior to oral argument—"he would consider it an unnecessary drain on resources."[30]

A few additional topics were never discussed between law clerk and justice: the results of the Court's weekly conferences and Brandeis's opinions of other justices. Unlike future justices, Brandeis did not come back from the Supreme Court's conferences and unburden himself to his law clerks. His docket book was kept locked, only to be burned at the end of the term by the marshal of the Court.[31] Nor did he complain or gossip about the other justices, perhaps due to what one clerk perceived as the justice's "adulation for the dignity of the Supreme Court."[32]

The other main responsibility for a Brandeis clerk: legal research. Not surprisingly, the inventor of "the Brandeis brief" gave his clerks daunting research assignments. "[W]e worked like hell for Brandeis checking cases and doing research," recalls Sutherland.[33] While Justice Brandeis expected his clerks to provide "the most exacting, professional, and imaginative search of the legal authorities," Acheson states that successful *legal* research "was more often than not the beginning, not the end, of our research." Thus Acheson's research time was spent equally in the Supreme Court Library as in the Library of Congress, collecting statistics and historical data "with civil servants whose only recompense for hours of patient help to me was to see an uncatalogued report of theirs cited in a footnote to a dissenting opinion."[34] A good example of the exhausting research projects assigned to the law clerks is found in the clerkship of Henry J. Friendly (October term 1927), who spent weeks at the Library of Congress preparing a report on the wiretapping laws of the forty-eight states.[35] Such visits were common to all clerks, who "came to know intimately the labyrinths of the Library of Congress."[36]

In short, "[t]he clerks went to Brandeis each year in trepidation, worked with exhilaration, and left in exhaustion."[37] Since Brandeis assumed that his law clerks would provide nothing less than excellence, they were not praised when they achieved that standard. Recalls Austern:

One time we had this case, the Jewel [*sic*] case, involving a question of radio copyrights.[38] And I set up this elaborate contraption with balls and pendulums to show the impact of frequency modulation. And [he] sat there, with his legs crossed, watching my little demonstration for 40 minutes. And after it was all over he just said thank you, and that was it. He rarely said anything you did was a great job. He assumed, since you were there, that you would do a great job.[39]

Adds Acheson: "Justice Brandeis's standard for our work was perfection as a norm, to be bettered on special occasions," a standard that the law clerk might not know if he ever achieved since the justice "was not given to praise in any form."[40] If the law clerks did receive praise for their work, it tended to come from either Frankfurter or Mrs. Brandeis. For a group of young men, fresh out of law school and working for a great man, operating without positive feedback from the justice must have felt akin to doing a high wire act without a net.

While former law clerk Friendly undeniably met the standard of excellence demanded by Justice Brandeis,[41] Friendly humorously lamented the fact that his skepticism about technology cost Justice Brandeis the opportunity to be the first jurist to pen a legal opinion that referenced television. The opinion was Justice Brandeis's famous dissent in *Olmstead v. United States* (277 U.S. 438 [1928]), a case involving whether the government's warrantless wiretapping of the telephone calls of a suspected bootlegger violated the Fourth Amendment. In support of his powerful argument that "[t]he progress of science in furnishing the government with means of espionage is not likely to stop with wire tapping," Brandeis originally pointed to the nascent technology of television in an opinion draft. Friendly recalls that in early drafts of the *Olmstead* dissent, Justice Brandeis argued that television would permit the government to look into people's homes—a technological point with which Friendly took issue:

And I said: Mr. Justice, it doesn't work that way! You can't just beam a television set out of somebody's home and see what they're doing. He said: That's just exactly what you can do. So we batted the ball across the net a few times, and I said: Well, I really think it's silly for two lawyers to be discussing this—why don't I go to the Library of Congress and get you some articles about this. Which will explain what television really is. Well, he said, that's fine. And of course you're going to be wrong. Well, I didn't say anything. So, I got the articles, and unhappily, I was right. And so, he had to strike that sentence.[42]

"Unhappily, the reference was deleted in deference to the scientific skepticism of his law clerk," writes Freund, clearly tongue-in-cheek, "who strongly doubted that the new device could be adapted to the uses of espionage."[43]

Cheerfully admits Friendly: "And in the course of events, he [Brandeis] was right! And I was wrong."

From the law clerks' perspective, Brandeis's natural remoteness was exacerbated by the justice's method of communication. Recalls former law clerk Louis L. Jaffe (October term 1933): "I worked in a little apartment at Stoneleigh Court. Brandeis worked in his own apartment, and I really saw very little of him. He would slip a paper under the door leaving me instructions in the morning before I got there, and I would slip my work under his door when I finished. He was really a very remote, distant person. I had very little direct personal contact with him. It took me a while to get over the pique of that, not having any contact with him."[44]

Brandeis typically met with his law clerks for a thirty-minute meeting around 8:30 a.m. and again in the early evening around 6:00 to 7:00 p.m. The law clerks usually continued working after the evening meeting. An early riser, Brandeis was often at work when the clerks arrived in the morning—a fact that made former clerk Freund "feel like a laggard keeping bankers hours."[45] Freund was not the only law clerk impressed by Brandeis's work ethic. Former clerk Austern commented: "I remember one time preparing a memo and staying up all night until about 5:30, going down to his apartment and slipping the memo under the door, and see it retrieved from the other side of the door."[46] Brandeis would sometimes work in his office in the second apartment before returning to his bedroom/study in his own apartment in the afternoon. Despite these meetings, at least one former clerk admitted that "it was a lonesome job."[47]

With the job, however, came freedom. Justice Brandeis did not impose set office hours on his clerks, and his only concern was that the assigned work be completed on time. Recalls Freund:

> It had become the custom by my time for clerks to work at all hours, but some had rather individual habits. One predecessor, who has since become an industrialist [Robert G. Page], made a practice of going out at night on the social circuit, then coming straight to the office in the early hours of the morning for a stint before returning home. On one occasion, having arrived at the office at one or two a.m., he was overtaken there at five o'clock, which was the Justice's opening of the work day.... The Justice entered the office, just above his residence in the apartment building, and greeting his clerk, "Good morning, Page," in a perfectly casual way, as if it were the most natural thing in the world for a law clerk to be about at five in the morning in white tie and tails.[48]

There is a sense that the limited interactions between the justice and his law clerk diminished over time, a pattern perhaps explained by Brandeis's slowly declining health. "You have to remember that we didn't talk much because this man was hoarding his energy," explains Fisher, Brandeis's last law clerk. "It was almost like being in Floyd Patterson's training camp. He [Brandeis] wasn't going to expend any energy on something he didn't have to do."[49]

The day-to-day ritual of clerking for Brandeis was shaped not only by the justice but also by his wife. "I should say that Mrs. Brandeis looked after him like he was a baby," recalls Sutherland. "She wouldn't let him work more than two hours in a row, for example. So every two hours he took the stairs down, took a quick walk around the block, came back for a five minute nap, and then started working again."[50] Mrs. Brandeis's protectiveness of her husband occasionally led to the odd job assignment for the law clerks. Freund recounts a time when Justice Brandeis was scheduled to meet president-elect Franklin Delano Roosevelt at the Mayflower Hotel in Washington, D.C. The day prior to the meeting, Freund was dispatched to the hotel by Mrs. Brandeis to "make sure that there were no open windows because Justice Brandeis was very susceptible to colds." Upon arriving at the hotel, the hotel staff told Freund that Mrs. Brandeis's fears were unfounded since FDR "did not like drafts either."[51]

The sense of isolation felt by some of the Brandeis law clerks was further exacerbated by Justice Brandeis's imposition of a strict duty of confidentiality, a precursor to the rules and norms that bind modern law clerks. "I remember the first thing he said. 'In this job you will hear and see a lot that's confidential,'" states Freund. "'There has never been a leak from this office and I don't expect there to be any leaks.'"[52] The duty of confidentiality extended not only to the general public but to the Supreme Court law clerks in other chambers as well.[53] Finally, Brandeis's sense of institutional loyalty meant that he imposed a duty of confidentiality upon himself. "Throughout the history of the Court there have been justices who in private conversation or correspondence have referred to colleagues in salty and not always complimentary terms," explains Calvert Magruder. "I never heard Justice Brandeis indulge himself in this relatively harmless sport. Nor did he ever betray any exasperation when his associates did not see things his way."[54]

The duties of the law clerks extended beyond the law. The clerks were drafted to help host the weekly teas that Washington society expected Mrs. Brandeis to hold.[55] At the teas, the law clerks served multiple roles—including guest, waiter, and bouncer. Landis explains that his duties included making sure "both that the guests were served and that the Justice should not be cornered too long by anyone of them."[56] The teas were not merely a social occasion, and the former clerks believed that the teas served multiple functions. Freund states that Brandeis "often invited people to tea who had just done something that he admired," adding that the invitation itself was a "sort of accolade" and that the invited guest would receive the justice's full attention and a volley of "penetrating questions."[57]

Brandeis's courtly side emerged at the teas. "Brandeis would never sit if a lady were in the room standing," states Austern. "So at these teas we had, Mrs. Brandeis had me running around making sure all the ladies were sitting down."[58] Law clerks remember that Brandeis could be charming to his guests, including the relatives of his law clerks. Former law clerk Nathaniel L. Nathanson (October term 1934) recounts a story of taking his mother to tea at the Brandeis residence: "He [Brandeis] was a pretty tough cookie, I thought, and I had told my mother about him . . . [but] he was as charming as could be at that tea, and afterwards my mother kept asking me how I could say all those things about him.[59] Mrs. Brandeis herself would make sure that visitors were not monopolizing the justice's time, often limiting the visitors to ten minutes with the justice before shooing them toward the tea tray. And Mrs. Brandeis would monitor the clerks to ensure they were following strict Washington protocol. "[S]he had learned how seriously people in Washington took their titles, and the clerk was admonished to be certain to get them right."[60]

Law clerks were also invited to join the Brandeises for dinner. Former clerk W. Graham Claytor Jr. (October term 1937) remembers that Mrs. Brandeis's protective nature extended to dinner as well, where she reminded guests that dinner started promptly at 7:00 p.m. and the justice was expected to retire by 9:30 p.m. While the conversation and company may have been first class, the food was not. Austern remarks that Mrs. Brandeis "would cut a slice of roast beef you could see through," and Riesman is even less charitable: "Dinner there was gastronomically ghastly."[61] The law clerks also served as bouncers at these evening functions. Landis states that the law clerk was responsible for guaranteeing that the Brandeis guests left at 10:00 p.m., and that any failure in this essential duty would result in an "accusing" stare from Mrs. Brandeis.

Besides teas and dinners, the daily grind was interrupted with trips between the Brandeis and Holmes residences. Because Brandeis and Holmes did not like the telephone, the law clerks' responsibilities included carrying materials between the two homes. This purely secretarial responsibility gave clerks the opportunity to interact with the great Holmes.

In his final years on the bench, the aging Brandeis may have leaned more heavily upon his law clerks. His last law clerk, Adrian Fisher, recalls working on both cert petitions and some opinion drafts, and the strapping former rugby player–turned–law clerk was pressed into service as an elevator:

> [Mrs. Brandeis] called in the afternoon and said the elevator was broken, Justice Brandeis was already on his way back from the Court, and what was I going to do about it. Clerks were expected to do everything. Well, I went down there and found the janitor . . . [a]nd we found a chair. And when Brandeis walked in, we had him sit in the chair, and we carried him up five flights of stairs. And I'll never forget that. Brandeis in his overcoat and derby hat, serene as could be, taking it all in stride as though there [was] not the slightest problem, looking straight ahead.[62]

Unfortunately for Fisher, his bout of manual labor was not yet complete. "Mrs. Brandeis came down in all a flutter, and she too had a weak heart, so after we took Brandeis up, we had to come back and carry Mrs. Brandeis up in the chair."

Unlike modern law clerks, but perfectly keeping with the Brandeis tradition, the justice and his former law clerks did not have formal reunions. Nor did Brandeis condone lavish celebrations or expensive gifts in his honor. Freund relates how the justice avoided one celebration:

> When, on the approach of his eightieth birthday, the former secretaries of Mr. Justice Brandeis planned a visit in his honor, word came that, more than the pilgrimage, the Justice would welcome a message from each of the group recounting the public service that he had of late been performing. The would-be pilgrims had known in their hearts that the devotion the Justice cherished most from them was devotion to his conception of the lawyer's calling.[63]

When recounting this story years later, Judge Calvert Magruder paused and added, "my letter was rather short."[64]

The Bonds between Isaiah and His Young Disciples

For the Brandeis law clerks, their relationship with Justice Brandeis took on a familiar pattern—distant, polite, and formal at first, with the chill of the early relationship replaced with warmth and occasional flashes of Brandeis's humor. Comments Nathanson: "[Justice Brandeis] did not immediately clasp

his law clerk to his bosom as a member of the family as well as a working associate. On the contrary, he seemed to keep personal relations at a minimum—
especially at first—and to be deliberately testing the mettle of his assistants."[65]
Once the law clerks passed Justice Brandeis's unspoken litmus test, however,
the Brandeis clerks discovered that "beneath that aloofness, there was a great
serenity—and also a sense of fun. But it was so distilled."[66] One example of
Brandeis's unique sense of humor: "I never forget asking him about an article
with which I disagreed strongly, and I said how could the author say those
things," states Austern. "And he said, 'Mr. Austern . . . you'll find this world is
full of sons of bitches, and they're always hard at work at it.'"[67]

Despite these flashes of humor, the law clerks remained in awe of Brandeis's emotional self-control, intellect, self-discipline, and formidable memory. While the clerks and Brandeis might grow closer over the course of their
year together, the relationship—with perhaps the exception of Dean Acheson
—did not evolve into friendship. "It was difficult to get to know him," recalls
Sutherland. "You could admire him, but he wasn't the kind of person to mold
in with as old friends."[68] Despite the distance between the justice and his law
clerks, Brandeis's assistants were fiercely loyal to "Isaiah." "There was some
quality about him that made people want to work for him and please him,"
adds Sutherland.

While aloof, Brandeis took an interest in each law clerk's life and well-being.
A touching example of this concern can be found when Brandeis retired from
the Supreme Court in 1939, and his primary concern was finding his current
clerk—Adrian Fisher—immediate employment. "Frankfurter told me that he
[Brandeis] called Felix in and told him, and after Frankfurter, who was then
a justice, went through how terrible it all was, Brandeis said, 'Well, that's not
why I called you here. What are we going to do with Adrian?'"[69] This concern is also reflected in Brandeis's correspondence with Frankfurter. For
example—upon learning that former clerk Landis would remain at the Security and Exchange Commission until he started teaching at Harvard Law
School, Brandeis wrote that Landis was "unwise" to work so hard and "needs a
vacation & time for meditation."[70]

Moreover, Brandeis took a keen interest in the career paths selected by his
law clerks, and his correspondence with Felix Frankfurter is sprinkled with references to the professional achievements of his clerks and suggestions regarding future advancement.[71] Brandeis preferred law clerks who might become
teachers or public interest lawyers, and he employed both direct and indirect

tactics in achieving these goals—often discussing with Frankfurter his own career plans for his law clerks *before* he shared said plans with the clerks themselves. During Harry Shulman's clerkship, Justice Brandeis quickly concluded that the young man "is too good in mind, temper, and aspirations to waste on a New York or other law offices. . . . Can't you land him somewhere in a law school next fall?" What Brandeis later referred to as "our plans for his teaching" were not revealed to Shulman until two months later, and subsequently it was Brandeis who "practically dictated" Shulman's letter of acceptance to Yale Law School.[72]

Brandeis voiced his displeasure when his former clerks did not follow his advice. In an October 13, 1929, letter to Frankfurter, Brandeis writes: "The satisfaction I had in having Page and Friendly with me is a good deal mitigated by the thought of their present activities [private practice]. Of course, it is possible that they, or at least Friendly, may reform and leave his occupation."[73] Brandeis was particularly vexed that Friendly did not become a law professor, referring to Friendly's time in private practice as a "trial period" and periodically pondering aloud about the "possibility of wrenching Henry Friendly loose" so he could make his preordained return to Harvard Law School.[74]

Riesman keenly recalls Brandeis's disappointment regarding his decision to enter private practice: "he was contemptuous of me because I wanted to go back to Boston to a law firm." Brandeis was "vehement" that Riesman must "be a missionary" who used his talents to benefit the less fortunate. "The fact that I had friends in Boston and had season tickets to the Boston Symphony was totally frivolous and unworthy of consideration. Friendship was not a category in his life."[75] Those law clerks who followed Brandeis's suggestions, however, found that the prophet was not infallible. "He never urged me to go into teaching," states Fisher, "but he did urge me to go back to Tennessee, which I did and it proved to be a real mistake."[76]

With his confidants, Brandeis could be sharply candid in his assessment of his law clerks. His first law clerk was Calvert Magruder, who later served as a federal appeals court judge. In a March 25, 1920, letter to Thomas Nelson Perkins about Magruder, Brandeis writes: "He has a good legal mind and good working habits—and is a right-minded Southern gentleman. He is not of extraordinary ability or brilliant or of unusual scholarship, but he has stability."[77] Upon learning that former clerk William Gorham Rice Jr. (October term 1921) was a candidate for a deanship, Brandeis observes to Frankfurter that "[d]espite his mental limitations, he [Rice] may be the best man available for Wisconsin," and he predicts that Louis Jaffe—having "found himself"—would be "much better at teaching than he was as secretary."[78]

Few law clerks became close enough to Brandeis to be considered confidants and friends. The one exception to this was Dean Acheson. Even during his clerkship Acheson was able to temporarily draw Brandeis's focus away from work and engage him in discussions on pressing political, social, and economic issues of the day, and in later years Acheson would ask Brandeis to swear him in as assistant secretary of state and would spend evenings with Justice Brandeis, gossiping and sharing "the latest dirt."[79] Moreover, Acheson and his wife often joined Justice and Mrs. Brandeis for holiday dinners. Brandeis's grandson Frank Gilbert recalls that Paul Freund also became close to the justice after his clerkship and visited Brandeis and his extended family at his summer cottage in Chatham, Massachusetts. The correspondence between Frankfurter and Brandeis contains multiple references to Freund and former clerk James Landis—including a discussion of Landis's engagement in 1926 and Brandeis's willingness to loan Landis $2,000 (presumably to cover expenses associated with the pending nuptials).[80]

Upon the justice's death, Acheson would be the Brandeis law clerk to deliver the eulogy at the justice's small memorial service at his California Street residence. Referring to the Brandeis law clerks as "the fortunate ones," Acheson revealed that Brandeis's affection for his law clerks ran deeper than they imagined. "I have talked, over the past twenty years, with the justice about these men. I have heard him speak of some achievement of one of us with all the pride and of some sorrow or disappointment of another with all the tenderness of a father speaking of his sons."[81] Walter B. Raushenbush, the grandson of Louis and Alice Brandeis, attended the memorial service, and over sixty years later still recalls being struck by Acheson's poise as well as his "moving and eloquent" remarks.[82]

While Justice Brandeis declined his law clerks' offers of celebration and tribute, after his death his law clerks honored the memory and service of their former employer in a variety of different ways. Several of the Brandeis law clerks published "tribute" pieces in law reviews and legal journals in the decades following the justice's passing—arguably becoming the originators of a literary tradition now followed by scores of former law clerks from all levels of federal and state courts. The clerks also commissioned a bust of the late jurist, which was presented to the Harvard Law School in January of 1943. At the presentation, Calvert Magruder spoke of Justice Brandeis's "'almost paternal concern' for and continuing interest in 'his boys.'" In short, these postclerkship activities are compelling evidence in support of Strum's assertion that the clerks "left Brandeis's service with admiration bordering on adulation."[83]

Conclusion

Justice Louis Brandeis left the United States Supreme Court in 1939, but in many ways his clerkship model has become the standard for the clerkship institution. While modern justices have admittedly deviated from the Brandeis model in terms of the types of job duties assigned to their law clerks,[84] what remains unaltered is Brandeis's expectation that a Supreme Court law clerk graduates from a top law school, possesses a strong work ethic, has superior legal writing and research skills as well as the internal fortitude to serve as a sounding board and critic to the justice's work product, and appreciates the importance of loyalty and confidentiality. In creating these standards, Brandeis—like Gray and Holmes—left his own distinct mark on the clerkship institution. As you continue through this book and read the essays regarding more recent law clerks and their justices, I would encourage you to compare the Brandeis clerkship model to the "modern" clerkship institution and ask whether the current Court's institutional practices are an improvement on the rules and procedures created by Louis D. Brandeis.

Notes

Portions of this essay are reprinted with permission from Todd C. Peppers, "Isaiah and His Young Disciples: Justice Brandeis and His Law Clerks." *Journal of Supreme Court History* 34, no. 1 (2009): 75–97.

1. Louis D. Brandeis, in *The Letters of Louis D. Brandeis,* vol. 5: *1921–1941: Elder Statesman,* ed. Melvin I. Urofsky and David W. Levy (Albany: State University of New York Press, 1975), 268.

2. Ibid., 320.

3. Brandeis, quoted in Philippa Strum, *Louis D. Brandeis: Justice for the People* (Cambridge, Mass.: Harvard University Press, 1984), 359 (correspondence with Felix Frankfurter).

4. Lewis J. Paper Interview with Adrian S. Fisher, August 11, 1980, Lewis Paper Papers, Harvard Law School Library, box 1, folder 3.

5. Law clerk Henry J. Friendly and his parents separately met with Justice Brandeis prior to Friendly's clerkship, apparently due to concerns over Friendly's future career plans. On October 28, 1926, Justice Brandeis spent one hour discussing with Friendly's

parents "[t]heir misapprehensions as to facts & relative values of Practicing Lawyer v. Professor of Law." Brandeis writes: "The only definite advice I gave them was to leave their son alone; to let him make up his own mind & not merely to say so, but let him see & know that they will be happy in whatever decisions he makes." Louis D. Brandeis, *"Half Brother, Half Son:" The Letters of Louis D. Brandeis to Felix Frankfurter,* ed. Melvin I. Urofsky and David W. Levy (Norman: University of Oklahoma Press, 1991), 257. Ironically, Brandeis did not follow his own advice and spent the next decade urging Friendly to become a law school professor.

6. Lewis J. Paper Interview with David Riesman, May 5, 1981, Lewis Paper Papers, Harvard Law School Library, box 1, folder 4. Of all the Brandeis law clerks, Riesman appears to be the only former clerk to speak critically of Justice Brandeis — or at the very least the one former clerk to view Justice Brandeis as mortal. During his interview with Paper, Riesman confessed: "I felt very ambivalent about my work with Brandeis. I was very critical of him. But I also felt that I had let him down, and I felt terribly guilty about that. I always had the impression that Freund and the other clerks had done so much for him, and I didn't feel like I made a real contribution." Riesman concedes: "I'm sure I didn't start things off on the right foot when I told him at the very beginning that I thought Zionism was nothing more than Jewish fascism. And he said he wouldn't discuss it with me because I had no understanding of history." According to Brandeis's grandson, Frank Gilbert, former law clerk Paul Freund recounted a slightly more nuanced exchange in which the justice first asked whether Riesman had read a specific list of books on the topic and, after Riesman's reply that he had not, then stated that there was no further purpose in discussing the topic. Frank Gilbert, telephone interview with author, January 15, 2008.

7. Lewis J. Paper Interview with H. Thomas Austern, January 12, 1981, Lewis Paper Papers, Harvard Law School Library, box 1, folder 4.

8. Fisher, interview.

9. Dean Acheson, *Morning and Noon* (Boston: Houghton Mifflin, 1965), 47.

10. Fisher, interview. Justice Holmes also had a strong preference for unmarried law clerks, but for a different reason — he wanted unattached clerks who could go to parties at night and return the next day to share the latest gossip with the justice.

11. Brandeis, *Half Brother, Half Son,* 574.

12. Felix Frankfurter and James M. Landis, *The Business of the United States Supreme Court: A Study in the Federal Judicial System* (New York: Macmillan, 1927); Charles Warren, *The Supreme Court in United States History* (Boston: Little, Brown, 1928); Brandeis, *Half Brother, Half Son,* 579.

13. Strum, *Louis D. Brandeis,* 355.

14. All of the justices continued working at home after completion of the Supreme Court building in 1935. Beginning with Hugo Black's appointment in 1937, all newly appointed justices and their staffs worked primarily in their chambers at the new court building. By the time Chief Justice Fred Vinson was appointed in 1946, all nine justices and their staffs were working full-time at the Court building.

15. Paul A. Freund, "Historical Reminiscence—Justice Brandeis: A Law Clerk's Remembrance," *American Jewish History* 68 (1978): 9.

16. Paul A. Freund, "The Supreme Court: A Tale of Two Terms," *Ohio State Law Journal* 26 (1965): 226.

17. Freund, "Historical Reminiscence," 9.

18. Alexander M. Bickel, *The Unpublished Opinions of Mr. Justice Brandeis: The Supreme Court at Work* (Cambridge, Mass.: Harvard University Press, 1957), 16.

19. Acheson, *Morning and Noon*, 80–81.

20. Ibid., 80.

21. Freund, "Law Clerk's Remembrance," 10.

22. Not surprisingly, the law clerk's duties often varied with Justice Brandeis's assessment of his young assistant's abilities. "His relationship with a particular clerk seemingly determined the degree of the clerk's independence," writes Strum. "To some, Brandeis merely gave drafts to check and flesh out with citations; others Brandeis encouraged to write first or later drafts, and the two would engage in mutual criticism of each other's ventures." Strum, *Louis D. Brandeis*, 356–57.

23. Paul A. Freund, "Mr. Justice Brandeis: A Centennial Memoir," *Harvard Law Review* 70 (March 1957): 776.

24. Acheson, *Morning and Noon*, 81.

25. Lewis J. Paper Interview with J. Willard Hurst, May 31, 1980, Lewis Paper Papers, Harvard Law School Library, box 1, folder 3. Landis felt the same, referring to himself as being in "a junior partnership with the greatest Justice of the Supreme Court." James M. Landis, "Mr. Justice Brandeis: A Law Clerk's View," *American Jewish Historical Society* (1957): 468.

26. Freund, " Mr. Justice Brandeis: A Centennial Memoir," 776.

27. Brandeis, quoted in Acheson, *Morning and Noon*, 80.

28. Lewis J. Paper Interview with William A. Sutherland, November 7, 1980, Lewis Paper Papers, Harvard Law School Library, box 1, folder 4.

29. Acheson, *Morning and Noon*, 96–97. See also Freund, "Law Clerk's Remembrance," 10: "Never in my experience did Brandeis invite the law clerk's view concerning how a case should be decided—that was distinctly the judge's responsibility —but the law clerk's ideas about the structure and content of the opinion were highly welcome."

30. Lewis J. Paper Interview with Paul Freund, February 11, 1981, Lewis Paper Papers, Harvard Law School Library, box 1, folder 3.

31. Dean Acheson writes that "one of the joys of being a law clerk was to open the [docket] book on Saturday afternoon and learn weeks ahead of the country what our masters had done," but it appears from Paper's interviews with subsequent law clerks that Justice Brandeis abandoned the practice of giving his law clerks access to his docket book at some undetermined time after Acheson's clerkship. Acheson, *Morning and Noon*, 85. Supreme Court historian Artemus Ward hypothesizes that Brandeis may have changed his docket book practices after a scandal involving allegations that

Ashton Embry, law clerk to Justice Joseph McKenna, was leaking information on pending decisions to a band of confederates. See John B. Owens, "The Clerk, the Thief, His Life as a Baker: Ashton Embry and the Supreme Court Leak Scandal of 1919," *Northwestern University Law Review* 95, no. 1 (Fall 2002): 271–308.

32. Lewis J. Paper Interview with Nathaniel L. Nathanson, December 17, 1980, Lewis Paper Papers, Harvard Law School Library, box 1, folder 4; Calvert Magruder, "Mr. Justice Brandeis," *Harvard Law Review* 55 (December 1941): 193–94; Austern, interview.

33. Sutherland, interview.

34. Acheson, *Morning and Noon,* 82. Landis describes a research project that required that he review every page of sixty-odd years of Senate journals. Landis, "Mr. Justice Brandeis," 471.

35. Leonard Baker, *Brandeis and Frankfurter: A Dual Biography* (New York: Harper & Row, 1984): 214. Baker adds: "A few days before the argument, to Friendly's chagrin, telephone companies filed an *amicus curiae* brief with identical information." Ibid.

36. Paul M. Freund, introduction to Bickel, *The Unpublished Opinions of Mr. Justice Brandeis,* xix.

37. Ibid.

38. *Buck v. Jewell-LaSalle Realty Co.* (283 U.S. 191 [1931]).

39. Austern, interview.

40. Acheson, *Morning and Noon,* 78.

41. Friendly clearly passed the high standards demanded of Justice Brandeis. In a May 20, 1928, letter to daughter Susan Brandeis Gilbert, Brandeis writes, "[t]here is even enough work on hand to satisfy my voracious secretary [Friendly]." Louis D. Brandeis, *The Family Letters of Louis D. Brandeis,* ed. Melvin I. Urofsky and David W. Levy (Norman: University of Oklahoma Press, 2002), 465.

42. Oral History Interview of Henry J. Friendly by David Epstein, July 1, 1973.

43. Paul. A. Freund, "The Evolution of a Brandeis Dissent," *Manuscripts* 10 (1958): 18–25, 34.

44. Lewis J. Paper Interview with Louis L. Jaffe, February 10, 1981, Lewis Paper Papers, Harvard Law School Library, box 1, folder 4. Alice Brandeis Popkin, granddaughter of Louis Brandeis, admits that she is surprised to hear her grandfather described in such terms. "He was not a distant person. Whenever I talked to my grandfather, he would look you straight in the eye. He was a very warm and loving person." Alice Brandeis Popkin, interview with author, April 16, 2008.

45. Freund, interview.

46. Austern, interview.

47. Hurst, interview.

48. Freund, "Supreme Court," 226.

49. Fisher, interview.

50. Sutherland, interview.

51. Freund, interview.

52. Freund, interview. Professor Urofsky suggests, however, that Justice Brandeis was not offended if his clerks shared gossip from other chambers with him. Urofsky, correspondence with author. Once all nine justices and their staffs began working exclusively at the new Supreme Court building, a "clerk network" quickly developed, and clerks were generally encouraged by the justices to aid in coalition formation. See Artemus Ward and David L. Weiden, *Sorcerers' Apprentices: 100 Years of Law Clerks at the United States Supreme Court* (New York: New York University Press, 2006): 159–70.

53. Nathaniel L. Nathanson, "Mr. Justice Brandeis: A Law Clerk's Recollections of the October Term, 1934," *American Jewish Archives* 15 (April 1963): 6–16.

54. Magruder, "Mr. Justice Brandeis," 193–94.

55. Acheson, *Morning and Noon,* 49.

56. Landis, "Mr. Justice Brandeis," 470.

57. Freund, interview.

58. Austern, interview.

59. Nathanson, interview.

60. Strum, *Louis D. Brandeis,* 362.

61. Austern, interview; Riesman, interview. Philippa Strum recalls Alger Hiss telling her the story of attending a dinner party at the Brandeis residence during his Holmes clerkship. "He remembered Poindexter, LDB's man of all work, taking a plate of asparagus around to the guests. Hiss got the plate relatively early and took what he thought was a reasonable helping. To his horror, he realized afterwards that the plate was not going to be replenished and his healthy helping meant that there would not be enough for everyone else." Strum, correspondence with author.

62. Fisher, interview.

63. Paul A. Freund, "Mr. Justice Brandeis," *Harvard Law Review* 55 (1941): 195.

64. Gilbert interview.

65. Nathanson, "Mr. Justice Brandeis," 9.

66. Nathanson, interview.

67. Austern, interview. Another example of Brandeis's sense of humor was found in his explanation as to why he had Acheson work for two—as opposed to one—year as his law clerk. "Whenever Brandeis was queried about it in Acheson's hearing, the latter recalled, 'He would speak of a concern for my prospective clients.'" Strum, *Louis D. Brandeis,* 362.

68. Sutherland, interview.

69. After helping Brandeis organize his papers, Fisher subsequently clerked with Frankfurter.

70. Brandeis, *Half Brother, Half Son,* 597.

71. See, generally, the correspondence in ibid.

72. Ibid., 395, 402, 410.

73. Brandeis, *Letters of Louis D. Brandeis,* 5: 404.

74. Brandeis, *Half Brother, Half Son,* 457, 531.

75. Riesman, interview.

76. Fisher, interview.

77. Ibid., 454.

78. Brandeis, *Half Brother, Half Son*, 371, 581.

79. Strum, *Louis D. Brandeis*, 358; Baker, *Brandeis and Frankfurter*, 185. Strum points out that Supreme Court scholars owe a debt of gratitude to Acheson, for it was during his clerkship that he convinced Justice Brandeis to keep copies of drafts and other related materials in his official court files. Strum, *Louis D. Brandeis*, 357.

80. Brandeis, *Half Brother, Half Son*, 248–49.

81. Dean Acheson, "Mr. Justice Brandeis," *Harvard Law Review* 55 (December 1941): 191–92.

82. Walter B. Raushenbush, interview with author, January 28, 2008.

83. Strum, *Louis D. Brandeis*, 359 (quoting from minutes of the presentation), 358.

84. See, generally, Todd C. Peppers, *Courtiers of the Marble Palace: The Rise and Influence of the Supreme Court Law Clerk* (Stanford, Calif.: Stanford University Press, 2006); Ward and Weiden, *Sorcerers' Apprentices*; Chester A. Newland, "Personal Assistants to Supreme Court Justices: The Law Clerks," *Oregon Law Review* 40 (1961): 299–317.

Benjamin Cardozo and His Law Clerks

Benjamin Cardozo was appointed to the Supreme Court of the United States to replace Oliver Wendell Holmes Jr. in February 1932. At the time he was chief judge of the New York Court of Appeals, widely thought to be the leading state court in the country. Cardozo had served on that court for eighteen years, the last six as chief judge. By common consent, he was the dominant figure on that court, but there were other strong voices—William Andrews, Irving Lehman, and especially Cuthbert Pound, to name just three.

Service as chief judge was the linchpin of Cardozo's life in 1932. His sister, Nellie, who had helped raise him and with whom he lived all his life, had died three years before. Life with his colleagues represented his professional and a major part of his personal life. While the New York Court of Appeals sat in Albany, most of its judges did not live there. During the regular two-week sessions throughout the court year, the judges lived together in the Hotel Ten Eyck in Albany. Cardozo's court was a friendly group; the judges ate and worked together. The other people he saw during the weeks between sessions and in the summer—family members and friends—were largely New York City residents.

Cardozo's New York law clerks did not figure large in his personal or even in his professional life during those years. He had just three clerks during his service as a New York judge. The first was Charles Evans Hughes Jr., the son of Justice (later Chief Justice) Hughes. Hughes Jr. later had a distinguished career at the New York bar, but he only served Cardozo during the month in which he sat as a trial judge after his election to the New York Supreme Court. When Cardozo was assigned to the court of appeals in 1914, he was importuned by his friend and mentor, the activist lawyer Louis Marshall, to hire a young man from his office, Abraham Paley. When Paley died unexpectedly four years later, Cardozo hired his brother, Joseph Paley, as his replacement. Paley served in that capacity for fourteen years, resigning a few months after Cardozo was appointed to the Supreme Court.

The jobs of his New York and Washington law clerks were very different. The three New York law clerks were officially called "secretaries," and that name described their role. Both Paleys obtained their law degrees while working for Cardozo. The voluminous correspondence between Cardozo and Joseph Paley indicates that the law work the clerks did was relatively minimal. They functioned as typists of drafts of opinions, as messengers, and generally as gofers. Sending court papers back and forth to Albany or to Cardozo's summer house in Allenhurst, New Jersey, buying office supplies and train tickets, and handling a whole variety of personal matters for the judge were accepted and substantial parts of their daily routine. Cardozo routinely dashed off a flurry of brief letters micromanaging Paley's performance of these small details of his personal and professional life, even to the point of checking to make sure that they had been done.

Once in a while Cardozo would have Paley look for a citation or a case from another jurisdiction to support a specific point, and Paley occasionally wrote memoranda on an undecided case. There was nothing, however, of the extensive research and analysis, not to speak of drafting opinions, that is associated with the work of most law clerks today, whether at the Supreme Court or at the state or lower federal courts.

That Cardozo did not use or even want a law clerk to help him much with his professional work is no surprise. He came to the bench after twenty-three years as a practitioner. Although he did a moderate amount of trial work and some advising of clients, his major work was as an appellate lawyer. While there were some young lawyers in his office, and at least one very good one (Walter Pollak), Cardozo did all his own research and writing. The photographic memory that had helped his education was of great use in his legal career, and his colleagues on the court of appeals would often exclaim in mock horror if Cardozo failed to produce from memory the citation of a case to which he or a colleague referred in their post-argument conferences. Thus, when he joined the Supreme Court of the United States, he had spent forty-one years as a practitioner and judge doing his own legal research and writing. The great success he enjoyed in the academic world as a judge and as a lecturer on the theory of judging doubtless created not only an established operational pattern for his professional work but also a confidence that he did not need much assistance.

Cardozo and the United States Supreme Court

Appointment to the Supreme Court wrenched Cardozo away from this colle-
gial life at the age of sixty-one. No wonder he constantly referred to his "exile."
No wonder he longed for the daily personal and professional companionship
of his former colleagues. Although he knew Chief Justice Hughes and Justice
Louis Brandeis, he had a personal relationship only with Justice Harlan Fiske
Stone when he arrived in Washington. While dean of Columbia Law School,
Stone had consulted with Cardozo about Columbia matters on a regular basis.

The atmosphere of the Supreme Court, however, was not collegial. There
were many tensions within the Court, and in any event the working conditions
were different. The justices worked in their own apartments or homes. That
practice continued for most of them even after the Supreme Court's own building was completed in 1935. In that setting, the only professional companionship available to Cardozo on a daily basis was with his law clerks. These young
men were of a different sort from the Paleys. They were neither of Cardozo's
generation nor experienced lawyers. They were, however, intelligent young
men who worked alongside him all week long, and Cardozo used them to fill
some of the gaps in his life created by the move to Washington.

Our knowledge of the relationship between Cardozo and his law clerks
comes almost entirely from the memories of the four regular law clerks and
Percy Russell, one of the two clerk-typists. Those memories were recorded
in the late 1950s and early 1960s from the vantage point of twenty years after
their service and at a time when all were well into their professional careers.
Mel Siegel was then a partner in a large (for the 1950s) Minneapolis law firm.
Ambrose Doskow was a partner at Proskauer, Rose, Goetz & Mendelson, one
of the leading Jewish firms in New York City. Alan "Bill" Stroock was also a
well-known lawyer in New York City, practicing in Stroock, Stroock & Lavan,
then in the process of broadening itself from a family firm to a major firm. Joe
Rauh had a more unusual career. Although a partner in a small Washington,
D.C., law firm, he developed a national reputation, in part for his legal work
representing unions and various civil rights causes, and perhaps in larger part
for his involvement in liberal and civil rights causes, in the Democratic Party,
and as one of the founders of the Americans for Democratic Action. Percy
Russell, the clerk-typist, had a fairly large communications law practice in
Washington, D.C.

When Cardozo was sworn into the Supreme Court of the United States in

March 1932, he moved to Washington right away, renting a three-bedroom suite at the Mayflower Hotel. Paley came with him and served as "law clerk" for the remainder of the term. He supervised the moving of Cardozo's personal belongings from his home in New York City to a spacious apartment at 2101 Connecticut Avenue and then departed the scene—"wisely," as Cardozo put it. Paley simply did not have the academic credentials of the other Supreme Court law clerks.

But the length of Paley's service did mean something to Cardozo, and he continued to correspond occasionally with his former clerk. Indeed, although Cardozo was quite discreet and careful in most of his correspondence, every once in a while he would express a substantive thought in a letter to Paley. Near the end of his first full term on the Court, in a letter dated March 29, 1933, he confided to Paley that "I still feel, however, that my work in the Court of Appeals was much more significant than any I am doing here. The system of distributing cases is at the root of the trouble." Only very occasionally did he complain about the assignments he received from the chief justice, and then only to people with whom he felt some degree of closeness. It is a tribute to Paley's long years of loyal service that he was favored with such a letter.

Cardozo immediately followed the practice of many other justices with respect to hiring Paley's replacement. He accepted an offer of help in the selection process from Felix Frankfurter, then a professor at Harvard Law School. Frankfurter had recommended law clerks to Justice Holmes and at the time was recommending clerks to Justice Brandeis. Frankfurter selected Mel Siegel, a recent graduate who had just obtained an S.J.D., for Cardozo, although he had originally told Siegel that he was going to recommend him to Brandeis. Subsequently, Cardozo was importuned by the deans at Columbia, his alma mater, where he had also served as trustee, and Yale, where he had delivered the lectures that became "The Nature of the Judicial Process," to hire their graduates. Ever accommodating, Cardozo decided to rotate his choices among the three institutions. In that fashion he ended up with just five law clerks (counting Paley) in the seven terms in which he served. Siegel and Ambrose Doskow, his second clerk (selected by Dean Young B. Smith of Columbia Law School), served one term each. Bill Stroock (selected by Dean Charles Clark of Yale) and Joe Rauh (selected by Frankfurter) served two terms each. Cardozo asked Stroock to stay an additional year after he had a heart attack in the summer of 1935. Rauh had been scheduled to come as law clerk for the 1935 term, but Cardozo did not want a new clerk so soon after his illness, and Stroock

reluctantly agreed to stay another year. Likewise, Rauh, who came the following term, agreed to stay another year and so was there to help care for Cardozo
in his final lengthy effort to recover from yet another heart attack and stroke.

In addition, Cardozo hired two combination law clerk-secretaries, Percy
Russell and Chris Sargent, both of whom were recent Harvard Law School
graduates. The former stayed four years, the latter two. They did all the office
typing, including handwritten law clerk memoranda, as Cardozo did not have
any other secretary. The law clerk and the clerk-secretary used a room in Cardozo's apartment as their joint work space.

During his first full term on the Court, Cardozo experimented with how he
might use his law clerk, but he eventually adopted a method of operation that
he retained more or less consistently for the rest of his service. The law clerks
read and prepared brief memoranda on the facts and issues in petitions for
certiorari. Depending on how busy he was, Cardozo occasionally took some of
the petitions at random and prepared his own handwritten memoranda. The
clerk-secretary also took some of the petitions and wrote the accompanying
memoranda. Cardozo sometimes had the law clerk prepare memoranda for
him in advance of argument on some difficult cases when he thought that the
law clerk could give him some help. Before a case was argued, he read all the
briefs himself and then discussed the cases with the clerk the morning before
they were to be heard. When he returned from argument, he reported on anything of interest that had occurred. Only occasionally, usually when the clerk
had worked on a matter or a leading lawyer was counsel, did the clerk travel to
the courtroom to hear a case argued. On Saturdays when there was a conference, the clerks would wait at Cardozo's apartment for his return shortly after
4:30 p.m. to hear Cardozo's report of the results of the day's work.

The pre-argument work was the major role of the law clerk. Opinion writing belonged to Cardozo himself. Once the assignment of the opinion was
made by Chief Justice Hughes, if he was in the majority, or the senior associate
justice in the majority if Hughes was not, Cardozo went to work immediately.
The law clerks reported that Cardozo had the unusual habit of writing out
his opinions longhand on lined pads of paper while walking back and forth,
turning the pages underneath as he wrote. The law clerks also reported that
if they came into the office on Sunday afternoon, Cardozo would often have
a rough draft ready then. By Monday, he was usually ready to have the draft
typed by the clerk-secretary. He would then ask the law clerk for reactions and
might assign some research on particular points. The law clerk was free to

raise particular points, expressing objections to the opinion or particular parts of it, and Cardozo was always ready to discuss the clerk's views. Once he had considered an argument, though, he was usually not open to re-argument from the clerk. Cardozo saw his job as requiring him to consider everything, but once he had done so, he had done his duty and was ready to move on to the next judicial task.

The law clerk would be rewarded if a citation he supplied wound up in the opinion. Rauh was thrilled once when a sentence that he suggested landed in the opinion. Siegel also remembered one occasion when Cardozo adopted a line of thought he had suggested in a tax case and how disappointed Cardozo was when Hughes assigned the opinion to himself after Cardozo suggested that line of argument to him.

Cardozo's use of his law clerks differed from that followed in other chambers. At least some justices did not talk with their clerks in advance of argument but did use them subsequently to do research, write memoranda, and even draft a piece of an opinion. It is clear that Cardozo made more use of his law clerks than he had in New York, perhaps because their skills greatly exceeded those of his New York law clerks and perhaps because many of the legal issues and materials were new to him. Nevertheless, when it came to writing the actual opinions, Cardozo did virtually all of that on his own.

The young men who worked with Cardozo occasionally saw him outside of working hours. Socializing was limited to a very few dinners each term and a night or two at the theater. After Mel Siegel and Herb Wechsler (Stone's law clerk) took Cardozo to an evening performance of Noel Coward's *Design for Living,* Wechsler reported that from the moment the curtain went up, it was obvious that Cardozo was uncomfortable with a play about adultery that was set in a bedroom. Cardozo's comment during intermission was that back in New York when he used to go to theater, he supposed that it wouldn't have been banned, but that a lot of people would have liked to see it banned. When Wechsler showed up for tea the next day at Cardozo's apartment, Miss Tracy (who had been nurse to two of his sisters and was later his housekeeper) was furious that the two clerks had taken the justice to such a play.

Cardozo reciprocated the invitation, taking the clerks to see Marc Connelly's Pulitzer Prize–winning *Green Pastures,* a play with an African American cast based on Old Testament stories seen through the eyes of African American children in New Orleans during the Depression. Wechsler reported that Cardozo appeared to enjoy that play a good deal. The story about *Design for Living* circulated from clerk to clerk, and subsequent law clerks contented themselves with the safe path of taking Cardozo to Gilbert and Sullivan operettas, usually *Iolanthe*.

The Cardozo that the law clerks came to know was in his sixties, and they were therefore wholly without experience of the younger Cardozo. In particular, none of them had any experience with Cardozo the tough lawyer and implacable professional opponent. They saw a man who had been mellowed first by eighteen years' experience engaging with collegial colleagues on a court that he came to dominate by force of intellect, persuasion, and accommodation and then further softened by declining health. All law clerks get to see only a portion of their justice's personality and life. Cardozo was an especially private person, and his clerks' reactions to their relationship reflected their different experiences, perceptions, and personalities.

Mel Siegel, Ambrose Doskow, and Joe Rauh were more uncritically admiring and appreciative of the relationship. Bill Stroock was different from the other clerks in two respects. His background was similar to Cardozo's. Although not of Sephardic Jewish origin, he came from a well-to-do New York Jewish family. His father, who had known Cardozo when both were practicing lawyers, had in fact referred matters to Cardozo, and therefore the two had worked together professionally. That created an element of shared experience between Cardozo and Bill Stroock. Cardozo talked with him about family and about Judaism in a way that he never did with his other clerks. Nevertheless, Stroock did not believe that he had a close relationship with Cardozo and believed indeed that Cardozo kept his clerks at arm's length.

The second respect in which Stroock differed from the other clerks is that, at least by the time he had matured into a leader in the New York Jewish community, his own personality led him to view Cardozo from a more critical perspective. When it came to writing a brief personal memoir of his clerkship, Stroock concluded with perhaps the obligatory enthusiastic appreciation: "It is, I am sure, unnecessary for me to expatiate upon the extraordinary experience it was for me as a young man to work intimately for two years with so brilliant, wise, cultured, and gracious a human being. In both law and manners, he was the greatest teacher I have known." Even that appreciation has the slight barb of combining "law" with "manners" to single out for praise. But the rest of the memoir dwells upon what he regarded as the warts of his subject. The significant human characteristics that he highlighted were "his extraordinary self-esteem" and "his sensitiveness to adverse comments or to any lack of respect from others," qualities that Stroock ascribed to Cardozo's

Sephardic upbringing in a family disgraced by the father's resignation from the bench just before he would have been impeached and in which social aloofness and female influence predominated.

Elsewhere, Stroock referred to Cardozo as "a vain and in many ways intolerant man." Vanity was reflected in the weekly visits of a barber who "studiously tended" to his "famously tousled hair" and in the fifteen identical black suits carefully brushed by the housekeeper. Moreover, this self-esteem was also reflected in the praise he heaped upon others and expected to receive in return. Cardozo praised everything Stroock did effusively, even the "bad stuff." It was likewise reflected in his refusal to engage in the ordinary give-and-take of political life that nearly cost him election to his first judicial office. Stroock even saw a sign of Cardozo's self-esteem in his willingness to sign a statement on Stroock's behalf if Stroock would sue to enforce a lease on a house in Washington. The lease contained a restrictive covenant against sale or lease to Jews. Stroock thought Cardozo reacted as he did because he viewed it as a personal attack upon himself, and Stroock stated that he saw his job as getting Cardozo to cool down. A more charitable and appreciative assessment of this incident might be that at least in part Cardozo was loyally supporting a law clerk against discrimination in suggesting a course of action that many, if not most, other justices would have hesitated to take. Whether a Supreme Court justice ought to speak out on a matter such as this is another question. Perhaps in the end Cardozo would have concluded that he should not, even if Stroock had not saved him from having to make that judgment.

I do not know whether Stroock's ultimate judgment about Cardozo twenty-five years later reflected his view at the time of his clerkship or was the product of the subsequent reflections of a successful lawyer from whom self-esteem was not lacking. Clearly, Stroock had not known Cardozo the tough-minded and tough-acting lawyer. Nor did he know that as a general rule judges running for office in New York in 1913 did not engage openly in electioneering. Nor did he know of the behind-the-scenes maneuvering in which Cardozo did engage when he was interested in judicial advancement. Such knowledge might have produced a more nuanced view of Cardozo's personal and professional character and might have led Stroock to place the warts he perceived in Cardozo's character in a more generous appreciation of the whole man.

Stroock thought that only Joe Rauh had a close relationship with Cardozo and attributed that to the justice's declining health. Certainly Joe Rauh was the only clerk who got Cardozo to call him by his first name instead of by Cardozo's usual form of address, "Mister Rauh." When Cardozo asked Rauh to stay a second year, Rauh responded willingly, but at the same time he importuned Cardozo to call him Joe. Cardozo did so, but it was an obvious effort.

Stroock's judgment that Cardozo was close only with Joe Rauh among his law clerks seems accurate. By the end of their first term together, Cardozo had progressed in his opening letter salutation from "Dear Rauh" to "My well beloved Rauh." And the tone of the letter was equally warm. "You were a comfort and a joy to the last minute. Whatever my Washington exile may have brought me in care and worry, there can be no doubt that it has won me some precious friendships, and of these there is none more precious than yours." This was followed by the closing, "Affectionately yours." Despite the fact that Cardozo was given to extravagant expressions of praise, this demonstration of closeness seems genuine. Whatever may have been his relations with his other law clerks, he was very fond of Joe Rauh—perhaps, as Stroock suggests, because his health made him more dependent on Rauh, but perhaps, and more importantly, because Joe Rauh had more in the way of personality, character, and kindliness to offer Cardozo. He gave more and received more than the others. Mel Siegel seemed to me to have possessed the necessary qualities for such a relationship, but it didn't happen—possibly because the justice was somewhat unsettled by his transition to Washington, and being new to the job, he didn't know what relationship he wanted with a real law clerk.

Joe Rauh addressed some of the same traits that Stroock noticed, but in a different vein. Referring to a memorandum he had written in an extradition case, Rauh reported:

[Cardozo] came in and said this was the most brilliant, magnificent thing he had ever read. This was obviously nonsense to a kid who knew as little about extradition as I could have learned in a few days. But I guess no one is as completely lacking in vanity as not to believe a small part of it. But this was a pattern . . . and I don't understand it. Whether it was a desire to be liked and reciprocated on his part, or a real belief, or what caused him to do this. . . . Miss Tracy said this, "You brought him a glass of water, he can't stop thanking you." . . . I can't ever remember his ever saying a quick word, or a harsh word in the entire time I was there.

Near the end of Rauh's first year as law clerk, he received an offer from Robert Jackson, then the solicitor general, to work in that office. Rauh had already indicated to Cardozo that he would stay a second year, but the solicitor general's office was every young lawyer's dream opportunity. When Rauh, at Jackson's suggestion, mentioned the offer, Cardozo indicated very quickly that he didn't want to make a change in law clerks, and Rauh stayed. Later, when Cardozo had a heart attack, shingles, and a stroke that left him incapacitated, Rauh was one of the people who managed his life. Cardozo's former colleague on the New York Court of Appeals, Irving Lehman, and especially Sissie Lehman, his wife, were very close to Cardozo and were heavily involved in choosing medical treatment and living arrangements for the ailing justice. At one point, Rauh raised the question of his leaving to pursue his own professional career, but Sissie Lehman made it very clear that she thought he was needed and should stay—and Rauh stayed. Indeed, he also participated in the selection of doctors and spent hours simply as a companion for Cardozo, sitting by the bedside and reading him light stories. Rauh accompanied the entourage that took Cardozo by train from Washington to the Lehmans' home in Port Chester, New York, and stayed with Cardozo until he died in July 1938. The story of Cardozo and his law clerks thus ended with the law clerk who was closest to the justice turning from professional aide to personal caregiver.

Biographical Note

The author conducted interviews with Cardozo's four Supreme Court law clerks, his long-term Court of Appeals law clerk, and his one living clerk-typist between 1957 and 1961. Transcripts of the interviews with the four law clerks and notes of the interviews with the others are contained in the Kaufman Cardozo Collection, in the Manuscript Division of the Harvard Law School Library. See box 3, folders 3-4–3-8, 3-13, 3-20, and 3-23. In addition, that collection contains transcripts of correspondence between Cardozo and Joseph Rauh and Joseph Paley. See box 13, folder 13-1 and vols. 1 and 2 bound red B. N. Cardozo Letters. These items form the source material for this essay. The four law clerks also wrote recollections of Cardozo, mostly brief summaries of the transcripts of the author's interviews: Joseph L. Rauh Jr., Melvin Siegel, Ambrose Doskow, and Alan M. Stroock, "A Personal View of Justice Benjamin N. Cardozo: Recollections of Four Cardozo Law Clerks," *Cardozo Law Review* 1 (1979): 5–22. More general information about Cardozo's career is contained in Andrew L. Kaufman, *Cardozo* (Cambridge, Mass.: Harvard University Press, 1998). The story of the career of Benjamin Cardozo's father is told in Kaufman, "The First Judge Cardozo: Albert, Father of Benjamin," *Journal of Law and Religion* 11 (1994–95): 271.

The Family of Stone Law Clerks

H arlan Fiske Stone was stricken on the bench and died on April 22, 1946. During his twenty-one-year tenure on the Supreme Court, he nurtured in his own way the talents of a total of twenty-two law clerks. I had the good fortune to be his senior law clerk during the first two terms of his chief justiceship and to enjoy close friendships with some—and at least cordial acquaintanceships with others—in our family of twenty-two.

From being sworn in as an associate justice on March 2, 1925, to his elevation to the chief justiceship on July 3, 1941, Stone conformed to the practice of some of his brethren by taking on for each term a new law clerk usually fresh out of law school. This young man would expect to be gone at the end of the term, moving on to the next phase of his professional career. But when Stone became chief justice, he felt the additional duties of that office made it desirable for him to have two law clerks at a time. That resulted in a two-year stint for some of us.

It is well known that Stone, before coming to Washington at President Calvin Coolidge's call to take up the reins as attorney general in the then-recently discredited Department of Justice, had been a notably successful practicing lawyer in major New York City law firms. He had also been a member of the faculty and, a little later—for thirteen years beginning in 1910—the dean of the Columbia Law School. This made it not unnatural that he should normally take his law clerks from young graduates of Columbia Law School. Two of us were otherwise. His first law clerk, for the tail end of October term 1924, was Robert F. Cogswell, a Georgetown Law School graduate whom he inherited from the retired justice Joseph McKenna. Cogswell had clerked for McKenna for about five years, and Stone asked him to stay on and finish out the term. I was a Harvard Law School graduate who came to Stone under the special circumstances that I describe later.

The other twenty law clerks were indeed Columbia Law School products. Six of them had been, in their turn, editor-in-chief of the *Columbia Law Review*, and all but one of the rest had been on the *Review*'s board of editors.[1] Even the selected bright law students who had served on the *Columbia Law Review* from time to time were by no means a homogeneous group; they had their individualized strengths and, at least occasionally, their individualized shortcomings. Stone adapted to them all and found each one helpful. For the most part, he accepted recommendations for the next term's incumbent from the Columbia Law School faculty, particularly from the dean and from Professor Noel T. Dowling, usually supplemented by a brief interview with the justice, and even some outsiders might zero in with suggestions. The acknowledged head of our law clerk family, until his untimely death in 1956, was Alfred McCormack, the law clerk for Stone's first full term on the bench (October term 1925).

Al McCormack certainly deserves a special word. He came to Columbia Law School already exhibiting enviable qualities of scholarship and leadership; he amassed an outstanding law school record and became his year's editor-in-chief of the *Columbia Law Review;* he established a high benchmark for successful relationships between Stone and his law clerk; and he later accepted with grace a kind of paterfamilias role over the law clerk family. No matter how deeply enmeshed Al might be in his career as an eminent practicing attorney or in his productive government service, he always had time and a friendly instinctive assist for one of his Stone law clerk successors.[2] In the memorial issue of the *Columbia Law Review* devoted to Stone, McCormack wrote a fascinating piece entitled *A Law Clerk's Recollections.*[3] One particular passage on the lifelong relationships that ensued expresses the thoughts of many of us:

> [Stone] delighted in his contact with young men fresh from the Law School; and they were the beneficiaries of his irrepressible desire to teach. He liked his law clerks. He followed their later careers, wrote to them at significant times in their lives, was never too busy to see them when they were in Washington, and every five years, on the anniversary of his accession to the Court, he entertained the group at dinner. Those were great occasions, and there are many stories connected with them. The older clerks love to tell, for instance, of the 1935 dinner, when the cook's husband dropped dead at five o'clock and Mrs. Stone and Miss Jenkins, the Justice's capable secretary, prepared a Lucullan feast, without anyone knowing of their part in it till it was over.[4]

After Stone's death we had an annual, less formal gathering with Mrs. Stone (no black tie). The gatherings were usually held at the home of one of the locally available law clerks, until Mrs. Stone informed us that she was no longer up to the reunions.

But, you might well wonder, what kind of interaction took place between

Stone and his law clerks during the term? Obviously, this would differ from time to time, and even during any single term it might well vary as Stone's needs would change and as the law clerk would develop a better familiarity as to how he could really be helpful.

First, however, a few words about the physical arrangements. When Stone became a justice the Senate was kind enough to find him some office space that he could use temporarily as chambers for himself and his small staff. Now that he knew his life was to be centered in Washington rather than New York, he and his wife Agnes arranged to build a substantial residence at 24th Street and Wyoming Avenue, NW. They were finicky in supervising its progress. To make sure that the result would be exactly what they wanted, Stone would make frequent visits to the construction site, often with his law clerk Milton Handler (October term 1946) trailing along. The edifice—for it was an edifice—when completed had a spacious wing to serve as Stone's chambers. At the far end of the wing was a small office for Stone's secretary, Gertrude Jenkins. The far end also had a balcony that was the law clerk's perch throughout Stone's associate justiceship. I do not mean that the law clerk was forever barred from visiting the Court or commingling with the other law clerks. Yet, the simple fact is that even when the new Supreme Court Building was completed in 1935, Stone refrained from using the chambers allotted to him and continued to work exclusively in his chambers at home. Thus, the situs for the law clerks through Allison Dunham (October terms 1939 and 1940) remained the balcony perch from which they were readily and conveniently available to the justice and where, without intentionally eavesdropping, the law clerk would often find himself a third-party listener to a conversation between the justice and some visitor.

The geography changed markedly when Stone became chief justice. In the Supreme Court Building the Court's large conference room leads at one end to a very comfortable, though not lavish, room for the chief justice and at the other end a room of ample size to accommodate at least two law clerks and even somewhat elaborate files. Stone found that his new duties made it essential that he spend a portion of his time down at the Court, not only to see occasionally some of his brethren, as well as various officials on the Court's staff and some of his visitors, but also to improve a draft of an opinion and to meet with his law clerks, whose main situs was now at the Court. From time to time, one or more of his law clerks would nevertheless meet with Stone at his house. In addition, there were frequent telephone conversations between the two locations with commendable caution, yet without too much concern as to whether some illegal wiretapping might be taking place.

What, then, did the law clerks really do for and with Stone? A primary responsibility, lasting throughout Stone's tenure on the Court, was to prepare "cert memos" on the growing volume of the petitions for certiorari and the much smaller number of jurisdictional statements on appeals. These memoranda were expected to be concise—usually a page or at most two—that disclosed the nature of the case, the questions presented, how the issues had been raised, and whether or not the law clerk thought the case was "certworthy" and why—that is, whether the law clerk's recommendation was that certiorari should be granted or should be denied. Stone, of course, had available the papers that had been filed in the case, but he quickly learned the extent to which the law clerk could be relied on to have views in tune with his and the extent, if any, that the justice might feel it desirable to dip into the formal papers in a case. The process was eased by the fact that it was true then, as it is now, that the great bulk of certiorari petitions clearly had no "certworthiness" whatsoever, and a law clerk's recommendation to "Deny" a petition was not often likely to be wrong.[5] Since the new law clerk traditionally would begin in the summer, his introduction to life at the Supreme Court would be to tackle the accumulating pile of "summer certs." And as the term opened and wore on, experience and conversations with the justice would give the law clerk surer footing as to where the justice would be looking for a recommendation to "Grant" certiorari.

Stone's tenure on the Court was completed well before the days of the much-discussed "cert pool." Under that regime subsequently instituted in 1972, the rapidly rising volume of petitions for certiorari convinced some of the justices that it would be advisable to divide up the certs so that a law clerk of one of the justices would prepare a presumably thorough memorandum with recommendation, and copies of that memorandum would be furnished to all the justices participating in the pool.[6] In Stone's time, however, each justice within his own chambers settled on his preferred process for handling the certs—whether to use the help of his law clerk almost always, or only sometimes, or not at all. Stone remained a firm believer in receiving a cert memo from his own law clerk. I think he would not have been satisfied to receive just one memo from another justice's law clerk. And when he became chief justice the usefulness of this in aiding his presentation of the discussed certs at the Court's conference was probably augmented.

One variant during my own experience relates to the handling of the in forma pauperis certs that had begun to increase noticeably during the time of Chief Justice Charles Evans Hughes. This was before the days when multiple copies of the in forma pauperis papers were required or even became available through duplication by the Clerk's Office. Chief Justice Hughes had established the practice that only those in forma pauperis petitions for certiorari that seemed to involve at least a remote possibility of some real question for the Court (the bulk of them did not) would be circulated to the other justices for examination. Stone as chief justice continued that practice, except that every capital case was circulated, and Stone took a somewhat more generous view of what additional cases deserved to be circulated. Whenever the papers were circulated in an in forma pauperis case, the memorandum of Stone's law clerk went along. This meant that the law clerk's memorandum to Stone carried an extra measure of responsibility, and even when it ended up with "Deny," it might also say "Circulate."[7]

Another practice during the Hughes Court was the distribution by the chief justice, before each conference, of what was formally named the Special List but was colloquially known to all insiders as the Dead List. This listed those petitions for certiorari that the chief justice thought all his brethren would agree were so obviously requiring denial that they did not warrant being discussed at conference. It was a benign measure to save conference time for those matters actually deserving discussion. Any one justice could remove a petition for certiorari from the Dead List if he felt otherwise, although this did not happen frequently.[8] Thus, while Stone was an associate justice it was open to his law clerk to suggest that Stone might wish to precipitate discussion of an otherwise condemned petition (though I do not know whether this ever did occur). When Stone became chief justice an added law clerk duty was to suggest to him what petitions should go on the Dead List.[9]

With respect to cases accepted by the Court for oral argument and decision on the merits, Stone was always open to discussion with his law clerk about how he would cast his vote at conference or even later. Usually after the oral argument he was clear on how he would vote, but there were exceptions. If a law clerk offered a new facet on a case, Stone would not only listen but would fairly consider it even though in the end the suggestion might not persuade him to change his vote or to accept the analysis.[10]

When Stone was elevated to the chief justiceship one of his inherited prerogatives—and for him a substantial new responsibility—was to decide on the assignment of opinions whenever he was in the majority, which would be most of the time. This, of course, was a function highly important to the Court's efficiency as well as to the contentment of the other members of the Court. I have elsewhere written about his practice of discussing the proposed assignments with me before the assignment sheet went out to the justices, and permitting me to make a suggestion here and there.[11] I assume (though I do not know for certain) that he continued to do this with my successors as senior law clerk.

We come now to the other main line of the law clerk's relationship to Justice Stone—how did his opinions evolve? Unlike some present and past members of the Court, Stone invariably produced the first draft of his opinions; he did not merely tell his law clerk what was wanted and instruct the law clerk to return with a draft. This was true throughout his career on the Court.[12] Even when he was a freshman justice, his knowledge of the law was broad; he thought he knew what he wanted to say, and his New England work ethic cultivated in him a strong desire to get something down on paper expeditiously. Once in a while he might have his law clerk prepare a memorandum on some point in advance of the first draft, but that was rare.

The style of the opinion's first draft was often a little on the cumbersome side. Stone's prose did not start out like that of Holmes or Brandeis or Cardozo or Learned Hand or Bob Jackson—the great masters of style in our twentieth-century judiciary. His sentence structures at their initial stages tended at times to be long and unwieldy—sometimes almost Germanic in appearance. He enjoyed the collaboration of his law clerk not only for improving ideas exhibited by the first draft but also for helping to smooth out form and sentence structure. And as time moved on and the justice and law clerk interconnected more comfortably with each other, Stone would welcome an additional sentence or even a paragraph drafted by his law clerk if he was satisfied that it fortified or improved the opinion. When successive drafts led to a version the justice circulated to his brethren, he would review with the law clerk the suggestions received back from the other members of the Court and discuss the extent to which accommodations ought to be made. As finally issued, Stone's opinions, whether for the Court or in dissent, displayed a sturdy elegance that has certainly contributed to their enviable life span.

Portions of this account might suggest that Stone's relationship with the incumbent law clerk tended to be stiffly formal, but that would be seriously wide of the mark. Stone was a man of many parts. Besides the law, which necessarily was central to his professional life, he had sophisticated interests in other areas—areas such as the arts, the sciences, government, and education, to name just a few. Moreover, he was vitally interested in people and was more gregarious than many of the justices who have graced the Court. This was the wide universe he enjoyed discussing, and his law clerk was a beneficiary of many lively conversations.

From time to time he would share with his law clerk reminiscences of events

large and small. For example, Stone told me that on the morning of Inauguration Day in 1929, when the White House was to shift from President Coolidge
to President Herbert Hoover, he had called on his friend Calvin Coolidge.
During the meeting, Stone observed that it might be just as well to be retiring
from the presidency at this time in view of some difficult economic problems
that might lie ahead. Stone added that he did not think Coolidge understood
what Stone was talking about.

A variety of additional duties might on occasion brighten the law clerk's
week. Over the course of the years it happened, though not very often, that a
law clerk would be called upon to assist on a speech or an informal talk Stone
had committed himself to give. By way of illustration I can mention three other
assorted matters that came up for me in consequence of Stone's chief justiceship. One was that when he first presided over the judicial conference, which
was the annual September gathering of the senior circuit judge from each of
the circuits (this was before the designation of a chief judge in each of the circuits). Stone asked me to sit in on the meeting and help to write his rather
extensive report.

A second additional duty occurred because the Court had farmed out to
an academician the task of producing a first draft of proposed *Federal Rules
of Criminal Procedure*. When the draft arrived the justices thought it was exceptionally poor, and Stone asked me to prepare a memorandum explaining
the many deficiencies so that he could pass it on to the draftsman with the
hope of stimulating the necessary repairs. A third task came about because
an unusual situation arose with respect to the staffing of the Supreme Court
Library; Stone asked me to interview the persons involved and report back to
him. I am sure a number of Stone's other law clerks would have been in a position to cite some special adventures of their own. And during Stone's associate justiceship, when as previously indicated the law clerk was stationed at the
Stone residence, the law clerk had the pleasure of assisting to officiate at Mrs.
Stone's periodic teas.

The indications I have given throughout this essay of the special responsibilities of the chief justice will help to explain why Stone, upon being informed
late in October term 1940 that he would be nominated to succeed to that office, decided that the chief justice should have not one but two law clerks, and
that the senior of the two should be someone who already was familiar with
the workings of the Court. That is how—largely on Justice Felix Frankfurter's recommendation when I was completing my tenure as Justice Reed's law

clerk—Stone selected me, even though I was a Harvard Law School graduate and not from Columbia.[13]

And how did professional afterlife turn out for those who had been a Stone law clerk? For many—probably too numerous to specify in detail—there were at least temporary periods of service either in the military or in responsible civilian posts in the federal government, or both. A strong majority of the twenty-two clerks spent at least a significant portion of their professional careers in private practice—some of them nearly totally—and with obvious distinction. Two of them became exceptionally talented and widely renowned federal judges—Harold Leventhal in the United States Court of Appeals for the District of Columbia Circuit (serving fifteen years) and Eugene Nickerson in the United States District Court for the Eastern District of New York (serving twenty-four years).[14]

Of the twenty-two, the academy made enduring claims on at least five who pursued law faculty careers in combination with other substantial accomplishments. Four of the five contributed to the core strength of the Columbia Law School faculty for a couple of generations. The fifth, Allison Dunham, made his considerable teaching talents available for a series of other law schools including particularly the University of Chicago.

Stone himself found special satisfaction and pride in the four who gave such strength to Columbia. The first, Milton Handler, served simultaneously for many years on the faculty and as an active practitioner in New York law firms and an author who became nationally recognized as an expert (Milton, however, thought he was *the expert*) on antitrust and trade regulation and trademark matters. Walter Gellhorn was a pioneer in the burgeoning subject of administrative law, as well as a successful advocate for establishing better links with foreign legal cultures. Herbert Wechsler, after serving as an assistant attorney general in the Department of Justice, became recognized as one of the nation's most eminent scholars and teachers in the fields of constitutional law and federal jurisdiction. He served as the reporter for the American Law Institute's influential Model Penal Code and thereafter was the ALI director, all concurrently with his post at Columbia. And Louis Lusky, after sixteen years of private practice in his native Louisville, Kentucky, joined the Columbia faculty in 1963 and stood out as a stalwart expert on civil rights matters.

I add a comment concerning Warner W. Gardner, the law clerk who had not been on the *Columbia Law Review* and who later resisted a tempting prospect of joining the Columbia Law School faculty. His outstanding performance in a series of federal positions, interrupted by two military years as a Special Branch officer in the European Theater, ended with his service as assistant secretary of the Interior. At that point he entered private practice as the co-founder of Shea & Gardner, a law firm that over the years became highly respected in Washington, and Warner was widely acknowledged to be one of the great lawyers of his time.[15] He had this to say about Justice Stone:

> For more than twenty-one years . . . [Chief Justice Stone] gave to the Supreme Court and the nation the inestimable benefits which have come from the service of an exceptionally wise and sensible judge. Perhaps no man of our time has done as much both to enrich our law books and to safeguard the integrity of our institutions.[16]

I feel confident that every one of our twenty-two law clerks would have been happy to subscribe to that verdict.

Notes

1. The exception was Warner W. Gardner (October term 1934), who spent much of his law school years engaged in teaching at Rutgers University and New York University, thus earning the money to pay for his law school education.

2. McCormack was for many years a major figure in the Cravath firm, and a biographical sketch is found in Robert T. Swaine, *The Cravath Firm and Its Predecessors, 1819–1947* (New York: Ad Press, 1948), 2: 476–79. During World War II McCormack was to a large extent the guiding spirit in assembling and running the famous Special Branch of U.S. Army Military Intelligence—a unit composed in no small measure of previously civilian professors, journalists, and lawyers, with the duty of preparing intelligence information from all sources ("top secret ultra" decodes and on down) that would be useful to many aspects of the war effort. Ronald Lewin, *The American Magic: Codes, Ciphers and the Defeat of Japan* (New York: Farrar, Straus, and Giroux, 1982), 141–52; Diane T. Putney, "The U.S. Military Intelligence Service: The ULTRA Mission," in *ULTRA and the Army Air Forces in World War II: An Interview with Associate Justice of the U.S. Supreme Court Lewis F. Powell, Jr.*, ed. Putney (Washington, D.C.: Office of Air Force History, U.S. Air Force, 1987), 65–97. And after hostilities ceased he served a turn in charge of the Bureau of Intelligence and Research at the State Department.

3. Alfred McCormack, "A Law Clerk's Recollections," *Columbia Law Review* 46, no. 5 (September 1946): 710–18.

4. Ibid., 717.

5. On an anecdotal basis, I mention that on one occasion I was able to prepare for Chief Justice Stone seventeen cert memos in one day. When I reported this statistic that evening to my wife Shirley, she was appalled.

6. The pool was started at the suggestion of Justice Powell, who felt strongly that it would increase the Court's efficiency; initially it had five justices as participants. See Chief Justice Rehnquist's description of its operation in Rehnquist, *The Supreme Court: How It Was, How It Is* (New York: William Morrow, 1987), 263–66; John C. Jeffries Jr., *Justice Lewis F. Powell, Jr.* (New York: Charles Scribner's Sons, 1994): 270–72. Although the number of participating justices gradually increased, Justice Stevens always remained outside the pool. And recently Justice Alito let it be known that he was withdrawing from the pool. The extent to which reliance is placed by any justice on the pool memo, without further investigation, may vary considerably from justice to justice and from case to case. See Eugene Gressman et al., *Supreme Court Practice: For Practice in the Supreme Court of the United States,* 9th ed. (Arlington, Va.: BNA Books, 2007): 316–19.

7. In a one-time-only experience, during a particular couple of weeks Justice Hugo Black's law clerk informed me that the time and effort of Justice Black and himself were deeply committed to opinion writing, and that Justice Black wondered if he could borrow the carbon copies of my cert memos. With Stone's permission this was done.

8. At some later date, as the volume of certs kept mounting, the procedure was modified to its current form so that the chief justice would circulate a Discuss List, and the rest of the petitions were denied without discussion. Any justice could have a case added to the Discuss List. As Chief Justice William H. Rehnquist said, leaving a case off the Discuss List "simply means that no one of the nine justices thought the case was worth discussing at conference with a view to trying to persuade four members of the Court to grant certiorari." Rehnquist, *Supreme Court,* 266–67.

9. I recall a period when Justice Black felt that the lower federal courts were rendering decisions needlessly hostile to farmers in cases arising under the Farm Bankruptcy Act. I recommended to Stone that a farmer's petition under the Farm Bankruptcy Act, no matter how uncertworthy the case appeared, should never be placed on the Dead List. Stone was of the same view, and this helped to preserve the credibility of the Dead List in a fortunately harmonious manner.

10. In the two years I was with Stone, I recall only one instance where I seriously disagreed with his position on the merits of a case and sought to persuade him to change his mind. The case was *Betts v. Brady,* 316 U.S. 455 (1942), where the majority of the Court, including Stone, in an opinion by Justice Owen J. Roberts, held that in a state court noncapital robbery conviction, the federal Constitution did not require that the indigent defendant on request be furnished appointed counsel. In trying to persuade Stone to modify his view, I collected a number of state statutes and constitutional provisions that I hoped would help. I was unsuccessful, and then I asked Stone whether I might turn over to the law clerk of Justice Black, who was working on a dissent, the materials I had collected. With Stone's permission, I did so, and the materials appear in the appendix to Black's dissenting opinion. About two decades later, in the light of more extensive experience, *Betts v. Brady* was overruled in *Gideon v. Wainwright,* 372 U.S. 335 (1963).

11. Bennett Boskey, "Opinion-Assigning by Chief Justices," *Supreme Court Historical Society Quarterly* 25, no. 1 (2004): 14, reproduced in Bennett Boskey, *Some Joys of Lawyering: Selected Writings, 1946–2007* (Washington, D.C.: Green Bag Press, 2007): 55.

12. What might be considered a slight exception would be some short per curiam opinions, particularly on jurisdictional points, he issued for the Court when he was chief justice.

13. I had not previously met Stone during my year with Reed, and I have elsewhere set forth an account of the interview at which I did meet him and he offered me the position. See Boskey, *Some Joys of Lawyering*, 68. It is only fair to add that although I might have caused some hiatus in Columbia's record, the fine Columbia man (C. Roger Nelson) whom Stone had already engaged came along as his other law clerk.

14. Before he was appointed to the bench, Nickerson was the first Democrat to serve as Nassau County Executive (Nassau County having traditionally been a strongly Republican segment of Long Island).

15. A far more detailed account of Gardner's career can be found in my remarks at the memorial service for Warner, January 9, 2003, reproduced in Boskey, *Some Joys of Lawyering*, 116.

16. Warner W. Gardner, "Mr. Chief Justice Stone," *Harvard Law Review* 59, no. 8 (October 1946): 1209.

Justice Horace Gray, photographed by Mathew Brady. Justice Gray was the first Supreme Court justice to hire law clerks to assist with the business of the Court. (Special Collections, Harvard Law School)

Thomas Russell, the first Supreme Court law clerk. Congress had not authorized funds for the hiring of law clerks, so Justice Gray personally paid his young assistant's salary. (Star Myles)

Justice Oliver Wendell Holmes Jr. in a field of flowers near Rock Creek Park, Washington, D.C., during an outing with law clerk Arthur E. Sutherland in the spring of 1928. Escorting Justice Holmes on field trips around the district was a traditional duty of the Holmes law clerks. (Courtesy of Historical & Special Collections, Harvard Law School Library)

Chief Justice Harlan Fiske Stone in a car driven by law clerk Bennett Boskey, on the opening day of the Court, October term, 1941. (Bennett Boskey)

Chief Justice Stone (front row center) and his "family" of law clerks during a black-tie reunion dinner, date unknown. (Diamond Law Library, Columbia University)

Justice Hugo Black (on left) with former law clerk Charles Reich. (Charles Reich)

Justice Hugo Black and Mrs. Elizabeth Black, with former law clerks and friends, on his eightieth birthday. (Library of Congress)

William T. Coleman Jr., the first African American law clerk, who clerked for Felix Frankfurter during October term, 1948. (AP Photo/John Rous)

Lucile Lomen, the first female law clerk, who clerked for William O. Douglas during October term, 1944. (Gretchen Van Tassel)

Justice William J. Brennan Jr. and his law clerks at their morning coffee meeting. (Lynn Johnson/National Geographic Stock)

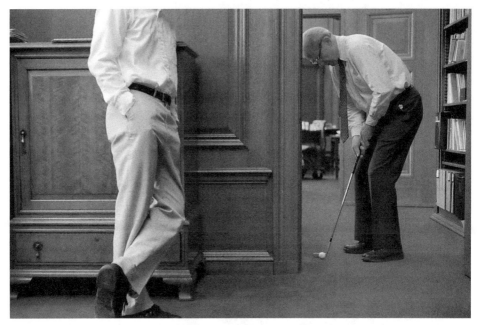

Justice Byron White putting in his chambers while a law clerk looks on. Justice White and his law clerks often engaged in various types of athletic competition, from basketball to putting. (Lynn Johnson/National Geographic Stock)

Justice Lewis Powell having lunch in chambers with his law clerks, who revered their courtly and soft-spoken justice. (Lynn Johnson/National Geographic Stock)

Justice Robert Jackson with then–law clerk William H. Rehnquist, date unknown.
Decades later, a memorandum written during his clerkship threatened to derail
Rehnquist's nomination to the Supreme Court. (Robert H. Jackson Center,
C. George Niebank Collection)

Associate Justice William
Rehnquist taking his daily
walk outside of the Court
with law clerk David Leitch.
(Lynn Johnson/National
Geographic Stock)

Associate Justice William H. Rehnquist with law clerks Dean Colson, Robert Knauss, and John Roberts (left to right), October term, 1980. Roberts is one of five former law clerks to return to the Supreme Court as a justice. (Supreme Court Curator's Office)

Justice Ruth Bader Ginsburg with her law clerks, October term, 2008. (Supreme Court Curator's Office)

II The Premodern Clerkship Institution

A Passion for Justice

Living with and Clerking for Justice Hugo Black

I served with David J. Vann as law clerk to Justice Hugo L. Black during the momentous 1953–54 term of the Supreme Court. This was the year when *Brown v. Board of Education* was decided.[1] It was the year when Chief Justice Fred Vinson died and was replaced by the governor of California, Earl Warren. And it was also a year in which the members of the Court divided bitterly in a series of cases with profound implications for the future, involving unlawful police surveillance, political restrictions on the right to work, and the use of psychiatry for "enhanced interrogation" of a suspect.

David and I lived with Justice Black in his Alexandria, Virginia, home and spent the entire day with him seven days a week, starting with breakfast cooked by "the Judge," as he was called, and served at the kitchen table, continuing with the drive to Washington and a day at the Court, and ending with dinner and an evening of discussion in the Judge's study upstairs. Justice Black had recently lost his wife, and his children were grown and had left home, so David and I were "family" as well as law clerks.

I was a third-year student at Yale Law School when I applied for a position with Justice Black. He was already an influential figure in Supreme Court history, having been appointed in 1937 by President Franklin D. Roosevelt, and having become the senior justice by the time that I applied. As a student I had been tremendously impressed by Justice Black's defense of civil liberties at a time when fear of communism had caused most judges, including many "liberals," to uphold the persecution and punishment of individuals who expressed dissenting views.

In the opinions I read while in law school, Justice Black made clear that he believed prior decisions had wrongfully diminished, diluted, and in some cases totally betrayed the Constitution's protections of individual rights and liberties. The most conspicuous example of such a betrayal was the Court's rewriting of the Fourteenth Amendment's guarantee of the "equal protection" of the laws, a guarantee adopted after the Civil War and specifically intended to grant equal status to former slaves. Instead of enforcing this provision as written, the justices had rewritten it to require "separate but equal" treatment—a formula for inequality that still remained the law in 1953.

Similarly, in Justice Black's view, the Constitution's mandate of "no law" abridging freedom of speech had been wrongfully rewritten by the justices to allow any law punishing speech that they considered necessary to prevent serious threats to the government. And in yet another example of judicial rewriting of the Constitution, to which Justice Black strongly objected, corporations had been given all the rights intended exclusively for persons. Such were the highly independent views of the justice with whom I had eagerly sought a clerkship.

The year previous to my clerkship had been an unhappy one for Justice Black. He was still grieving from the death of his wife Josephine, he had suffered a physically painful case of shingles, and he was an increasingly isolated dissenter on the Vinson court. Just before my clerkship began the Court had suffered the trauma of the *Rosenberg* case,[2] in which a hastily convened "special session" of the Court had allowed the execution of Julius and Ethel Rosenberg to proceed. Justice Black repeatedly objected that the session itself was not authorized by the rules of the Court. Moreover, he contended that the Court had failed to consider substantial issues concerning the legality of the death sentences. When David and I started work, Justice Black was still angry that the Court had failed to follow its own procedures. He refused to have lunch with "them," and instead the three of us had lunch downstairs in the Court's public cafeteria.

Recently Linda Greenhouse described the activities of the current Supreme Court justices as follows: "in this media-saturated age, the Justices are everywhere. If they are not on book tours, they are opining on the authorship of Shakespeare's plays, or mingling with their peers in Europe, or on C-SPAN addressing high school students, or at least delivering named lectures at law schools."[3] Justice Black did none of these things. David and I sat in his office and watched him open his mail, heavy with invitations to official functions, embassy receptions, and offers of honorary degrees from universities. On each he wrote one word: "regret."

He was home seven nights a week, and he insisted on doing all of his own work. He wrote his own opinions, did his own legal research, made his own decisions on petitions for certiorari, read the lengthy printed record of cases when necessary, and made his own preparations for hearing cases on the bench and for the justices' weekly conferences. Thus David and I did none of the work usually assigned to law clerks. For example, incredible as it may seem, we never did any legal research. Only where the Judge's work ended did ours begin. We read certiorari petitions and discussed his choices for cases that the Court should review. We discussed his opinions line by line as well as the opinions of other justices when they were circulated. We even listened to the angry letters he received from people in Alabama who thought he was a Communist. In fact, we were busy all day long, but never did we do *his* work.

Occasionally David and I wandered next door to the chambers of Justice Felix Frankfurter, where F.F.'s clerks, Frank Sander and Jim Vorenberg, offered the hospitality of the large room with a fireplace intended for the justice himself, while F.F. preferred the smaller office intended for his clerks. Often our law clerks' gossip sessions were interrupted by the sudden appearance of the excitable Justice Frankfurter himself, who treated everyone as one of his students and sometimes backed me into a corner with demands that I "explain" something to "your judge" who was, in F.F.'s view, a bit slow to catch on to certain matters, such as the proper criteria for granting or denying petitions for certiorari. Justice Frankfurter seemed to think that my Yale Law School education might enable me to correct some of the flaws in my judge's education. Needless to say, I never undertook to "correct" Justice Black.

The area of the Supreme Court Building that included the chambers of the nine justices, their secretaries, their messengers, and their law clerks made up a small self-contained village where the clerks wandered freely, carts loaded with cert petitions were rolled along, and a relaxed atmosphere prevailed. Everyone was on friendly terms, and the clerks had their own dining room where David and I would go when our judge finally decided it was time to have lunch with "them." There were no female law clerks in our year; the Court convened at noon; and government lawyers still wore formal dress. On one memorable occasion we all dressed in rented white tie outfits for a formal reception at the White House. We all were in the courtroom to hear two of the greatest lawyers of the day, Thurgood Marshall and John W. Davis, argue *Brown v. Board of Education*. But thereafter, none of the law clerks except the chief justice's worked on these cases.

I have previously written about Justice Black, but always with a sense of constraint imposed by the confidentiality of a law clerk's position. But now that more than fifty years have passed, now that the Court is a constant subject of political debate, I feel that the claims of history and the study of law have become paramount. For historians, the story of how the new chief justice began as a "law and order" judge but by the end of the term had been transformed, with the crucial intervention of Justice Black, into the "liberal" judge of the "Warren Court," needs to be recorded while there is still a witness able to do so. For aspiring legal academics, a close-up of one justice's thought processes and tactics should prove valuable. For law students, I would like to provide a picture of one individual who truly loved the law. For all of the above and for the public as well, there is the ultimate test of what makes a good judge: a passion for justice.

In the Judge's Study

David and I occupied our own quarters on the ground floor of Justice Black's beautiful old home at 619 South Lee Street in Alexandria, Virginia. Our windows looked out on a grape arbor and tennis court. Our day began when the Judge, in his bathrobe, knocked on our door to tell us that breakfast, which he prepared, was almost ready. At breakfast, in the kitchen, he liked to read aloud from the *Washington Post,* with many humorous asides. He especially enjoyed the Herblock cartoons. We each had a car, and we rotated cars and drivers for the daily trip to Washington and the Court. Usually we had lunch together in the Court's public cafeteria. Between 12:00 p.m. and 12:10 p.m. the line was open to Court employees only, and the Judge liked to time our trip downstairs so that we just made the tail end of the employees' line. At precisely 3:50 p.m., just ahead of the afternoon rush hour, we departed for Alexandria. Dinner was served at about 6:00 p.m. by Lizzie Mae Campbell, the Judge's longtime cook and housekeeper. Then the three of us would climb the stairs to the Judge's second-floor study for a session that would last until bedtime. For me, this was the most remarkable and inspiring part of our day together.

The study was filled with books, including a full set of *U.S. Reports,* containing all previous Supreme Court decisions and opinions. There was space on the walls for many framed photographs, usually autographed, of individuals the Judge had known in his long public career as a senator and justice. My favorite, in a place of honor, was a photograph of Senator George Norris of Nebraska, inscribed "To my friend Justice Black with admiration and love." The books revealed a great deal about the Judge's concept of what it meant to be a Supreme Court justice. To him, it was a position that went far beyond merely voting on cases. To begin with, the job required a scholar, one who had studied history all the way back to the Greeks and the Romans, with particular emphasis on the history of liberty and tyranny and the rise of the rule of law. The framers of the Constitution were well represented, as was the history of English law going back to the Magna Carta.

The spirit that pervaded this remarkable room was best expressed in Edith Hamilton's *The Greek Way,* a book beloved by Justice Black and frequently referred to. The Greeks, writes Hamilton, were the first to practice "the supremacy of mind in the affairs of men . . . the first intellectualists. In a world where the irrational had played the chief role, they came forward as the protagonists of the mind. . . . The Greeks said, 'All things are to be examined and called into question. There are no limits set to thought.'"[4]

In this spirit, there were no limits set to what David or I could say or ask as the Judge sat behind his desk, rocking gently back and forth, and David and I occupied two easy chairs facing him. Most frequently the subject was a case on which we were working, with the printed record on the desk and perhaps the first draft of an opinion or dissent in our hands. But before we reached the subject of any specific case, the Judge gave us some insight into how he viewed the job of being a Supreme Court justice and how he prepared for that job. A justice must have a judicial philosophy. He saw his role as a defender of the Constitution, and as a protector of the individual, to whom the Constitution belonged. Essential to this role was knowledge of history, in particular the intentions of the framers of the Constitution and the fears of power that concerned them. This led back to English history, to the injustices that the framers knew about and sought to prevent, and further back to the long struggle between tyranny and the rule of law. Much as he loved his country, Justice Black believed that the rise of tyranny was always a possibility, that exaggerated fears, such as the fear of communism, pose an ever-present threat to liberty, and that freedom remains, in the words of Stephen Vincent Benet, "a hard bought thing."

Crucial to the Judge's judicial philosophy was his invariable practice of looking directly at the words of the Constitution itself, rather than at previous Supreme Court interpretations of those words. Most judges are inclined to follow precedents; he was never satisfied with precedents if he thought the words of the Constitution did not support them. Justice Black opposed any interpretation of the Constitution that allowed broad leeway to judges. He repeatedly objected to any view of the First Amendment that allowed judges to engage in "balancing" the interests of government against the interests of the individual. To him, "balancing" was judge-made law, never intended by the framers. Likewise, he rejected vague and shifting interpretations of the phrase "due process of law," seeking to give the phrase a definite meaning limiting the discretion of judges.

For the same reason, Justice Black was also determined to restore to their full vigor sections of the Constitution that had been allowed to fall into disuse, notably the prohibition against bills of attainder and the prohibition against ex post facto laws. He was keen to find present-day examples of both these abuses, while other justices treated them as archaic remnants. Finally, Justice Black was acutely sensitive to the injury done to any individual and the harm done to society in any given case. While other justices stated the facts of a case in abstract and legalistic terms, in opinions and particularly in dissents he made sure to present the facts as a vivid narrative.

During our sessions there were no interruptions. When David and the Judge were having an exchange, I liked to sit back and watch the Judge's expressive face register his feelings. When we discussed a case where power had been abused and an individual had suffered harm, the Judge's face showed pain and anger. Too often in law school my teachers, many of them "legal realists," made law seem like a game or even a joke, and any answer was just as acceptable as the opposite answer. This made for good, lively classroom teaching, but ultimately it left students cynical and disillusioned about the law as a profession. Later, when I became a teacher, I often wished that my students could have shared my experience in Justice Black's study. It profoundly renewed my idealism and belief that justice is the foundation of society. Yet I have never heard a senator ask a Supreme Court nominee, "Do you have a passion for justice?"

Exercising the Mind

Justice Black was a great believer in exercise—both physical and mental. If he could not find a tennis partner, when he got home from the Court he would go directly to the tennis court with a large basket of tennis balls that he would hit from one side to the other, pick them all up, and repeat the process by hitting them all back. He was unlucky to find that neither David nor I played tennis, but we at least partly made up for that deficiency by enthusiastically participating in mental exercise. David was the first to recognize that the Judge enjoyed a good argument. Apparently David had taken a course in admiralty law at the University of Alabama, because he came out swinging as the Judge prepared a lengthy dissent in *Maryland Casualty Co. v. Cushing*,[5] a case where a towboat named *Jane Smith* hit a railroad bridge and sank in the Atchafalaya River, causing five crew members to lose their lives. For many evenings the Judge's study was filled with arguments concerning maritime law.

I had never taken a course in this subject; in fact, I didn't even know where to find the Atchafalaya River on a map, but I saw that the Judge would allow a law clerk to make a full-blown argument just like a lawyer in court, and when the time came I too made a full-blown argument in a later case that interested me deeply. David showed me how far the Judge would go in granting equality to his law clerks so they could challenge him with full vigor. Of course, the Judge made clear that he would not readily change his own long-held views. But he was a great believer in hearing the other side, and he clearly considered that kind of openness to be an essential part of being a judge.

In many ways, David helped to make the whole experience with Justice Black possible. Certainly the wrong person in his position could have made it impossible. David was a native of Alabama and a graduate of the University of Alabama School of Law who served as mayor of Birmingham during the most difficult days of desegregation. He understood the Judge's foibles and rituals far more easily than I could have.

During our serious sessions in the study David was thoughtful, congenial, and more than able to hold his own when the discussion grew serious. It was David, not me, who asked Justice Black about his early membership in the Klu Klux Klan, whether that membership carried with it racism, and why the Judge had quit the Klan when he did. I would never have dared to ask these questions. David also asked about some of the Judge's more questionable early decisions such as the first flag salute case and the Japanese internment case, both of which might be seen in hindsight as mistakes.[6] Many people have asked me what the Judge had to say about the Klan. He told us that it was just a social and fraternal organization, like many others he belonged to. David and I found this answer frustrating, but the Judge would go no further—and we were left to wonder.

After an evening in the study, when the Judge had retired for the night, David and I sometimes talked about the events of the day, the interplay among the justices, and Justice Black's own stubborn streaks. David had both tact and humor, but he was fully prepared to argue his views strenuously when he thought the Judge was wrong. Spending seven days and nights together week after week could have been a disaster instead of an extraordinary experience. David was an indispensable part of that experience.

Of course, every one of Justice Black's law clerks must have played the role of mental exercise partner, and some were tennis partners as well. I never got to observe them in action. But during 1953–54 the Judge had occasional guests, and it was interesting to see that they too provided him with mental exercise, although Court business was never discussed. Each guest was invited to come alone. The dinner table was set for four instead of three, the guest got the tenderloin part of the steak, and upstairs David and I were quieter than usual, although we were always welcome to talk. Otherwise, the routine in the study was much the same for four as it was for three.

Among the guests, I remember Senator Lister Hill of Alabama, Benjamin V. Cohen, Justice William O. Douglas, Professor Edmund Cahn of the New York University School of Law, Tommy "The Cork" Corcoran, who brought his accordion and sang for us, and Chief Justice Earl Warren.

I found Justice Douglas fascinating from the moment that he walked in the door, with his ruddy outdoorsman face, battered western hat, and intense energy. From Justice Douglas, we learned how he had been ready to leave for the summer (after the Court ended its term in June), when he was approached by lawyers with a last-minute plea in the Rosenberg case.[7] He reluctantly agreed to listen. Even more reluctantly, he concluded that their argument—that the Rosenbergs had been convicted and sentenced under the wrong statute—required a full Court hearing. Accordingly, Justice Douglas issued a stay of execution until the Court's fall season, jumped into his car, and started the long drive to his summer cabin in Goose Prairie, Washington. When he stopped for the night at a motel on the Pennsylvania Turnpike, he turned on the television news and was stunned to learn that Chief Justice Fred Vinson had called a special session of the Court to overturn the stay. The next morning, he headed back to the hearing—a hearing that both he and Justice Black believed was improperly called.

When Chief Justice Warren came for dinner, I was dispatched in my used blue Dodge to call for him at his temporary residence in the Wardman Park Hotel in northwest D.C. This forty-five-minute drive with the famous ex-governor of California, ex-presidential candidate, and new chief justice, plus the return trip, was just about as exciting as things can get for a twenty-five-year-old who had just graduated from law school—and today at the age of eighty-one I can still feel the thrill.

With each guest Justice Black was his usual self, rocking back and forth behind his desk, perhaps taking a volume of Tacitus down from the shelves, asking questions and making sure that there was serious talk. I marveled at the calming effect that the Judge had on Justice Douglas, who could be restless, brusque, and impatient, but when asked about his travels he became eloquent and even flashed his winning smile at David and me. The chief justice and Justice Black found common ground in running for office and winning elections, and with Senator Hill the talk was about politics in Alabama. Otherwise these evenings resembled our regular sessions to a remarkable degree. The words might be different, but the music was the same.

Courting the Chief

In case after case during the 1953–54 term, the Judge found himself on the opposite side from the new chief justice, Earl Warren. On this painful subject, the Judge said nothing at all. Meanwhile, Justice Frankfurter was making an obvious and very public attempt to instruct his newest "student" in the duties of a Supreme Court justice. The odd couple was frequently seen in the hall, with F.F. holding the Chief's arm with one hand while gesticulating with the other hand in a professorial manner. David and I often saw the chief justice as he came through our door on his way to discuss some matter with Justice Black. The Chief was hearty and outgoing, but David and I each suspected that F.F.'s teacher-student relationship would not last. We often talked about this late at night after our session with the Judge in the study, and especially after the evening when the Chief came out to dinner. The Chief was a proud man. But, we both suspected, he might be thin-skinned. The Judge certainly did not treat him like a student. The Judge called him "Chief" and made no attempt to "teach" him anything.

Other justices also made a play for Chief Justice Warren. Justice Jackson evidently had the Chief's ear in *Irvine v. California*,[8] but Jackson was soon taken ill and vanished from the scene. Justice Douglas invited the Chief to go walking on the C&O Canal towpath, but this effort proved disastrous. We all heard that the Chief had returned with sore feet and blisters, and that Mrs. Warren had said never again.

Justice Black finally found a case with which he could win over Chief Justice Warren. I have already mentioned that the Judge read and decided petitions for certiorari himself, contrary to the practice of most justices. One day the Judge picked a case that no law clerk would have ever chosen. In an earlier form, it had already been denied review by the Supreme Court. The case seemed to meet none of the criteria of "public importance" required for review by the Court. It was a sordid murder case, in which a middle-aged man had beaten his elderly parents to death with a hammer, a crime to which he had confessed and for which he had been sentenced to death in New York.

But the Judge had studied the record in the case, and he was deeply troubled by the confessions introduced into evidence because they had been obtained by the use of a police-employed psychiatrist pretending to "help" the defendant. The Judge called us into his office, where he was seated with the printed record on his desk. He said that he had discovered that a tape recording had been made of the psychiatrist talking to the defendant. "Don't you think we ought to hear that recording for ourselves?" he asked. David and I nodded. "Why don't we ask the clerk's office to send for it?" We nodded again. And in due time a tape recording arrived from New York, the clerk's office supplied a machine to play it, and the three of us sat down to listen.

The defendant, Camilio Leyra, had already undergone lengthy questioning by the police, but had admitted nothing. On the day that his parents' bodies were found, a Tuesday, Leyra was questioned by the police until 11:00 p.m. On Wednesday he was questioned from 10:00 a.m.to midnight. On Thursday he was questioned from 9:00 a.m. through the day and the night until 8:30 a.m. the following morning, when he was taken to his parents' funeral. After the funeral he was allowed to sleep for an hour and a half after which questioning resumed. During his absence a concealed microphone had been installed, enabling the police to listen to and record any further conversation. At no time was a lawyer present, and Leyra made no admissions.

Leyra had been suffering from acute sinus pains, and after the concealed microphone had been installed the police promised to get a physician to help him. He was introduced to Dr. Helfand, supposedly a doctor who would help with the sinus pain. In fact, Dr. Helfand was a psychiatrist who had considerable experience with hypnosis. We heard Dr. Helfand saying:

> I want to see if I can help you . . . Sometimes we do things in a fit of anger or temper that we aren't really responsible for . . . I am going to make you recollect . . . thoughts you might have forgotten . . . I am going to put my hand on your forehead, you are going to bring back these thoughts . . . Your thoughts are coming back to you . . . Don't be afraid now. We're with you. We're going to help you. You're going to feel lots better after you talk to me . . . We're with you one hundred percent . . . Don't be afraid. Your conscience will be clear. God will be with you, and everybody will help you if you tell the truth . . . A lot of people do things that they are not responsible for while in a fit of temper . . . Speak up. Everybody will help you . . . We're all with you one hundred percent. We'll help you . . . I'm your doctor. I'm going to help you . . . We know that morally you were just in anger. Morally you are not to be condemned . . . You are a nice fellow.

As the session continued and Dr. Helfand repeated his suggestions over and over again, Leyra's voice sounded so slow and dazed that he seemed drugged, hypnotized, or just plain exhausted, like a person barely awake, barely able to answer. The doctor kept saying, "I have my hand on your forehead . . . I will help you remember."

The Judge was able to get three votes in addition to his own for a grant of certiorari. But the outcome was still in doubt. Justice Jackson was ill and unable to take part in the case. Three other justices were determined to uphold the verdict. A four-four split would affirm the death sentence. The Judge stayed home for several days to prepare an opinion. Meanwhile, I imagined that this would be a famous case, a "case of first impression," the first case on mental coercion by the use of psychiatry and hypnosis, a landmark. It would be noted in every law review, included in every casebook, taught in every class in both criminal and constitutional law, and in medical school as well, cited in every future decision on interrogation . . . but only if we could get five votes, and that would require the vote of the chief justice, who up to that time had yet to vote in favor of a criminal defendant.

When the Judge showed us the draft opinion he had prepared, my daydreams about a landmark case were suddenly dissolved. The *Leyra* case would not be famous.[9] It would never be taught in law school or noted in the law reviews. The Judge had written the simplest possible opinion. It was almost entirely factual. It appeared to make no new law. Instead, the opinion made the case seem like long-established law. The Judge's special ideas about due process were relegated to the inconspicuous last sentence of a footnote: "Some members of the Court reach this conclusion because of their belief that the Fourteenth Amendment makes applicable to the states the Fifth Amendment's ban against compulsory self-incrimination." For those who might be interested, an appendix was included, running twenty-two pages in *U.S. Reports,* containing excerpts from the tape recording, without further comment. The opinion itself took up only five and a half pages. Not a word in the opinion was the least bit novel or controversial.

The Chief signed on! The Judge's strategy worked. He had read the Chief's character perfectly. The Chief was not prepared to make new law, but he would not tolerate the duplicity of a Dr. Helfand. The Warren Court had begun.

On June 1, David and I went down to the courtroom. The Chief was graciousness itself as he presided over the usual admissions to the bar. Then he nodded to Justice Black on his right. The Judge leaned forward. "I am authorized to announce the Opinion and Judgment of the Court in Camilio Leyra v. Wilfred Denno, Warden of Sing Sing prison, on writ of certiorari to the Second

Circuit of Appeals." Anyone who ever heard Justice Black deliver an opinion from the bench will never forget the effect his soft but perfectly clear and distinct voice had on the packed courtroom. It was still the custom to read opinions in full. The Judge related the facts at length, while the legal conclusion was condensed into a single sentence that made no mention of psychiatry: "We hold that the use of confessions extracted in such a manner from a lone defendant unprotected by counsel is not consistent with due process of law as required by our Constitution."

Finally, the Judge read the judgment, overturning a death sentence and the holdings of four courts below: "It was error for the court below to affirm the District Court's denial of petitioner's application for habeas corpus. *Reversed.*"

Two weeks before *Leyra, Brown v. Board of Education* had been decided. David and I were in Court for the announcement, but we had not worked on the case. After the dramatic events at the Court, we returned to Alexandria and the Judge sat down with us under the grape arbor for at least two hours to tell us his thoughts about *Brown.* His first words were, "Earl Warren has made his place in history." The Judge apologized to David and me for the extraordinary secrecy with which the case had been handled, but he also said that if there had been a leak, we would have thanked him for keeping us uninformed. Now, however, the Judge seemed eager to speak out.

He had agreed to make the opinion unanimous, but, in fact, he had disagreed with the enforcement part of the decision (namely, implementation was delayed for further arguments). The Judge said that the South would resist no matter how cautiously the Court proceeded, so he would have preferred to dispose of the case like any other ordinary lawsuit by ordering the plaintiffs to be admitted to the schools they applied to "forthwith" with no further delay and no general hearing on the broad issue of implementation. "I should simply have ordered them in," he told us. But he had nothing but praise for the chief justice's skill in bringing the Court together. From the depths of the *Rosenberg* case, the year had seen the Court rise to one of its greatest challenges.

Postclerkship Years

After my clerkship was finished I remained in Washington, D.C., for the next five years, working at the law firm of Arnold Fortas & Porter and living in an apartment house on Connecticut Avenue. The firm was a small one near DuPont Circle, in a private mansion formerly occupied by the late Justice Pierce Butler. The three founding partners were all prominent former New

Dealers—insiders. Justice Black remarried, his new wife, Elizabeth, was warm and outgoing, and for me a huge bonus was the fact that the wonderful evenings at South Lee Street continued.

I would be working at my desk in the mid-afternoon when the phone would ring and the familiar voice of Justice Black would say, "Charlie! Can you come out to dinner at six? Elizabeth has a steak that looks perfect for three." Occasionally there would be another guest, but most of these evenings were just the three of us. We never talked Court business, and we never mentioned current cases. Sometimes a neighbor from across the street came over after dinner to make a fourth for bridge.

In 1960 I joined the faculty at Yale Law School and moved to New Haven. Only rarely did I travel to Washington, D.C. I wrote law review articles. Justice Black read them, and I received comments in the mail, but we saw each other only a few times a year, and this was a great loss for me. But there were much greater losses to come.

A photograph in the *Yale Daily News* shows a group of shivering protestors on a sidewalk in downtown New Haven on a typical wet, cold, snowy winter day. I am bareheaded in the first row of protestors, carrying a hand-painted sign reading "No More Napalm." According to the caption, the protest was directed at the presence of a Dow Chemical Co. recruiter on campus. This was hardly the role I imagined for myself when I became a law professor. But the discomfort I felt was overridden by the inhumanity of dropping flaming chemicals from the air on human beings in Vietnam as the newest escalation in the depravity of war. A law professor does, after all, have a legitimate concern with what is being done in the name of constitutional government.

President Lyndon Johnson gave a reception at the White House to honor Justice Black, and I did not attend because of my opposition to the Vietnam War. In retrospect, this was a mistake. Justice Black was hurt by my absence, and no one else was helped in the slightest. I had met and listened to President Johnson at private dinner parties on two previous occasions when he was still vice president and admired him greatly then, so my objections had only to do with Vietnam. My compass was swinging wildly.

In 1970, I published *The Greening of America*. Justice Black read his copy carefully and filled it with his usual comments and underlining. Meanwhile my colleagues at the Law School maintained a silence that, if it had been translated, might have been expressed as "What's a law professor doing writing a book like this?"

And so matters stood when the news of Justice Black's death reached me in

New Haven. With another of the Judge's law clerks, Guido Calabresi, I traveled to Washington for a state funeral in the National Cathedral, attended by official Washington with a row of seats near the front reserved for former law clerks, into which Guido and I slipped, side by side. The service was a formal one, with readings from sources familiar to all of us in the Justice Black community. Then, as the service almost ended, one of the former law clerks at the podium began reading from the Judge's personal copy of *The Greening of America*—not just what I had written but critical comments that the Judge had written in the margin and that I had never seen. I remember standing in the cathedral feeling shocked and hurt. This was totally out of place at a formal state funeral. It was personal and private, something the Judge might have shown to me in his study with a smile. In the cathedral, no other person had been singled out for mention, and I felt attacked at a time and place when response was impossible. Fortunately, a hymn began, and Guido and I stood and wept as the coffin and its honor guard passed us on its way out of the cathedral.

Notes

1. *Brown v. Board of Education*, 347 U.S. 483 (1954).

2. *Rosenberg v. United States*, 346 U.S. 273 (1953).

3. "Week in Review," *New York Times*, May 3, 2009.

4. Edith Hamilton, *The Greek Way* (New York: W. W. Norton, 1942), 20, 36–37.

5. *Maryland Casualty Co. v. Cushing*, 347 U.S. 409 (1954).

6. *Minersville School District v. Gobitis*, 310 U.S. 586 (1940); *Korematsu v. United States*, 323 U.S. 214 (1944).

7. Julius and Ethel Rosenberg were convicted and sentenced to death for conspiring to violate the Espionage Act of 1917. The full court eventually held a special term to decide whether to vacate the stay of execution issued by Justice Douglas. See *Rosenberg v. United States*, 346 U.S. 273 (1953).

8. *Irvine v. California*, 347 U.S. 128 (1954).

9. *Leyra v. Denno*, 347 U.S. 556 (1954).

DANIEL J. MEADOR

Clerking for Justice Hugo Black

The eighteen law clerks for the Supreme Court justices in October term 1954, as in all terms, shared many experiences, although the experience in no two chambers was exactly the same. But clerking for Justice Hugo Black was unique, decidedly different from that of clerking for other justices. There were similarities, of course. Like those in other chambers, Black's clerks reviewed certiorari petitions, read and discussed opinion drafts circulated by other members of the Court, assisted in editing the justice's drafts, sat in from time to time on oral arguments, and ate lunch with their fellow clerks. Yet clerking for Black was a very special experience, made so by the force of his personality, his distinctive interests in books, and his legal views.

Justice Black's Law Clerks

Hugo Black's clerks were a distinctive group. What made them so was the group's noticeable, but not exclusively, southern character. It was often said that Black gave preference to applicants from Alabama, he being a native of the state and its former United States senator. That was to an extent true, but it could be overstated. During the thirty-four years that he was on the Court, from 1937 to 1971, he had a total of fifty-five law clerks. Of those, only eighteen came from Alabama. But another seventeen came from elsewhere in the South. Thus southerners accounted for about two-thirds of the total. Nothing even approaching that pattern could have been found in any other chambers. Indeed, as far as I know, in that era no other justice had an Alabama clerk, and southerners of any breed were rare. Being from Alabama gave a clerk a special relationship with the justice, deriving from a common awareness of places, people, and events. Alabama clerks probably appreciated some aspects of Black's make-up that eluded clerks from elsewhere.

Another somewhat overstated claim is that Black hired only clerks who played tennis. He was indeed an enthusiastic tennis player. Within the walled premises of his eighteenth-century Alexandria house, an unusually large space for an otherwise tightly packed neighborhood in Old Town, he had built a clay tennis court (he disdained hard surface courts). Over the years numerous clerks did play tennis with him, but as many or more did not. Those who did testified to his inexhaustible energy, usually outlasting them on the court. High energy and determination to prevail, both at work and at play, were among his most striking characteristics.

In terms of law schools attended, the Black clerks were not much different from those in several other chambers. Twenty-six attended either the Harvard or Yale Law Schools, about equally divided between the two (fourteen Harvard, twelve Yale). Ten other geographically dispersed law schools were represented. Only three clerks graduated from the justice's alma mater, the University of Alabama Law School. Most clerks came to Justice Black directly from law school. It was not usual in those days for an applicant to have clerked for a judge on a lower appellate court.

Clerking for Justice Black

While there was a high degree of similarity over the years in the experiences of all the Black clerks, there may have been subtle differences, depending on the number of clerks per term, the nature of the cases dealt with, and the stage of the justice's life. For his first thirteen years on the bench, Black had one clerk per term. Then for the next nineteen years, there were two each term. In his last two terms he had three. The increases in the number of clerkships resulted from authorized increases for all the justices. William O. Douglas alone held on to one clerk.

In the nature of things, a single clerk probably had a more intense relationship with "the Judge," as we all called him, than two or three would have had. Moreover, the relationship was somewhat different during those years between the death of his first wife, Josephine, in 1951 and his marriage to Elizabeth in 1957. In that interim he was alone in his large and quiet Alexandria house, except for the constant services of his cook and housekeeper, Lizzie May Campbell. He then saw more of his clerks, especially at night, than in other times. Yet despite whatever differences there may have been over time, the recollections of all the clerks about the Judge and their experiences with him are remarkably similar. They all saw him as a teacher, and they all remembered their time with him as being highly educational, often as the best year of their lives. For many, the relationship was quite personal, the clerk coming eventually to feel like a member of the Black family.

A clerk's first contact with Black usually came during the application process, with the interview. This was an awesome prospect for a law student or recent law graduate. Most were apprehensive over whether they would be able to answer all the legal and constitutional questions they anticipated being asked. But such matters were rarely discussed. Instead, the conversation would likely range over a wide variety of nonlegal topics, such as tennis, life in Alabama, some social or political problem of the day, or books the applicant had read. Generalities or superficial comments by the nervous applicant were often met by a quiet "Why?" and then another "Why?" as the Judge would not be willing to let him off easily.

One has the impression that in most instances Black had already decided to engage the applicant before the interview, based on background (Alabama or southern), law school record, and recommendations. He was known to have said that he was more interested in what he could do for the clerk than what the clerk could do for him. I think this was especially true in picking his Alabama clerks. A year at the Court, in his view, would broaden the clerk's mind and provide an important educational experience, helping to prepare him for future leadership in Alabama, where enlightened leadership was sorely needed. Several clerks became leading Alabama lawyers, and four held significant public service posts in the state: Truman Hobbs, federal district judge; David Vann, mayor of Birmingham; Drayton Nabers, chief justice of the Alabama Supreme Court; and myself, dean of the University of Alabama Law School. Others achieved distinction elsewhere.

A major aspect of the Judge's life that his clerks quickly came to know was his reading interests and unique collection of books. Introduction to this fascinating side of the Judge often came in the interview before the clerk even had the job. "Have you read *The Greek Way*?" the Judge would ask. "No, sir" was the usual answer. As all came to know, this book by Edith Hamilton, published in 1942, truly delighted the Judge, probably *the* favorite of all his books.[1] It expressed much of his view of life. For the clerks, it was required reading. In the course of the year, numerous other favorites would be brought to the clerks' attention and in effect made assigned reading. Certain books were so much an integral part of the Judge's life that in the memory of most clerks the Judge and those books are inseparable.

High on his list of favorites were books about ancient Greece and Rome. He was enamored with those civilizations. He was especially fond of the writings of Thucydides, Plutarch, Livy, Pliny, and Tacitus. They were occasionally cited in his opinions for the Court. In reading them (in English translation), as he did with all his favorite books, he underlined passages, made marginal notes, and penciled in his own index in the back. Those writings validated one of his basic theories—that over several thousand years human nature had not essentially changed. He saw that people in those long-ago times faced problems similar to those around him in the twentieth century and often reacted in much the same way.

Alongside the writings of ancient Greece and Rome were those of the founding period in American history. In the Judge's library and in his mind one man stood out from all the others—Thomas Jefferson. He had read everything written by Jefferson himself; he owned most of Jefferson's writings and many books about Jefferson. He had cited Jefferson often in his Senate speeches and cited him from time to time in his judicial opinions. Among his books on this subject, he particularly liked Claude Bowers's *Jefferson and Hamilton*.[2] He saw the contrasting views of government portrayed there as still very much alive in his own time. In the course of the year clerks would frequently hear about Jefferson, or at least the Judge's thoughts about Jefferson. Anthony Lewis wrote in the *New York Times* that Black was an "unreconstructed Jeffersonian."[3] In short, it was impossible to clerk for Black and not become well acquainted with Thomas Jefferson.

Also looming large in the library in the Alexandria study and in Black's mind were books dealing with the English constitutional crises in the seventeenth century. There he saw one of his favorite themes being played out, the struggles of the people against the overweening power of government. He was attracted to *The Levellers*, by Joseph Frank, published in 1955.[4] It featured one of his heroes of that time, John Lilburn, a leader in the fight for liberty of "plain people," as he called them.

One of the distinctive—perhaps idiosyncratic—aspects of Black's interest in books was his zeal for ferreting out little known, or completely unknown, books, mainly dealing with his abiding interest in human liberty. He would peruse rare book catalogues looking for such or for some well-known volume he had not been able to find. One of those largely forgotten books was *Our Ancient Liberties*, by Leon Whipple, published in 1927, on the historical origins of civil and religious liberty.[5] Judging from the way he spoke of it, one would have thought it was an all-time classic. He was fond of Saul Padover's *To Secure*

These Blessings, an account of the debates in the 1787 constitutional convention, and Vernon Parrington's *Main Currents in American Thought.*[6]

On a few occasions the Judge read aloud a favorite passage. One I especially remember was the description of the friendship of Thomas Jefferson and Dabney Carr in Thomas E. Watson's biography of Jefferson. It told of how in their youth they wandered over the mountaintop that later became Monticello, sharing their dreams of the future, and how they sat together under a great tree vowing that they both would one day be laid to rest there, to sleep together for eternity. Black read in an emotion-laden voice and said when he finished that he never read this without tears coming to his eyes. Just as he was an effective public speaker, Black was a persuasive reader. It was not hard to see how he had been a superb jury trial lawyer.

There were many other books, too numerous to mention here, that Black read and reread, marked, indexed, and mentioned to his clerks from time to time. Altogether there were 953 titles in his study, not counting law books. Some of those titles consisted of multiple volumes, so there were well over a thousand books in his personal library.

The Judge's three-room suite in the Supreme Court Building was in the northeastern corner. His room, actually in the corner, had a window on each side. The rear window provided an uninspiring view of 2nd Street, and the other looked out on Maryland Avenue. There was a private bathroom. On the inner wall was a fireplace, which he never used. In the middle of the room was his huge desk, behind which was a tall swivel chair in which he would lean back much of the time. The shelves held an entire set of the *United States Reports,* the United States Code, and miscellaneous other books. Very few of his favorites were there; instead they remained in his study at home. A door beside the fireplace opened into the clerks' room. It too looked out on 2nd Street. There was a desk and typewriter for each clerk. On the shelves was a set of the *Federal Reporter, 2nd Series,* known as "Fed second."

On the Maryland Avenue side of the chambers was the room for the secretary and messenger. Multiple file cabinets lined the wall, containing all of the Judge's correspondence, past opinions, and much else. A door connected it to the Judge's room. The clerks' room and the secretary's room each had a door opening on to the main corridor, but the Judge's room did not. To reach the Judge, a visitor had to enter the secretary's room and then proceed into the Judge's room.

The job of messenger dated from earlier years before the Court had a building housing all of the justices. They then lived all over Washington and worked at home. A messenger was necessary to circulate draft opinions from one to another. With the coming of the building in 1935 the work of a messenger was considerably diminished, yet he still delivered draft opinions to the various chambers. Beyond that, however, he was a general utility man for the justice. In his entire thirty-four years on the Court, Black remarkably had only one messenger—Spencer Campbell, brother of Lizzie May, the cook and house-keeper. Black had brought both up from Alabama. Spencer assisted in garden-ing (the Judge was especially fond of growing roses), drove the Judge around, and handled whatever other jobs came along.

In his time on the Court, Black had only four secretaries. First there was Ann Daniel (1937–46), who came from Alabama. She was followed by Gladys Coates (1946–56). Then came Elizabeth DeMeritte, who held the job only one year, as she married the Judge. Hugo Jr. had sent her up from Birmingham, where she had been working in the office of the clerk of the federal district court, to replace Gladys. She was followed by Frances Lamb (1957–71).

The Judge, the clerks, the secretary, and the messenger made a tightly knit little group, in effect a family, with the addition of Lizzie May. All of the clerks for thirty-four years knew Spencer and Lizzie May, and they knew the secre-tary well during their year of service. As the number of clerks jumped from one to two to three per term, they became an extended family, holding re-unions from time to time, often on the Judge's birthday. Most reunions took place at the Alexandria house. Frequent special guests included Thomas G. Corcoran ("Tommy the Cork" of New Deal fame) playing his accordion and singing "Happy Days Are Here Again," the New Deal marching song. In later days Justice Potter Stewart was often there, playing the piano. Judge J. Skelly Wright, one of the Judge's ardent admirers, was sometimes present.

During my year, the 1954 term, Gladys Coates was the secretary. She was a serious-minded woman, though not without a sense of humor, a former mem-ber of the WAVES (Women Accepted for Volunteer Emergency Service), who admired the Judge but did not have him on a pedestal. She understood his foibles and peculiar habits, and she would frankly discuss them with me and my co-clerk, Bill Stewart. Bill was married, and I was not, so we did not see much of each other outside of work. That year was during the time between the Judge's marriages when he was living alone. During the previous year his two clerks, David Vann and Charles Reich, actually lived in the Judge's house. For reasons known only to himself, the Judge did not want to continue that arrangement. As far as I am aware, no clerk thereafter was invited to share the Alexandria house.

Job Duties of Justice Black's Clerks

The major work of the clerks, day in and day out, was preparing memoranda on certiorari petitions. Once a week a stack would be delivered from the Court clerk's office. In that year there would be about forty a week. We would divide them, one of us taking the odd numbered and the other the even numbered. The Judge had a rigid rule about cert memos: they must be no more than one page in length. And this was not normal-sized typing paper; rather the page was less than half that size. The paper was punched with holes for insertion into a three-ring binder. This one-page rule forced us to devise creative abbreviations. Every word was shortened as much as possible. Fortunately, in hope of one day holding this job, I had taught myself touch typing in law school.

There was a set format for the memo. The name and number of the case were at the top, followed by the court in which the case had been decided. If it was a U. S. court of appeals case, the three judges who had participated in the decision were listed, by last name only. The name of the judge writing the opinion was underlined. Then came a highly succinct statement of the case and the contention of the petitioner as to why certiorari should be granted. Finally came the clerk's terse reasoning and conclusion. The last line of the memo was one word: either "Grant" or "Deny."

Preparing a memo involved reading the petition, the response, and as much of the record as seemed necessary to understand the case. If the brief in response had been filed by the Solicitor General's Office on behalf of the United States, we normally read that before reading the petition, because it was typically better written and presented the case more clearly and understandably than the petition. The question we focused on was the "certworthiness" of the case. To be certworthy the petition usually had to show a conflict between the circuits, a decision below in conflict with Supreme Court decisions, or some unusually important and unsettled question of national law that ought to be resolved.

We would feed the memos to Gladys as we finished them, and she would put them into the binder for the Judge. Sometimes when the Judge was in our room, he would see the petitions stacked up and sense that we were struggling to keep up, so he would scoop up a handful, saying, "I'll just take a few home and do them." He could review and decide on a petition in a fraction of the time that it took us to do a memo.

In the mornings Bill and I would usually be in our room before the Judge arrived. He could be heard coming down the spacious marble corridor whistling and moving fast. He had a kind of loping gait, always carrying a well-filled briefcase. During the day it was not unusual for him to pop into our room to tell us about some passage he had just read in one of his books and to comment on its current relevancy or to call our attention to an item in the morning newspaper that was reminiscent of something that Tacitus or another of the ancients had said.

The Court's weekly conference was then on Saturday mornings. Gladys and Spencer would load a large cart with all the cert petitions to be taken up and the records and briefs in the cases to be decided. A Dead List would have been circulated in advance, listing the cert petitions that would be denied without discussion unless some justice wanted a petition discussed. This considerably winnowed down the number of petitions to be dealt with. Spencer would roll the cart down the corridor and into the conference room, parking it beside the Judge's chair.

When the Judge came back from conference, which would be noon or later, he would drop on the desk the binder with all of our cert memos. On the back of each he made notes as to how each member of the Court had voted, sometimes adding brief comments. He used abbreviations, such as FF for Felix Frankfurter and CJ for the chief justice. We eagerly paged through to see what the Court had done and to see how well our recommendations had accorded with the Judge's vote and the Court's action. The results were mixed.

One of the most memorable experiences of the clerkship was the process of editing drafts of the Judge's opinions. When he was assigned a case for an opinion he immediately plunged into reading the record and all the briefs. He did not call on the clerks for much research. Occasionally he would send us to the library to run something down or look into the background of some rule or concept. He did not seem to need much help of that sort. He had then been on the Court for seventeen years and had confronted almost every type of question that could arise and had his views fairly well worked out. He did not use us to draft opinions. Instead, he did a first draft himself in longhand. Gladys typed the draft and gave each of us a copy. We usually had overnight to review it and make editorial suggestions. Then the fun began.

The two of us would sit in his room, in chairs facing his desk, and he would begin going through the draft line by line, even word by word. Usually the Judge had his mind made up on the substance, so there was not often room for debate on that. We did talk about the issues, though, and it was in the course of those discussions that I learned more about his constitutional views than could be gleaned from his published opinions alone. Debate was mainly on choice of words and organization. There was a surprising amount of controversy about commas. The Judge disfavored them, whereas my co-clerk wanted to insert them rather liberally. My own view was somewhere in between. I thought the Judge used too few, but I did not favor a comma at every point for which Bill argued. This was a slow, painstaking editing process, often running for hours through the day, but I never tired of it. More than once the process continued in the evening in the upstairs study at his house, lasting to midnight. Sometimes we would eat dinner there, cooked and served, of course, by Lizzie May. Steaks were the Judge's favorite.

In his writing the Judge was insistent on clarity and brevity and the use of words as simple as possible. He disliked Latinisms, legal jargon, and abstract legal concepts. An opinion should be written, he said, so that "they" could understand it. By "they" he meant the average nonlawyer citizen, "plain people," as he often put it. I conjured up in my mind unrealistic visions of store clerks, bus drivers, farmers, and housewives reading Supreme Court opinions. But that was the audience he liked to imagine.

Justice Black had a knack for cutting through a complicated situation to get to the heart of the matter, at "what is really involved." He could see right through pretentiousness and make-weight arguments. Bill Stewart was attracted to legal concepts, and he and the Judge had some lengthy discussions in which the Judge tried to get him to forget the concept and think about who did what to whom and who was being hurt by what had happened. The judge had a strong practical, commonsense understanding of life derived from his long experience in law practice and politics.

His memory of past Supreme Court decisions was extensive. He remembered them in various ways, not always by the full name. Sometimes he recalled only the volume where a case appeared. He would say, "Get 326," meaning volume 326 of the *U. S. Reports*. We would jump up and pull it off the shelf, and he would page in and find the case. Sometimes he would say, for example, "that case Bill Douglas wrote about that longshoreman hurt on the docks, around 1947." When he did recall the case name he often referred to it by the name of the respondent, the only person I have known who followed that practice. When I first heard him speak of the *Tompkins* case, I did not realize that he was talking about *Erie Railroad v. Tompkins*.[7]

His views on the Constitution sometimes led him to see a constitutional problem from an angle different from the way other justices saw it. An example that stands out in my mind is *Toth v. Quarles*.[8] An airman had been honorably discharged from military service but was thereafter arrested, tried by court-martial, and convicted of an offense committed while he had been on active duty. Justice Stanley Reed was assigned the opinion. His draft viewed the constitutional question as one under the Fifth Amendment, that is, whether the requirement of indictment by grand jury applied to this military offense. If it did, the conviction could not stand. He held that it did not, so the conviction was upheld.

The Judge took quite a different view of the issue presented. He saw it as a question of congressional authority under Article I, that is, whether Congress had authority to subject to military trial a discharged serviceman who was now a civilian. He thought it did not, so he drafted a dissent. Editing this opinion was of special interest to me, as I had served on active duty with the Judge Advocate General's Corps in Korea, trying court-martial cases. *Toth* had been argued before an eight-man court because Justice Robert Jackson had died. While the case was pending decision John Harlan was appointed to the vacancy. The Court then set the case for re-argument in the fall. By the time it was decided I had left the clerkship, but I was pleased and pleasantly surprised that the majority opinion was what had been Black's dissenting opinion that we had edited.

Jackson died in October 1954, just one week into the new term. I had seen him only twice, as he was walking along the corridor. The law clerks attended his memorial service in the National Cathedral, sitting as a body in the north transept. The entire Court then went to Jamestown, New York, for the burial. While Jackson was in Nuremberg in 1946 prosecuting the war crimes cases, he had attacked Black in a serious way, for reasons that have not been clearly understood. But apparently by the time of his death they had reconciled. I never heard Black say anything critical of Jackson. For that matter, I never heard him say anything derogatory about any of his colleagues, although he could make humorous comments about some.

He did, of course, have differences with them on various issues. Free speech cases had been prominently before the Court in recent years, and Black had insisted on holding that the First Amendment's protection of speech was "absolute." He attacked Frankfurter's view that protection should be "balanced" against other interests, such as national security. Frankfurter was inclined to apply a "reasonableness" test in determining the constitutionality of a speech regulation. Black said the only provision in the Constitution that authorized him to decide what was "reasonable" or "unreasonable" was the Fourth Amendment prohibiting "Unreasonable searches and seizures." He differed with Frankfurter and others on the right to jury trial. It was my perception that Black never saw a directed verdict for a defendant in a personal injury case that he approved. This view undoubtedly stemmed from his many years in representing injured plaintiffs in jury trials. There was a running fight between Frankfurter, on the one hand, and Black and Douglas, on the other, as to whether certiorari should be granted in FELA (Federal Employer's Liability Act) cases where the only question was whether the trial judge had correctly directed a verdict for the defendant. Frankfurter was adamant that certiorari was improper.

Much of the disagreement between Black and Frankfurter over "balancing" First Amendment rights and the relationship between judge and jury reflected Black's unusual distrust of judges. He believed that too much leeway for a judge to decide a matter, too little constraint on his discretion, was dangerous to legal rights. This led him to think that it was unwise to let the meaning of "due process" to be determined by what a judge considered "fair." His solution was to conclude that the due process clause of the Fourteenth Amendment incorporated the specific restrictions of the Bill of Rights. He was unsuccessful in persuading the Court to adopt that position wholesale, but over time the Court did so piece by piece, a great tribute to Black's long-range influence.

The Judge one day received an application for stay of execution of a death sentence. It came to him as the Circuit Justice for the Fifth Circuit. It was customary for the justices to act on such applications on the papers presented, without oral argument. The Judge denied the stay. But then word came from the Court clerk's office that the two lawyers representing the prisoner were there and were strongly urging that because of some unusual features in the case, it was especially important that they have an opportunity to address the Judge in person. The Judge relented and said he would receive them. He invited me to sit in. They sat there in front of his desk for twenty minutes making what seemed to be a heartfelt argument for the stay. The Judge sat back in his chair impassively, fingertips together, a position he often assumed when he was reflecting on something. He did not interrupt and asked no questions. When their presentation was concluded, he said quietly, "I have read all your papers, and I understand what you say. I had made up my mind to deny the stay, and see nothing here to change it." In this I saw an illustration of the Judge's decisiveness, his ability to decide a matter without a great deal of anguish or vacillation, and then to put it behind him.

One of the benefits of a clerkship was the privilege of sitting in on oral arguments. The clerks sat in chairs between the columns (spaces reserved for them) on the south side of the courtroom. Every now and then a messenger would hand a clerk a note from his justice, making a humorous comment about what was going on or asking him to look up something later. In the course of the year I heard advocates of varying quality and picked up useful pointers about appellate argument.

The most highly publicized argument of the term was in *Brown II,* the implementing stage of the holding a year earlier that racial segregation in public schools was unconstitutional.[9] The Court had waited until Justice John Marshall Harlan was in place before scheduling the three-day session. Argument for the petitioners was presented by Thurgood Marshall, who had been their chief counsel ever since the cases—there were five—reached the Supreme Court. He was followed by a parade of counsel for the states, mainly the states of the Old South, arguing in various ways for additional time—time for adjustment of physical facilities, time for the people to adjust to such a far-reaching social change, and so on. It was hard to escape the feeling that we were at an historic moment.

Black never mentioned these school cases to us. One reason for his silence was the Court's self-imposed secrecy. The decisional process functioned under wraps different from that in any other cases; draft opinions were not circulated in the usual way, and with very few exceptions law clerks were not involved. I think the Judge would have considered it inappropriate to talk to us about those cases. Also, I think he knew all along what his position was and saw no point in discussion. It was typical of him generally to make up his mind early on and not thereafter stew over the matter. After the decision came down announcing the famous standard of "all deliberate speed," he commented that he thought it would have been better to have ordered immediate desegregation of the schools involved.

In that spring of 1955, the Judge's daughter, Josephine, called Jo Jo, was scheduled to graduate from Swarthmore College. He had been invited to deliver the commencement address. He took the occasion to expound his view that human nature had not changed much over time and the problems of long ago were not unlike those today. To prove the point, he sent us to the library to copy headlines from newspapers in 1906, the year he graduated from law school. Sure enough, a number of them could have come from the morning's papers.

Other Aspects of the Clerkship for Justice Black

At irregular intervals, perhaps once every week or two, we would get together with the Judge to eat lunch in the public cafeteria on the ground floor of the

Supreme Court Building. We would go through the line with Court employees and then take our trays to a table like all other diners. The conversations that ensued were among the most entertaining and interesting of the year. The Judge, of course, did the talking, recalling incidents from his law practice, his campaigns for the Senate, and his time in the Senate. He had a fine sense of humor. He could imitate with mock seriousness statements by his opponents or by those who took positions different from his. He would often break out into laughter after such imitations, which made his opponents seem ridiculous. Most of his stories related to Alabama. I have wondered how much they meant to the clerks from elsewhere. Because we were in a public place, surrounded by strangers, we never discussed pending cases or any aspect of Supreme Court work.

On most days when we were not eating with the Judge we ate with other law clerks in the clerks' private dining room. We would go through the cafeteria line and take our trays a short distance down a corridor to the room. That year there were eighteen clerks. The chief justice had three, Douglas had one, and the other justices had two each. On any given day a majority of the clerks would be present. There we could freely discuss pending cases, which we often did, with the clerks' arguments among themselves tending to reflect the positions of their justices.

In the course of the year we invited each justice to join us as a guest. The justice I remember most vividly was Felix Frankfurter. He announced that he wanted us to go around the table, with each of us asking him a question, and he would then answer these questions. He listened to all the questions before undertaking to answer any. It was a remarkable performance, as he did not forget any question. The luncheon was unusually long, lasting about three hours. When we returned to our chambers, Black said in a slightly sarcastic tone, "Well, is school out?" Frankfurter never got out of his professorial mode with colleagues or clerks.

It was also customary for the clerks to invite prominent Washington figures to be our guest at lunch. Among them, I remember Dean Acheson, Eric Sevareid, Simon Sobeloff, Henry Cabot Lodge, and Harold Stassen. Acheson, having been secretary of state, was then in private practice. He reminisced about his clerkship with Justice Louis Brandeis and talked about the first case he argued before the Supreme Court. Sevareid, the CBS TV newsman, mused about the news business. He advocated having the TV evening news appear only every other day, saying that there was not real news every day. Sobeloff, the Solicitor General, described the work of his office. Lodge, a former U.S.

senator and then the U.S. ambassador to the United Nations, explained that although there were legal questions under the Charter, his job at the UN was much more political than legal. Stassen, the former governor of Minnesota, was then serving in the Eisenhower administration, coordinating U.S. operations abroad. I do not now recall what he talked about. Being exposed in informal luncheons throughout the year both to the justices and to men of that caliber in high places was a major benefit of the clerkship.

Another highlight of the year was the annual reception for the judiciary, hosted by the president at the White House. All the justices were invited along with their clerks. What sticks in my mind about meeting President Eisenhower is that his face had a much ruddier appearance than his photographs revealed. Of my meeting with Vice President Nixon, I retain the impression of an unusually long, thin hand. Justice Black was absent as he had gone to Florida, as usual, for the Christmas holidays.

Traditionally the clerks held a reception for their justices in the nearby Washington Hotel after the White House event. Being one of three bachelors among the clerks, I was designated to engage the room and see to it that setups were provided. Each clerk was responsible for providing liquor for his justice. I left the White House a bit early to see that all was in order at the hotel. The first to arrive was Chief Justice Earl Warren, with his wife and daughter, Honey Bear. We chatted for about ten minutes before anyone else appeared. Honey Bear struck me as well above average in looks, and I ended up taking her home after the reception was over.

I next saw President Eisenhower a few weeks later at his State of the Union address before a joint session of Congress. The Judge had given me one of his guest tickets. He himself did not attend. I sat in the House gallery two rows behind Mamie Eisenhower, trying to see how many senators I could identify as they assembled. The occasion was memorable, but the speech must not have been, as I do not recall what the president said.

Justice Black did not have many visitors. His chambers were a relatively quiet workplace. Chief Justice Warren dropped in a few times. I never knew what they talked about. Warren was then in his second term on the Court, still feeling his way to some extent. Douglas came by once, as I recall. The other members of the Court that term were Stanley Reed, Felix Frankfurter, Tom Clark, Harold Burton, and Sherman Minton. I do not recall any of them stopping in. Between Jackson's death in October and John Harlan's appointment in March, the Court functioned with eight members.

By happenstance I witnessed the Senate's confirmation of Justice Harlan. Working late and alone in chambers, I suddenly realized that the Senate was scheduled to take up the nomination that evening. I dropped everything, hurried across Capitol Plaza, found a seat in the Senate gallery, and heard about an hour of the debate. Harlan was opposed on the ground that he had been a "world federalist." He was confirmed comfortably but with a significant vote in opposition. I returned to chambers and telephoned the Judge at home to give him the news. His reaction was noncommittal and almost uninterested. Whatever Black's initial view of Harlan, in the last years of their lives they became close friends and died, within months of one another, in the Bethesda Naval Hospital.

The End of a Clerkship

The end of June brought the end of my clerkship, the close of the most memorable year of my life. On the day of my departure, I drove out of Washington down to 619 South Lee Street in Alexandria to say good-bye. The Judge had been at home all day, tending to his roses and reading. I found him in his upstairs bedroom, resting on the bed in his tennis outfit. I do not remember exactly what we said. The conversation was brief. I tried to thank him for the grand experience. He wished me well and said something about better days for Alabama. We shook hands, and then I was gone.[10]

Notes

1. Edith Hamilton, *The Greek Way* (New York: W. W. Norton, 1942).

2. Claude G. Bowers, *Jefferson and Hamilton: The Struggle for Democracy in America* (New York: Houghton Mifflin, 1925).

3. Anthony Lewis, "The Authentic Voice," *New York Times*, October 5, 1970.

4. Joseph Frank, *The Levellers: A History of the Writings of Three Seventeenth-Century Social Democrats; John Lilburne, Richard Overton, William Walwyn* (Cambridge, Mass.: Harvard University Press, 1955).

5. Leon Whipple, *Our Ancient Liberties: The Story of the Origin and Meaning of Civil and Religious Liberty in the United States* (New York: H. W. Wilson, 1927).

6. Saul K. Padover, *To Secure These Blessings: The Great Debates of the Constitutional Convention of 1787* (New York: Washington Square Press, 1962); Vernon L. Parrington, *Main Currents in American Thought: An Interpretation of American Literature from the Beginnings to 1920*, 3 vols. (New York: Harcourt, Brace, 1927–30).

7. *Erie Railroad v. Tompkins*, 304 U.S. 64 (1938).

8. *Toth v. Quarles,* 350 U.S. 11 (1955).

9. *Brown v. Board of Education II,* 349 U.S. 294 (1955).

10. *Mr. Justice Black and His Books* (Charlottesville: University Press of Virginia, 1972), by Daniel J. Meador, contains a complete catalog of Justice Black's personal library, together with an essay on his reading interests and habits, a detailed description of his study, and a list of all his clerks. Most of the books in that collection are now in the Hugo Black Room in the University of Alabama Law Library.

Half Clerk, Half Son

Justice Felix Frankfurter and His Law Clerks

As the earlier essays in this book demonstrate, Justices Horace Gray, Oliver Wendell Holmes Jr., and Louis D. Brandeis each played an important role in the creation and early evolution of the clerkship institution. A complete analysis of the origins and early history of the law clerk institution, however, must also include Felix Frankfurter. Not only did Frankfurter, as a Harvard Law School professor, send scores of his brightest young law students to clerk on the Supreme Court (Frankfurter alone accounted for over one-half of the law clerks sent to Holmes and all the clerks employed by Brandeis), but Frankfurter, as a Supreme Court justice, placed his own unique stamp on the law clerk institution by combining Holmes's "noble nursery of humanity" with a clerkship model in which the clerks were assigned substantive job responsibilities. The result was a clerkship in which the best and brightest graduates from Harvard Law School became Frankfurter's valued assistants, intellectual foils, social companions, and lifelong law clerks.

Selecting the Frankfurter Law Clerks

No longer selecting law clerks for other justices, Frankfurter relied upon his own set of Harvard Law School professors to select clerks—primarily Henry M. Hart Jr. (himself a former Brandeis law clerk) and, in later years, Albert M. Sacks.[1] Former law clerk Andrew Kaufman (October terms 1955 and 1956) writes that Frankfurter gave the professors "carte blanche" to select law clerks, an assessment echoed in Frankfurter's letters to Henry M. Hart Jr.[2] Frankfurter, however, did provide the selectors with some minimal instructions. In a December 27, 1946, letter to Professor Hart, Frankfurter writes: "I now write merely to suggest that if you could manage to 'channel'—I think it is a loathsome word—people like Bill Bundy and [Elliot] Richardson . . . to Calvert and one of the Hands, so that they could have had the experience of work in the Circuits before they come down here, it would greatly enhance their usefulness to me."[3]

In the letter, Frankfurter was referring to United States Court of Appeals judges Calvert Magruder (himself a former Brandeis law clerk), Augustus Hand, and Learned Hand; in doing so, Frankfurter became the first Supreme Court justice to rely upon "feeder court judges," namely, trusted associates who could train law school graduates to be appellate court law clerks before they arrived at the Supreme Court.

Frankfurter, however, professed no preference for a law clerk's ethnic or religious background.[4] As discussed in the following essay, Frankfurter hired the first African American law clerk—William T. Coleman Jr. In contrast to Frankfurter's lack of prejudices involving race, however, the justice could not bring himself to break the clerkship institution's gender barrier. He thus missed the opportunity to select a young Columbia Law School graduate named Ruth Bader Ginsburg as only the second female law clerk in the history of the Supreme Court. Former law clerk Paul Bender (October term 1959) recalls the justice discussing the fact that Harvard Law School professor Sacks was recommending that Frankfurter consider Ginsburg:

> One day during the term Justice Frankfurter comes into our office and announces "guess who Al Sacks wants to send me as a law clerk next year—Ruth Bader Ginsburg." My co-clerk and I told him that it was a wonderful idea, but Justice Frankfurter replied that 'she has a couple of kids, and her husband has been ill, and you know that I work you guys very hard, and I do curse sometimes' as reasons why it wouldn't be a good idea. Well, that wasn't the case. We had the softest job of all the law clerks at the court—we didn't work nights or weekends—and the Justice did not use four letter words. I concluded that the Justice wasn't comfortable with a female law clerk. This was odd since the Justice had strong intellectual relationships with a number of women, including the wives of some of his law clerks.[5]

When asked about Justice Frankfurter's decision not to hire a female law clerk, Justice Ginsburg recalls that Professor Sack's recommendation was "entirely unexpected" and that she was "elated that he [Sacks] had such faith in me." Ginsburg adds, however, that she was not taken aback by Frankfurter's reticence to hire a female law clerk. "[I was] not really surprised that

Frankfurter wasn't up to hiring a woman. After all, neither was Learned Hand, the federal judge for whom I wanted to clerk beyond all others."[6]

By the 1940s, the law was no longer a jealous mistress who forced her young charges to forgo marriage before entry into the Marble Palace. In short, the institutional norm that clerks be bachelors had been abandoned (a norm firmly enforced by Holmes and more benignly followed by Brandeis). Katharine Graham writes that her late husband, Philip Graham, did discuss his marriage plans with Justice Frankfurter. "[H]e drove the justice home from the Court one night and told him of our decision to be married and even asked his permission, for there had been an unwritten rule that the law clerks remain single, so as to be at the complete service of the justice, day or night. By this time that tradition had broken down, but Phil still felt the need to ask."[7]

The Daily Activities of a Frankfurter Law Clerk

Former law clerk John H. Mansfield writes that "an invitation to be a Frankfurter clerk was an invitation to life, to a wider, richer life than one had supposed oneself capable of."[8]

> What shall I tell you of being his law clerk? Shall I tell you of the warm, sun-lit study of the house on Dumbarton Avenue, with books open everywhere, and an invitation to sit in the old Morris chair that used to be Holmes'? Shall I tell you of walks in the Washington springtime ... Shall I tell you of talk and talk and more talk on a thousand subjects? Work? I can hardly remember any work at all in the usual sense of the word. The door to his office would burst open, and in he bounced with some new idea to try out, some new experience to share. What did we think about this? Had we heard about that? Look at this new book! Come and meet so and so, the ambassador from somewhere or the author of something, or just an interesting person. He certainly observed his own advice that a really good lawyer spends only a small portion of his time at specifically legal work. Most everything in life was relevant to law, grandly conceived.[9]

The cornerstone of the Frankfurter clerkship was lively conversation and noisy debate, not unlike the intellectual equivalent of a rugby match between teams of unequal ability.[10] Former Frankfurter law clerk Alexander Bickel describes debates during which Frankfurter "gave it to you with both barrels ... there were no holds barred."[11] These exchanges, often interrupted with the justice's "explosive" laughter and his cries of "good—isn't that good!" extended beyond Frankfurter's chambers to social engagements and the justice's daily car rides with his clerks.

He often tested his clerks' intellectual mettle by goading them into long arguments over legal history, current events, constitutional doctrine, and music: Name ten milestones in Anglo-American law and defend your choices. Who was Home Secretary in the Atlee government? Who was the greater composer, Bartok or Bruch? To win these debates, he did not hesitate to intimidate his young opponents by invoking his seniority or his intimate knowledge of the persons and events under discussion. Sometimes sensing defeat, he would bolt from the office in disgust, leaving a shaken law clerk behind. But by next morning, within earshot of the same clerk he would tell his secretary: "Wasn't that a terrific argument last night? Wasn't Al just great? Did you hear what he said to me?"[12]

For the current clerks, the candor between justice and law clerk was always tempered with awareness of status and position. "You were careful [with your comments]," observes Kaufman, "but you were encouraged to speak up." The exchanges were "entirely professional and intellectual," but could also be rather loud.[13] "The shouts of the Justice and his law clerks could often be heard through closed doors in the hallways of the Supreme Court."[14]

Frankfurter strove to remain in the middle of the action in his chambers, a fact symbolically represented by the justice's decision to place his office in the middle of the three rooms that made up his chambers. This arrangement meant that the law clerks shared the office normally reserved for the justice, an office that featured a private bathroom. Any trepidation that former law clerk William T. Coleman Jr. (October term 1948) felt in working for a larger-than-life figure like Frankfurter was dispelled during Coleman's first day at the Court, when Frankfurter crossed through the clerk's office to use the bathroom. For Coleman, it was a reassuring sign that the legendary justice was a mere mortal.[15]

The interactions between Frankfurter and his clerks were not limited to his judicial chambers. The duties of the Frankfurter law clerks started early in the morning, as a clerk would arrive at Frankfurter's Georgetown residence to drive him to work.[16] "Justice Frankfurter expected us to have read the morning newspaper," remarks Kaufman, and law clerk and justice would have an "animated conversation" about current events.

On one occasion, inclement weather provided the justice with a new conversation partner. Former law clerk John French (October term 1960) recalls driving Justice Frankfurter to work and getting stuck in traffic due to the snow. Justice Frankfurter looked out the window and discovered that the car was stuck in front of Alice Roosevelt Longworth's home. "Oh, is that Mrs. Longworth's home? I'm going to go in and see her,'" exclaimed the justice. When he returned fifteen minutes later, "the car hadn't moved one foot."[17]

Banter did not cease when the clerks delivered Justice Frankfurter to his chambers. "There were also random conversations and a stream of questions at any time of day, and sometimes at night, about history, the law, philosophy, politics, personalities, the Harvard Law School, music—in short, any subject whatever."[18] The law clerks drove the justice home at night, and Kaufman recalls "often sitting in the driveway and talking for a half-hour." Debates would be extended into the weekends as well, as clerks received calls and shared dinner with the justice.

Finally, Frankfurter was not above appealing to outside sources to win an argument with his clerks. Former law clerk Coleman recalls that "Frankfurter, above all, was a good lawyer. He could be very persuasive. Sometimes he even called my wife to get her to change my mind."[19] On another occasion, after a particularly grueling argument Frankfurter called the wife of a current clerk—not to enlist her aid in convincing her husband, but to warn her of the verbal row and to ask her to prepare a martini for her husband upon his return home.

During the year, it became a tradition for the current clerks to invite the justice (and, in earlier years, Marion Frankfurter) to their homes for lunch or dinner. When it came time for current clerk Roland S. Homet Jr. (October term 1961) and his wife to have Frankfurter over for lunch, they arranged for a babysitter for their two small children—but the babysitter canceled, and the two children were at home when Justice Frankfurter arrived. "Justice Frankfurter was completely unphased," recalls Homet. Lifting the Homet children up to the sky in his arms, the justice laughed and said, "saying that you cannot understand children unless you have children of your own is like saying that Shakespeare could not write about the War of the Roses without being there." Later during the lunch, Justice Frankfurter asked Mrs. Homet the following question: "Does your husband come home and let you know about the great stuff that he does?" When Mrs. Homet replied in the affirmative, Justice Frankfurter teasingly responded, "you shouldn't let him get away with that."[20]

Frankfurter enjoyed meeting with the extended members of his clerkship family, and occasionally conversations with the wives of his law clerks turned harmlessly flirtatious. John French remembers that Frankfurter was very fond of his first wife, and once during a visit with the young couple, he told Mrs. French that "if I were younger, I would take you to Vienna and get lost in your eyes." Adds French: "my wife and I were a bit stunned."[21] Other wives also found themselves at the center of the justice's courtly attentions. Writing to the wife of former clerk Elliot Richardson, Frankfurter states: "You must have noted when you were here last how intensely I kept looking at you. I hope that you merely noticed it and were not offended, but the reason I stared at you so is because I thought I never saw you look lovelier." Noting that he now understood why "Elliot had so many rivals for your hand," Frankfurter adds, "[w]hen you left, I felt more intensely than ever before how glad I was that it was Elliot who won out!"[22]

While Frankfurter's clerkship model may have incorporated elements of Holmes's "institutionalized mentorship," the Frankfurter law clerks did have substantive job responsibilities as well. Here Frankfurter considered the law clerks to be his "junior partners, " with Frankfurter describing himself as the "very exacting task master" who would not tolerate "nonsense," "short-cuts," or "deference to position."[23]

In carrying out their formal duties, the Frankfurter law clerks followed a set of chamber rules that evolved over time. Originally, one of Justice Frankfurter's law clerks took a few yellow pages of notebook paper and typed out some basic instructions regarding how the justice ran his chambers. In subsequent terms, the new clerks reviewed the sheets and amended the notes to reflect changes in the justice's rules.[24] In essence, each new set of Frankfurter law clerks drew upon the collective wisdom of past law clerks as they carried out their assignments.[25] These notes are the equivalent of a time capsule, with the original typed comments crossed out, amended, and fleshed out by subsequent groups of Frankfurter clerks. Playwright and Frankfurter friend Garson Kanin recalls Frankfurter joking about the informal handbook:

> He laughs as he related that it has become a custom for his departing clerks to leave a memorandum for the incoming clerks about "all my eccentricities and idiosyncrasies and peculiarities, and each clerk finds new ones, and by now I suppose it must be an enormous, fat file, because there have been about forty clerks, and each one has doubtless discovered *something!*"[26]

Since Frankfurter—like Brandeis—believed that his most important responsibility was monitoring the activities of the lower courts and deciding which cases to hear, Frankfurter normally did not have his law clerks review cert petitions.[27] Kaufman estimates that he reviewed no more than a half dozen cert petitions in the two terms of his clerkship, explaining that Frankfurter regarded such assignments as an "inefficient use of his law clerks' time." Occasionally, Frankfurter had his law clerks write bench memos in cases that interested him. When asked to quantify the number of bench memoranda he drafted, Kaufman replied, "I wouldn't say it was a steady diet."[28] Other former law clerks do not mention bench memoranda as part of their job duties.[29]

The in-chamber rules discovered in the Frankfurter papers, however, reveal that the Frankfurter law clerks were far more involved in opinion writing than some Court scholars suspected. The rules state, in relevant part:

> Normally, one of you will write a memorandum on each case assigned to the Justice, as well as on many of his concurrences and dissents. A memorandum is a memorandum is a memorandum. Usually, it should be in the form of an opinion, and in the form in which you would be willing to see it go down. Sometimes, a more discursive and perhaps introspective essay is in order... Most frequently, however, when the Justice writes, he will dictate with your memorandum in hand. You may recognize much of yourself in the final, or nothing. Don't let either get you down... As to both substance and style, feel free to suggest and to argue; on the other hand, remember that it is the Justice who is responsible for the opinion and everything in it (except with your fellow law clerks) and use your discretion as to when you've done all you could to make him see the light.[30]

The recollections of the law clerks reflect the aforementioned procedures. "We always talked to Justice Frankfurter before writing an opinion draft, but we did not receive written instructions," stated French. "He would tell you what the case was about, where he stood, and what he wanted. Then you went and wrote the draft opinion. He would review the opinion draft and tell you what he didn't like. You would make the necessary changes, and then it went to print."[31]

Not all law clerks were delighted with the responsibility of preparing a draft opinion and the extensive research related to the opinion. Former law clerk Frank A. E. Sander (October term 1953) prepared the draft of the majority opinion in *St. Joe Paper Co. v. Atlantic Coast Line Railroad Co.*, a complicated case involving the question of whether the Interstate Commerce Commission had the power under § 77 of the Bankruptcy Act to submit a reorganization plan requiring a corporate merger.[32] Justice William O. Douglas would ultimately file a dissent, so the case had Frankfurter's full attention. Prior to drafting the opinion, Frankfurter "banished" Sander to the Supreme Court library with the instruction that he "go and learn the relevant provisions of the Bankruptcy Act until you know more about it than anybody else and then come back and write the opinion."

When a forlorn Sander kept complaining about the assignment and asked Justice Frankfurter if he wanted him "to resign from life" and cloister himself in the library in order to learn the law, Justice Frankfurter simply said, "that's just what I want you to do. Give yourself to the task and you will know more about bankruptcy law than anybody else in the world." Looking back upon the episode, Professor Sander stated, "it impressed upon me that one can learn almost anything" through sufficient careful study.[33]

One should not come away with the impression that Justice Frankfurter did not subject the drafts to a thorough vetting, however. Former law clerk Fred Fishman (October term 1949) recalls one instance when he prepared the first draft of either a dissent or concurrence for Justice Frankfurter. "I worked hard on it, and I thought that it was pretty good, but when I received the draft back from the Justice it had been all marked up. I told the Justice 'I'm glad to see that you used some of my words.' When the Justice, surprised, said 'Oh, which ones,' I responded 'the' and 'a.'"[34]

On a few occasions, the instructions from the justice to the clerks, and the edits, were minimal. Homet recalls that in one case involving interstate commerce the justice gave his law clerk a note card with only a few notations and citations. After Mr. Homet prepared the first draft, he received a one word note from Justice Frankfurter—"Good!" "You can imagine what that note meant to me," stated Mr. Homet. "It lifted my heart . . . If he accepted your ideas, you felt received into exalted company and that you were, for that moment, a colleague."[35]

Frankfurter's native exuberance colored the drafting process, and often the justice would hover over his clerks as they worked. Former law clerk Elliot Richardson writes: "I remember a day early in my year with him when he was waiting for a citation or two to be added to a draft opinion he wanted to circulate among the other members of the Court before opposing views had a chance to solidify. Bouncing with impatience—and I do mean bouncing—he said, 'This is a war we're fighting! Don't you understand? *A war!*'"[36]

Frankfurter's avowed preference for law clerk candor extended to the opinion-writing process. In a 1949 note to law clerks Fred N. Fishman and Albert M. Sacks, Frankfurter states: "When I ask you lads to read a draft of mine, I expect you to read it critically—i.e., to deal with substance and style unmercifully and put your questions and objections to me."[37]

Sander sometimes found the debates between clerk and justice to be "exasperating." As an example of how frustrating it could be to a Frankfurter law clerk, Sander recounted an instance when both he and co-clerk Jim Vorenberg told Justice Frankfurter that he should remove a sentence out of a slip opinion because it was offensive to another justice. Justice Frankfurter told his clerks, "I will not compromise my standards out of politeness" and refused to remove the offending sentence, only to walk into the chambers the next morning and blithely announce, "I should take that sentence out" as if the previous day's conversation had never occurred.[38]

Sometimes, in the face of a particularly vigorous intellectual assault by his clerks, the justice beat a strategic retreat. Former law clerk Harry Wellington (October term 1955) recalls that while driving Frankfurter home one time, a heated debate ended when the justice ordered Wellington to stop the car, and he exited and caught a taxi home. Wellington drove home, believing that he would be fired, but he returned to work the next day to find Frankfurter had drafted an opinion that contained the very changes the young man advocated. "That was the nature of the relationship," concluded Wellington, "one argued about everything."[39]

Wellington was not the only clerk to drive the justice into a temporary retreat. Recalls former clerk Homet: "When I scored a point in argument, the Justice would so signify by sticking his hands in his pockets and whistling. Or he might repair to his private bathroom for thought. On at least one occasion, very rarely, he might actually whistle and go into his bathroom at the same time. No matter what the tactic, he would emerge with a fresh idea or a new argument, ready for the fray. For a much younger law clerk, it was a great compliment and much intellectual fun."[40]

In such jousting matches, the justice was not above using the verbal equivalent of brass knuckles. Homet recalls that if Frankfurter disagreed with his law clerks, he might bitingly comment, "I don't like it when graduates from the Harvard Law School think in such a shallow way." Homet added, however, that Justice Frankfurter would remove the sting from his words "by then putting his arm around you."

Frankfurter, however, was remarkably tolerant of his law clerks' mistakes. During October term 1939, law clerk Edward F. Prichard Jr.—a law clerk whose intellect was not matched by an eye for detail—failed to shepardize all the cases contained in a Frankfurter opinion draft, resulting in the case being set for rehearing. Despondent over the error, Prichard left Washington, hid in New York City, and did not return to the Supreme Court until he learned that Frankfurter had forgiven his error. Writes Tracy Campbell: "Within a few days, the justice was at work in his chambers when a tearful Prichard appeared at the door. The bulky figure was soon on his knees crawling on all fours to Frankfurter, begging forgiveness. The two embraced in a scene that has probably never been re-created at any time in the history of the U.S. Supreme Court."[41]

Ironically, it would be Prichard who tried—but failed—to protect Justice Frankfurter from what some believe to be his greatest mistake, namely, the majority opinion that Frankfurter drafted in *Minersville School District v. Gobitis*.[42] In the opinion, the Supreme Court held that school children could be forced to salute the American flag regardless of their religious beliefs. "I tried desperately to get him to take a different view, and I couldn't do it," recalled Prichard years later. "I did something that could have got me fired . . . I took the draft of the opinion to his house [home of Joseph L. Rauh Jr., Frankfurter's first law clerk] in the dead of night with tears in my eyes, and I said, 'Joe, is there anything we can do to prevent this disaster?' And we stayed up until the wee hours in the morning and concluded there wasn't anything we could do."[43] In the eyes of his loyal clerk, the *Gobitis* decision irrevocably changed Frankfurter's judicial reputation: "it absolutely blasted Frankfurter's reputation as a great liberal jurist," concludes Prichard, "[and] he was never the same again."

Finally, the law clerks were privy to Frankfurter's unvarnished views on his fellow justices. "Frankfurter did not hide his lack of regard for some of his colleagues," stated Bender. "He was most frustrated with Brennan, who, as a Harvard graduate, should have known better, and who, when I was there, was winning almost every battle about issues that Frankfurter cared deeply about—federalism related issues mostly."[44] Frankfurter's suspicions extended to Hugo Black as well. Former clerk French recalled an instance in which he recommended that Frankfurter join a Black opinion. "He refused," recalls French. "He told me that 'you are dealing with the most devious mind in America,' and he didn't want to be 'tricked' into joining an opinion that could be used against him later."[45]

Frankfurter, however, was a bit more generous in assessing his own place at the Court. French recalls a second instance when the justice returned from conference and announced to his clerks, "I wish you fellows could have been at conference today." When co-clerk Daniel Mayers asked, "why, did someone say something foolish," Justice Frankfurter responded: "I talked for an hour, and I was brilliant."[46]

In keeping with the life-time tenure of the Frankfurter clerkship, his work assignments did not cease after the clerks left the Supreme Court. "You never stop being a Frankfurter law clerk," writes former clerk Irving J. Helman (October term 1947).[47] While a new associate at the law firm of Dewey Ballantine, Fishman received notes from Frankfurter asking that he "run down the elusive legislative history of the New Jersey escheat law" or "find time to put on paper what you would deem the proper content for such a phrase [as institutional awareness]."[48] Helman was asked to research why some states had abolished the death penalty. As an inducement to Helman, Frankfurter writes: "it [the project] also might still your conscience for spending most of your time in serving the ogres of Big Business from just punishment."[49]

"Seducing" Law Clerks from Other Chambers

No account of Frankfurter and the clerkship institution could be complete without a brief discussion of his interactions with clerks from other chambers. During his years on the Court, Frankfurter had rigorous and constant debates and discussions with clerks from other chambers on a wide range of legal and nonlegal issues. "I know that there was a feeling at the Court that Justice Frankfurter was like the Pied Piper and would attract law clerks from other chambers into his office and conduct law school seminars," states former law clerk Vincent McKusick (October term 1951).[50] The question remains as to the intent of the justice's interactions: was he a former professor looking for any opportunity to teach, or, more troubling, was the justice attempting to influence his brethren by converting their clerks?

A handful of law clerks to Justice Stanley Reed believed it was the latter explanation. Former Reed law clerk Edwin Zimmerman (October term 1950) states: "Frankfurter felt that Stanley Reed was an apt pupil, and Frankfurter . . . was forever trying to seduce Reed's law clerks in the expectation that they would help seduce Stanley Reed." His comments are seconded by former Reed law clerk Roderick Hill (October term 1955), who recalls that Frankfurter was "quite fond of using Justice Reed's law clerks as an avenue to the justice's opinions . . . [He] was quite likely to walk into our chambers . . . and discuss issues with us that he never talked to the justice about."[51]

Most former Frankfurter law clerks, however, reject the notion that Frankfurter was "lobbying" the other justices through their clerks, although former law clerk Bender believes that the justice would not have hesitated to point out the errors in the judicial philosophies of his fellow justices: "What he

[Frankfurter] probably did do is to try to get to know other justices' clerks, especially if they were from Harvard, and to talk to them about jurisprudential issues, and specifically to suggest to them that their boss's view of the world was wrong. . . . I don't think FF would have intended that kind of thing to be destructive—although he should have known and cared that it would not be welcomed by the other justice."[52]

At least one former law clerk to Justice Robert H. Jackson, however, did feel that Frankfurter was using him (unsuccessfully) as conduit through which to influence his justice. Former Jackson law clerk E. Barrett Prettyman Jr. (who would later briefly clerk for Frankfurter) recounted: "He was in my office [in Jackson's chambers] a lot during the first term, proselytizing me because for some reason he thought I might have some effect on Jackson—which was just not true, but he chose to think so."[53]

Bender offers another explanation for Frankfurter's lecturing of the clerks. Frankfurter "had a hard time accepting that smart law clerks, especially smart Harvard law clerks, could actually believe that Black, or Douglas, or Brennan, who was the main enemy when I was there, was right about something really important where FF held a different view." Regarding a bright young Harvard Law School graduate who clerked for Justice Brennan during the same term that Bender clerked for Frankfurter, Bender states: "I know that he thought . . . [the young clerk] had sold out his soul to the devil—something hard to accept about someone who had done brilliantly at Harvard."[54]

Finally, the justice also availed himself of the "law clerk network" to gain information on the activities of the other chambers. The law clerks typically dined together in the clerks' special dining room. "Justice Frankfurter would often ask us to 'tell me what you have learned about what is going on in the other chambers' while simultaneously reminding us not to tell the other law clerks what was going on in the Frankfurter chambers."[55]

The Lifelong Bonds between Frankfurter and His Clerks

Many have referred to the forty-one men who clerked for the childless Frankfurter as his "surrogate sons," a "common, easy suggestion" that former Frankfurter law clerk Louis Henkin writes "is less than a half-a-truth." He explains that "we all had other fathers, but he had no other, 'permanent' sons. He gave us something of what a second father might give to sons; he took for himself little of what sons can sometimes give to a father."[56]

Whether the former clerks were surrogate children, devoted friends, or loyal courtiers, however, the undisputable fact remains that a Frankfurter clerkship was a life-time appointment to what former clerk John H. Mansfield characterized as "the golden circle of his acquaintance."[57] As Kaufman explains:

> [Frankfurter] was loyal to his friends. Once he admitted you to that circle —and the circle was very large—you were his friend for life. There was one group that was admitted en masse: his law clerks. Frankfurter treated us like colleagues; he was interested in our lives; he included our families in his interest; and he kept his clerks as his friends and as his colleagues forever. It is hard not to reciprocate the affection of someone who cares passionately for you.[58]

Kaufman adds that the law clerks uniformly returned this affection, although the affection was tempered with "a current of tolerant criticism about his personal foibles and professional missteps."[59]

Frankfurter's interest in his former clerks extended to their professional and personal lives, and he did not hesitate to pepper his clerks with unsolicited advice. "I think FF spent a good deal of thought and energy in deciding what career his clerks should follow," explained Bender. "He was a powerful personality, and hard to say no to, especially because it was very clear—to me at least—that his advice was sincerely intended to be for my benefit, not his."[60] Some former clerks did not follow Frankfurter's advice to go into teaching, instead becoming attorneys at large law firms—a fact that Frankfurter would often bemoan. "'Do you really want to spend your life living in a Park Avenue apartment with seven bathrooms?' was a typical FF sally" when faced with a law clerk who wanted to enter private practice.[61] For those clerks who ignored the justice's guidance, they occasionally found themselves the targets of their mentor's sharp tongue (and sharper pen). Disappointed in Fred Fishman's announcement that he could not continue to prepare summaries of Supreme Court cases for his former employer, Frankfurter writes: "You will forgive me for saying so, but one of the things that makes a difference between a narrow-minded and a broad-minded lawyer is that the former allows his immediate professional demands to eat up the whole." Frankfurter, however, is not finished scolding his pupil. "While I am in this moralizing mood I venture to suggest to you that a lawyer who is merely a lawyer is not a good enough lawyer, certainly not with the demands of modern society." While Frankfurter reassures Fishman that he recognizes the "central tragedy" of life, namely, that "there are only twenty-four hours in the day," the justice is not sympathetic to this fact. "But it is a limitation which binds everybody and one must somehow or other break through that limitation to the extent of not letting oneself be imprisoned by the immediate demands of daily living or daily working."[62]

The evidence of the lifelong relationship between Justice Frankfurter and his clerks can be literally measured by the bulging law clerk correspondence files in the Frankfurter papers. The letters between the justice and his former clerks cover an endless array of personal, political, and legal topics—not to mention healthy doses of gossip—and touch upon the major political and legal figures of the twentieth century. Figures such as long-time Harvard Law School dean Erwin Griswold, who Frankfurter describes as "just gauche" and "utterly and completely devoid of grace" when writing to former law clerk Alexander Bickel (who felt patronized by Griswold).[63] Or Thurgood Marshall, about whom Bill Coleman writes a "disappointed" Frankfurter (who was displeased with Marshall's nomination to the Second Circuit Court of Appeals) and reassures him that "Marshall will be an adequate judge" and worthy successor to Learned and Augustus Hand.[64] Or Katharine Graham, the wife of former law clerk Philip Graham and the daughter of *Washington Post* owner Eugene Meyer. In a wartime letter to Katharine, Frankfurter urges her to stop publishing society news in the *Washington Post* because it entices members of Washington's glittering social set to engage in acts of "frivolity and waste and snobbery." "There are not many influences stronger than the seductions of publicity—silly as it may appear to you—for taking people's thoughts and time and energies into frivolities like cocktail parties and dinners and whatnot ... [and] the fact that they will appear in print the next day is too often magnetic for too many people." For Frankfurter, national morale depended on a Washington in which the "dominant atmosphere" was "austere."[65]

Frankfurter's affections extended to the wives and children of his former law clerks. In a poignant letter to Elizabeth "Lally" Graham written shortly after her father's suicide, Frankfurter reassures her that her father would have wanted to attend her upcoming wedding. "I know how much he loved you, how deeply he hoped that you would know happiness and fulfillment, and how grateful he was for his delight in you and the happiness you gave him," writes Frankfurter. "If I were not disabled, I would actually dare to invite you to put your arm through mine and walk you through [sic] the aisle." Frankfurter concludes the letter as follows: "I have always liked your daring in calling me 'the little judge' but I have a big heart and it belongs to you today. Bless you, my dearest Lally, and may all the favoring angels attend you and guide you."[66]

The bonds between the justice and his clerks were renewed and strengthened through yearly reunions, typically black-tie affairs held at exclusive clubs in Washington that featured liberal amounts of food and drink. For example, the 1959 reunion dinner for Justice Frankfurter and his law clerks was held in the Tamerlaine Room of the Shoreham Hotel in Washington, D.C. The dinner included shrimp cocktail, cream of mushroom soup, roast beef, string beans, potatoes au gratin, a mixed green salad, and Baked Alaska. Beverages included manhattans, martinis, Scotch, and Bourbon before dinner, a glass of sherry for each participant at the start of dinner, red wine served with the roast beef, Scotch and Bourbon after the dinner, and champagne with dessert.

Not surprising given the wide array of liquid refreshments, the reunions also featured raucous conversation. Commented one former clerk:

> The Justice does not regard the [reunion] dinners as gatherings of former apprentices to salute their old master. We are his children and heirs to whom he feels an obligation to render periodic accounts of his judicial stewardship. And so, cigars and brandy come around, the Justice rises. But what begins as a message on the state of the Court finished as a joyously uninhibited free-for-all in which it is utterly futile to try to enforce any rule of germaneness or uninterrupted discourse. Only at 3:00 or 4:00 a.m., after one of the older clerks seizes him *vi et armis* to take him home—the Justice protesting all the while that the evening is still young—does the party end.[67]

Decades later, the former Frankfurter clerks have vivid memories of these gatherings. Fishman recalls one reunion where Frankfurter, frustrated that he wasn't being heard, shouted, "Will you please listen?" Former law clerk Stanley Silverberg (October term 1943) immediately responded, "It's pretty hard to make your point when you are being interrupted all the time, isn't it?" which drew laughter from the audience and prompted former clerk Philip Graham to walk across the room and shake Silverberg's hand for the witty verbal thrust. Never at a loss for words, Justice Frankfurter immediately shot back, "Well, it is for judges—but it shouldn't be for lawyers."[68]

On other occasions, the clerks skewered themselves. John French vividly recalls one reunion where former Frankfurter law clerk Elliot Richardson described what it was like to campaign for lieutenant governor of Massachusetts. Richardson told the audience that campaigning in the election "reminded me of being at Harvard College, when I was trying to get into one of the houses [social clubs]." As part of his hazing, Richardson was made to stand on the

street corner in Cambridge and introduce himself to passersby in the following fashion: "How do you do. My name is Elliot Richardson, and I am a lovely
boy."[69]

The only nonlaw clerks to attend the reunions were Dean Acheson (former law clerk to Louis Brandeis) and, in earlier years, Marion Frankfurter.
Summarizing Mrs. Frankfurter's role at the reunions, Coleman writes: "After
dinner Mrs. Frankfurter made humorous remarks, classifying each law clerk
from barbarian to milquetoast."[70] The reunions of the former Frankfurter
law clerks continue today, although on a semi-annual basis, and are often
held on the anniversary of the justice's appointment to the Supreme Court on
January 30, 1939.

In Frankfurter's illness and death, as in life, his current and former law clerks
continued to answer the call to service. Before his death, the ailing Frankfurter
sent for former student Paul Freund and former law clerk Lou Henkin (October term 1946) to discuss his funeral arrangements. The two men met with the
wheelchair-bound Frankfurter and his weeping wife, Marion. "Felix wanted
plans to be made because he had seen what happened in the absence of plans
when Chief Justice Stone died leaving no directions and placing needless burden on the survivors," Freund writes. "He would have Marian [sic] avoid that
ordeal." After telling Freund and Henkin that he wanted a simple service with
a quintet of musicians, the agnostic Frankfurter asked Lou Henkin to recite
the Kaddish, the Hebrew prayer for the dead, at the service:

> "I came into the world a Jew and I want to leave it a Jew" [Frankfurter
> explained]. And then, addressing Lou he said, "There will be those in the
> room who will not understand the meaning of the prayer. Perhaps you
> can explain it. Perhaps you can compare it to the Catholic Magnificat."
> And I thought: a teacher to the end—and beyond.[71]

At Justice Frankfurter's memorial service at his home on February 24, 1965,
his former law clerks were joined by President Lyndon Johnson and former
secretary of state Dean Acheson. The lasting effects of the Frankfurter clerkship were reflected in Paul Freund's eulogy at the service, where he poignantly
asked: "Who of us will not continue to feel that iron grip on the arm, to hear
the full-throated greeting, to be rocked with the explosive laughter, and to be
moved by those solicitous inquires about ourselves and our dear ones that
seemed to emanate from some miraculous telepathic power on his part?"[72]

For the Frankfurter law clerks, the call to service was not finished with the
death of the justice. Frankfurter did not leave behind a large estate, and the

$10,000 a year annuity received by Mrs. Frankfurter as the widow of a Supreme Court justice failed to cover her considerable medical expenses. Thus many of the early Frankfurter law clerks banded together and created the Marion Frankfurter Trust to care for the ailing widow of Justice Frankfurter.

Conclusion

So how can one succinctly summarize the Frankfurter clerkship model? Is it possible to boil down the essence of the clerkship experience to a single sentence? We believe that the answer is found in the traditional signed photograph that Frankfurter presented to former law clerk Frank Sander at the end of his clerkship. Frankfurter and Sander shared the bond of being German immigrants, and to honor their common heritage, the justice signed Sander's photograph with the German phrase *es war so schön*—"it was so beautiful." This simple phrase applies with equal force to the Frankfurter clerkship institution.

Notes

1. Leonard Baker, *Brandeis and Frankfurter: A Dual Biography* (New York: Harper & Row, 1984): 415; William T. Coleman Jr., Louis Henkin, and anonymous Frankfurter law clerk, interviews with Peppers.

2. Andrew Kaufman, interview with Peppers. In an April 14, 1952, letter to Hart, Frankfurter writes: "I think I ought to add that not only have I given you an unqualified power of appointment, but my experience with your exercise of it is such that I am quite happy to put that power into your hands. Each year the men are so good in their varying ways that I say to myself that Henry and Mary won't be able to do as well next year, but you always come up with trumps." Henry M. Hart, Jr. Papers, box 4, Harvard Law School.

3. Frankfurter to Hart.

4. In fact, Frankfurter embraced qualified, diverse candidates. Kaufman remarks: "I remember how pleased he [Frankfurter] was when Al Sacks appointed John Mansfield. He was happy to have a Catholic law clerk at last and said so." Kaufman, interview.

5. Paul Bender, interview with Peppers.

6. Ruth Bader Ginsburg, correspondence with Peppers, June 10, 2011.

7. Katharine Graham, *Personal History* (New York: Alfred A. Knopf, 1997): 118. Luckily for the couple, Justice Frankfurter was "'heartily in favor' of the union." Ibid.

8. John H. Mansfield, *Felix Frankfurter: Talks in Tribute* (Cambridge, Mass.: Harvard Law School, 1965): 15.

9. Ibid., 16.

10. Kaufman took issue with our description of the relationship between Frank-

furter and his law clerks being the equivalent of an athletic competition, pointing out that the justice and his law clerks were not equal competitors in regard to intellectual ability. He added, however, that Frankfurter treated his clerks as equals. Kaufman, interview.

11. Baker, *Brandeis and Frankfurter,* 415.

12. Michael E. Parrish, "Justice Frankfurter and the Supreme Court, "in *The Jewish Justices of the Supreme Court Revisited: Brandeis to Fortas,* ed. Jennifer M. Lowe (Washington, D.C.; Supreme Court Historical Society, 1994): 67.

13. Kaufman, interview.

14. Andrew Kaufman, "The Justice and His Law Clerks," in *Felix Frankfurter, the Judge,* ed. Wallace Mendelson (New York: Reynal, 1964): 224.

15. Coleman, interview.

16. In earlier years Dean Acheson and Justice Frankfurter walked from Georgetown to Acheson's office at Covington and Burling. One of the law clerks would then be dispatched to pick up Justice Frankfurter by car and bring him to the Supreme Court.

17. John D. French, interview with Peppers.

18. Kaufman, "Justice and His Law Clerks," 225.

19. "Quirks and Clerks: A Short History," *Juris Doctor* 41 (1972): 41.

20. Roland S. Homet Jr., interview with Peppers.

21. French, interview.

22. Felix Frankfurter to Anne Richardson, letter, July 14, 1964, Personal Papers of Felix Frankfurter, Library of Congress.

23. Baker, *Brandeis and Frankfurter,* 415.

24. Kaufman, interview. The notes are contained in Frankfurter's personal papers, bearing the title "To be passed on and kept up to date." Felix Frankfurter Papers, Harvard Law School.

25. In view of the limited responsibilities granted to the Frankfurter clerks, as well as the strong, personal relationship between the justice and his law clerks, we would have expected to find few rules or practices designed to prevent the agent/clerk from violating the duty owed to the justice/principal.

26. Garson Kanin, "Trips to Felix," *Atlantic Monthly* (1964): 57.

27. Coleman, French, Henkin, and Kaufman, interviews; Irving Helman, correspondence with Peppers.

28. Kaufman, interview. Former law clerk French states that he only prepared a few bench memoranda during the October 1960 term. French, interview.

29. Helman specifically states that he did not prepare bench memoranda. Helman, correspondence.

30. Frankfurter chamber rules.

31. French, interview.

32. *St. Joe Paper Co. v. Atlantic Coast Line Railroad Co.,* 347 U.S. 298 (1954).

33. Frank A. E. Sander, interview with Peppers.

34. Fred Fishman, interview with Peppers.

35. Homet, interview.

36. Elliot Richardson, "A Personal Appreciation," *Harvard Law School Bulletin,* March 1965, 4.

37. Fred Fishman Papers, Harvard Law School. Fishman was a partner at the New York law firm Kaye Scholer and served as the president of the Bar Association of New York City. Albert Sacks worked briefly at the law firm of Covington and Burling, leaving private practice to teach at Harvard Law School. From 1971 to 1981, Sacks served as dean of Harvard Law School.

38. Sander, interview.

39. Harry Wellington, interview with Peppers.

40. Homet, interview.

41. Tracy Campbell, *Short of the Glory: The Fall and Redemption of Edward F. Prichard, Jr.* (Lexington: University of Kentucky Press, 1998): 64–65.

42. *Minersville School District v. Gobitis,* 310 U.S. 586 (1940).

43. Edward F. Prichard, Jr. Oral History Project, Kentucky Historical Society, November 29, 1982, 35.

44. Bender, interview.

45. French, interview.

46. Ibid.

47. Helman, correspondence. Frankfurter's lifelong interpretation of the clerkship meant that the justice had no reservations about advising former law clerks about matters that later came before the Supreme Court. See Philip Elman, "The Solicitor General's Office, Justice Frankfurter and Civil Rights Litigation, 1946–1960: An Oral History," *Harvard Law Review* 100, no. 4 (February 1987): 817–44; Norman I. Silber, *With All Deliberate Speed: The Life of Philip Elman* (Ann Arbor: University of Michigan Press, 2004).

48. Fishman Papers.

49. Irving J. Helman Papers, box 1, Harvard Law School.

50. Vincent McKusick, interview with Peppers.

51. The comments of Zimmerman and Hills are contained in the *Stanley Forman Reed Oral History Project,* University of Kentucky.

52. Bender, interview.

53. "Legends in the Law: A Conversation with E. Barrett Prettyman," *District of Columbia Bar Report,* April/May 1997.

54. Bender, interview.

55. Sander, interview.

56. Louis Henkin, "Felix Frankfurter: A Very Private Person," in Catalog to *Felix Frankfurter, 1882–1965: An Intimate Portrait,* prepared by Erika S. Chadbourn (Cambridge, Mass.: Manuscript Division, Harvard Law School Library, 1982).

57. Mansfield, *Felix Frankfurter,* 15.

58. Andrew L. Kaufman, "Constitutional Law and the Supreme Court: Frankfurter

and Wellington," *New York Law School Law Review* 45 (2001): 141. The Prettyman papers contain copies of a few memos written by Prettyman to the justice.

59. Kaufman, *Frankfurter and Wellington,* 142.

60. Bender, interview.

61. Ibid.

62. Felix Frankfurter to Fred Fishman, letter, November 27, 1951, Personal Papers of Frankfurter Papers, Library of Congress, Reel 33.

63. Felix Frankfurter to Alexander Bickel, letter, August 29, 1956, Personal Papers of Felix Frankfurter, Library of Congress, Reel 14.

64. William T. Coleman Jr. to Felix Frankfurter, letter, December 29, 1961, Personal Papers of Felix Frankfurter, Library of Congress, Reel 30.

65. February 13, 1942 letter from Felix Frankfurter to Katharine Graham, Personal Papers of Felix Frankfurter, Library of Congress, Reel 36.

66. November 5, 1964 letter from Felix Frankfurter to Elizabeth Morris Graham, Personal Papers of Felix Frankfurter, Library of Congress, Reel 36.

67. Kaufman, "Justice and His Clerks," 226 (quoting former law clerk Philip Elman).

68. Fishman, interview.

69. French, interview.

70. William T. Coleman Jr. (with Donald T. Bliss), *Counsel for the Situation: Shaping the Law to Realize America's Promise* (Washington, D.C.: Brookings Institute Press, 2010): 88.

71. Freund, *Reminiscences and Reflections,* 12.

72. Fishman Papers.

TODD C. PEPPERS

William Thaddeus Coleman Jr.

Breaking the Color Barrier at the United States Supreme Court

O n April 15, 2007, baseball fans celebrated the sixtieth anniversary of Jackie Robinson's debut with the Brooklyn Dodgers—an event that broke the color barrier and integrated major league baseball. In stadiums across America, professional baseball teams honored the memory and accomplishments of Robinson as managers and players donned Robinson's retired jersey number, hall of famers threw out ceremonial first pitches, and tributes boomed from video displays. The tributes to Robinson, however, like his legacy, went far beyond the ball parks, as newspaper and television journalists debated Robinson's role as a civil rights pioneer while lamenting the dwindling number of minorities playing baseball, and elementary school children read stories of Robinson's stirring feats.

On September 1, 2008, the United States Supreme Court quietly celebrated a similar anniversary—the sixtieth anniversary of the arrival of the first black law clerk at the United States Supreme Court. His name is William T. Coleman Jr., and on September 1, 1948, Coleman began clerking in the chambers of Felix Frankfurter. A graduate of Harvard Law School, Coleman used his Supreme Court clerkship as a stepping stone to a legal and political career whose highlights include working as the first black lawyer in a major Philadelphia law firm, volunteering his time and expertise for the desegregation cases collectively referred to as *Brown v. Board of Education,* running the NAACP Legal Defense and Educational Fund, serving as the secretary of transportation in the Ford administration, and receiving the Presidential Medal of Freedom.

The purpose of this essay is twofold—to succinctly summarize the important events of Coleman's life and professional career while making the argument that these achievements were as groundbreaking to the legal community as Robinson's were to baseball. Admittedly, looking to our national pastime is hardly an original literary maneuver—the myriad similarities and links between baseball and the law have offered rich material for many legal writers. Moreover, this article does not wish to diminish Coleman's accomplishments by comparing them to a mere "game." By drawing up the sixtieth anniversary of Jackie Robinson's debut, my hope is to give Coleman his due and place his laudable achievements in the proper perspective. Not only did the two men do much to dispel the pernicious stereotype that they belonged to a race that was doomed to second-class citizenship, but the efforts of the two men to integrate their respective professions and to use their talents to effect change reverberated throughout society.

The Early Life of William T. Coleman Jr.

William Thaddeus Coleman Jr. was born on July 7, 1920, in Germantown, Pennsylvania, to parents William Thaddeus Coleman Sr. and Laura Beatrice Coleman. One of three children, Coleman grew up in a middle-class home where education and hard work were encouraged. Social activism and public service were practices engrained into Coleman's family—his father, William Coleman Sr., a graduate of the Hampton Institute, balanced his work as the executive director of the Wissahickon Boys Club—an organization originally founded to provide educational and recreational opportunities for minorities and poor whites—with his duties as a field secretary for the Boys Club of America and as a director of a local summer camp, while his maternal great-grandfather was an Episcopal minister who operated the Underground Railroad in St. Louis, Missouri.

Coleman's mother, Laura Beatrice Coleman, was a former German teacher who also greatly influenced her son. "My mother always said what redeemed her living in a world where blacks and women were second place was that when she got to heaven, God would be a black woman."[1] One pattern of Coleman's childhood was exposure to "a great many worldly people," including civil rights pioneer W. E. B. Du Bois—a friend of Coleman's maternal aunt who would occasionally join the Coleman family for dinner—and author Langston Hughes. The result of this exposure to the world—"I knew we were as good as anybody. I never felt inferior."[2]

The lessons learned around the dinner table would prove to be important as Coleman began moving into a segregated world that did not push young black students to fulfill their potential. Recalling his time at Theodore Roosevelt Junior High School, Coleman recounted the following incident. "I finished tops in my class at Roosevelt. I made what I thought was a good speech and my teacher said, 'You'll make somebody a good chauffeur.' I won't tell you what I told her, but I was suspended for saying it. My mother and father had to tell her, 'You don't talk to a Coleman kid that way.'"[3]

Coleman subsequently enrolled in the predominately white Germantown High School, where he was one of fewer than ten black students. An outstanding student, he would nevertheless be suspended when he demanded to become a member of the all-white swim team. When Coleman's suspension was lifted, the swimming team disbanded rather than be forced to integrate and accept Coleman. Remarks Coleman: "The day I graduated, they posted a note saying they were starting up the swimming team again. But the coach wrote me the best recommendation [letter] for the University of Pennsylvania."[4] When asked why he decided to become an attorney, Coleman pointed to his experiences of sitting in Philadelphia courtrooms as an adolescent and being impressed that the lawyers got "paid to argue," as well as a visit as a high school student to an operating ward at a local hospital, where Coleman watched a stomach cancer operation and quickly decided "that wasn't for me."[5] It was as a teenager that Coleman learned of the efforts of attorney Charles Hamilton Houston and the NAACP to attack and defeat segregation, a fight that appealed to Coleman's own sense of justice and equality. Coleman graduated summa cum laude from the University of Pennsylvania in 1941.

Coleman originally planned to major only in political science but added an economics major after a lawyer told his father that economics was a good field of study for future lawyers. Coleman describes his time at the University of Pennsylvania as "sort of a blur," adding, "We studied, and we were all glad when Friday came. If we didn't have a theme due by ten o'clock Monday morning, we loved to spend the weekend taking the ladies out."[6]

Coleman arrived at Harvard Law School in the fall of 1941, one of only four minority law students in the first-year class.[7] Although Harvard Law School had admitted its first black law student—George Lewis Ruffin—shortly after the Civil War, minority students had a minimal presence there in the following decades. Approximately nine black students attended Harvard Law School throughout the decade of the 1920s, and in the 1930s and 1940s no entering Harvard Law School class had more than five black students. As the first half of the twentieth century drew to a close, Harvard Law School graduated a class of 520 students—of those, only 2 students were black.[8]

Coleman quickly immersed himself into his legal studies, going so far as to attend extra classes just to hear lectures by some of Harvard Law School's legendary professors. His hard work paid off in the spring of 1941, when his high grades (he was second in his first-year class) propelled him to the staff of the *Harvard Law Review*. Coleman was only the third black to serve on the law review, following in the footsteps of previous graduates Charles Hamilton Houston and William Henry Hastie. While Coleman does not recall feeling any trepidation at being one of the first minorities to serve on the law review, he surely, like his predecessors, felt the historic weight of his selection and the consequences if he stumbled. Only twenty years earlier Charles H. Houston wrote his parents: "The editors on the Review didn't want me on this fall; now all is one grand harmony. But I still go on my way alone. They know I am just as independent and a little more so than they. My stock is pretty high around these parts. God help me against a false move."[9] And when William H. Hastie became the second black selected to the *Harvard Law Review* in 1928, the editor-in-chief declined to invite Hastie to the traditional dinner held to welcome the new members—a decision that was reversed when fellow Harvard law student Paul Freund organized a boycott of the dinner.[10] Neither Coleman nor his contemporaries on the law review, however, recall Coleman receiving similar treatment.[11] States fellow law review member Jerome E. Hyman: "Bill was a well regarded member of the Review. If anything I think there was a great deal of satisfaction that the Review was becoming more diverse in its membership." While subsequent minorities followed the path laid by Houston, Hastie, and Coleman, it would not be until 1990 that the law review selected its first black president—Harvard Law School student Barack Obama.[12]

Coleman worked during the summer and fall semesters on the law review, typically attending classes until 1:00 p.m. and then walking to the law review offices at the historic Gannett House and working there until 8:00 p.m. His studies at Harvard Law School and his work on the law review were interrupted by the entry of the United States into the Second World War. Coleman was originally conflicted about serving in the military and sought counsel from then Howard Law School dean Charles H. Houston. Recounts Coleman:

> Like ten percent of the American population, I struggled with the idea whether it made sense to fight for freedom and liberty in Europe and Asia when racial segregation was still so rampant in the United States. I got an appointment to see Mr. Houston in Washington, D.C. . . . [he] gave me sound advice. He said that with all its faults, the United States is still the

best country in the world. Through the use of training, knowledge, and commitment by dedicated lawyers, businessmen, and those members of other disciplines, someday the United States would be free of the scourge of racial segregation. In the meantime, if persons wanted to demand full citizenship in their country, they had to risk their lives and fortunes when the very security and being of their country was being seriously challenged by a formidable foreign force.[13]

Coleman subsequently enlisted in the Army Air Corps, and in 1942 he traveled to Biloxi, Mississippi, for basic training before going to Tuskegee, Alabama, to train with a group of black aviators that would gain fame as the Tuskegee Airmen.

When Coleman stepped off the train platform in Biloxi, however, he was quickly reminded that his country's struggle against fascism had not wiped away its own racist propensities. At the Biloxi train station, Coleman was greeted by a belligerent white sergeant who called out "hey, nigger, where are you going?" Coleman wouldn't respond to the hated racial epithet and started walking away from the train station, until the sergeant called out "hey, boy." Coleman "settled" for the slightly less offensive term (a decision about which he professes "shame" sixty years later), turned around, and learned that the sergeant was assigned to transport Coleman to a nearby military base. During the dusty ride to the base, the army truck picked up several white soldiers returning from a weekend of leave. After spying Coleman, one of the soldiers turned to his compatriot and said wonderingly, "Why do I see all these well-dressed niggers in town—what are they doing here?" Responded his buddy: "You know, that Mrs. Roosevelt—she taught that dumb President that those black people could fly." Concludes Coleman, with a smile: "So that was my introduction to the U.S. Army."[14]

After basic training, Coleman trained to be an aviator at the Tuskegee Army Air Field in Tuskegee. Describing his fellow airmen as "very good people who were good at everything," Coleman completed his basic training before "washing out in advanced training" and deciding that "I better do something else."[15] Coleman's failure to become a fighter pilot is arguably the only professional accomplishment that he would ever fail to achieve. Coleman, however, found another way to serve as a wing man to the Tuskegee pilots; in 1945 he helped defend a group of black airmen who were arrested for challenging the segregation of an officers' club at Freeman Field in Seymour, Indiana.[16] Coleman spent the remainder of his military service defending soldiers during court-martial proceedings and by his own count won sixteen out of eighteen acquittals (with one of the two convictions reversed on appeal).

The end of the war saw Coleman's return to Harvard Law School and his final year of studies. Despite his strong academic record, he fully recognized the institutionalized prejudices that raised hurdles in the path of any young black lawyer. Coleman's sober assessment of these barriers is reflected in a handwritten letter to Associate Justice Hugo Black, a letter in which Coleman applied to be Black's law clerk. "Despite my training due to the fact that I am a negro I have encountered considerable difficulty in getting a suitable position. Your efforts and expressions in your judicial utterances led me to inquire if you would consider me for the position as your legal clerk."[17] Recalling his motivation for writing the letter, Coleman commented: "I was married and had one kid and I had to do something. I figured if I made enough ruckuses something would open up to me."[18] In his reply, Black congratulated Coleman on his "excellent" record but stated that the law clerk for the coming term "was selected some months ago."[19] When Coleman arrived at the Supreme Court in the fall of 1948, he would become friends with both Justice Black and his law clerk, Truman M. Hobbes.[20]

When Coleman graduated magna cum laude from Harvard Law School in the fall of 1946, he faced the bitter reality that graduating first in his class, serving on the law review, and winning the John H. Beale Prize (awarded to the Harvard Law student with the highest grade in Conflicts of Law) did not guarantee legal employment. His first break came from his hometown of Philadelphia, when Judge Herbert Goodrich of the Third Circuit Court of Appeals offered Coleman a clerkship for the spring of 1947. Coleman was able to secure a Langdell Fellowship at Harvard Law School to cover the interim period between graduation and the start of the clerkship, and Coleman returned to Philadelphia in 1948 and began serving as Judge Goodrich's sole law clerk.

Clerking on the United States Supreme Court

In December 1947, Harvard Law School professor Paul Freund wrote Frankfurter and recommended that Coleman serve as one of his two law clerks. Frankfurter quickly responded to the letter. After noting that "I have heard a good deal about [Coleman] on the occasion of the Sixtieth Anniversary Dinner of the Law Review, and I am not surprised at the weighty commendation that you give me," Frankfurter clearly dispelled with any concerns that race might disqualify Coleman: "I don't have to tell you that I don't care what color a man has, any more than I care what religion he professes or doesn't."[21] Frank-furter's pronouncement had historical precedent—as a Harvard Law School professor, he had mentored both Charles H. Houston and William Hastie. With Frankfurter's declaration in hand, it was Professor Hart who placed the telephone call that arguably changed the course of Coleman's career.

> One day I got a call from Professor Hart, asking me if I wanted to clerk next year for Justice Frankfurter. I, of course, said yes. Then he hung up. I never got any call on when I should report to Justice Frankfurter. So a month and a half later I called Paul Freund, who was my best friend at law school, who said I'll check. So Freund went and talked to Hart, who said "Oh, gee, that Coleman must not be as bright as everybody says he is if he doesn't think he has the job." So that is how I got the job.[22]

Although Coleman had previously met Justice Frankfurter at the aforemen-tioned *Harvard Law Review* dinner, he did not know the justice and had never interviewed with him prior to receiving the clerkship offer.

While Coleman appreciated the historic nature of his clerkship with Justice Frankfurter, he modestly points to changing social conditions, not his own abilities, as the main explanation for his selection. "I knew that I was the first . . . but I knew that under different circumstances Charlie Houston and Bill Hastie would have been the first because they were brighter, more able people . . . but they lived in a different time and didn't have the same opportunities."[23] Cole-man's hiring was sufficiently noteworthy to merit mention in the *New York Times* and the *Washington Post,* and Frankfurter's personal papers contain con-gratulatory letters from the General Alliance of Unitarian and Other Liberal Christian Women, the Race Relations Committee of the American Friends Service Committee, the Christian Friends for Racial Equality, and Congress-man John W. McCormack.[24]

In response to the letters, Frankfurter penned a simple reply:

> Mr. William T. Coleman was named as one of my law clerks for next year precisely for the same reason that others have been named in the past, namely high professional competence and character. You are kind to write me, but I do not think a man deserves any praise for doing what is right and abstaining from the wrong.[25]

The extended members of the "Frankfurter family" also praised the selec-tion. In a March 29, 1948, letter to Justice Frankfurter, former law clerk Harry Mansfield applauded the hiring decision. "He is a first rate choice in every respect. His mind is brilliant and with brilliance he combined judgment. And his winning personality—full of confident ease and good humor—enabled him to overcome readily whatever obstacles were raised because of his color . . . it is gratifying to me that you can be the first to give someone like Bill his opportunity without relaxing in any measure the standards ordinarily applied."[26]

The selection of Coleman was also praised by Frankfurter's African American messenger, Tom Beasley. Former Brandeis law clerk Paul A. Freund recalls an exchange that took place between Frankfurter and Beasley shortly after the selection of Coleman. Writes Freund:

> After it was announced in the press [that] Justice Frankfurter was to take as his law clerk the first black law graduate to be so appointed, Tom Beasely said to the Justice, "That's a mighty fine thing you're doing, Mr. Justice, taking one of our people to be your law clerk." Frankfurter said, "Tom, I've heard others say that, but I never thought I'd hear that from you. Don't you know that I selected Mr. Coleman because on the basis of brains and character he deserves it?" As Felix described it, "Tom looked at me pityingly and said, 'Mr. Justice, in this world do you think our people get what they deserve.'"[27]

During October term 1948, Coleman shared his clerking duties with fellow Harvard Law School graduate Elliot Richardson.[28] Richardson—a Harvard graduate who served as a medic during the invasion of Normandy and as a law clerk to Judge Learned Hand (and who would go on to serve as the secretary of health, education and welfare, secretary of defense, U.S. attorney general, secretary of commerce, and ambassador to Great Britain)—and Coleman quickly established a daily practice that has become unique in the lore of Supreme Court law clerks. Each day Richardson and Coleman spent one hour reading Shakespeare or poetry. "Elliot went to private schools before college, and I had gone to public schools," explains Coleman. "I felt like my education was lacking, which led to reading Shakespeare and such during our lunch breaks."[29] The young men also recognized the need for physical as well as mental exercise, and Coleman writes that approximately three mornings a week the two clerks "played badminton on the roof [top floor] of the court to clear the mind and work off excess energy."[30]

For the modern Supreme Court law clerk, buried in a mountain of cert petitions and opinion drafts, the notion that an earlier generation of Supreme Court law clerks spent an hour each day reading literature (as well as heatedly debating the political issues of the day with their justice) must undoubtedly seem bizarre. Such a practice, however, was only in keeping with the Frankfurter clerkship tradition of challenging his clerks to broaden their intellectual horizons.

When Coleman arrived at his clerkship in the fall of 1948, he found himself working with a dynamic, larger-than-life personality who joyfully embraced his law clerks as members of his family. Coleman keenly remembers his first encounter with Felix Frankfurter:

> On September 17, Justice Frankfurter made his grand entrance as he dashed through our offices on the way to the bathroom. In the presence of my new employer I felt like Manasseh Cutler, a Massachusetts minister, when he first met Benjamin Franklin: "My knees smote together." Yet, I thought to myself, he is human like the rest of us, having to answer the call of nature.[31]

Of his relationship with Frankfurter, Coleman states that "from the day we came to the day he died, Felix Frankfurter was the nearest thing to a father or a brother that I had outside of my own family."[32]

Justice Frankfurter's enthusiasm and affection extended to the families of his clerks. He invited Coleman's parents to visit with him in his chambers, and the children of his clerks were also welcomed. "When my first child, Billy, was three years old, he visited the chambers," writes Coleman. "[B]efore long the justice was rolling on the floor pushing Billy's red toy car around the carpet."[33]

As with most Frankfurter law clerks, Coleman attended meals at the Frankfurter home, and he become close with Marion Frankfurter—whom he referred to as a "second mother." In the early months of Coleman's clerkship, Marion Frankfurter took on the role of writing tutor. Justice Frankfurter originally felt that Coleman's writing skills were not on par with Richardson's, so Coleman started getting up at six o'clock in the morning to meet with Mrs. Frankfurter for writing tutorials prior to the start of his twelve-hour work day. Comments Coleman: "That lasted about two weeks, until she called Justice Frankfurter and told him 'he writes better than you.'"[34]

While Coleman found a welcoming home within Justice Frankfurter's chambers, it is instructive to remember the political and social climate in which he clerked. Not only was Coleman the first black law clerk at the Supreme Court (and most likely the first minority law clerk in the entire federal and state court system), but he was also a member of a federal judiciary that had never had a minority as an Article III judge and a member of a profession that firmly closed its doors to minority lawyers.[35]

Moreover, the marble walls of the Supreme Court could not shelter Coleman from the forces of bigotry and segregation that still held sway over the District of Columbia. In the 1940s almost two hundred thousand blacks lived in the District, but they were carefully segregated from the approximately five hundred thousand white citizens in every aspect of daily life. The two races lived in separate neighborhoods, attended separate schools, played in separate parks, and swam in separate pools. The vast majority of restaurants, theaters, hotels, dance halls, skating rinks, and bowling alleys completely denied blacks entry, and even some hospitals refused treatment to blacks. The only places where blacks and whites freely mixed were on the District's buses and trolleys, in its federal buildings and their cafeterias, and at Union Station.[36]

Coleman recounts one instance of the state-sanctioned racism that he endured during his clerkship at the Supreme Court. It was during a day when the Supreme Court was open, but the Court cafeteria was closed. Coleman was working in Frankfurter's chambers on an antitrust opinion, when Elliot Richardson announced that the law clerks were going to lunch at the Mayflower Hotel and wanted Coleman to join them. Richardson, however, would subsequently call ahead to the hotel and discover that its restaurant would not serve Coleman. Richardson did not share this information with Coleman, but instead he nonchalantly announced that the late hour made dining at Union Station a better choice. Coleman remembers that after lunch a distraught Richardson told Justice Frankfurter what had happened, and that both men were "near tears" over the incident.[37]

There is an interesting footnote to the story. In recent years scholars have written much about the influence that law clerks do or do not wield over their justices, with some authors suggesting that law clerks influence their justices through a variety of means—from educating the justices as to the dispositive facts in the record to making novel new legal arguments.[38] Influence, however, can be more indirect and diffuse. In Coleman's case, one wonders if his experiences as a black man living in a segregated city affected Felix Frankfurter when the NAACP mounted its frontal assault against segregation in the early 1950s.

A tantalizing hint of such benign influence can be found in a law review article by Harvard Law School professor Mark Tushnet, who writes that during the Supreme Court's conference discussions on the case *Bolling v. Sharpe*, a case that challenged segregationist practices in the District of Columbia, Justice William O. Douglas's conference notes record that Felix Frankfurter discussed "the experiences of colored people here especially [William T.] Coleman, one of his old law clerks."[39] While Frankfurter's main attack on segregation in the

District of Columbia turned on legal, not factual, grounds, one might suggest that the passion underlying his argument that segregationist practices violated the due process clause of the Fifth Amendment was fueled by seeing a former law clerk struggle to live in a segregated community.

Coleman's clerkship with Justice Frankfurter ended in the summer of 1949, and Coleman—like the law clerks before him—became a lifetime member of the Frankfurter family. He faithfully attended the reunions of Justice Frankfurter and his former clerks and occasionally traveled from Philadelphia to Washington, D.C., to visit his former employer and exchange the latest news and gossip. Written evidence of Frankfurter's affection and respect for Coleman is found in two historical artifacts: (1) in the traditional, leather-bound volume of opinions that Justice Frankfurter presented to Coleman, the inscription reads "I know never will you pursue false gods let alone false men. It was a joy to have worked with you for a year and I shall watch your future with confident great hopes"; and (2) in a postclerkship letter, in which Frankfurter drew upon the words of his own hero to further praise his former clerk: "What I can say of you with great confidence is what was Justice Holmes' ultimate praise of a man: 'I bet on him.' I bet on you, whatever choice you may make, and whatever the Fates may have in store for you."[40]

Subsequent Professional Career: Being "Counsel for the Situation"

Charles Houston is commonly quoted as remarking that an attorney is "either a social engineer or he's a parasite on society."[41] While Coleman's career has embodied Houston's challenge to all lawyers, especially minority lawyers, to use their legal training to improve their communities and the lives of the politically dispossessed, Coleman has moved back and forth between private practice and public service. "It is a tragedy in the [civil rights] movement that you have got a mind like Bill Hastie or Charlie Houston . . . that had to spend all their time on one thing and not just being a lawyer," observes Coleman. "As [Justice] Brandeis once said, 'a good lawyer is counsel for the situation.'"[42] In short, Coleman's wish is to be remembered first and foremost as an attorney, not a civil rights activist.

Despite his Supreme Court clerkship and impressive academic credentials, Coleman's hopes of becoming a lawyer at a top law firm were not immediately realized. For today's modern law clerk, a clerkship at the United States Supreme Court opens up a world of professional opportunities—including teaching at the elite law schools or working in the country's most prestigious law firms (the latter coming with $200,000 signing bonuses).[43] It was a very different story for a minority law clerk in the late 1940s. Armed with letters of recommendation from Justice Frankfurter, Coleman returned to his home-town of Philadelphia and quickly discovered that prospective employers were not color blind. "I tried like hell to get a job in Philadelphia and no local law firm would hire me."[44] Most of Philadelphia's law firms refused to give Cole-man an interview. When Coleman personally visited the firms with résumé in hand, receptionists stonewalled him, and hiring partners were simply too busy to see him. And if Coleman managed to secure an interview, the outcome was always the same—a suggestion that he consider the local black law firms that specialized in run-of-the-mill tort cases.[45] When asked how he reacted to the rejection, Coleman simply remarked: "You just knew that life would change and things would get better . . . I'm pretty sure at that time I got indignant."[46]

Giving up on Philadelphia, and with only one week remaining before he left the government payroll as a law clerk, Coleman turned his attention to New York and the law firm of Paul, Weiss, Rifkin, Wharton and Garrison—the one firm that had extended an employment offer when he was clerking for Judge Goodrich—and secured a position there. Having already purchased a Phila-delphia home for his young and growing family, Coleman would spend the next three years commuting by train between Philadelphia and New York.

After three years, he was approached by attorney Richardson Dilworth and offered a position at the all-white Philadelphia law firm of Dilworth, Paxson, Kalish and Levy. Coleman relates: "When I came back to Philadelphia, all the secretaries threatened to walk out. Mr. Dilworth told them, 'You ought to stay; he's a nice guy.'" Coleman's hiring at Dilworth, Paxson, found one important supporter—client and media mogul Walter Annenberg. Coleman remarks: "Annenberg said, 'If you don't keep Coleman, I will take my business wher-ever he goes.' I had never met Mr. Annenberg," adds Coleman, "but that was one of the great moments of my life."[47] Coleman stayed and flourished. And he enjoyed a small measure of revenge. "Coleman betrays no bitterness about his early rejections by Philadelphia law firms. But he relished the times when Dilworth, in an effort to needle competitors, sent him to the offices of competi-tors to collect files of clients that had chosen to switch to Dilworth's firm."[48] Coleman would remain with the Philadelphia law firm until 1975, when he was nominated to be secretary of transportation by President Gerald Ford. When Coleman was sworn in as secretary on March 7, 1975, long-time friend—and now associate Supreme Court justice—Thurgood Marshall administered the oath at Coleman's request.

After President Ford's defeat in the 1980 presidential election, Coleman joined the Washington office of the law firm O'Melveny & Myers, where he still practices law. During his almost sixty years as a lawyer, Coleman has represented such clients as Chase Manhattan, Ford Motor Company, Goldman Sachs, and United Airlines. He has argued nineteen cases before the United States Supreme Court—including when the Supreme Court appointed Coleman amicus curiae in the cases of *Bob Jones University v. United States* and *Goldsboro Christian Schools, Inc. v. United States.*[49] "It was the first time in history the Supreme Court had called on someone to represent the judges below," explains Coleman. "[W]e spent the whole summer on it, running up about 780,000 billable hours, and it was all pro bono."[50] The brief and oral arguments made by Coleman produced an 8–1 decision in his favor.

While Coleman has characterized his civil rights work as representing less than one-fifth of his professional career, it is in his willingness to donate his time and energy that Coleman has arguably made the greatest impact on society. In approximately 1950, Coleman received a telephone call from Thurgood Marshall. Then heading the Legal Defense Fund, Marshall asked Coleman to join an elite group of lawyers in formulating legal strategy and drafting the legal briefs in the five cases commonly referred to as *Brown v. Board of Education.* For the next four years, Coleman would maintain a grueling schedule of work—spending a full day in his law office before returning home for dinner and devoting his evening to legal research and writing for the NAACP. Coleman would prove to be a critical member of the team of lawyers and advisers that Marshall had assembled, and he would sit by Marshall's side when *Brown v. Board of Education* was reargued before the United States Supreme Court in December 1953. Coleman's civil rights work did not end with *Brown.* Coleman subsequently represented a group of minorities seeking admission to Philadelphia's all-white Girard College, and from 1977 to 1997 Coleman served as chairman of the board of the NAACP Legal Defense and Educational Fund.

Coleman has also responded to the call for government service. He proudly points to the fact that he has served as an adviser to seven American presidents, starting with Dwight Eisenhower. A brief (and incomplete) list of Coleman's service includes being a member of the Presidential Commission on Employment Policy (1959–61), a senior consultant and senior counsel to the President's Commission on the Assassination of President Kennedy (1964), a member of the United States Delegation to the 24th Session of the United Nations General Assembly (1969), a consultant to the United States Arms Control and Disarmament Agency (1963–75), a member of the National Commission on

Productivity (1971–72), and cochairman of the secretary of state's Advisory Committee on South Africa (1985–87). As secretary of transportation in the Ford administration, Coleman became only the second black to serve in a presidential cabinet.[51] The list could be longer—Secretary of State Dean Acheson wanted Coleman to be an assistant secretary of state, President Lyndon Johnson wanted to nominate Coleman to the federal appeals court, and Attorney General Elliot Richardson asked Coleman to take the position of special prosecutor in the Watergate scandal. Coleman declined all these offers.[52]

Conclusion: Just Be in the Room

Now ninety years old, William Coleman has received an endless list of awards from a wide range of organizations: the Presidential Medal of Freedom; the Thurgood Marshall Lifetime Achievement Award from the NAACP Legal Defense and Education Fund; the Chief Justice John Marshall Award from the American Bar Association Justice Center; the Judge Henry J. Friendly Medal from the American Law Institute; the Marshall-Wythe Medallion from the Marshall-Wythe Law School of the College of William and Mary; the Thaddeus Stevens Award from the Public Interest Law Center of Philadelphia; the Lamplighter Award from the Black Leadership Forum; the "We The People" award from the National Constitution Center; the Fordham-Stein Prize from the Fordham University School of Law; the David A. Clarke School of Equal Justice Award from the University of the District of Columbia Law School; honorary degrees from twenty-one American colleges and universities.[53]

Moreover, Coleman has been present when some of America's most prominent political figures have both come into power and have stepped away from the political arena and into the pages of history. Coleman was present when Thurgood Marshall was sworn in as a Supreme Court justice in 1967, and Coleman was at the Supreme Court's east conference room twenty-four years later when an aging Justice Marshall announced his retirement from the Court.[54] Coleman would complete the journey with Marshall in January 1993, when Coleman stood before an assembled crowd of dignitaries at the Washington National Cathedral and eulogized his departed friend.[55] Coleman would serve in a similar capacity in 2007, when he joined former secretary of state James Baker III, then vice president Dick Cheney, former senator Robert Dole, former Federal Reserve chairman Alan Greenspan, former secretary of state Henry Kissinger, former secretary of defense Donald H. Rumsfeld, and former national security adviser Brent Scowcroft as honorary pallbearers at the funeral of President Gerald Ford.

The honors and awards are arguably validation for Coleman's philosophy that the key to breaking down racial barriers is for minorities to be "in the room" when important decisions are made and deals are brokered. Coleman rejects the idea that the solution to racial problems are practices that separate the races, and he cringes at such labels as "African American" and "affirmative action." Speaking of race relations today, Coleman states that he is "disturbed when black kids go to these great universities. They spent most of their time on African American studies or something. They don't get involved in traditional studies. You have to be a good scholar to be a good lawyer. They can do that [African American studies], but that shouldn't be your major focus."[56]

Jackie Robinson got on the field. The result was a hall-of-fame career that saw Robinson break into major league baseball as a twenty-eight-year-old rookie, compile a lifetime batting average of .311, steal home plate nineteen times, appear in six World Series, and win the National League Most Valuable Player award in 1949. While Robinson's accomplishments alone are impressive, they do not do justice to Robinson unless they are placed within the social and racial context of American in the late 1940s.

William T. Coleman Jr. got on the field—and to the Supreme Court. Like Robinson's achievements, Coleman's accomplishments take on a deeper meaning when placed in the context of a segregated society. Refusing to accept the barriers placed within his path by the forces of racial animus, Coleman used his intellect and will power to generate lifetime statistics that rival Jackie Robinson's. On April 15, 2007, baseball fans across America celebrated the sixtieth anniversary of Robinson taking the field as a Brooklyn Dodger. On September 1, 2008, the legal community should have held a similar celebration for the sixtieth anniversary of the day that Coleman walked up the stairs of the Marble Palace and broke the color barrier of the Supreme Court law clerk corps.

Notes

Portions of this essay are reprinted with permission from Todd C. Peppers, "William Thaddeus Coleman, Jr.—Breaking the Color Barrier at the United States Supreme Court," *Journal of Supreme Court History* 33, no. 3 (2008): 353–70.

1. William T. Coleman Jr.," National Visionary Leadership Project, Washington, D.C.

2. Annette John-Hall, "William T. Coleman, Jr.—Lawyer, Social Activist," *Philadelphia Inquirer*, May 16, 2004.

3. Ibid.

4. Ibid.

5. "Coleman," National Visionary Leadership Project.

6. Patty Dornbusch, "Flashback: William T. Coleman, Jr.," *Columns* 27 (Spring 1980).

7. The other minority students entering Harvard in the fall of 1941 included Wade H. McCree Jr., who later served as a judge in the United States Court of Appeals for the Sixth Circuit and as United States solicitor general, and George N. Leighton, who subsequently became a federal district court judge in Illinois.

8. "Harvard Law School Celebrates Its Black Alumni," *Journal of Blacks in Higher Education,* April 30, 2001, 85–87.

9. "Many of the Nation's Most Prestigious Law Reviews Have Lily-White Editorial Boards," *Journal of Blacks in Higher Education,* April 30, 1998, 55.

10. Karen Hastie Williams, "William Hastie: Facing Challenges in the Ivory Tower," *Journal of Blacks in Higher Education,* July 31, 1999, 122–23. While the prejudices of the times undoubtedly denied William H. Hastie a chance to clerk at the United States Supreme Court, his daughter—Karen Hastie Williams—became the first black female to clerk at the Court.

11. William T. Coleman Jr., interviews with author; author's correspondence with former Harvard Law Review members Phil C. Neal, Jerome E. Hyman.

12. Anthony Flint, "First Black Chosen Head of Harvard Law Journal," *Boston Globe,* February 6, 1990.

13. William T. Coleman Jr., "In Tribute: Charles Hamilton Houston," *Harvard Law Review* 111 (June 1999): 2148, 2156–57.

14. "Coleman," National Visionary Leadership Project; Coleman, interviews.

15. "Coleman," National Visionary Leadership Project.

16. Charles E. Francis, *The Tuskegee Airmen: The Men Who Changed a Nation,* 4th ed. (Boston: Branden Books, 1997).

17. Letter from William T. Coleman Jr., to Hugo Black, June 20, 1946, Hugo LaFayette Black Papers, Manuscript Division, Library of Congress, box 442.

18. Coleman, interviews.

19. Letter from Hugo Black to William T. Coleman Jr., June 24, 1946, Black Papers.

20. As with Justice Frankfurter, Coleman was not afraid to disagree with Justice Black. On one occasion, Justice Black called Coleman into his chambers to argue about a particular point of law. Coleman politely listened to Justice Black before telling him "if you listen to what you are saying, you will see that you are wrong." Black later told Frankfurter that he had a "very relaxed" law clerk. Coleman, interviews.

21. Personal Papers of Felix Frankfurter, Harvard Law School, reel 9.

22. "Coleman," National Visionary Leadership Project; Coleman, interviews.

23. "Coleman," National Visionary Leadership Project.

24. "Supreme Court Justice to Have a Negro Clerk," *New York Times,* April 27, 1948, 22; "Frankfurter's Negro Clerk to Be First in Court History," *Washington Post,* April 27, 1948, 1.

25. Personal Papers of Felix Frankfurter, Harvard Law School, reel 9.

26. Ibid.

27. Paul A. Freund, *Felix Frankfurter: Reminiscences and Reflections* (Cambridge, Mass.: Harvard Law School, 1982): 12.

28. Of course, many Americans know Richardson for his role in the Watergate scandal, when as attorney general Richardson refused President Richard M. Nixon's order to fire Watergate special prosecutor Archibald Cox. Like Coleman, Richardson would be awarded the Presidential Medal of Freedom by President William J. Clinton.

29. Coleman, interviews.

30. William T. Coleman, Jr. (with Donald T. Bliss), *Counsel for the Situation: Shaping the Law to Realize America's Promise* (Washington, D.C.: Brookings Institute Press, 2010): 87.

31. Ibid., 79.

32. Coleman, interviews.

33. Coleman, *Counsel for the Situation,* 80.

34. Coleman, interviews.

35. It would not be until 1949 that President Harry S. Truman became the first president to nominate a minority to an Article III judgeship, in this case his nominee would be the aforementioned William Hastie. Professor Walter Gellhorn writes that in the 1930s and 1940s "[w]hite law firms, government, business, and bar associations were closed to the Negro. The Negro lawyer had to operate on the fringe of the profession." Walter Gellhorn, "The Law Schools and the Negro," *Duke Law Journal* 1968, no. 6 (Dec. 1968): 1069–70.

36. Constance McLaughlin Green, *The Secret City: A History of Race Relations in the Nation's Capital* (Princeton, N.J.: Princeton University Press, 1967); Flora Bryant Brown, "NAACP Sponsored Sit-ins by Howard University Students in Washington, D.C., 1943–1944," *Journal of Negro History* 85 (2000): 274–86; Irene Osborne, "Toward Racial Integration in the District of Columbia," *Journal of Negro Education* 23 (1954): 273–81.

37. Coleman, interviews.

38. See, generally, Todd C. Peppers, *Courtiers of the Marble Place: The Rise and Influence of the Supreme Court Law Clerks* (Stanford, Calif.: Stanford University Press, 2006); Artemus Ward and David L. Weiden, *Sorcerers' Apprentices: 100 Years of Law Clerks at the United States Supreme Court* (New York: New York University Press, 2006); Edward Lazarus, *Closed Chambers: The First Eyewitness Account of the Epic Struggles Inside the Supreme Court* (New York: Times Books, 1998).

39. *Bolling v. Sharpe,* 344 U.S. 873 (1952); Mark Tushnet, "What Really Happened in *Brown v. Board of Education,*" *Columbia Law Review* 91 (1991): 1867.

40. Coleman, interviews; Steve Neal, "Coleman Was Better Top Court Choice," *Chicago Sun Times,* October 18, 1991.

41. Genna Rae McNeil, *Groundwork: Charles Hamilton Houston and the Struggle for Civil Rights* (Philadelphia: University of Pennsylvania Press, 1983): 218.

42. "Coleman," National Visionary Leadership Project.

43. Linda Greenhouse, "Women Suddenly Scarce among Justices' Law Clerks," *New York Times*, August 30, 2006.

44. Coleman, interviews.

45. Chris Mondics, "Tenacity & Power," *Philadelphia Inquirer*, April 8, 2007.

46. "Coleman," National Visionary Leadership Project.

47. John-Hall, "William T. Coleman, Jr."

48. Mondics, "Tenacity & Power."

49. *Bob Jones University v. United States and Goldsboro Christian Schools, Inc. v. United States*, 461 U.S. 574 (1983).

50. Jay Horning, "A Passion for Law That Never Waned," *St. Petersburg (Fla.) Times*, September 8, 1996.

51. The first black to serve in a cabinet-level position was Robert C. Weaver, secretary of housing and urban development from 1966 to 1968.

52. Steve Neal, "Private, Powerful Bill Coleman Goes Public," *Philadelphia Inquirer*, January 26, 1975.

53. Coleman received honorary degrees from the following colleges and universities: Amherst College, Bard College, Bates College, Central Michigan University, College of William and Mary, Columbia University, Drexel University, Georgetown University, Harvard University, Howard University, Lincoln University, Marymount University, Roanoke College, St. Joseph's College, Saint Michael's College, Swarthmore College, Syracuse University, Tulane University, University of the District of Columbia, University of Pennsylvania, Williams College, and Yale University.

54. Joe Burris, "One Supreme Day, Recalling the Swearing-In of Thurgood Marshall 40 Years Ago," *Baltimore Sun*, October 2, 2007.

55. Joan Biskupic, "One 'Whose Career Made Us Dream Large Dreams,'" *Washington Post*, January 29, 1993.

56. Coleman, interviews.

Fifty-Two Weeks of Boot Camp

What kind of clerks have I got this year, Datch?" Justice William O. Douglas would ask Harry Datcher, his messenger and chauffeur, every year as he rode from the airport to the Supreme Court Building before the opening of the Court on the first Monday in October, leaving behind his summer home in the Pacific Northwest.

"Oh, you've got a good batch this year," Datcher would always tell him, having seen them work slavishly in the office all summer long on piles of appeal petitions, and knowing also that his answer meant little to the man whose mind was already made up on the question.

"I hope so. I hope they are better than last year's," Douglas would always say.[1]

Datcher knew what was coming next. On his first day back to the Supreme Court Building, Douglas liked to slip quietly into his inner office without the clerks noticing. Then the justice would sit in his office and decide how long to wait that first day before summoning that year's victims. Finally, he decided the time had come. "Brrraaacccckkk! Brrraaacccckkk!" sounded the teeth-chattering buzzer on everyone's desk that kept them at Douglas's beck and call, summoning his new assistants into his inner chambers. It was the buzzing sound of a bad dentist's drill that would haunt them for years thereafter.

"I once woke up in the middle of the night, just bolt upright, because I heard that buzzer in my dream," recalls former clerk Lucas A. "Scot" Powe (October term 1970).[2] One buzz summoned a secretary (and heaven help them if the wrong one responded). Three buzzes meant that he wanted Datcher, whose response varied depending on the nature of their working relationship at the time. But two buzzes—*two buzzes*—meant that the Judge wanted "the law clerk." Douglas did not differentiate among his assistants; no matter how many he had, he referred to each of them simply as "the law clerk." Speed in answering the buzzer—summoning them either for more work or a tongue lashing, but never praise—became the most important skill for a Douglas clerk. If a clerk liked to work in shirt sleeves, he would have to develop the dressing skills of a firefighter, wriggling into his suit coat as he ran through the secretary's office heading for the justice's office door.[3]

"After that first buzz it was like a load off their back," Harry Datcher remembered years later with a chuckle. "Until then, they waited and looked like they . . . were waiting to be electrocuted. . . . Oh the Judge loved to terrorize those clerks."[4]

And that was just how Douglas wanted them to feel. His treatment of the clerks in his office was so demanding, frequently so harsh, and so renowned throughout the building that William Coleman, a clerk in Felix Frankfurter's office, later said, "When we came to the Court, all of us thought Douglas was the person we most wanted to work for, but when we finished our clerkship we all agreed that he was the person we least wanted to work for."[5] Even other justices took notice. Justice Harry Blackmun said of Douglas's relationship with his clerks, that he treated them "in ways I couldn't accept. He went too far with them."[6]

Making the First Impression

When the clerks arrived at their job during the summer, they learned that their justice was vacationing in the Pacific Northwest, enjoying the mountains. Their training, provided by the previous year's clerk, was typically brief. Keep up with the work. Be prepared to work through lunch. Keep the memos short and on point. And, if you are married, don't plan on seeing your spouse for the year. Then the pile of petitions for certiorari and appeal were handed over. The new clerk was expected to write a memo on each petition, summarizing its contents so that the justice could decide from his vacation spot whether to vote to accept or reject it. And each memo had to be written just the way the justice liked them.[7]

Douglas liked to make a strong first impression on his new law clerks in an initial treatment that his secretaries called "The Terror."[8] Peter Kay Westen, a prize law school graduate of the University of California at Berkeley, learned firsthand about this process after he survived the rigorous screening to become Douglas's law clerk for October term 1968. Trained by the previous clerk, William Reppy, Westen had been on the job for only a few weeks during the summer, sorting and summarizing certiorari petitions and sending his memos to

Douglas in Goose Prairie when he faced "The Terror." Westen got a message from the secretary at the close of business that he should wait to receive a call from Justice Douglas. Since this would be his first official meeting with his new boss, he was, quite understandably, nervous. Everyone left the building, and Westen waited for the call. Hour after hour passed, and the phone remained silent. When no call had come by 9:00 p.m., Westen wondered whether he should leave the office or continue to wait, but he maintained his vigil.

Finally, at 9:30 p.m., the phone rang. Westen picked it up in the middle of the first ring. "This is Peter Kay Westen in Justice Douglas's chambers," he answered.

"Where's my goddamned pouch!" barked the disembodied voice at the other end of the line. Westen was too stunned to do anything but mumble something while he tried to figure out who was on the phone. "Where's my goddamned pouch!" the voice yelled again. Finally, Westen realized that it was Douglas calling from Goose Prairie, and he was referring to that week's pouch filled with the certiorari petitions that had not yet arrived by mail.

"Mr. Justice Douglas," the young man said quietly, "This is Peter Westen, your new . . ."

"I don't give a damn *who* you are. Where's my goddamned pouch!"

Westen explained the reasons for the holdup, careful to point out that it was not his fault.

"Well, don't let it happen again," yelled the voice. And without further comment the phone went dead.[9]

Westen was hardly alone in knowing from the very beginning that his year with the justice would be challenging. A little more than a month after Lucas A. "Scot" Powe began work for the justice reviewing petitions and sending them off to Goose Prairie, a harsh letter came back along with the latest batch of appeals. Unhappy for some unknown reason with the quality of Powe's memos, Douglas wrote that this was not the sort of job where "we take it off the top of the head," and asked his clerk whether he believed that he was capable of performing his duties adequately. Recognizing that he was being threatened with possible dismissal before he even met his boss, Powe told his wife that it was going to be "a very, very hard year on her" and went on to give a distinguished year of service as a clerk. Much later, after becoming a chaired professor at the University of Texas Law School, Powe still kept the framed letter on his office wall as a reminder of his year of "boot camp" in the justice's service.[10]

The Law Clerks: Selection and Job Duties

Serving as a law clerk for William O. Douglas was a hard year's labor for anyone. Douglas's use of his law clerks changed over the years, as he got older and
as his career changed, but his opinion of them, throughout his thirty-six and a
half years of service on the Supreme Court, never did. After the Court began
increasing the number of clerks in each office in the 1950s, Douglas was always slower to increase the number he hired, because he believed that multiple
clerks "would just talk to each other." Still, whether he had one, two, or three
law clerks in a given year, the justice viewed them the same way—as necessary
and sometimes expendable foot soldiers in his personal judicial army. Douglas
once told his colleague Harry Blackmun, "Law clerks are the lowest form of
human life."[11] And he treated them that way.

"It is common knowledge that clerking for [Douglas] could be like 52 weeks
of boot camp," explained former Douglas clerk Richard Jacobson (October
term 1971). "It is difficult to convey, unless you went through it, the absolute
terror that a Douglas clerk felt at the thought of making a mistake."[12] To this
point Douglas's long-time secretary, Fay Aull Deusterman, added: "Ten thousand dollars a year did not seem enough for what those boys had to put up
with. We all thought they, and we, for that matter, should get combat pay in
addition."[13]

Everyone in the office feared Douglas's unpredictability and wrath over missteps, both real and perceived. "He wasn't the sweetest person you'd ever want
to meet," said Harry Datcher. "He didn't give a damn what people thought of
him. No, William O. Douglas was only happy when he had everyone, his wives,
his clerks, the workers in the building, in his total control."[14]

For all of these young people, some of the brightest young legal minds of
their time, selection as William O. Douglas's law clerk represented the highest honor of their young careers. But they could not know that it would also
become for many of them the most challenging year of their career, even from
the beginning of his tenure on the Court. When Douglas first came to the
Court, he brought with him an assistant from the Securities and Exchange
Commission named C. David Ginsburg (October term 1939) to finish out the
partial first-term in office. Even having worked for Douglas in the executive
branch, Ginsburg found the new job demanding indeed. As Ginsburg recalled,
the pressure came from his boss's compulsion to remain current with the work
of the Court. "When [Douglas] was in the office and in the room, he worked.
. . . He got at it. And did it. He put pencil to paper. And he started writing right

away; just as soon as he had finished [reading] the record of the case. Or he called me and said I want a memo on this subject. He didn't tell you enough to [figure it out]. You would have to guess at it. . . . And he had his yellow tablets and sent it [sic] to [his secretary] Edith [Waters] to get it typed. I always had the feeling of 'get it done.' . . . Any undone job was just hovering at him. He had to get it finished."[15]

Thereafter, upon learning that nearly all of the other jurists selected their law clerks from three eastern law schools—Harvard, Yale, and Columbia— the naturally independent and contrarian Douglas, who was raised in Yakima, Washington, a place he still considered his home, decided that *his* clerks would come from the Far West and Southwest, with the first three coming from the University of Washington Law School. And likely in part because of their lack of prior experience with Douglas and his partial year of experience on the Court, those first clerks, selected initially by Max Radin, a professor of law at the University of California at Berkeley, and from 1950 on by former law clerks, became hard-working, cite-checking assistants, rather than the authors of case memos to help in the writing of opinions as Ginsburg had been.[16]

"He didn't really discuss very many things with me," recalls his first full-term clerk, Stanley C. Soderland (October term 1940). "What I was doing was organizing things for him. I would get notes from him, [saying] 'find me a case on such and such,' and I would get over to the library and look. He wrote his own opinions in long-hand. . . . My job was to read it over and make a suggestion here or there, [and] make sure all citations were right . . . and that is just mechanical."[17]

Partly because of the proximity in age between Douglas, who had come to the Court at age forty, and his clerks, their role continued to be a limited one, as Jed King, who served with Douglas from 1941 to 1942, recalls. "Douglas was young, and wasn't nearly as secure, I don't think, as he got to be later on. . . . If you got a word or two into one of his opinions, you were damn lucky. . . . Douglas would write his own opinion and you had to footnote the past cases, check the records to make sure that the facts were properly stated, and things of that sort. It wasn't very exciting."[18]

By the middle of the war years, Douglas began to develop enough self-confidence in his position that his relationship with his law clerks began changing. Newly hired law clerk Vern Countryman discovered this fact in working on an opinion written by Douglas in a federal robbery case. "I didn't think very much of his opinion and I rewrote the whole damn thing and took it in to him," recalled Countryman, who served as Douglas's law clerk in 1942–43. "He didn't suggest that I had not been appointed to the Supreme Court as a justice, but he just thanked me and took it. When the final version of the opinion came down, there was one sentence [of mine] as a footnote. So that's the only effect I had on that opinion."

Unlike other clerks at the time, who were accustomed to socializing with their justice in and outside of the Court building, Douglas was still all about one thing—work. "He worked me like a goddamned dog," recalls Countryman. "But that seemed fair. I only had to do it for a year. He was doing it for life. So, I never had any trouble with it at all."[19]

Lucile Lomen, the first woman to serve as a law clerk for the Supreme Court when she worked for Douglas during the 1944–45 term, recalled her own observations of Douglas's work ethic and brilliance. "You worked 'til you dropped, and then you picked yourself up and you worked some more. . . . He himself was the fastest, most accurate researcher I've ever seen. He could pull a case out just like that. I'd be researching for three or four days to get what he'd get in three minutes. I don't know how. But he had a very retentive memory. Of course, he'd only been on the Court for five years. And he could remember every line of cases and every opinion he'd written, as far as I could tell. . . . He could tell me at the end of a conference how things were going to go."[20]

But much as they admired his work, his early law clerks could not say the same about his personality. "[H]e was not a warm man," recalled Vern Countryman. "I usually got to the office just a few minutes before he did. He would come through my office to go to his own, and he would come in the back part of the Court. He never stopped to chat. He would say hello and keep on going. But that didn't bother me any. It bothered other people, I know. The only thing he ever talked to me about at the time I was clerking were the cases we had to decide. . . . But that was it. That was it. There were no extraneous social gestures whatsoever."[21]

But as the years went on, and the age gap between the justice and his assistants grew, and his interest in the job began to wane compared to his other outside political interests, his use of his clerks began to change. The man who never saw himself going to the Supreme Court, but rather set his life's goal on becoming president of the United States, evolved over time toward a more liberal and more absolutist position as he got further and further removed from the prospect of ever entering the White House.[22] As he made this transition, he became more and more engaged in extrajudicial political activities, book publishing, and public speaking, and less and less interested exclusively in the technical aspects of his work on the Court. As a result, his assistants' duties also changed. By the late 1950s, in addition to the usual preparation of summaries of appeals petitions, opinion writing, and cite-checking duties, Douglas began asking his clerks to draft occasional majority opinions and one or two dissents, which he would rework extensively before they were released.

Beyond these duties, the clerks became research gofers, searching out answers to the justice's steady stream of questions during oral arguments on all manner of topics. One problem in deciphering the justice's notes, written on three-by-five-inch Supreme Court notepaper, was in trying to figure out what Douglas was working on while he was supposed to be listening to oral arguments, and why he wanted this information, as a clue to where to look for the answer. Since he was rarely giving full attention to the argument before him, and later claimed that he had already "decided all of the cases that would come before the Court," the now somewhat unchallenged and bored jurist might be writing on another case, working on a speech or new book, or just playing with a new idea, while the attorneys dueled before him.

A typical note came to law clerk Charles A. Miller, who served during the October term 1958, during one oral argument session: "Find out the name of the chief of that Indian Tribe in Nebraska. What's the score of the World Series game? What was the year of the Japanese invasion of Manchuria?" Then one day Miller got an even more enigmatic request: "What was the case we decided a couple of decades ago when the dissent said something about the overbearing arm of government bureaucrats?"[23] In the days before computer-assisted legal research, such a request was virtually impossible as the clerks did not even have a list of cases in which he had participated as a starting point for the answers.[24]

Because of their crushing workload, Douglas's clerks had little time to eat lunch and socialize with the other clerks and exchange views about the Court and its work. And should any of the members of his office want to see the historic oral arguments that were occurring in the Court's chambers, they would have to stand behind "The Douglas Pillar," so named because the justice could not see members of the audience in that section of the courtroom from his vantage point on the bench. "Douglas clerks had to do this because their presence in Court during argument always seemed to pose a challenge to him. It meant that the clerk had run out of work and, since that was intolerable, a note with a research project would shortly arrive by one of the messengers," recalled former law clerk Charles Ares (October term 1952).[25]

While the clerks worked around the clock, seven days a week, Douglas could not live with the thought that they might not always be busy. So, in the beginning of the Court term, he would assign them "The Term Project." This

186 | BRUCE ALLEN MURPHY

was a book-length research project, such as "the history of Fourteenth Amend-ment in race relations," on which the clerk had to work and report at the end of the year. To the best of anyone's knowledge, no one ever had the time to finish one of these projects.

By the 1960s, with Douglas still refusing to hire a second law clerk as the other justices had done, and the workload increasing, and with the observation of one Douglas clerk, Jared Carter (October term 1962), that for his boss "court work was low on his list of interests," life in his chambers became even more challenging.[26] Douglas explained his unhappiness to his colleague Justice John Harlan: "The first five years were great; all the great issues came before the court and I had to decide how I felt about them and how I would vote. The second five years were also great, because the issues came around again, and I got to reconsider my views and decide what I really thought. After that it was boring as hell. After fifteen years it was just great tedium."[27] To make matters worse for him, after John F. Kennedy was elected president, the much older Douglas knew that he was destined to remain on the Court for the rest of his life and not serve as president. So he began to take some of that career disap-pointment out on his assistants and his office staff.

Everyone would make sure that they were at the office five minutes before Douglas arrived, always at 7:00 a.m. "Work is energizing!" he would yell at his exhausted office staff as he marched double speed by their desks. Work for the justice had to be done immediately, and without a single mistake. His secretaries would watch in terror at the end of the day as he flipped through the day's letters to sign them. Whenever he found the smallest typographical error, rather than give them a chance to make a correction, he would scrawl a giant X on the letter, and force them to retype it completely.

After a day of hard work dealing with Douglas, everyone would wait until he departed before bolting from the office themselves—sometimes as late as 8:00 p.m. When Douglas found out about this practice, he began leaving, and then returning ten minutes later to see if the work was still underway. Seeing no one, Douglas asked his secretary the next day, "Where was everyone last night? I came back and no one was in the office." The worst nights, though, were the ones when Douglas would leave the lights on in his office to make them think that he was still working, and quietly sneak out the back door. Since no one dared to peek in Douglas's office, that meant they all stayed until well into the night before they realized he had fooled them.[28]

Frequently, clerks were asked to search out material for extended case foot-notes. Law clerk Thomas Klitgaard remembers being asked in the October term 1961: "TJK: If you have time (and not otherwise) would you send me . . . a paragraph for each case in recent years on the procedural requirements for dealing with obscene literature. You might start with Manual Enterprises and work back. I remember Kingsley from New York and the one from Missouri involving a search warrant so broad that the Sheriff could seize anything that was offensive to him (and by Presbyterian standards that could include everything except algebra)."[29] But Douglas, who prided himself on doing all of his own work, still drafted nearly all of his opinions.

Law clerks in this era all learned that none of Douglas's rules were ever to be ignored. "Brrraaaccckkk! Brrraaaccckkk!" rang the buzzer one day in 1965, summoning Jerome B. Falk Jr. "Did you write in this volume?" asked a furious Douglas, his voice quivering with anger as he held up a *United States Reports* volume containing Supreme Court opinions.

"No sir," responded the concerned young clerk.

"I'm relieved to hear that," said the still angry justice. "Books are treasures. They are temples of the intellect. They must be cherished and protected. I couldn't imagine that you were the sort of person who would write in a book." That said, Douglas turned, as was his practice, and pitched the book in the direction of the extended window seat behind him, where Harry Datcher would find them for reshelving at the end of the day. But Douglas was so pumped with adrenaline after his fiery speech that he overshot the seat and instead fired the book right out of the open office window to its loud, cracking demise on the concrete patio a floor below. Falk spun to return to his desk, simply acting as if the incident had never happened, and book preservation was never spoken of in the office again.[30]

By the mid- to late 1960s, Douglas was so involved in his search for other sources of income to subsidize the costs of his three divorces, including his book writing and his outside speaking engagements, and so much less engaged in the work of the Court after realizing that he would never make it to the White House, that he began asking his clerks to write "quite a few" first drafts of judicial opinions.[31]

However, in performing their duties, the clerks inevitably learned that one never went beyond what the justice perceived as being the limits of his assistant's job. Just a week after William Reppy began his year of service with the justice, he learned this lesson well. Having amassed a sterling record at Stanford, and having spent a very pleasant year clerking for Justice Raymond Peters of the California Supreme Court, Reppy did not fully comprehend what Tom Klitgaard, the San Francisco attorney and former Douglas clerk who hired him, meant when he warned that "there would be nastiness" during the year. Reppy was working on a loyalty oath case, *Whitehill v. Elkins*.[32] The justice had drafted an opinion just one day after receiving the assignment, ruling the oath unconstitutional, and told his clerk to "check it." For Douglas, this meant checking the accuracy of the recitation of the facts of the case and the case citations and supplementing footnote sources where the support might be weak. But Reppy decided to go one step further, as his previous employer would have wanted, and redrafted a couple of paragraphs that were a bit garbled, even adding a few sentences resolving a point that had been ignored in the draft. All of these ideas were typed up and carefully stapled to the draft and attached for the justice's consideration.[33]

"Brrraaaccckkk! Brrraaaccckkk!" went the buzzer, as soon as the justice saw the result. When he entered the inner sanctum, Reppy got "The Speech," which a great many of the clerks heard at least once. Have you been appointed by the president and confirmed by the Senate? Douglas asked. No sir, came the automatic response. To which Douglas responded, since that is the case, you are not a Supreme Court justice and should not be writing opinions. Having divested himself of this judgment on this "impertinence," Douglas added, "I'll just throw this in the trash then." Then, like so many other clerks before him, Reppy was told to "get out" and never to return.

"Don't worry," said Douglas secretary Nan Burgess upon being told of the encounter. "We get fired all the time. Just go home now and come back tomorrow." And, when he returned the next day, responding to the first double "Brrraaaccckkk!" Reppy found a cheerful Douglas, who told him, "Keep giving me your ideas." Indeed, when the next draft of the opinion was circulated, the offending paragraphs had somehow been retrieved from the office wastebasket and found their way into footnote 2 of the final text. "You know," explained Fay Aull Deusterman, "that's the way he treated them. He kept them on their toes by doing things like that."[34]

By the late 1960s, as Douglas became increasingly unhappy with the outcome of his career, the declining nature of his health, and the direction of his judicial colleagues' decisions, Douglas's treatment of his clerks became even more harsh. Law clerk Peter Kay Westen saw this change in the October 1968 term when Black Panther Eldridge Cleaver appealed to the Court after the California Adult Authority revoked his parole without a hearing for being in a house where a weapon was present. Because both the California Supreme Court and the U.S. Supreme Court had denied his appeal, Cleaver's lawyers appealed to Douglas for relief as the supervisory justice of the Ninth Circuit.[35]

Douglas asked Westen for a memo on the issue. The young assistant studied all of Douglas's earlier due process opinions before writing his advisory memo to grant the appeal. Unable to locate any Supreme Court precedent to support Cleaver's claim, Westen bolstered his argument by pointing out that his celebrity status, connections, and access to money would prevent him from fleeing and forfeiting the heavy bail.[36]

"Brrraaaccckkk! Brrraaaccckkk!" clacked the buzzer on Westen's desk, commanding him to enter the justice's chambers. "Where did you go to law school, in the gutter?" yelled the justice. "Even if I voted this way, I would be the only one on the Court who would vote this way. As long as Earl Warren is chief justice, this Court will never do anything with the California Adult Authority, which deals with paroles. Earl Warren has been an attorney general under the California system and he regards it as a great liberal advance. The last thing I need is to go out on a limb once more. I'm going to be overturned by the Court anyway. I don't have time to grant this; give it to Thurgood [Marshall]."[37] So Cleaver's appeal was denied.

Douglas wasn't through with this matter. Peering at his assistant coldly he said, "By the way, I've got to leave for a speech and on Monday there will be a woman from the Labor Department in here. She will be my new law clerk, and I'd like you to prepare for her to take over."[38] Fully versed from the secretaries that nearly every law clerk had been fired and rehired at least once in their term, as the hours wore on Westen began to fear that he may well have been fired permanently. "What do I do?" he asked secretary Fay Aull Deusterman, explaining that it was Friday, and on Sunday he was being married with a reception in the Supreme Court Building, to which Douglas had been invited. "Hold the reception anyway," she said, "and see if the justice shows up. Douglas is eccentric, and loves to bully his clerks." "But", she added, "I have never seen anything quite like this."

So Westen held the reception. When Douglas appeared with his wife, Cathy, Westen held his breath and waited for the announcement that he was no longer in the justice's employ. But it never came. The justice simply came up, all smiles as they shook hands, wished the couple much happiness, and the incident was never spoken of again.[39]

Life for many of the clerks became a challenge as Douglas's career began to wind down. By this time, Westen and other clerks were noticing that Douglas did not seem to want to be on the Court. "I always got the impression that he was a very unhappy man, but I never knew what it was that was missing. I suspect that he wanted to be something other than what he was."[40] Two years later, after the appointment of Warren Burger to chief justice along with three other Nixon appointees, and a conservative majority took over on the Court, some sets of Douglas clerks were asked in the summer appeals petition review process to draft hundreds of dissents to denials of certiorari, in anticipation of the Court voting not to hear cases of interest to Douglas. Once Court was in session, they were also asked to write greater numbers of drafts of majority, concurring, and dissenting opinions than in past years. As law clerk Jay Kelly Wright explained the process, "[Douglas] would tell me generally what he wanted, review my draft, and then edit it, usually also asking me to do more work and produce another draft. There was never any doubt about who was deciding the case (him, not me) and whatever I wrote got carefully reviewed. He was not rubber-stamping my work."[41]

On occasion, just to keep his clerks off balance and perhaps thinking that it would motivate them to work harder, Douglas would stop speaking to one of his clerks for no apparent reason. In 1970–71, "Scot" Powe of the University of Washington and a UCLA grad named Dennis Brown were chosen as clerks. But for some unknown reason Douglas decided that he was not going to deal with Brown. "The buzzer would come and the doors [to his office] would swing [as you entered] and then close automatically," recalls Powe. "Dennis would get up once [a day].... Douglas would look up at some point while Dennis was walking in and say, 'Where's Powe?' Dennis would then wheel on one foot because the goal was to be able to make it back through the door without having to retouch it.... As the door would close, Dennis would say to me, 'Shithead wants you.' And so it went for the rest of the year."[42] This treatment was not a negative reflection on Brown. Year after year now, Douglas "froze out" somebody in his office for some perceived transgression, whether it be one of his clerks, a secretary, a Court page, a librarian, or a Court marshal.

Just why Douglas treated these talented young people so harshly was unclear to those around him. Some thought that he was toughening them up by creating adverse circumstances, so that they could succeed in life. "He was an enigma," explained Deusterman. "[H]e was the type of person that felt that you should be working fifty hours a day, you know. I mean he just pushed, pushed, pushed."[43]

Others believed that this genius in the law was less patient with those who were supposed to be brilliant in his field but could not keep up with him. "He had a hard time respecting people that were in his own profession that weren't up to his beat," said Yakima, Washington, buddy Cragg Gilbert, "But you get him off with someone else like a good old sheepherder or a cow-herder or a hiker or climber, any person that he couldn't quite be as good as they . . . and he had a tremendous respect for these kinds of people."[44]

Still others argued that the workaholic justice just wanted someone who was as efficient at "getting the work done" as he was, and that he was impatient with those who could not do so.[45] Or perhaps this was simply a chance for Douglas to vent his frustration at a life and career that he viewed as having gone sour by lording over his office staff in a tyrannical fashion.[46]

Whatever the reason, not every Douglas clerk considered the year's treatment excessive. Thomas J. Klitgaard, one of the men who for a time selected these law clerks, recalled of his year of service in Douglas's office: "Before starting my clerkship, I had heard rumors that the justice was a fearsome taskmaster. I never found this to be so. He was demanding, but fair. He expected the very best, but in looking back through my old certiorari memoranda and other notes to him, I was reminded how tolerant he was of a young clerk's lack of experience."[47]

Whatever Douglas's motivation for treating his assistants the way he did, after watching generations of them come and go, messenger Harry Datcher said, "When you left the judge's office as a clerk, you were prepared for anything."[48]

When Douglas died in 1980, his remains were removed to the First Presbyterian Church of Washington, where he would lie in state in the building's great hall for the next day's viewing by the general public. Groups of his law clerks were asked to stand in an around-the-clock vigil next to the coffin, much like a military honor guard. "This often amused me," recalled former secretary Fay Aull Deusterman. "I often wondered after all the hell he had put them through what the law clerks talked about at three in the morning when nobody was there." Perhaps, she decided, they considered opening up the coffin and peering inside just to make sure that Douglas was not being buried along with his buzzer.[49]

Justice Douglas and His Law Clerks: The Debate Continues

The continuing discussion of the portrait of Douglas's relationship with his law clerks seems to have developed a life of its own. In response to the publication of this author's biography, *Wild Bill: The Legend and Life of William O. Douglas,*[50] twenty-three of Douglas's fifty-four former law clerks gathered in San Francisco in August 2003, seeking to rehabilitate the public image of William O. Douglas in the face of what one clerk complained was "an unflattering portrait of the justice, including the manner in which he allegedly treated his law clerks." More than four years later, based on a survey of thirty-six of Douglas's former clerks, a re-revisionist article, along with a new set of recollections from the clerks, was published in the Supreme Court Historical Society's *Journal of Supreme Court History.*[51] While these newly crafted, "rose-colored" recollections are understandable given the passage of decades since the clerks' service with Douglas, can they be taken as complete and accurate? Knowing that responses to the survey would be used in an article containing their fellow clerks' recollections, respondents might well have succumbed to the very natural, human impulse to avoid making it seem as though their time of service was unusual, less worthwhile, less supportive, or less productive than that of their colleagues. That, and their desire to reassert their own role in shaping American legal history, created a curious result, since they were hardly writing on a blank slate. This was not the first set of personal recollections that had appeared from these clerks, with the first set dating back to 1989 and 1990. In addition, their extensive personal written commentary was bolstered by nineteen extended taped interviews by documentarian Walter Lowe for his 1988 film *William O. Douglas: A Life on the High Court,*[52] and another eighteen interviews of law clerks and Douglas office personnel for the writing of *Wild Bill.*

As flattering as it is for an author that, years later, people are still trying to answer one's work, for all of their efforts to reshape the image of Douglas's treatment of his law clerks, the countercharges are insubstantial, both in their number and nature. They argued the following:

Douglas did not use the term "the law clerk" to refer to all of his clerks;

Douglas was not so casual about his judicial duties in his later years that he prepared short drafts of some of his opinions while traveling to speaking engagements that were dubbed "plane-trip specials";

Douglas did not really tell Harry Blackmun that "law clerks are the lowest form of human life," or, if he did say it, he did not believe it;

Douglas did not use the buzzer to summon and thus terrorize his law clerks; and

Douglas's clerks were not so overworked that they were unable to eat lunch with other clerks or interact with the justice outside of the office.

While the memories and personal feelings of these clerks are very real, they are not the entire record on William O. Douglas. One of the advantages of the biographer is the ability to consult widely, and research extensively, in order to move beyond the recollections of individual characters and to assemble a more comprehensive view of the subject. For instance, while several clerks correctly detected that Douglas did not enjoy being a justice, very few of them were aware that the source of Douglas's diminishing satisfaction came from his frustrated ambition for the presidency. And none of them were contemporaneously aware of Douglas's casual acquaintance with the truth when writing his multiple memoirs, a fact that was clearly evident to his long-term acquaintances and family members who were characters in his narratives.

In seeking to reset the historical record with this new set of recollections, the clerks fail to acknowledge the memoirs of the other firsthand witnesses to their office encounters with William O. Douglas: the members of the Supreme Court staff and his colleagues on the Court. These people, who had the benefit of observing the patterns of behavior over successive years, concluded that the justice "terrorized" his assistants and relished doing so. They were the ones to whom Douglas used the generic phrase "the law clerk," and secretaries, such as Fay Aull Deusterman, were the ones who coined the term "plane-trip special" for the short judicial opinions. There is absolutely no doubt about Justice Blackmun hearing Douglas describe his clerks as the "lowest form of animal life," a comment that Blackmun repeated in my presence, the presence of other Douglas biographers, and a roomful of Douglas law clerks, in his keynote address for the fiftieth anniversary conference on Douglas hosted by the William O. Douglas Institute at the University of Seattle in April 1989. And while some would like us to believe that Douglas did not summon his law clerks with the office buzzer, even this new article concluded otherwise, with at least six of the assistants responding to the most recent survey, whose service ranged from 1939 to 1975, mentioning being buzzed. This is consistent with the recollections of seven other clerks who recalled the buzzer in their 1989 recollections.

While the clerks, in these new recollections, seek to portray a more supportive and sociable Douglas extant during their year of service with him, it is a curiously ambivalent defense of the record. Even though the question was not among those asked by the survey, several clerks acknowledged that Douglas had threatened to fire them, or actually fired them, during their year of service; five of them remembered being "fired" for a time, and others discuss living in fear of being fired or reprimanded.[53]

Was Douglas a different man from the one portrayed in *Wild Bill* and this article? Even in their most recent accounts, with the clerks well knowing that their colleagues would be reading their recollections, it is instructive that the words of several of the clerks offer no reason to think so. Dennis Brown (October term 1970) says that his clerkship was "not a personally rewarding time," recalling that Douglas spoke no more than ten minutes to him in the office during his entire year of service. Carol Bruch (October term 1972) writes, "I have an abiding sadness that the year was so unnecessarily marred by the Judge's unkindness." Stephen Duke (October term 1959) said that Douglas "treated me like a machine," adding that he "never expressed any interest in me or my family and never told me I did a good job on anything." Finally, Alan Sternstein (October term 1975) added, "I have ambivalent feelings about WOD."[54]

That leaves the question of how overworked the clerks might have been, how many times the clerks lunched with clerks from other offices, and how many times they lunched with Douglas or saw him on social occasions outside the office. While I sincerely doubt that history's verdict on Douglas will turn on this argument, I do concede that in some of his more than thirty-six years on the Court, *some* of the clerks had greater associations with clerks from other offices and with the justice than others. In my work, I portrayed what appeared to be the norm, but not necessarily the only experience of a Douglas law clerk. It is interesting to note, in reading all of these accounts, the variation in the extent of these encounters, with some meeting with Douglas only once or twice in a year, while others, who might have had the good fortune of working for him when he was in a good mood or whom he apparently liked better, saw him more frequently.

While the reader can construct his or her portrait of Douglas by assessing the evidence in this essay, *Wild Bill,* and the recollections in the *Journal of Supreme Court History,* perhaps the clerks can concede, despite their shifting recollections, that when former clerks recall being fired, when office staff recall how Douglas relished it when he "terrorized" his assistants, and when fellow justices say that Douglas "went too far with them," that, whatever their individual experience, the overall description of Douglas's behavior is sound. And, individually, it was probably not the rosy year for each of them that some would now like us to believe—memorable, yes; life-altering, to be sure; but rosy, clearly not.

The real issue, then, is not just how Douglas treated his law clerks and others around him, but, more importantly, *why* he did it. Why did a Supreme Court justice, the defender of the rights of the common man, treat those individuals closest to him, including members of his own family, his wives and ex-wives, so poorly? Why was he so unhappy, and how does it help us understand his work and his legacy? Perhaps we can all agree that while some of these clerks await a hagiography of the justice that is more to their liking, Douglas himself was an unhappy genius who felt misplaced on the Court and became disappointed that his life ended up there rather than in the White House. And however the clerks were treated individually or as a whole by Justice Douglas, thanks in part to each of their years of service, his enthralling vision of a free America, a more protective Bill of Rights, greater environmental protection, and a safeguarded right of spatial privacy and personal autonomy was chiseled into case law.

Notes

1. Harry Datcher, interview with author, May 5, 1990.

2. Lucas A. "Scot" Powe, interview with author, June 20, 1989.

3. Fay Aull Deusterman, interview with author, March 3, 1991.

4. Datcher, interview.

5. William T. Coleman Jr., interview with author, July 11, 1979.

6. Quoted also by Melvin Urofsky, "Getting the Job Done: Collegiality in the Supreme Court," in *"He Shall Not Pass This Way Again": The Legacy of Justice William O. Douglas*, ed. Stephen Wasby (Pittsburgh: University of Pittsburgh Press, 1990), 42.

7. This summary is based on the law clerk interviews done by the author for Bruce Allen Murphy, *Wild Bill: The Legend and Life of William O. Douglas* (New York: Random House, 2003).

8. George Rutherglen Recollection, found in "Remembrances of William O. Douglas by His Friends and Associates," edited by William Tod Cowan and Catherine Constantinou and later published as "Remembrances of William O. Douglas on the 50th Anniversary of His Appointment to the Supreme Court," *Journal of Supreme Court History: 1990 Yearbook of the Supreme Court Historical Society* (hereinafter "Douglas Remembrances").

9. Deusterman, interview; Walter Dellinger, interview with author, November 1, 1991.

10. Powe, interview; William O. Douglas to Lucas A. Powe, August 3, 1970, Lucas A. Powe personal papers, Austin, Texas. While Powe bases his account on his year of service for Douglas during the October 1970 term, it became clear after speaking with other clerks that this treatment was a common part of WOD's treatment of his assistants.

11. Address on William O. Douglas by Justice Harry Blackmun, at "The William O. Douglas Commemorative Symposium, 1939–1989," Seattle, Washington, April 16, 1989. Quoted also by Urofsky, "Getting the Job Done," 42.

12. From Richard L. Jacobson recollections in "Douglas Remembrances."

13. Deusterman, interview.

14. Datcher, interview.

15. David Ginsburg, interview with author, August 28, 1989.

16. Melvin Urofsky reports in "Getting the Job Done" that Stanley Sparrowe, the Douglas clerk in the 1947 term, chose the clerks from 1950 to 1967. Thomas Klitgaard, Douglas's law clerk in the 1961 term, screened the candidates from 1967 to 1970. For the

remainder of Douglas's time on the Court, his clerks were screened by a committee of former clerks, Charles E. Ares (1952), William Cohen (1956), and Jerome Falk (1965).

17. Stanley Soderland, interview with author, June 12, 1990.

18. Jed King, interview by Walter Lowe, for his documentary *William O. Douglas: A Life on the High Court*, KYVE-TV, Yakima, Washington (1988), hereinafter "Lowe Videos."

19. Vern Countryman, interview with author, November 14, 1989.

20. Lucile Lomen, interview with author, September 9, 1990.

21. Countryman, interview.

22. For Douglas's "love-hate" relationship with his White House ambitions, see Murphy, *Wild Bill*; and for his move toward an absolutist judicial philosophy, see Lucas A. Powe Jr., "Evolution to Absolutism: Justice Douglas and the First Amendment", *Columbia Law Review* 74 (1974): 371–411.

23. Charles Miller Recollections, "Douglas Remembrances."

24. Such research tasks were made easier for clerks in the 1970s after a case list was reproduced in the Special Subcommittee of the House Judiciary Committee inquiry into Douglas's impeachment in 1970.

25. Charles E. Ares Recollections, "Douglas Remembrances."

26. Jared Carter recollection, in Marshall L. Small, "William O. Douglas Remembered: A Collective Memory by WOD's Law Clerks," *Journal of Supreme Court History* 32, no. 3 (2007): 297–334, hereinafter "Douglas Memory."

27. Ibid.

28. Deusterman, interview; and Datcher, interview.

29. Reminiscences of Thomas J. Klitgaard, "Douglas Remembrances."

30. Reminiscences of Jerome Falk, "Douglas Remembrances."

31. Lewis Merrifield recollection, "Douglas Memory." Other law clerk interviews make clear that on occasion they were asked to assist in book research and writing outside speeches.

32. *Whitehill v. Elkins*, 389 U.S. 54 (1967).

33. William Reppy, interview with author, November 1, 1991. See also Joseph L. Rauh Jr., "An Unabashed Liberal Looks at a Half-Century of the Supreme Court," *North Carolina Law Review* 69 (1990): 213–49.

34. Deusterman, interview. When the opinion was later released and the *Washington Post* criticized the result, taking special care to attack the argument in this one footnote, Douglas chose not to lord this small victory over his clerk. Reppy, interview with author, November 1, 1991. See also William Reppy, "Justice Douglas and His Brethren: A Personal Recollection," *North Carolina Central Law Review* 12 (1980–81): 424–25; and the Reminiscences of William Reppy in "Douglas Remembrances."

35. *Cleaver v. Frank M. Jordan* 393 U.S. 810 (1968).

36. Peter Westen, interview with author, September 26, 1990.

37. Ibid. In making his recommendation, Westen expected Douglas to go along, remembering the *Rosenberg* case in 1953 when the courageous Douglas was willing to

act on his own, issuing an injunction to halt the execution of the atomic bomb spies. But Douglas, remembering the same incident, recalled how quickly he had been reversed by the whole Court. When Douglas refused to agree with a memo saying where he *wanted* to go, relying on how he had voted in the past, Westen realized that he had made it hard for the liberal justice to say no to the appeal. Douglas was so frustrated that he might be opening himself up to attack by the Nixon administration.

38. Ibid. Also, Fay Aull Deusterman, interview with author, March 3, 1991.

39. In the end, Thurgood Marshall did deny the appeal, and Cleaver did skip out on the bail.

40. Westen, interview.

41. Recollection of J. Kelly Wright, in "Douglas Memory."

42. Powe, interview.

43. Deusterman, interview.

44. Cragg Gilbert, interview with author, August 17, 1990.

45. See Urofsky, "Getting the Job Done."

46. Walter Lowe, interview with author, April 27, 1989.

47. Thomas J. Klitgaard Reminiscence, Supreme Court Reminiscences.

48. Datcher, interview.

49. Deusterman, interview.

50. Murphy, *Wild Bill.*

51. Small, "Douglas Memory." While the reader is led to believe that this "collective memory" is a representative sample of the entire group of clerks on all of the questions at issue, that impression can be challenged. It is interesting that some of those clerks found in past interviews to be most critical of their year of service with Douglas either did not participate in this survey or had died, freezing their accounts in past recollections. Furthermore, many of the recollections that were reproduced are limited to short recitations of social encounters with the justice during their year of service and afterward, leaving many of the central questions completely undiscussed.

52. Lowe, "William O. Douglas," KYVE TV Yakima, Washington, 1988.

53. On being "fired," see the Recollections of Bernard Jacob, William Cohen, Ira Ellman, Montana Podva, and William Reppy, and on working under the threat of being fired, see the Recollections of Lucas A. Powe and Richard Jacobson, in "Douglas Memory."

54. Recollections of Dennis Brown, Carol Bruch, Steven Duke, and Alan Sternstein, in "Douglas Memory."

JENNIE BERRY CHANDRA

Lucile Lomen

The First Female United States Supreme Court Law Clerk

Helen Lucile Lomen, the first female to clerk on the U.S. Supreme Court, was thrust into the national spotlight when she joined the chambers of Justice William O. Douglas in September 1944. Subject to a flurry of press coverage, Lomen's arrival at the Court was "widely hailed by women lawyers as a significant step forward in their slow, uphill climb in a profession largely dominated by men."[1] There were high hopes that Lomen would stand out as a female, to blaze trails for women seeking future positions at the Supreme Court.

Lomen, however, sought to deflect attention away from her gender. Publicly, Lomen repeatedly emphasized that she was "just one of ten" clerks.[2] And inside the Supreme Court, Lomen worked tirelessly through many nights, dispelling any notion that she suffered from "feminine frailty." Soft-spoken, but determined, Lomen did not seek special treatment for herself or other females. Across each stage of her legal career, Lomen only asked that her work be judged by the same standards as those applied to her male counterparts.

This essay focuses on Lucile Lomen and assesses her impact—on the legal profession generally, and on female lawyers in particular. With respect to the first inquiry, this essay delves into Lomen's advancement of legal scholarship and constitutional doctrines. There are few published reports of her life, and even in those accounts, her contributions to the legal profession are largely overlooked. This essay seeks to fill that void.

And while the second inquiry perhaps would be contrary to her wishes, any assessment of Lomen's performance before, at, or after the Supreme Court would be incomplete without note of her gender. In an era before the women's rights movement had yet to fully form, Lomen's presence in the workplace challenged professional norms. Lomen faced many critics and skeptics, including Justice Douglas, and she would need to placate and overcome naysayers to advance and establish herself as a leader within the legal profession.

Expanding the Search for a United States Supreme Court Clerk

On December 14, 1943, Justice William O. Douglas wrote University of Washington Law School dean Judson F. Falknor in search of a top law student to serve as his clerk.[3] Douglas required that his clerks be "sharp, clearheaded, [and] hard-hitting."[4] He further narrowed the applicant field with an additional restriction: his clerks could come from only Ninth Circuit law schools. Douglas was circuit justice for the Ninth Circuit for most of his tenure, so he thought it appropriate to limit clerks to that circuit.[5] Applicants who met these criteria then were subject to a careful review of their academic performance. Candidates' letters of recommendation, transcripts, and publications were scrutinized by Douglas personally.

Dean Falknor had a good track record for finding clerks for Justice Douglas: Falknor had supplied four of Douglas's prior five clerks. All were male. Two years before, due to what Lomen later called "a sex problem," the dean had passed over the top student of the law school class (a female), and instead opted to recommend a male student who was close behind in the rankings.[6]

Dean Falknor's focus on male candidates may have been in response to Justice Douglas's preferences. While Douglas later would claim publicly that the war's effect on manpower had no influence on his decision to consider a female clerk,[7] his personal letters and hiring decisions tell a different story. Douglas informed his confidants that he strongly preferred a male clerk from the Ninth Circuit.[8] Despite his need for clerks to type documents in short order, Douglas even had resorted to hiring a one-armed male clerk for the 1943 term.[9]

Justice Douglas, however, reconsidered his preferences when his "canvass of law schools . . . turned up very little" for the 1944 term.[10] World War II had drained law schools of many of their best male candidates. When Lomen enrolled in the fall of 1941, there were six women in her entering class of eighty-four. But by her third year, many male students had been drafted onto World War II battlefields, and Lomen's class dropped to thirty-five students, with women constituting approximately one quarter of the class.[11] Given these conditions, Douglas expanded his search to include female candidates—but he would hire a woman only if she was "absolutely first-rate."[12]

The Makings of a "First-Rate" Candidate

It would be no exaggeration to say that Lucile Lomen was destined to be a pioneer. Lomen, the second of five children, was born in Nome, Alaska, in 1920. As described by Lomen, Nome at that time was "a rather raw town."[13] Snow, which could exceed seventy inches in depth, would coat the ground from September until June. Often the weather would make car travel impossible, so residents would have to travel by foot for extended distances. There was no garbage collection or running water, except in the summertime. Lomen's maternal grandparents, who owned the town's general store, would have to buy food in late September that would last through the following June. Eggs for sale typically turned green by April or May. The water was owned by the richest man in town, and he would charge one dollar (the equivalent of approximately ten dollars today) for sixty gallons. Children were educated in a one-room school house.

In this environment, weakness was not tolerated. The Lomen children were taught to be self-reliant. Lomen's father, Alfred J. Lomen, was a well-known Alaskan entrepreneur who hoped to get rich by selling reindeer meat and clothing items. At a young age, Lucile and her brother Al were enlisted as help for their parents' regular dinner parties (one of the few forms of entertainment possible in Nome). The youngsters would stand on chairs to reach the sink and would wash dishes for twenty or thirty people at a time. According to Lomen's sister Marian Gravenslund, "the family talked about war, education—but not about personal struggles. If you were sick, you stayed in bed, dealt with it, got over it, and went to work. People didn't get angry. They just got on the job, and moved on."[14]

In elementary school, Lomen decided to become a lawyer. She was inspired to join the legal profession by her grandfather Gudbrand J. Lomen, who served as a U.S. district court judge from 1921 until 1932.[15] Observing her grandfather regularly read for long stretches without interruption, Lomen decided that she should be a lawyer, so that she too "could read to my heart's content without anybody bothering me."[16] Later Lomen admitted, "The reason I wanted to be a lawyer really wasn't the best, but it did carry me in the conviction I would be one for many, many years until I found other reasons I should become one."[17]

Scholastic Achievement

Lomen tested her legal aptitude as a student at Whitman College and the University of Washington Law School. The schools, both located near Lomen's (relocated) family, offered financial assistance.[18] Also unlike many institutions of the time, both welcomed women and featured professors willing to devote time to a female student's scholastic development.[19] Lomen, in particular, found mentors and supporters in Whitman College professor Chester Maxey and University of Washington Law School dean Judson F. Falknor.

Lomen gained the respect of Chester Maxey when she penned a notable thesis titled "Legal Restraints on the President."[20] Written while President Franklin D. Roosevelt expanded executive powers, Lomen's manuscript described, but then largely dismissed the importance of, various congressional and judicial restraints that could be used to limit such powers.[21] Instead, Lomen reached a novel conclusion: "The confidence which is felt in a Chief Executive today is the greatest factor in determining which restraints will be applied—though legal restraints do exist, if they are not used they are of little value. So long as he retains the public confidence he may continue to be the principal source of our governmental policies, but history indicates that a President will ride on the crest of power only so long as he has the backing of the people."[22] In effect, Lomen recognized that a president's power is largely derived from personal skills and persuasion.

Lomen's emphasis on the president's ability to garner public support was far ahead of legal scholarship at the time. Literature prior to 1960 focused on the theory and practice of the president's formal authority.[23] Most prominent in this line of work was Edward S. Corwin's *The President: Office and Powers,* which was first published in 1940 (the year of Lomen's thesis).[24] Corwin viewed presidential power as a function of the framers' intentions, constitutional language, and judicial interpretation.[25]

It was only in 1960 that Richard E. Neustadt published *Presidential Power: The Politics of Leadership*[26] and led a shift in the general scholarly emphasis "from formal rules and procedures to . . . actual political behavior of individual leaders."[27] Neustadt—an adviser to Presidents Harry S. Truman, John F. Kennedy, and Lyndon B. Johnson—found that his political experience did not square with traditional presidential scholarship's emphasis on legal formalities, and instead he wrote that presidents' authority is best defined by their individual power to persuade.[28] *Presidential Power* continues to be recognized as the seminal work on the presidency.[29]

Well before Neustadt's book reinforced Lomen's analysis, Lomen's undergraduate adviser, Chester Maxey, concluded that Lomen was "one of the most outstanding major students I have ever had. . . . Miss Lomen is not only exceptional in native mental ability, but also has a prodigious capacity for exhaustive and detailed labor."[30] Lomen had made an ally in Maxey, and Lomen later stated it would prove to be a "very helpful relationship."[31]

Lomen forged a second, very helpful relationship while working as a University of Washington Law School student. For Lomen and other professional women, one positive result of the otherwise trying times during World War II was that it became more respectable for women to work. The number of women working in the civilian labor force increased from 11.97 million in 1940 to 18.61 million in 1945—amounting to an increase of 55 percent.[32] During World War II, 60 percent of American women and men approved of married women's employment, at least as an emergency wartime measure.[33] This public opinion was significantly different from prewar sentiment: in the 1930s, 75 percent of American men and women were opposed to married women working.[34]

When she was in law school, Lomen worked thirty hours per week as a secretary for University of Washington Law School dean Judson F. Falknor. Due to Falknor's position as a War Production Board compliance commissioner, Lomen typed countless opinions—and learned a good deal of administrative law, as the dean briefed her on his decisions. But Lomen's position involved a trade-off: since her job and classes consumed her daytime hours, Lomen regularly had to study late into the night to keep her grades up and meet her goal of finishing the law school's four years of required course work in three calendar years.[35]

Dean Falknor, who took a personal interest in Lomen, was impressed that she led her "class scholastically by a very substantial margin" in spite of demands on her schedule.[36] Lomen studied through the summers and stayed on track to finish her courses in three calendar years. She was the only member of her law school class to be named "Honor Graduate in Law" and member of Order of the Coif, a legal honorary society.[37] "The only fly in your ointment," the dean informed Lomen, "is your sex."[38]

Lomen even managed to devote substantial time to the *Washington Law Review*. She served first as a member and then as vice president of the law review board, and she authored two comments and two law review articles.[39] Both of Lomen's articles received critical acclaim—a notable achievement for any law student, but particularly for one who was working thirty hours per week while shouldering a heavy course load.[40]

Lomen's most noteworthy article focused on controversy surrounding the scope of "Privileges and Immunities under the Fourteenth Amendment."[41] At least some framers of the Constitution held that the Privileges and Immunities

With the SC's striking down of the Voting Rights Act (June 2013) can DOJ still protect the voting rights of the citizens in those states that have passed restrictive — voting laws — in the wake of the SC's decision? (YES)

Clause, which declares that "[n]o State . . . shall abridge the privileges and immunities of citizens of the United States," allows the federal government to intervene if states encroach upon civil rights.[42] But the U.S. Supreme Court, in the *Slaughter-House Cases,* held that the clause only protects privileges incident to national citizenship, privileges the Court limited to rights outside of the "entire domain of the privileges and immunities of citizens of the states."[43] The Court categorized all rights preexisting "the Federal government, its National Character, the Constitution, or its laws" as state rights, so state governments retained sovereign domain over protection of civil rights.[44] Under this interpretation, as Justice Stephen J. Field stated in his dissent, the Privileges and Immunities Clause was reduced to "a vain and idle enactment, which accomplished nothing."[45] *voting in national elections is a civil right.*

Most authors of Lomen's time favored the Supreme Court's narrow construction of the Privileges and Immunities Clause. They predicted that a more literal reading of the clause would lead to dire results, such as "an extremely centralized government."[46] The legal scholars found comfort in the Court's many refusals to find a Privileges and Immunities violation and "[t]rends discernable in recent decisions . . . [that] point to another period of judicial self-restraint in dealing with the enactments of legislative bodies."[47]

Lomen challenged this mainstream perspective. She traced the judicial history of the amendment and found that while "the cases during the past decade have not served to broaden the interpretation of the privileges and immunities clause . . . they serve to indicate that some members of the Supreme Court are thinking of that Clause as a purposeful phrase."[48] Lomen then argued that the Privileges and Immunities Clause, indeed, *should* be treated as a purposeful phrase. She observed that the clause, "on its face, emancipates citizens from state supervision of civil rights," and framers of the clause "intended it should be broadly construed, with full meaning to be given to each word just as it was written."[49] According to Lomen, it was incongruous for Congress to have conceived the clause for protection of the African American man, but then to give him little protection against "state impairment."[50] Lomen criticized a state where "all of the fundamental rights 'which belong to [an African American] as a free man and citizen'—those rights which affected his whole manner of living—were left to the unfettered discretion of the local governments."[51]

Lomen's article, which was awarded the University of Washington Law School's prize for best student essay on constitutional law, attracted the attention of a wide variety of legal scholars. *Tulane Law Review* listed it as one of nineteen "articles of interest" in 1943 periodicals.[52] Lomen was not only the sole female author, but also the sole law student afforded this acknowledgment. And more than fifty years later, Lomen's article continues to receive acclaim. Justice Ruth Bader Ginsburg has commented that the piece "has had remarkable staying power."[53] Lomen's article even is quoted in the text of renowned Harvard Law School professor Laurence H. Tribe's *American Constitutional Law* textbook, and as noted by Justice Ginsburg, Tribe also has included Lomen's article in his Constitutional Law seminar reading list.[54]

Lomen's law review article, as was the case with her constitutional law thesis, was ahead of the legal scholarship of her time. Many preeminent legal scholars subsequently have adopted her position. John Hart Ely, in his renowned book *Democracy and Distrust,* maintains that the Privileges and Immunities Clause "was a delegation to future constitutional decision-makers to protect certain rights that the document neither lists, at least not exhaustively, nor even in any specific way gives directions for finding."[55] Likewise, Harvard Law School's Tribe advocates for a broader construction of the Clause, as he argues that it "seems doubtful that the 125–year-old *Slaughter-House* precedent should continue to command the respect that pre-1999 courts consistently accorded it."[56]

While comprehensive in many respects, Lomen's analysis, however, notably omitted any discussion of how a revitalized Privileges and Immunities Clause might affect women.[57] In the first few years after the Fourteenth Amendment was passed, Reconstruction Era feminists proposed a broad interpretation of the amendment, under which they claimed women were enfranchised.[58] Characterized as the New Departure, the feminists' argument focused on the fact that the framers spoke of "persons" and "citizens" when defining citizenship in Section 1 of the Fourteenth Amendment, and from that inferred that "all persons born or naturalized in the United States" were equally entitled to privileges and protections of citizenship.[59] This argument was marginalized after *Slaughter-House* and other Supreme Court decisions, in particular *Bradwell v. Illinois* and *Minor v. Happersett.*[60] Ultimately feminists concluded that women were far more likely to win rights through an act of Congress, than a Court decision.[61]

There is no clear explanation for why Lomen overlooked this significant dimension to the debate over the Privileges and Immunities Clause. Perhaps her final product is best explained by practical concerns: Lomen may have limited her assessment to racial implications so as to provide a clear focus for her article. She may have predicted race concerns were more likely to garner sympathy during World War II, as many minorities were serving in the military. Alternatively Lomen, like many women after *Minor,* simply may have not thought about the clause having an impact on women, or at least not an impact as great as that for minorities. Or Lomen may have worried that discussing revolutionary implications for women could appear self-serving or could dissuade would-be male supporters from taking up her cause.

Letters of Recommendation

Dean Falknor decided that Lomen's credentials made her a viable candidate for a U.S. Supreme Court clerkship and wrote a glowing letter of recommendation on Lomen's behalf.[62] The letter included what one would expect to see in a letter recommending a law student: a long recitation of achievements in the classroom, journal leadership, and scholarship.[63] But it also contained a few atypical notes. One regarded the applicant's looks, as Falknor remarked that Lomen "had a pleasing appearance."[64] He also made it clear that there were no male candidates close to her caliber. The last line in his letter was explicit: "We do not feel there is any other member of this year's class whom we can recommend to you."[65]

For good measure, Dean Falknor enclosed a copy of Lomen's "Privileges and Immunities under the Fourteenth Amendment."[66] The article was useful to her application in three ways. First, it showed that Lomen was an excellent researcher and writer. Second, it proved she was willing to adopt a minority position, as Justice Douglas often did on the Supreme Court. Third, the article informed Douglas that Lomen approved of his approach to civil rights. Lomen's article cited Douglas's concurrence in *Edwards v. California* for the position that the general right of free transit is a component of national citizenship that is protected by the Privileges and Immunities Clause—an expansive interpretation that Lomen praised and urged others to adopt.[67]

There is no evidence of what motivated Lomen to write her article on the Privileges and Immunities Clause. Perhaps the topic was prompted by Justice Douglas's concurrence in *Edwards* (written two years before Lomen's article), because Lomen wanted to write an article that would support a campaign to make her Douglas's Supreme Court clerk.[68] Regardless, one thing we do know is that Lomen's article, coupled with Dean Falknor's endorsement and her stellar credentials, convinced Douglas that Lomen was worthy of further consideration.

Justice Douglas first contacted Whitman political science professor Chester Maxey, a former fraternity brother, to get an outside assessment of Lomen's abilities. Douglas impressed upon Maxey that "[t]he job of being a law clerk is a pretty mean one. . . . It entails tremendously long hours and is very exacting. As you can imagine, fumbles are costly."[69] Lomen's undergraduate thesis adviser replied almost immediately to the justice's letter.[70] Maxey assured Douglas that Lomen was one of his best major students and stated he had firsthand knowledge that she had done a "brilliant job" in law school.[71] "If you are reconciled to a girl as a law clerk," Maxey stated, "I doubt if you can find one more competent than Lucile Lomen."[72]

Justice Douglas next wrote to former clerk Vern Countryman, whose last year at University of Washington Law School was Lomen's first.[73] Here Douglas made his central concern evident, and asked for Countryman's "reaction as to how you think a girl would fair as a law clerk in these surroundings which you know so well."[74] In response Countryman provided a glowing report of Lomen: "She is a very intelligent woman . . . and she is an indefatigable worker. . . . She appears to be a very healthy young woman, with stamina enough to keep on working long and busy hours. In addition, she is a very pleasant girl, and gets along well with everyone."[75] Countryman concluded by allaying Douglas's concerns about hiring a woman. Although Countryman admitted a female clerk might not be as well informed on other justices' activities as well as a male clerk, Countryman said this factor should not influence Douglas's decision "unless you are satisfied that the man is absolutely first rate, because I'm sure Miss Lomen is just that."[76] History suggests that these words from Countryman, one of the justice's favorite clerks, resonated with Douglas.[77]

With Countryman's recommendation in hand, Justice Douglas finally had enough information to make his decision. On January 29, Douglas wrote Dean Falknor and stated that he would take Lomen as his clerk for the 1944 term.[78] It was the first time in the 154-year history of the U.S. Supreme Court that a woman was made a U.S. Supreme Court clerk.[79]

Working at the United States Supreme Court

Lomen arrived in Washington, D.C., in September 1944. The appointment of the first female clerk made national news, and United Press and Associated Press coverage of Lomen's selection was featured in newspapers across the country.[80] Lomen, however, downplayed the fact that she was the first female clerk. Her remarks to press inquiries were staid and bookish. Lomen stated that she appreciated the appointment most because "there is no finer opportunity for a person serious about the law."[81] And when asked to give advice to other women considering a legal career, the young Lomen responded, "I have no advice to give to women lawyers because I think that any woman desiring to enter into the profession should concentrate on the fact that she is becoming a lawyer. If she is conscientious and sincere, the fact that she is a woman will not interfere too much with her career."[82] Reporters quickly concluded that Lomen most certainly was "not a militant feminist."[83]

At the Supreme Court, various attachés dropped in to "look her over," but Lomen paid no mind to the special attention.[84] Instead she promptly went to work. Lomen's responsibilities included drafting certiorari memoranda that recommended votes on petitions for review; checking first drafts of Justice Douglas's opinions for factual accuracy, style, and logic; and writing memoranda on legal questions that arose when Douglas reviewed a case. Through these tasks Lomen effectively "acted as a sounding board" for Douglas.[85]

Lomen especially enjoyed working on questions involving political and civil rights. As Lomen explained, "It became impossible to remain passive about such questions after close association with one actively and aggressively committed to invoking the full measure of the law to secure those rights."[86]

One of the most significant political and civil rights cases that Lomen worked on was *Ex Parte Endo,* involving a challenge to Japanese internment camps.[87] For *Endo,* Lomen prepared a number of memoranda. One briefed Justice Douglas on the duty of the Supreme Court to construe a statute, if possible, so as to avoid the conclusion that it is unconstitutional. Another considered whether the due process clause of the Fifth Amendment provides a right to equal protection. The Court previously had not ruled that individuals possess a right to equal protection under federal laws.[88] After succinctly summarizing judicial precedent, Lomen, however, urged the novel conclusion that "inferences in . . . [prior] cases" indicate that "the due process clause covers discrimination."[89]

Although the latter analysis ultimately proved moot for the case at hand (Justice Douglas, writing for a unanimous Court, based the decision on statutory grounds),[90] Lomen's expansive interpretation of the Fifth Amendment appeared in subsequent U.S. Supreme Court cases.[91] In particular, Douglas returned to Lomen's argument in another case involving disparate treatment of naturalized citizens. Citing the Fifth Amendment as support, Douglas, writing for the Court, struck down a "statute [that] proceed[ed] on the impermissible assumption that naturalized citizens as a class are less reliable and bear less allegiance to this country than do the native born."[92]

Working on *Endo* and other cases, Lomen served as a Supreme Court law clerk at a time when the role of clerk was expanding, a movement that ultimately changed "the very nature of the Supreme Court."[93] In the early years of the Court there were no clerks, and when Congress first funded the position in 1886, clerks were assigned a rather lowly station.[94] Each justice was allowed to hire one law clerk. These clerks were anything from research aides to "baggage carriers," but substantive issues were almost entirely off limits.[95] William Rogers, clerk to Justice Stanley F. Reed, described the duties of the clerks as "performing the drudgery of judging—looking up citations, examining old cases for apt quotations, and doing general research."[96]

Only in the middle of the twentieth century were law clerks recognized as "proximate to the opinion writing process."[97] According to former clerk John P. Frank, clerks began making substantive contributions to the justices' opinions in the 1940s, and "sometimes clerks [were] allowed to do the bulk of the serious writing for the Justice."[98] Clerks were going from being secretaries and assistants to what Justice Douglas called a "Junior Supreme Court," which now performs a substantive role in producing decisions.[99] This expanded role of clerks was and still is a contested development.[100]

For his part, Justice Douglas preferred to rely less on clerks than his colleagues. Lomen and other Douglas clerks penned certiorari memoranda and occasionally wrote substantive memoranda (like those for *Endo*), but Douglas continued to draft all of his own decisions long after his colleagues had assigned drafting to law clerks.[101] Douglas had a distinct writing style. Critics alleged his writings showed signs of haste;[102] defenders of Douglas admired "the forceful and blunt manner by which he reached the core issue in each case."[103] Churning out more opinions than any other justice, Douglas rarely lobbied for support of his position; he was more interested in getting his opinion heard than accepted.[104]

Lomen, at the end of her career, stated that Justice Douglas was "the fastest worker in the legal field that I have ever encountered."[105] Yet she did not echo those who accused the justice of sloppy work. In a letter to her parents, Lomen expressed her admiration for Douglas: "It was for me a great delight to see [Douglas] break down a complicated case, discard the unimportant and irrelevant, and go to work on its main proposition. His steady devotion to finding the real substance and refusal to be content with accepting the superficial appearance of any case established a standard of professional excellence which cannot be ignored."[106]

Lomen, like other Douglas clerks, hustled to keep up with Justice Douglas's pace.[107] Lomen recounted that it "was generally accepted that the Douglas clerk put in longer hours than the others" and "[y]ou never got any breaks in the office."[108] She worked harder than she did at any other point in her life.[109] Most days she was at the Supreme Court for sixteen hours and would escape to the YWCA to sleep for only a few hours each night.[110] On the weekend she would go to sleep at nine o'clock on Saturday night and not wake up until noon the next day.[111] Lomen later recounted that the 1944 Court decisions represented "a heck of a lot of hours of grief and work and worry for me—and also some of the best hours I ever had."[112]

Lomen found many friends at the Supreme Court. Because she was a woman, Lomen explained that she "got a double dose of whatever social life there was."[113] Lomen was invited to attend baby showers and other social events with the secretaries,[114] and she was befriended by the Court's African American staff.[115] Lomen was the only clerk the staff had known who was not a white male.[116] More typical for clerks, Lomen also was included in the law clerks' dinner parties, but she never felt like she was thought of the same as the other clerks.[117] Rather than focus on the fact that she was a female, Lomen surmised that her differences from the other clerks could be attributed to the fact that she was younger, started later, or, unlike most, attended a West Coast law school.[118]

Justice Douglas did not engage in any office small talk. Lomen, however, was invited to attend several dinner parties at the justice's house, and she reported that there he transformed into "a delightful fellow."[119] Douglas regularly socialized with top Democrats (including Lyndon Johnson, whom Lomen met at one of Douglas's dinner parties), and Democratic leaders seriously considered making Douglas their vice presidential nominee.[120]

Back at work, Justice Douglas was "distant" and "all business."[121] He "never said good morning or goodnight."[122] Lomen and Douglas both studied at Whitman, but she later stated that "he never mentioned Whitman as far as I can remember."[123]

Justice Douglas failed to provide much, if any, feedback on Lomen's performance. When working at the Supreme Court, Lomen wrote to Professor Maxey at Whitman College, because she was concerned that she "never heard [Douglas's] salty language for which he was reputed."[124] Maxey replied to her and said, "You're doing all right then."[125] Douglas, according to Maxey, never said anything good.[126] For Lomen, Maxey's reply was "the closest [she] ever came to having an evaluation."[127] Lomen came to the conclusion that "I don't think any of us did as well as he did, so there was no reason to praise anyone."[128]

Justice Douglas later told Dean Falknor that Lomen got along "very well."[129] This account was reaffirmed in his autobiography, which characterized Lomen as "very able and very conscientious."[130] In his future hiring decisions, Douglas seemed much more responsive to hiring a female clerk after his experience with Lomen. Starting in 1946, Douglas relied on a committee (comprised of friends and former clerks) to select his clerks, and while the committee did not hire another woman until two were employed in 1972,[131] the justice made it clear that his only stipulation was that the clerk come from the Ninth Circuit.[132] Women were given serious consideration.[133] And on learning his committee hired two females in 1972, Douglas enthusiastically replied, "That's Women's Lib with a vengeance!"[134]

At the end of Lomen's clerkship, Justice Douglas offered to find Lomen a job. But she informed him she already had two offers. Lomen was deciding between a position at the U.S. Department of Justice and another at Graham, Green, Burnett, Howe & Dunn, a Washington State law firm. Douglas recommended that she return to her roots, and Lomen decided to heed his advice.[135] She headed back west.

The Washington State Attorney General's Office

Lomen's career plans changed soon after she returned to Seattle. Lomen dreamed of being a judge like her grandfather, and she believed that a successful local law firm practice was an ideal stepping stone to such an appointment.[136] But upon arriving in Seattle in 1945, Lomen soon "learned that the law firm really was not the place for me at this time."[137] She explained, in a letter to Justice Douglas, that several men had returned from military service, and she now was slated to become an understudy for the partner in charge of tax work.[138] "The firm was somewhat embarrassed," she added, "because they had offered me $250 whereas the returned veterans . . . were getting only $200."[139] So even before she started work at the firm, Lomen began to look for a new job.[140]

"One by one my haphazard dreams," the young Lomen wrote, "are blown away by the cold wind of this practical world."[141] She contemplated practicing law in Alaska and getting into politics, but she doubted that she could attract any really good clients.[142] Lomen also dabbled with the idea of teaching. She considered the idea of applying for a Sterling Fellowship to get a postdoctoral degree at Yale, but she dismissed this idea as impractical too: "The horrible part of it is that I know I could not get the fellowship on my own merit," concluded Lomen.[143]

Lomen's story is unusual given positions for which she vied, but the trends it represents were common for the 1940s. In his seminal history of American women, William Chafe states that "temporarily at least, the war caused a greater change in women's economic status and outlook than a prior half century of reform and rhetoric," but after the war many women confronted the same sort of disappointments as before the war.[144] Within one year after the war ended, the female labor force shrank to a size closer to that of 1940 than to that of 1944.[145] Women in higher-wage industrial jobs were forced out of their positions by seniority rules and institutional changes adopted after the war.[146] Similarly the female professional workforce shrank in size.[147] Susan B. Anthony characterized this decline in female attorneys and school superintendents as evidence of the "crack-up" of the U.S. women's movement.[148]

In the end, Lomen was one of the luckier women. While she did not attain the promised law firm job and never claimed an academic or political position, Lomen did find professional employment at the Washington State attorney general's office in the fall of 1945. Attorney General Smith Troy, who was just back from the European Theater, hired Lomen to be an assistant attorney general. After Lomen was hired, one of the oldest men in the office told her, "I don't know anything about you but you must be good."[149] Attorney General Troy apparently had a bad experience with a female lawyer in the past, and after the female lawyer left the office, the tenured employee recounted that Troy said "he would never hire another woman lawyer."[150]

It is unclear how exactly Lomen got the job in the attorney general's office. Perhaps her impeccable credentials, such as the Supreme Court clerkship, convinced Troy to change his mind. Or perhaps Vern Countryman persuaded Troy to hire Lomen. After serving in the army, Countryman took a position in the Washington attorney general's office, and given his high opinion of Lomen, Countryman again may have interceded on her behalf.

In any event, Lomen's position at the attorney general's office was not glamorous—she was the "lowest paid member of the attorney general's staff"— but the "extremely interesting and varied" work offset her small salary.[151] While her Supreme Court clerkship seemed to have little influence on her formal position,[152] informally Lomen benefited by being assigned work on appellate cases. Senior attorneys would come to her, because according to Lomen, "they knew I had seen more briefs in my year with Douglas than they would see in a lifetime."[153] Lomen preferred appellate work to trial work and was happy to take on the additional assignments.[154] She ended up representing the state before the Washington State Supreme Court in more than a dozen cases, both on briefs and in oral argument.

From all reports Lomen was a model employee,[155] and once he saw her work product, Attorney General Troy worked hard to keep her in his office. When she took a leave of absence to accompany her grandparents to their Northern European homeland, Troy sent Lomen a telegram that reiterated his promises that increased responsibility and a raise awaited her upon returning home.[156] (Sending the telegram overseas was a costly proposition: Lomen recounted that a seven-word telegram back to Seattle cost her grandfather fifteen dollars —an amount equivalent to more than one hundred dollars today.)[157] When Lomen returned to his office, Troy made good on his word.

Lomen's able performance in the attorney general's office challenged negative stereotypes of women in the workplace, and here too her example likely helped open doors for future female attorneys. Troy found Lomen to be an "attorney of outstanding ability as trial lawyer and keen legal analyst."[158] And despite the alleged declaration that he would never again hire a woman, Troy employed two more female attorneys during Lomen's tenure.[159]

A Legal Career at General Electric

In early 1948 Lomen decided to leave the attorney general's office to assume what was to be the first of a series of positions at General Electric (GE). GE needed an attorney to handle legal matters for Richland, a mill town of 27,000 that served as part of the company's Hanford Atomic Products Operation (Hanford Works). The position was a cross between a city attorney (advising the community council) and an attorney for a landlord owning stores and thousands of dwelling units. A local attorney recommended Lomen for the job because of her familiarity with Washington State law.[160]

Lomen almost was passed over for the GE position. The vice president in charge of the Hanford Works operation "had a couple of sad experiences with women" and refused to give Lomen a hearing.[161] Hanford Works chief counsel Lewis F. Huck, however, wanted to hire Lomen and believed that the "prejudices of his superior [could] be overcome."[162] Huck requested that Lomen solicit letters of recommendation from Justice Douglas and others for whom she had worked. Lomen complied and asked the justice to write a letter on her behalf.[163]

Within days, Justice Douglas mailed out a letter of recommendation in support of Lomen's application.[164] Writing to Huck, Douglas praised Lomen both personally and professionally: "Miss Lomen is a person of high character and integrity and a lawyer who practices the high ideals of the profession. She has a fine mind and a firm foundation in the law. She has a great capacity for work, is thorough, reliable and dependable in every respect. She is straight-forward, honest and loyal. I am confident that all those who know Miss Lomen would likewise testify as to her ability, industry, and character."[165] In summary Douglas recommended Lomen "without any qualifications whatsoever."[166] With this and other ringing endorsements,[167] Huck's superior acquiesced, and Lomen joined the Law Division of the GE Nucleonics Department.

In ensuing years Lomen became a literal poster child for GE's self-proclaimed "policy of offering opportunity to many young people . . . who can achieve personal success."[168] In 1950 GE included a full-page advertisement on Lomen in four weekly *Scholastic* magazines, which at the time were read by 761,000 high school students across the United States.[169] Both the background and responsibilities of the female "Atomic Town Attorney" were featured, and GE reported that the advertisements "rival[ed] the editorial part of the magazines in interest."[170]

Lomen subsequently received a series of promotions. She was transferred to San Jose, California, to serve as a lawyer for GE's first private nuclear operation, where she applied for and received many first-ever licenses for building nuclear reactors.[171] Lomen also drafted contracts for the sale of nuclear reactors, a challenging practice that lacked any framework of accepted commercial assumptions and practices domestically or abroad.[172] Lomen next was marked for promotion to the top legal post at GE's Aircraft Nuclear Propulsion Department, where she served as the first female chief counsel for a GE department.[173] This role was followed by GE appointments as counsel for the Aircraft Accessory Turbine Department, nuclear energy projects counsel for the International General Electric Export Division, and counsel for the General Learning Corporation.

Lomen, despite these professional advancements, never exhibited much outward interest in obtaining a better title or salary.[174] For example, Lomen, even in retirement, stated that it was "all right by me" that GE general counsel Ray H. Luebbe had refused to consider her (or any other woman) for a counsel role; when hiring restrictions were in place, Lomen said that she "was enjoying the legal questions that I had" in San Jose.[175] This positive attitude helped Lomen gain acceptance among male coworkers. Unlike raw ambition, her apparent focus on "finding interesting legal work" was not inherently threatening.[176] Fritz Heimann, who was Lomen's supervisor in San Jose and ultimately rose to second in command in the GE legal department, recounted that Lomen "gave almost no indication of being driven by ambition. She gave the impression that she really enjoyed being a team player rather than being a leader of the group, and to a point, that helped offset concerns about her being a woman."[177]

For her final promotion, Lomen was moved to GE headquarters to serve as the company's corporate affairs counsel. This role, among other responsibilities, required Lomen to oversee all of GE's executive compensation and benefit programs and tackle yet another cutting-edge legal topic: the Employee Retirement Income Security Act of 1974 (ERISA).[178] ERISA's far-reaching regulation of private employee pension plans was a significant new development, as before 1974 there was minimal federal regulation of employee pension plans. With little government guidance on how to implement specific statutory provisions, Lomen, just as she had in addressing nuclear energy issues, devised novel compliance strategies. Her work ultimately affected thousands of GE employees and billions of dollars in corporate assets.[179] Other companies looked to GE as a model for their own best practices.

Lomen's decisions on how to administer the pension portfolio led her to clash with GE chief executive officer Jack F. Welch. When he took the helm in 1981, Welch "set out on a mission to see GE become the world's most valuable company,"[180] and he refused to increase payouts or add an automatic cost-of-living adjustment to pension checks of GE retirees.[181] While the plan's surplus grew to more than $20 billion under his watch, Welch directed that interest earned from pension plan funds be allocated to corporate revenues instead.[182] Lomen protested. According to her sister Ann Sandstrom, Lomen viewed it her duty to remain "squeaky clean and very idealistic," and she sympathized with retirees who suffered a significant loss of purchasing power.[183]

In her capacity as corporate affairs counsel, Lomen stood out as an "elder statesman" for other female lawyers.[184] In the 1970s and 1980s, it was rare to see a woman in the upper echelons of business, and Lomen's colleagues consistently applauded her work.[185] Recognizing her accomplishments, *Business Week* named Lomen one of the "Top 100 Corporate Women" in 1976.[186] Looking at the other women featured in the magazine's list further highlights how unique Lomen's role was: only five of the women listed (including Lomen) were practicing lawyers.[187]

As Lomen rose to a position of prominence, however, she never doled out special favors to women behind her. She cautioned that only women of a certain "temperament" should aspire to be a lawyer: "There has to be a willingness to consider that the job is your life—it can't be shut off after eight hours. It means taking brief cases home for work in the evening. It means putting the job first all the time."[188] By all accounts, Lomen never adopted a set of beliefs more "revolutionary" than "if you work harder, you can get anywhere."[189] Indeed, the only women's cause that Lomen is known to have supported was adoption of the Equal Rights Amendment[190]—advocacy that, at the time, placed Lomen at odds with many prominent feminist organizations, which feared a constitutional guarantee of equal rights could be used to invalidate protective labor laws applicable only to women.[191]

Effectively Lomen expected female lawyers to follow her example—and it was not an easy one to follow. She was careful not to draw any attention to the fact that she was female.[192] Lomen regularly worked long hours and through weekends,[193] and she devoted relatively little time to organizations that promoted advancement of females in the workplace.[194] Lomen also never assumed the traditional female roles of wife and mother. Instead she shared her home with close friend Ruth Hill—a living arrangement that attracted little scrutiny, because it was common for single women to live together for financial reasons.[195] Observed Lomen's sister Ann Sandstrom, decisions Lomen made in her personal life helped facilitate her career advancement, because male superiors could "deal[ ] with her like she was one of them" and never had to worry about whether she could devote time to her work.[196]

Despite Lomen's best efforts, Lomen's friend Ruth Hill admitted that Lomen surely "wasn't promoted as if she . . . were a man."[197] But Lomen "accepted life as it came . . . and made the best of it."[198] Lomen did not complain about any discrimination she faced as a woman.[199] She firmly believed that a female lawyer "had to pull [her]self up."[200]

Conclusion

After working for GE for thirty-five years, Lomen retired in 1983, and she and Ruth Hill relocated to Seattle in 1989.[201] Lomen's return to Washington was to be her final move. On June 21, 1996, Lomen died of esophageal cancer.

Lomen's obituary ran in the *Seattle Post-Intelligencer* on June 27, 1996.[202] The week after her death the Seattle newspaper reported upon and published detailed obituaries of some select individuals, including a health economist and a local mountain climber.[203] But Lomen was not featured similarly. Instead her obituary ran among the paid obituaries, and her life achievements were listed in one short paragraph.[204] There was no mention of the fact that Lomen had achieved a number of notable firsts, including serving as the first female U.S. Supreme Court clerk and first female corporate counsel at GE.[205]

Lomen, however, might not have been offended by her obituary's modest treatment. She received many awards over the years,[206] but according to her sister Marian Gravenslund, they meant "nothing to her. Lucile just had [her] awards . . . stuck in a box."[207] Lomen did not seek out special recognition for being a female professional in a workplace dominated by men. "I was just a lawyer," Lomen remarked close to the end of her life, "and that's all I wanted to be."[208]

Notes

The author thanks Ann Sandstrom and other members of Lucile Lomen's family, Lomen's friends, and the Whitman College and Northwest Archives for providing a wealth of information about Lomen's life; Stanford Law School professor Barbara Allen Babcock, Stanford Law School Library deputy director Erika Wayne, Stanford professor David J. Danelski, Eric Einhorn, and Mary Ann Berry for thoughtful comments on my research and analysis; Roanoke College professor Todd Peppers for ensuring this essay meets the high standards of this book; and my husband Ravi Chandra for offering encouragement and valuable feedback during each stage of research and writing.

1. Ray Pierre, "Girl Has Clerkship in Supreme Court," *Eastern Chronicle*, December 21, 1944, 8. Other news stories include the following: United Press, "Miss Lomen to Be First Girl to Aide Justice," *Seattle Times*, April 28, 1944, 4; United Press, "Woman Gets High Court Clerk Post," *Portland (Ore.) Journal*, April 27, 1944; United Press, "Woman Shatters 154–Year Record," *Charleston (S.C.) Courier*, April 27, 1944. Some of the press clippings found in Lomen's personal records, such as those referenced here, did not contain all the information needed for complete citations.

2. Lucile Lomen, interview by Marilyn Sparks, May 20, 1991, transcript, Whitman College and Northwest Archives, Penrose Library, Walla Walla, Wash. (hereafter Sparks Oral History).

3. William O. Douglas to Judson F. Falknor, December 14, 1943, William O. Douglas Papers, Manuscript Division, Library of Congress (hereafter Douglas Papers).

4. William O. Douglas to Thomas J. Klitgaard, November 25, 1968, Douglas Papers.

5. William O. Douglas to Jerome B. Falk, November 4, 1977, Douglas Papers.

6. Sparks Oral History.

7. United Press, "Miss Lomen," 4 ("Douglas says he appointed Miss Lomen . . . not because of the war's effect upon the manpower situation").

8. See, e.g., William O. Douglas to Chester C. Maxey, December 27, 1943, Douglas Papers.

9. The clerk was Eugene A. Beyer Jr.

10. Douglas to Falknor, December 14, 1943.

11. Campuswide only 400 undergraduate and graduate students, including 285

women, completed their degrees in May 1944, as compared to 1,150 students in 1940. "400 Graduates in Smallest U. of W. Class in 10 Years," *Seattle Times,* May 21, 1944, 12.

12. William O. Douglas to Judson F. Falknor, March 24, 1943, Douglas Papers.

13. Lucile Lomen to Ray Pierre, March 28, 1947, Lucile Lomen Collection, Department of Special Collections and University Archives, Stanford University Libraries (hereafter Lomen Papers).

14. Marian Gravenslund, telephone interview with author, March 14, 2004 (hereafter Gravenslund Interview).

15. Judge Lomen previously served as mayor of Nome, Alaska.

16. Pam Pallis, "Woman Named to Top Legal Post," *Daily Advance,* May 6, 1970, 8.

17. Sparks Oral History. Reasons notwithstanding, Lomen's unwavering conviction to become a lawyer was of no surprise to her family. All of the Lomen females sought out independent careers. Of Lomen's three sisters, Jean wanted to be an interior decorator, Ann received a degree in physics, and Marian went on to own a retail store. And, in fact, Lucile Lomen would not be the first female lawyer in the family. Lomen's aunt Laura Volstead graduated from George Washington University Law School in 1918. "Aunt Laura," as she was known to Lomen, was the only child of the famous protectionist U.S. senator Andrew J. Volstead, and she used her legal knowledge to be a better host to her father's guests after her mother died at a relatively young age. Laura Volstead also served as a legal adviser to her father and clerk of the Judicial Committee of the House of Representatives.

18. When she was fourteen, Lomen moved to Seattle, Washington. Her parents wanted her older brother Al to be exposed to life outside of Alaska before starting college at the University of Washington, and they decided Lucile should join him. Eventually Lomen's entire family moved to Seattle.

19. For example, Harvard Law School began accepting women only in 1950.

20. Lucile Lomen, "Legal Restraints on the President" (A.B. thesis, Whitman College, 1941), Lomen Papers.

21. Ibid., 1–2.

22. Ibid., 90.

23. Kenneth R. Mayer, *With the Stroke of a Pen* (Princeton, N.J.: Princeton University Press, 2001), 12.

24. Edward S. Corwin, *The President: Office and Powers* (New York: New York University Press, 1940).

25. Corwin's discussion of the president's office and powers was expressly intended to be "primarily a study in Public Law—in American constitutional law, to be precise." Ibid., vii.

26. Richard E. Neustadt, *Presidential Power: The Politics of Leadership* (New York: Wiley, 1960).

27. Joseph M. Bessette and Jeffrey Tulis, "The Constitution, Politics, and the President," in *The Presidency in the Constitutional Order,* ed. Joseph M. Bessette and Jeffrey Tulis (Baton Rouge: Louisiana State University Press, 1981), 4–5.

28. Neustadt contends that a president's power "is the product of his vantage points in government, together with his reputation in the Washington community and his prestige outside." Neustadt, *Presidential Power,* 150.

29. For an assessment of Neustadt's book, see Charles O. Jones, "Richard E. Neustadt: Public Servant as Scholar," *Annual Review of Political Science* 6 (June 2003): 8 ("Published over 40 years ago, [*Presidential Power*] is still assigned in undergraduate and graduate courses. Why? Possibly because it is a good, persuasive, enduring book that reads well. It defies standard political science classification, yet compels political scientists' notice. No one had written a book like it then. No one has since").

30. Chester Maxey to William O. Douglas, January 4, 1944, Douglas Papers. Maxey was not alone in his assessment. Stephen B. Penrose, who served as Whitman's president for forty years, stated that Lomen was "one of my favorite Whitman daughters": she demonstrated a "rare combination of brains, character, and common sense." Stephen B. Penrose to William O. Douglas, January 5, 1945, Douglas Papers.

31. Sparks Oral History.

32. U.S. Department of Commerce, Bureau of the Census, *Statistical Abstract of the United States: 1952* (Washington, D.C.: U.S. Government Printing Office, 1952), § 8, 178 (hereafter *1952 Census*).

33. Rochelle Gatlin, *American Women since 1945* (Jackson: University Press of Mississippi, 1987), 1.

34. Ibid.

35. This was before the University of Washington Law School limited its coursework requirements to three years.

36. Judson F. Falknor to William O. Douglas, December 20, 1943, Douglas Papers.

37. It should be noted, however, that Lomen's graduating class was particularly small. University of Washington Law School graduated only eighteen students in May of 1944, and only three of those students had completed an L.L.B. degree. University of Washington, Program of Exercises for the Sixty-Ninth Commencement, May 12, 1944, Lomen Papers.

38. Sparks Oral History.

39. Lucile Lomen, "Recovery of Damages for Private Nuisance," *Washington Law Review and State Bar Journal* 18 (1943): 31–38 (comment criticizing a contemporary Washington State Supreme Court decision that held a factory did not owe damages to local residents when it caused them discomfort or annoyance); Lomen, "Privileges and Immunities Under the Fourteenth Amendment," *Washington Law Review and State Bar Journal* 18 (1943): 120–135; Lomen, "Union Security in War-Time," *Washington Law Review and State Bar Journal* 18 (1944): 133–159 and *Washington Law Review and State Bar Journal* 19 (1944): 188–203 (published in two parts in two volumes); Lomen, "Resolving Ambiguities against the Conditional Sale," *Washington Law Review and State Bar Journal* 20 (1945): 112–121 (comment attempting to define circumstances that would cause the Washington Supreme Court to construe a conditional sales agreement as a chattel mortgage).

40. See, e.g., "Practising Lawyer's Guide to the Current Law Magazines," *American Bar Association Journal* 30 (1944): 634 (stating that Lomen's article titled "Union Security in War-Time" was "the most comprehensive review which has been published, as to both the decided cases and the development and history of the highly controversial policy of 'union security' by government fiat").

41. Lomen, "Privileges and Immunities."

42. U.S. Const. amend. XIV, § 1. Representative John Bingham, principal architect of the amendment, and Senator Jacob Howard, the amendment's sponsor in the Senate, both asserted that the Privileges and Immunities Clause requires the states to obey the Bill of Rights, and not a single senator or congressman contradicted them. Michael Kent Curtis, *No State Shall Abridge* (Durham, N.C.: Duke University Press, 1986), 91.

43. Slaughter-House Cases, 83 U.S. 36, 77 (1873).

44. Ibid., 79.

45. Ibid., 96 (Field dissenting).

46. D. O. McGovney, "Privileges or Immunities Clause: Fourteenth Amendment," *Iowa Law Bulletin* 4 (1918): 226. See also Pendleton Howard, "The Privileges and Immunities of Federal Citizenship and *Colgate v. Harvey*," *University of Pennsylvania Law Review* 87 (1939): 279; Stanley C. Morris, "What Are the Privileges and Immunities of Citizens of the United States?," *West Virginia Law Quarterly* 28 (1921): 54–56.

47. Howard, "Privileges and Immunities," 279.

48. Lomen, "Privileges and Immunities," 135.

49. Ibid., 121.

50. Ibid., 124.

51. Ibid.

52. "Articles of Interest in Current Legal Publications," *Tulane Law Review* 18 (1943): 179.

53. Ruth Bader Ginsburg, "The Supreme Court: A Place for Women" (Wilson Lecture, Wellesley College, Wellesley, Mass., November 13, 1998), http://www.wellesley.edu/PublicAffairs/Releases/1998/111098.html.

54. Laurence H. Tribe, *American Constitutional Law*, vol. 1, 3rd ed. (Mineola, N.Y.: Foundation Press, 2000), 1309; Ginsburg, "Supreme Court."

55. John Hart Ely, *Democracy and Distrust: A Theory of Judicial Review* (Cambridge, MA: Harvard University Press, 1980), 28.

56. Tribe, *American Constitutional Law*, 1: 1321.

57. Lomen only cited two related women's rights cases in a footnote, in a manner that was surprisingly ungendered: Lomen characterized *Bradwell v. Illinois* (83 U.S. 130 [1873]), which denied women the right to practice law, as a decision that held that the Privileges and Immunities Clause did not provide the right to practice law in a state court; she described *Minor v. Happersett* (88 U.S. 162 [1875]), which refused to grant women suffrage rights, as a decision that ruled the right to vote in an election was excluded from the Privileges and Immunities Clause. Lomen, "Privileges and Immunities," 125n16.

58. Ellen Carol DuBois, *Woman Suffrage and Women's Rights* (New York: New York University Press, 1998), 116.

59. Ibid., 118.

60. *Bradwell v. Illinois*, 83 U.S. 130 (1873); *Minor v. Happesett*, 88 U.S. 162 (1875).

61. After giving up on the Privileges and Immunities Clause argument, *Minor* suffragists instead pushed for a separate constitutional amendment that would give women the right to vote. DuBois, *Woman Suffrage*, 131. This alternate approach proved successful with the ratification of the Nineteenth Amendment in 1920.

62. Falknor to Douglas, December 20, 1943, Douglas Papers.

63. Ibid.

64. Ibid.

65. Ibid.

66. Ibid.

67. Lomen, "Privileges and Immunities," 133–34 (citing *Edwards v. California*, 314 U.S. 160 [1941]).

68. This motivation would help explain why Lomen did not mention how women are affected by a narrow reading of the Privileges and Immunities Clause.

69. Douglas to Maxey, December 27, 1943.

70. Maxey to Douglas, January 4, 1944.

71. Ibid.

72. Ibid.

73. William O. Douglas to Vern Countryman, January 10, 1944, Douglas Papers.

74. Ibid.

75. Vern Countryman to William O. Douglas, January 12, 1944, Douglas Papers.

76. Ibid.

77. Justice Douglas characterized Countryman, who later became dean of the University of New Mexico Law School at Albuquerque and a noted Harvard Law School professor, as an "extraordinary" man. William O. Douglas, *The Court Years, 1939–1975: The Autobiography of William O. Douglas* (New York: Random House, 1980), 170. Lomen described Countryman as "over the years the one [clerk] who seemed closest to Douglas." Lucile Lomen, "Lucile (Lucy) Lomen" (unpublished manuscript, 1991), 4 (used to create an entry on Lomen in the Class of 1941 Reunion Booklet (1991), 15, Lomen Papers), Lomen Papers [hereafter Lomen Autobiography]. Countryman, it appears, held a similarly high opinion of Douglas. Writing a flattering book on Douglas, Countryman discussed how to evaluate the performance of a jurist and concluded that "Justice Douglas passes the test with flying colors." *The Judicial Record of Justice William O. Douglas* (Cambridge, Mass.: Harvard University Press, 1974), 381.

78. William O. Douglas to Judson F. Falknor, January 29, 1944, Douglas Papers.

79. Lomen, however, was not the first woman to be employed at the U.S. Supreme Court: all the justices' secretaries in 1944 were women. United Press, "Miss Lomen," 4.

80. See, e.g., ibid.; United Press, "High Court Clerk Post"; United Press, "154–Year Record."

81. "First Woman Law Clerk of High Court Likes Her Job," *Evening Star,* October 3, 1944.

82. Lomen to Pierre, March 28, 1947.

83. "First Woman Law Clerk."

84. Ibid. (quoting Lomen).

85. Pallis, "Woman Named," 8.

86. Lucile Lomen, April 15, 1964 (testimonial on the 1944 term written for an unknown purpose—perhaps related to Justice Douglas's twenty-fifth anniversary on the bench) (hereafter Lomen Testimonial).

87. *Ex Parte Endo,* 323 U.S. 283 (1944).

88. The U.S. Supreme Court had only held that the Fourteenth Amendment prohibited states from violating equal protection.

89. Lucile Lomen to William O. Douglas, memorandum, October 26, 1944, Douglas Papers.

90. Justice Douglas held that Endo was entitled to immediate release from internment. 323 U.S. at 304. Soon thereafter the World War II exclusion orders were suspended, and Japanese Americans were allowed to return home.

91. For example, *Bolling v. Sharp,* 347 U.S. 497, 499 (1954), held that D.C. schools could not practice racial segregation, because the Fifth Amendment prohibited discrimination that is "so unjustifiable as to be violative of due process."

92. *Schneider v. Rusk,* 377 U.S. 163, 168 (1964).

93. Bernard Schwartz, *A History of the Supreme Court* (New York: Oxford University Press, 1993), 369.

94. The Sundry Civil Act of August 4, 1886 (ch. 902, 24 Stat. 222, 254), described the clerk's position as a "stenographic clerk."

95. Bradley J. Best, *Law Clerks, Support, Personnel, and the Decline of Consensual Norms on the United States Supreme Court, 1935–1995* (New York: LFB Scholarly, 2002), 95.

96. William Rogers, "Do Law Clerks Wield Power in Supreme Court Cases?," *U.S. News and World Report,* February 21, 1958, 114.

97. Best, *Law Clerks,* 39.

98. John P. Frank, *The Marble Palace: The Supreme Court in American Life* (New York: Knopf, 1958), 118, 117.

99. William O. Douglas, *The Douglas Letters: Selections from the Private Papers of Justice William O. Douglas,* ed. Melvin I. Urofsky (Bethesda, Md.: Adler & Adler, 1987), 146.

100. The debate over the clerks' proper function was reignited in 1999 when Edward P. Lazarus, a former clerk of U.S. Supreme Court Justice Harry A. Blackmun, published a book contending that "ideologically driven" U.S. Supreme Court clerks could exercise "sometimes inappropriate influence over the law." Edward P. Lazarus, *Closed Chambers: The First Eyewitness Account of the Epic Struggles Inside the Supreme Court* (New York: Times Books, 1998), 516, 314–15, and 322. A number of other prominent commentators also have indicated concern related to justices' increased reliance on

their clerks. See, e.g., Kenneth W. Starr, "The Supreme Court and the Future of the Federal Judiciary," *Arizona Law Review* 32 (1990): 215. Critics have responded that these concerns are overblown. For example, Ninth Circuit judge Alex Kozinski, while admitting that Lazarus "may have raised a legitimate issue," contends that "[j]udges generally maintain control by giving law clerks detailed instructions and carefully editing and revising the drafts prepared by the clerks." Alex Kozinski, "Conduct Unbecoming," *Yale Law Journal* 108 (1999): 870. See also Erwin Chemerinsky, "Opening Closed Chambers," *Yale Law Journal* 108 (1999): 1108 ("While Lazarus contends that the Court's clerks play too great a role in its decisionmaking, his description of specific cases belies this criticism. In case after case, Lazarus documents the Justices' personal involvement in their decisionmaking through their attempts to persuade others, their internal memoranda, and their draft opinions").

101. According to Justice Douglas, "Court assignments—opinions I had been chosen to write on behalf of the majority—were always my own creation." Douglas, *Court Years,* 172.

102. See David J. Garrow, "The Tragedy of William O. Douglas," *Nation,* March 27, 2003, http://www.thenation.com/article/tragedy-william-o-douglas (stating that "most of Douglas's . . . clerks" agreed that the justice's decisions were easy to ignore, because they were too hastily written).

103. William O. Douglas Biography, *Oyez,* http://www.oyez.org/justices/william_o_douglas.

104. According to U.S. Supreme Court justice Tom Clark, "Bill believed that rather than seeking harmony, one should seek disharmony. . . . Bill Douglas, the dissenter, was a catalyst at conference; indeed, his role was a crucial one." Clark, qtd. in James F. Simon, *Independent Journey: The Life of William O. Douglas* (New York: Harper & Row, 1980), 353.

105. Lomen Autobiography, 6.

106. Lomen Testimonial. See also Valerie Barnes, "Corporate Law Her Specialty," *Newark (N.J.) News,* May 15, 1970 (quoting Lomen as stating, "Justice Douglas was a tremendous man to work for" and "[d]oing research on opinions for the justice was like having a personal tutor").

107. See Simon, *Independent Journey,* 225 (describing the long work hours the Douglas clerks endured).

108. Lomen Autobiography, 3; Sparks Oral History.

109. Lucile Lomen, interview by Thomas Edwards, October 12, 1994, transcript, 25, Whitman College and Northwest Archives, Penrose Library, Walla Walla, Wash. (hereafter Edwards Oral History).

110. Ibid.

111. Ibid.

112. Lucile Lomen to Mother and Dad (written during her post–World War II trip to Europe with her grandparents).

113. Sparks Oral History.

114. After her clerkship concluded, Lomen stayed in touch with Justice Douglas's secretary Edith Allen and Justice Stanley F. Reed's secretary Helen Gaylord.

115. Lucile Lomen to Blanche, November 26, 1946.

116. William T. Coleman Jr., the first African American clerk on the U.S. Supreme Court, served four years after Lomen.

117. Sparks Oral History.

118. Ibid. All the other law clerks had been out of school for at least one year (they had served in circuit courts or government agencies), and Lomen began work on October 1, a full three months after the other clerks started working.

119. Ibid.

120. There is good evidence that Justice Douglas was given serious consideration for the Democratic vice presidential nomination in 1944 and 1948. See generally James L. Moses, "William O. Douglas 'Political Ambitions' and the 1944 Vice-Presidential Nomination: A Reinterpretation," *Historian* 62, no. 2 (2000): 325–42 (surveying Douglas's involvement in political affairs). Douglas's personal affairs, however, ultimately would ensure he never held a political office. He married four different times, each time to an increasingly younger woman. His last wife, Cathleen, was a twenty-three-year-old waitress whom he married when he was sixty-seven.

121. Sparks Oral History.

122. Ibid.

123. Ibid.

124. Ibid.

125. Ibid.

126. Ibid.

127. Lomen Autobiography, 4.

128. Sparks Oral History.

129. William O. Douglas to Judson F. Falknor, December 1, 1944, Douglas Papers.

130. Douglas, *Court Years,* 171.

131. The clerks were attorney Janet Meik Sigler and law student Carol Myer.

132. William O. Douglas to Max Radin, December 24, 1947, Douglas Papers.

133. See Thomas Klitgaard to William O. Douglas, November 25, 1968, Douglas Papers (noting consideration of a female candidate for a clerkship); Max Radin to William O. Douglas, March 10, 1944, Douglas Papers (same); Max Radin to William O. Douglas, Jan. 25, 1944, Douglas Papers (same); Max Radin to William O. Douglas, March 29, 1943, Douglas Papers (same). There is evidence that one woman, Jeanyse Snow, was offered a Douglas clerkship in 1970, but she turned it down. Thomas Klitgaard to William O. Douglas, August 22, 1970, Douglas Papers. See also William O. Douglas to Anne Dix, June 17, 1947, Douglas Papers (Justice Douglas offers to help a female law student from Columbia attain a clerkship in Washington, D.C.).

134. William O. Douglas to Thomas Klitgaard, November 11, 1971, Douglas Papers. The second female U.S. Supreme Court clerk was Margaret Corcoran, who was hired by Justice Hugo L. Black in 1966.

135. Sparks Oral History.

136. Marian Gravenslund Interview.

137. Lucile Lomen to William O. Douglas, November 20, 1945, Douglas Papers.

138. Ibid.

139. Ibid. Lomen had to be surprised about the turn of events. In the summer of 1945 Colonel Donald G. Graham, a senior partner at the firm, had asked University of Washington Law School dean Falknor "to assure [Lomen] . . . that the offer to you is to be considered a permanent one and the return of these men from the service will not prejudice [her] position if the association is otherwise mutually satisfactory." Judson F. Falknor to Lucile Lomen, June 6, 1945, Lomen Papers.

140. Lomen to Douglas, November 20, 1945.

141. Lucile Lomen to Maurine, September 11, 1946 (written from Bergen), Lomen Papers.

142. Lucile Lomen to Al and M. E., October 4, 1946 (written from Denmark), Lomen Papers.

143. Lomen to Maurine, September 11, 1946.

144. William H. Chafe, *The Paradox of Change: American Women in the 20th Century*, rev. ed. (New York: Oxford University Press, 1991), 121.

145. *1952 Census*, 178.

146. See generally Sherrie A. Kossoudji and Laura J. Dresser, "Working Class Rosies: Women Industrial Workers during World War II," *Journal of Economic History* 52, no. 2 (1992): 431–46 (describing and offering support for the proposition that women after the war did not voluntarily surrender their jobs, but rather were pushed out of their positions).

147. Chafe, *Paradox of Change*, 153.

148. Ibid. (recounting Anthony's quote, which was included in a 1948 article in the *Saturday Evening Post*). See also Lucile Lomen to Lura Robinson (*Career Guide for Women* production manager), August 9, 1946, Lomen Papers (hereafter *Career Guide for Women* Letter) ("It is true that during the war many women were given responsible legal positions, but now that men are returning home, the average woman will be kept in the background").

149. Lomen Autobiography, 6.

150. Ibid.

151. Lomen to Al and M. E., October 4, 1946; Lucile Lomen to Jean, December 29, 1946 (written from Norway), Lomen Papers.

152. Assistant attorney general was the starting position for all junior attorneys in the office. In all, thirty-six individuals held the same role as Lomen during her period with the office. Lomen Autobiography, 6.

153. Ibid., 7.

154. Ibid.

155. According to State of Washington Supreme Court judge Walter B. Beals, Lomen always "acquitted herself with credit. She is an able and discriminating lawyer,

and the briefs which she has written have been excellent, both in form and substance. Her arguments are clearly and forcibly presented, in concise form." Walter B. Beals to Lewis F. Huck, April 30, 1948, Lomen Papers. State of Washington director of vocational education Harry G. Halstead, whom Lomen represented, also held a high opinion of her abilities: "Though the work of this department is highly specialized, Miss Lomen has readily grasped our technical problems, and has given us legal representation with which we are completely satisfied. She is a credit to her profession, and an asset to any community in which she lives." H. G. Halstead to Lewis F. Huck, May 3, 1948, Lomen Papers.

156. Telegram from Smith Troy to Lucile Lomen, December 20, 1946, Lomen Papers. See also Lucile Lomen to Byron, February 1, 1947 (from Bergen), Lomen Papers (describing how the telegram restated past promises).

157. Lomen to Byron, February 1, 1947.

158. Smith Troy to H. P. Hudspeth, (spring 1948?), Lomen Papers (in which he further commented that "every confidence" expressed in Lomen was "borne out by the excellence of her work and her unfaltering loyalty").

159. Lomen Autobiography, 5.

160. Charles L. Powell, a prominent local lawyer who recommended Lomen, observed Lomen's legal abilities when they worked together to arrange care for a Native American cemetery that was located within the Richland city limits.

161. Lucile Lomen to William O. Douglas, April 29, 1948, Douglas Papers. Lomen also had to get past General Counsel Ray H. Luebbe. At the time GE employed approximately seventy lawyers, and all of the operation counsel had been interviewed by the general counsel. Lomen Autobiography, 8. This interview would be a problem for Lomen. She recounted that Luebbe "did not want to participate in the hiring of a woman" (9). Lomen, however, avoided Luebbe's opposition because of the limited scope of her application. The Richland town attorney job, which Lomen vied for, was not a "regular GE attorney" job. Fritz Heimann (former GE associate general counsel), telephone interview with author, April 22, 2004 (hereafter Heimann Interview). It was considered a two-year position with no hopes of leading to advancement in the company. Lomen Autobiography, 8–9. GE officials expected the Richland facility would soon be privatized. Luebbe, therefore, was willing to give more discretion to the Hanford officials (9). While Luebbe would not participate in the hiring of a female lawyer, he would not veto one being employed for a temporary job (9).

162. Lomen to Douglas, April 29, 1948.

163. Ibid.

164. Lomen wrote Justice Douglas on April 29, 1948; Douglas mailed his letter of recommendation in less than one week. William O. Douglas to Lewis F. Huck, May 5, 1948, Douglas Papers.

165. Ibid.

166. Ibid.

167. University of Washington Law School Dean Falknor wrote another glowing

letter in support of Lomen's application: "[Lomen] is tops in every respect and I sincerely hope that the fact that this applicant is a woman will not prevent a consideration on the basis of her ability, experience and promise. . . . Were I to re-enter the practice of law . . . I would deem myself very fortunate to have this young woman associated with me in the practice, and I assure you that I would not consider her sex a militating circumstance in any degree." Judson F. Falknor to Lewis F. Huck, May 3, 1948, Lomen Papers. Subsequent University of Washington Law School dean Roland L. Hjorth, who was a student under Falknor at New York University, recalled that Falknor "was not lavish in his praise and I would have been greatly honored to have received from him the kind of recommendation he gave Ms. Lomen" when she applied to GE. Roland L. Hjorth, "From the Dean," *Condon Crier,* University of Washington Law School, March 3, 1997, 1–2, Lomen Papers. Washington State Supreme Court judge Walter B. Beals (before whom Lomen appeared while in the Washington State attorney general's office) and State of Washington director of vocational education Harry G. Halstead (whom Lomen represented in the attorney General's office) also submitted letters of recommendation in support of Lomen. Beals to Huck, April 30, 1948; Halstead to Huck, May 3, 1948.

168. "This Hanford Works Career Woman Chooses Law . . . ," *Hanford Works News* (Richland, Wash.), January 13, 1950, 6. Lomen garnered respect from local community members and individuals within GE's Nucleonics Department. Charles F. Steele, one of Lomen's Richland colleagues, reported that Lomen's "performance at Hanford was excellent." Charles F. Steele to Walter Powers, January 11, 1963, Lomen Papers. See also Affidavit of George C. Butler (former member of GE's legal staff in Richland), In the Matter of the Application of Lucile Lomen for Admission on Motion to Practice as an Attorney and Counsellor-at-Law in the State of New York, June 1, 1965, Lomen Papers ("I have been able to judge from the closest personal knowledge that Miss Lomen is an attorney of unusual professional ability and of the highest moral character"); Affidavit of Richland Operations Office chief counsel Chester G. Brink, In the Matter of the Application of Lucile Lomen for Admission on Motion to Practice as an Attorney and Counsellor-at-Law in the State of New York, May 21, 1965, Lomen Papers ("Lomen's moral character and professional ability are of the highest order"); Washington State Superior Court Judge Orris L. Hamilton to Board of Bar Examiners, Massachusetts State Bar Association, October 29, 1962, Lomen Papers ("Upon each such occasion [that Lomen presented matters in Judge Hamilton's court], she demonstrated professional ability and integrity far above average").

169. "Hanford Works Career Woman," 6.

170. Ibid.

171. Given widespread support for Lomen, GE general counsel Ray H. Luebbe, who previously had refused to hire a permanent female attorney, scaled back his opposition so that Lomen at least could receive transfers and raises (but still could not be made department counsel). Sparks Oral History. This change allowed Lomen to become a regular GE attorney and better aligned Luebbe's policies with the opinion of GE president Ralph J. Cordiner, a Whitman College graduate who knew Lomen through their

mutual involvement in the Whitman Alumni Association. Ibid. At a party celebrating Luebbe's twenty-five years at GE, Cordiner personally introduced Lomen around the room full of GE attorneys, and among those lawyers she met was a surprised Luebbe, who had never met Lomen in person prior to the party in 1953. Ibid.

172. Lomen delivered an address at Boalt Hall's Symposium on Atomic Energy and the Law that provided an excellent survey of special issues faced in drafting nuclear energy contracts. Lucile Lomen, Address at the Symposium on Atomic Energy and the Law (School of Law, University of California, Berkeley, November 15, 1957), transcript, 7–11, Lomen Papers.

173. Lomen was able to join the ranks of corporate counsels only after GE general counsel Ray H. Luebbe retired. Luebbe consistently had refused to allow a woman to become a corporate counsel. In 1983 Lomen and eighty-four-year-old Luebbe reunited at a meeting of GE headquarters lawyers, and Lomen reminded Luebbe that he did not support her hiring. Sparks Oral History. According to Lomen, Luebbe replied that he "thought it was all right to hire" her, but he explained that he "didn't think [his] managers would want to be represented by a woman." Ibid.

174. See Pallis, "Woman Named," 8 (characterizing Lomen as a "modest unassuming woman").

175. Sparks Oral History.

176. Heimann Interview.

177. Ibid. Similarly, former General Learning Corporation president John D. Backe recalled that Lomen struck a difficult balance: "She was tough, smart, competent . . . and she was a lady. She didn't try to outdo or compete with the men." John D. Backe, telephone interview with author, March 28, 2005 (hereafter Backe Interview).

178. Employee Retirement Income Security Act of 1974, 29 U.S.C. §§ 1001 et seq.

179. Benefits like unemployment compensation and workers compensation cost GE close to $2.25 billion in 1980 alone; these costs were equal to more than 40 percent of pay for time worked. Lucile Lomen, "Implications of Company-wide Benefit Plans," Address at the Negotiations/Strike Seminar (March 3, 1982), transcript, 1, Lomen Papers. At the end of 1981 there were more than 86,000 GE employees on the pension payroll, and 99 percent of all eligible employees participated in the GE pension plan. Ibid. By 2001 the GE pension plan covered 485,000 people, approximately a third of whom were retirees, and the assets of the pension plan had grown to $49.8 billion. Vincent Lloyd, "Penny Pinching the Retirees at GE," Multinational Monitor 22, no. 7 (July/August 2001), http://www.multinationalmonitor.org/mm2001/072001/lloyd.html.

180. Janet Lowe, Welch: An American Icon (New York: Wiley and Sons, 2001), 37. See also Thomas F. O'Boyle, At Any Cost: Jack Welch, General Electric, and the Pursuit of Profit (New York: Knopf, 1998), 14–15 (describing Welch as "intimidating, tough, and unrelenting in his pursuit of ever higher profits").

181. GE employees' pension benefits were fixed from the day they retired, and benefits could only be increased at the company's discretion. Lloyd, "Penny Pinching."

182. Ibid. (reporting that the GE plan's assets in 2001 were $49.8 billion, while the company estimated that it would have to pay out just $28.5 billion to retirees).

183. Ann Sandstrom, telephone interview with author, March 4, 2004 (hereafter Sandstrom Interview 1). See also Lloyd, "Penny Pinching" (finding that some GE pensioners experienced losses in purchasing power of as much as 22 percent).

184. Heimann Interview.

185. GE corporate counsel David E. Bamford, Evaluation and Development Summary, April 30, 1981, Lomen Papers ("Miss Lomen's performance in assigned areas continues to be excellent. Lucy works effectively in employee benefit plan area. She also continues high level of service in counseling in public affairs area. . . . Extensive and varied legal experience within the Company and broad knowledge of Company operations give Miss Lomen special strengths in assigned area. An excellent lawyer!"); Raud E. Johnson, Evaluation and Development Summary, May 7, 1974, Lomen Papers (recognizing Lomen's "[s]ubstantial ability to work with people, experience, general 'common sense'"); R. H. Jones (GE chairman of the board) to Lucile Lomen, June 25, 1973, Lomen Papers (congratulating Lomen for "assuring [a] sound legal position" on the GE Supplementary Pension Plan).

186. "The Top 100 Corporate Women," *Business Week*, June 21, 1976, 58 (recognizing that Lomen's position as counsel for corporate affairs was a "key spot" at GE).

187. See generally ibid. Approximately one dozen of the women, however, held law degrees. Ibid., 57.

188. Pat Hanna, "It's Long Way from Nome to the Title of Counsel," *Post & Times-Star*, August 12, 1960, 26 (quoting Lomen). Lomen repeatedly noted that being a lawyer is "never" a "9 to 5 job." See Barnes, "Corporate Law" (quoting Lomen); Pallis, "Woman Named," 8 (quoting Lomen).

189. Ann Sandstrom, telephone interview with author, March 12, 2004 (hereafter Sandstrom Interview 2).

190. The proposed amendment to the United States Constitution, H.R.J. Res. 208, 92d Cong., 2d Sess., 86 Stat. 1523 (1972), would have established that "[e]quality of rights under the law shall not be denied or abridged by the United States or by any state on account of sex."

191. See "Kennewick B & PW Club Hears of Equal Rights Amendment," *Tri-City Herald* (Kennewick, Wash.), September 25, 1951 (recounting that Lomen had argued that the passing of the Equal Rights Amendment was of "pressing importance"); Serena Mayeri, "Constitutional Choices: Legal Feminism and the Historical Dynamics of Change," *California Law Review* 92 (2004): 762 (describing initial opposition to the Equal Rights Amendment). In the early 1950s the American Association of University Women, American Civil Liberties Union, and League of Women Voters were among the many organizations opposing the Equal Rights Amendment.

192. Lomen dressed in an understated fashion, donning simple white blouses and rarely wearing jewelry. Marian Gravenslund Interview; Sandstrom Interview 1. She also made sure that she was the first to arrive at GE meetings, so that she could avoid being singled out by well-intentioned men who, if seated before her, would stand and offer her a seat. Ruth Hill, interview with author, July 17, 2004, Seattle (hereafter Hill Interview).

193. Lomen's nephew Will Gravenslund, who regularly visited Lomen's Connecticut home, recalled that there was a distinct "pattern" to his aunt's weekend: Lomen would run errands on Saturday morning, go to work on Saturday afternoon, return home for dinner, and retire to the office to read after dinner. Will Gravenslund, telephone interview with author, April 22, 2004 (hereafter Will Gravenslund Interview). There was no TV in the house; as in Lomen's years in Nome, music, reading, and friendly company offered the only forms of entertainment. Lomen especially enjoyed quizzing younger relatives on their studies and professional lives. Ibid. According to Lomen, "[w]atching changes in society, the law, the places where I live or have lived, technology which goes unnoticed becomes a part of our lives, differences in my family from one generation to the next, etc., is to me a hobby. I don't have any of the conventional ones such as tennis, jogging, or collecting something." Lucile Lomen to Sharon Johnson Schneider, Alpha Chi Omega National Headquarters, June 27, 1979, Lomen Papers.

194. Lomen showed sustained interest in only one such organization: the YWCA. This involvement, however, may have been due to her appreciation for housing provided to her as a Supreme Court clerk (as suggested by her nephew Will Gravenslund), or a more general desire to help the poor, encourage peace, and improve race relations (as suggested by her sister Ann Sandstrom and friend Ruth Hill). Will Gravenslund Interview; Sandstrom Interview 2; Hill Interview. Lomen also was active in the Association of University Women and League of Women Voters when she served as a community lawyer in Richland. This participation, which Lomen ended when she left Richland, likely was at least in part a response to GE's expectation that she engage in local affairs. Lomen Autobiography, 10 (describing her role at GE). These organizations were some of the few offering women the opportunity to be community leaders at that time.

195. Ruth Hill, who met Lomen at a YWCA meeting in 1948 and later became a senior official in the YWCA, stated that the two were never questioned regarding their decision to start living together in 1971. Hill Interview. Indeed, John Backe, former president of General Learning Corporation, recalled that "I never knew anything about [Lomen's] personal life. I knew that she was a single lady, but that was it." Backe Interview. According to GE colleague Fritz Heimann, "I don't think people pried into Lucy's personal life, and Lucy didn't pry into theirs." Heimann Interview.

196. Sandstrom Interview 1. See also Will Gravenslund Interview (echoing the sentiment that Lomen "probably had a more accomplished career at GE than if she'd ever been married," because "people would say . . . she can devote time to the company").

197. Hill Interview.

198. Ibid.

199. Throughout her career Lomen denied that she faced any significant prejudice in the legal profession. See Barnes, "Corporate Law" (quoting Lomen: "I recognize that there is discrimination but it has not prevented me from doing work I enjoyed and I was not aware of having been rebuffed in my career because of being a woman"); Hanna, "It's Long Way," 26 (quoting Lomen: "Of course, some places won't employ

people with red hair or flat feet. But I've found that once a place will have me, they don't limit the character of the work assigned to me"); "Company Lawyer," *Mortar Board Quarterly,* May 1950, 165 (quoting Lomen: "One of the questions I am frequently asked is whether women in the legal profession meet with much prejudice. I have had the opportunity to know many women in the profession, and I believe that I can state with certainty that while there may be some who object to them on general principles, there is no avenue in the profession which is closed to a woman merely because she is a woman"); Lomen Autobiography (commenting that while the GE general counsel believed managers would resist working with her, she "did not find that to be the case").

200. Marian Gravenslund Interview. See also *Career Guide for Women* Letter ("Too many women in the legal profession have been discriminated against to make it a worth-while enterprise for one who is not interested in good hard work. . . . On the other hand, anyone who is willing to work hard and who has a good background and better than average ability can, if she will, have a successful and interesting career at the bar").

201. For Lomen, however, retirement did not mean ceasing work altogether. She took classes through Fairfield University's Institute for Retired Professionals, and she served on the institute's advisory board from 1983 until 1987. Later in Seattle Lomen served on the board of trustees of Horizon House, a continuing care retirement community where she resided.

202. "Lucile Lomen," *Seattle Post-Intelligencer,* June 27, 1996, B3 (the obituary also ran in the newspaper's June 28 and June 30 editions).

203. "Thomas Burke, Health Economist, Dies at 57," *Seattle Post-Intelligencer,* July 4, 1996, B10 (announcing the death of a Virginia resident best known for coauthoring the Reagan administration's failed effort to extend Medicare coverage to catastrophic illness); Arthur C. Gorlick, "Climber Louis Ulrich Dies: For 60 Years, Legendary Hiker Showed the Way," *Seattle Post-Intelligencer,* June 27, 1996, B1 (describing the life of a Washington state guide who scaled the Cascade Range for many decades).

204. "Lucile Lomen," B3.

205. See generally ibid.

206. Recognition of Lomen's professional achievements include the following: the Whitman Board of Trustees' naming a dining room and meeting room in her honor (1995), a certificate "for outstanding service" awarded by the Whitman College Alumni Association (1980), Whitman's Alumni of Merit Award (1977), the Alpha Chi Omega Award of Achievement (in recognition of her achievements in law in 1962), a plaque from the Richland Chamber of Commerce for "an outstanding record of leadership" (1956), and Richland's "Woman of the Year" award (from the Richland Toastmistress Club in 1950).

207. Marian Gravenslund Interview.

208. Sparks Oral History.

JOHN M. FERREN

Wiley Blount Rutledge Jr. and His Law Clerks

The last of eight justices Franklin D. Roosevelt appointed to the Supreme Court, Wiley Blount Rutledge Jr., became one of the strongest proponents of civil liberties and civil rights in the Court's history. On these issues Justice Rutledge, with Justice Frank Murphy, took more expansive views of individual rights than those of two other liberals on the Court in the 1940s, Hugo Black and William O. Douglas. Rutledge, however, served only six and a half years, dying suddenly in 1949 at age fifty-five after a cerebral hemorrhage; thus, he is less well known than illustrious colleagues who served much longer: Harlan Fiske Stone, Felix Frankfurter, Robert Jackson, Black, and Douglas. Recently, however, the judicial legacy of Wiley Rutledge has received significant attention, especially because of its relationship to Supreme Court decisions written by Justice John Paul Stevens, a Rutledge law clerk, granting habeas corpus rights to suspected terrorists held at Guantanamo Bay, Cuba.[1] The story of Justice Rutledge, therefore, and of his law clerks' role in that story, is of particular interest today.[2]

Wiley Rutledge: Education, Professional Career, First Clerkship

The Kentucky-born Rutledge, son of a Baptist preacher, arrived at the Court from the U.S. Court of Appeals for the District of Columbia Circuit. He had served there for four years, since 1939—a judicial consolation prize after he had been runner-up twice when President Roosevelt appointed Frankfurter and Douglas to the high bench. Before that, Rutledge, a University of Colorado Law School graduate, had served as the law dean first at Washington University in St. Louis and then at the University of Iowa. From a Southern Baptist he became a Christian humanist, much like a Unitarian, focused on solving human needs—an outlook reflected in his professional career.

Politically, Rutledge was always a Democrat and, as early as his college years, was stressing the civil liberties of individuals over the demands of majorities. In St. Louis, Rutledge sought reform of the criminal justice system and campaigned against the many abuses of child labor and the unrestrained power of public utility holding companies. In Iowa, he urged support of legal aid for the poor and warned the legal profession against monopolizing services that lay persons could offer as well at less cost. In 1937, Rutledge was one of the few law deans in the country to support President Roosevelt's "Court-packing" plan. As an appellate judge he established himself, mainly in dissent, as a strong supporter of the "free exercise" rights of Jehovah's Witnesses under the First Amendment and of the rights of indigent prisoners to appointment of counsel under the Sixth Amendment. And as FDR's advisers had anticipated, he demonstrated a solid grasp of administrative law and labor relations.

Wiley Rutledge almost hired the first woman to clerk on the Supreme Court.[3] His close friend from Washington University, Professor Ralph Fuchs, had recommended the school's top student and editor-in-chief of the *Washington University Law Quarterly*, Virginia Morsey, for a clerkship on the court of appeals. Rutledge had tentatively offered her the position, contingent on his incumbent clerk's leaving for military service. Upon his nomination to the Supreme Court, however, Rutledge was importuned by Fuchs to take as his clerk Victor Brudney, a law review graduate from Columbia who had clerked for Rutledge's predecessor, Justice James F. Byrnes. Reluctantly, with obvious anguish, Rutledge informed Morsey that he had hired Brudney. He was "wholly 'green'" on the Supreme Court, Rutledge wrote, and thus needed "the assistance of all the experience" he could get from a clerk.[4] Morsey graciously wrote Rutledge that he was "absolutely justified" in choosing Brudney.[5] For Rutledge, Brudney—who served for one and a half terms and later became a distinguished law professor at Rutgers and then Harvard—was a godsend, indeed the benchmark against whom every clerk thereafter was measured. Self-described as "something of a wise ass" from New York City, Brudney would argue legal points with Rutledge endlessly—and loudly—once offering, unsuccessfully, to resign over their differences. But that kind of intellectual combat was exactly what Rutledge relished—and expected. Probably as secure, personally, as any middle-aged man could be, Rutledge knew that he could not do the best job of which he was capable without the aid of considerable intellectual firepower from an assertive law clerk.

Fondly, Rutledge later referred to the "Vic Brudney type who will fight you to 11:59 on Monday morning before the decision comes down to get you and sometimes make you change your vote"—and make you "darn glad he wouldn't take No."[6] Brudney, for his part, had unbounded affection and respect for his boss. He considered Rutledge not only a "wise" justice but also an unusual, very special human being. He was "immensely friendly"; he "simply liked people, with great gusto and pleasure"; there was "nothing fake" about him; he "had absolutely no side or cant," and "no image of himself as a great man." Added Brudney, "He showed me there are more complicated, richer dimensions to law and to people than I had ever thought about." And "in our relationship he was really open in ways that I feel certain few of his colleagues were with their clerks."[7]

The Duties of the Rutledge Clerks

Brudney and all later Supreme Court clerks have said that their principal work for Rutledge was review of cert (for certiorari) petitions followed by cert memoranda summarizing each petition and recommending disposition, either grant or deny. Every clerk has reported that Rutledge was super-conscientious, not only reviewing cert memos but also often reading the cert petitions themselves and even more frequently the in forma pauperis petitions filed by prisoners in their own handwriting. The other justices typically relied on a single memorandum on carbon paper, called a "flimsy," from the chambers of the chief justice when voting on prisoner petitions. But not Rutledge. And he agonized over those petitions, sometimes writing his own supplementary cert memos in prisoner cases.[8]

Former law clerk Harry L. Shniderman reported that Rutledge was reluctant to let cert petitions "go back to the clerk's office after they had been decided."[9] Edna Lingreen, the justice's secretary, "had to sneak them out," Shniderman added, because Rutledge kept wanting "to rethink them." According to Justice Stevens, Rutledge "was always concerned that his chambers would overlook a meritorious claim."[10]

Rutledge, not his clerk, would typically write the first draft of an opinion, although Brudney has reported that if the justice left the Court's Saturday conference with more than one opinion to write, he might say to his clerk, "You pick one, and I'll pick one." Then each would prepare a draft, "swap them," and critique the other, followed by Rutledge's completing a final draft of each. Nothing that Brudney wrote, he said, "emerged full blown," although Brudney occasionally would recognize some of his prose in places, shifted around.

Most of his clerks have reported that decisions came hard to Rutledge. Even as late as the October term 1947, former Rutledge law clerk Stanley L. Temko once observed to his co-clerk, John Paul Stevens: "He's in there beating his head against the wall" trying to decide.[11] Rutledge and his clerks would spend each Friday night before the justices' Saturday conference—sometimes until early in the morning—poring over the cert petitions and argued cases pending decision. Experience, to be sure, increased the justice's knowledge and matured his judgment, enlarging year by year his confidence about where to go on a case; and yet his regard for the facts and for the persuasive arguments on each side would continue to leave him, on occasion, in equipoise until the decision day, when even then he might change his mind.

For the decisions that came hard, so did the opinions, and the process was laborious even for those that evolved more smoothly. Aside from special concurrences that made a point or two briefly, a Rutledge opinion tended to be more comprehensive than those of his judicial colleagues. Rutledge "wrote long," as Court observers would say, because—unlike the other justices—he felt obliged to answer every argument presented, not just the large legal questions. "By the time the lawyer and litigant get to the Supreme Court," he told Brudney, "they have lived years with the case, and the lawyer has put a big piece of himself into it." So "however foolish or trivial his arguments, I want them to know that I heard him" by responding to each point raised. Rutledge was fond of saying that a losing litigant never complained that the opinion was too long.

The justice also wrote long as the only way he knew to sort out his thinking; he could not finally decide an outcome without elaborating in writing his thought process in detail sufficient to convince himself that all relevant facts had been identified and the issues resolved correctly and coherently. To that end, continuing from Brudney days, Rutledge sometimes would solicit a first draft from a clerk and, according to former law clerk Louis H. Pollak—in contrast with Brudney's recollection—might even incorporate a "good deal" of it; indeed, the justice added but a few sentences to Pollak's draft of the dissent in *Wolf v. Colorado*.[12]

Similarly, John Paul Stevens supplied significant material for the Rutledge dissent in *Ahrens v. Clark* rejecting the majority's restrictive view of habeas jurisdiction.[13] (Stevens himself later relied on this dissent in writing the Court's opinion in *Rasul v. Bush* granting habeas rights to Guantanamo detainees.)[14] Rutledge also included paragraphs written by Stevens for the justice's concurring opinion in *Marino v. Ragen,* where he urged his colleagues to ignore the petitioner's failure to exhaust Illinois's "merry-go-round" (Stevens's expression) of state remedies.[15] All this said, however, typically only a paragraph or two from a clerk's cert memo or draft opinion would survive verbatim; the clerk's principal written contribution would be the footnotes. (Justice Stevens recalled a common notation on a Rutledge draft: "J.P.S. get cites." According to Stevens, "Sometimes they weren't so easy to prove.")

The justice's clerks were amused, on not a few occasions, when Rutledge would ask for a short draft, and the opinion he then wrote—in hand on yellow foolscap, with a clerk's typed language sometimes stapled in—would be many times longer than the clerk's effort. For Rutledge, then, a clerk's writing was rarely thorough enough in scope or expressive enough in language to become a substantial part of the opinion itself. A clerk's submission often showed a splendid economy of language, clear and precise; another justice might well have adopted it without change. But the Rutledge style, commonly eloquent but often more splendorous than a clerk would have dared to offer, tended to embrace long sentences, as well as redundant clauses and unnecessary adjectives. Rutledge feasted on duplication to achieve emphasis. If one were to read the entire collection of Rutledge Supreme Court opinions, the reader would surely conclude that one person had written them—except for a handful or two that offer a plain, concise explication. This latter group may reflect the Rutledge practice of offering each clerk an opportunity to write a complete, polished opinion during the term, which the justice sometimes accepted with little change.[16]

While recognizing that Rutledge crafted virtually all his own opinions, one should not underestimate the influence of Rutledge law clerks on those opinions. The clerks' cert memos and chambers conferences with the justice, from Brudney through Pollak and Philip W. Tone (October term 1948), were often vital to his decision making, even in the later years when Rutledge's experience often minimized his need for the kind of extended discussions he had experienced with Brudney. John Paul Stevens, for example, in his analysis for the *Ahrens* dissent, proffered an approach granting federal judges substantial leeway to find habeas jurisdiction when the prisoner was not confined in their districts—leeway greater than Rutledge and Black had agreed upon after the Court's conference. Rutledge was persuaded by Stevens's suggestion, and Black joined.[17]

A year later, Rutledge returned from a Court conference with an opinion to write for a 5–4 majority holding the United States liable for damages to farmland attributable to a rise in the water of a non-navigable tributary after the Army Corps of Engineers had raised the level of the Mississippi River. Pollak convinced his boss to change his mind.[18] Rutledge, of course, did not delegate his thinking to his clerks, but like all careful judges he was always open to, and more than occasionally influenced by, their suggestions.

Even the influential Brudney found that his arguments went only so far with the justice. During Rutledge's first full term, his impulse for civil liberties yielded to the curfew imposed on West Coast Japanese nationals and Japanese Americans and, in the next term, to the evacuation program that resulted in their internment.[19] Before the curfew case, *Hirabayashi v. United States,* was pending, Brudney had learned from his days in the solicitor general's office that the FBI, like Attorney General Francis Biddle, had expressed serious doubts about the necessity for imposing sweeping restrictions that applied, without differentiation, to all persons of Japanese ancestry.[20] Brudney suggested to the justice that the Court might benefit from receiving that FBI analysis. More in astonishment than anger, Rutledge confronted his clerk (as Brudney recalled the words):

> What do you think you are doing? Don't you understand that there are only nine of us sitting here, and that the generals have said this [curfew] is necessary for the preservation and security of the country? Pearl Harbor was attacked and more may happen. Who are we to question this? What makes you think any of us will question this? Too much is at stake, and we are too far removed from the realities. Cut it out.

compare to reactions to Patriot Act post-9-11

Remembered Brudney, "This was well before the tides had turned in the war, . . . and the pressure in these matters was simply unbelievable." The Court upheld the curfew 9–0.

The Personal Relationships between Rutledge and His Clerks

Brudney and former law clerk Richard F. Wolfson (October terms 1945 and 1946) have written that Justice Rutledge, aware of his isolation as a justice, "looked, in part, to his law clerks to bridge the gap between the Court and the outside world." More specifically, "[h]e wanted to know the ideas of a different generation, and he wanted someone around him who would feel free to offer these ideas" and, when prodded, "to defend them."[21] The justice, it would appear, desired a close relationship with his clerks similar to those he had forged with his law students. He had enjoyed his students; welcomed them for conversation, legal or personal, at virtually any time; lunched with them on the law school lawn and at local hangouts; found ways to help finance their education and find them jobs, rooms, and meals during Depression days; condemned

how much do shifting societal norms affect $ decision on such social issues as abortion, gay rights, etc.?

anti-Semitism on campus; created opportunities for African American students; and, unlike many of his colleagues, gave female students his respect and special attention. When he joined the U.S. Court of Appeals and invited an Iowa student to come to Washington as his clerk, Rutledge also invited the young man to live at his home.

The former student analogy, however, is inapt. Inherently, teacher and student are not equals, whereas Rutledge established an intellectual partnership with Brudney and Wolfson akin to that with former faculty colleagues. Both clerks recalled that, "[i]n their intellectual relationship, the clerk was constantly made to feel equal."[22] On the other hand, Brudney has acknowledged that their relationship was "pretty much" business, in contrast with the personal connections Rutledge achieved with students. Later clerks agreed with Brudney's characterization. Stanley Temko could recall no time for leisurely "jurisprudential discussions" with Rutledge during the 1947 term. Temko's co-clerk, John Paul Stevens—who received the clerkship after a coin flip with his co-editor-in-chief of the law review at Northwestern[23]—put it this way: "We didn't spend an hour a day chatting."

Furthermore, unlike Justice Black, for example, who played tennis with his own and other clerks, Justice Rutledge did not socialize with his aides outside the courthouse, aside from a dinner or two each year at his home. The social ties and extracurricular musings that the justice had experienced with students and faculty, therefore, were missing for the most part from Rutledge clerkships. "Law clerks were not in his intimate circle," according to Tone.

It is interesting to note, moreover, that the Rutledge clerks after Wolfson did not describe their interactions with the justice in the language of equality that Brudney and Wolfson used. While affirming that Rutledge invited and listened respectfully to their views on all matters before the Court, these later clerks have described relationships with their boss that were somewhat more hierarchical, more businesslike, and thus less intimate than those spelled out by Brudney and Wolfson. This shift, though slight, may have occurred for three reasons. First, beginning in the October term 1947, Rutledge and three of his colleagues, for the first time, employed two clerks (Chief Justice Vinson had three).[24] This change created a somewhat different dynamic as these justices now had to reduce the time available for each clerk, account for two personalities, and, in some instances, allocate the workload according to perceived differences in efficiency if not ability (Rutledge, however, allocated his assignments randomly).

Second, Pollak has observed that Rutledge had been five years closer in age to Brudney during his clerkship than to Pollak and Tone during theirs. And, of course, Rutledge had garnered five more years of experience before he worked with Pollak and Tone. Not surprisingly, therefore, during the 1948 term Pollak had been "in awe" of Rutledge and considered him "more of a father figure" than a colleague.[25] Tone experienced the justice as "self-confident." Rutledge, in short, had become an older, more self-assured justice by the time that Pollak and Tone had come on board.

Third, Pollak, in 1948, regarded Rutledge as "very old," although only in his middle fifties. That observation reflected a consensus among those who knew Rutledge well that his health had begun to decline during the 1946 term. Writing virtually around the clock over four days, he became drained, physically and emotionally, while writing his most celebrated opinion, dissenting from the Court's decision in *In re Yamashita* denying habeas corpus relief from the military commission conviction of the Japanese commander in the Philippines for war crimes near the end of World War II.[26] A law clerk for Chief Justice Vinson during October term 1947 recalled that Rutledge seemed "haggard and worn."[27] As a result, he began to lose some of the zest that had characterized his earlier relationships with his clerks.

These developments did not suppress the clerks' affection and respect for Rutledge, nor did they seriously inhibit access to him, but the joint-venture nature of the relationship became less equal. Temko called Rutledge a "wonderful boss," who was "always approachable," and Justice Stevens added that Rutledge "welcomed disagreement." Stevens, however, also stressed that the justice typically did not seek law clerk opinions on his drafts, a marked change from the Brudney/Wolfson experiences.

In October term 1948, Philip Tone found in Rutledge a man of "great intellectual integrity," a "very warm, kind person" who was "direct, without hurting feelings." Tone could not recall any argument with Rutledge. "If there was a difference of opinion I don't think we would argue about it; we would yield immediately to his views." His colleague, Pollak, echoing Temko and Stevens, recalled that the justice was "very respectful" toward his clerks and "receptive to hearing us." Rutledge would "go over cases pretty carefully" with him and Tone "before and after argument," and the three would "almost always reach consensus." Unlike Tone, however, Pollak remembered one occasion when "Phil and I were strongly of the view that Frankfurter was right," and they argued with Rutledge, to no avail, "for a very long time." Thereafter, according to Pollak, Rutledge took a "dim view" of his clerks approaching him together.

As a result, when Pollak wanted to question the justice, he would "talk out" the matter first with Tone and then see Rutledge alone.

More relaxed, collegial relationships with his clerks might have been possible had the justice reduced his other engagements. But Rutledge continued to make time for old friends and former students; he never would shut them out. Indeed, they showed no hesitation in coming unannounced to chambers (or even to his home) for a visit, to the consternation of the justice's secretary and clerks, who worried about his backlog of unwritten opinions. Nor could Rutledge refuse requests to speak, whether before bar associations or at Rotary Club meetings. Thus, longtime friendships and commitments outside the Court, when added to the workload of a justice in poor health who continued to labor hard on his opinions, combined increasingly to pressure his life in a way that limited his clerkship relationships to the work itself.

Rutledge enjoyed the personal, as well as the intellectual, respect of the clerks from the other chambers, whom he would occasionally join for lunch, offer a ride home from work, or otherwise encounter informally. These clerks saw him as "conscientious" and "hard working," almost to the point of "affliction." With amazing uniformity they have described him as "warm" and "down to earth," typically "smiling" and "outgoing." He was "gentle." The words "modest," "common touch," even "old shoe" were used. He was "informal," "friendly," a "big bear of a guy" who chuckled with a "deep, husky voice." (He "sounded like a cowboy," recalled his own clerk, Shniderman.) To the other clerks there was "no arrogance"; "he seemed to have no ego." He showed no "meanness"; he was not "rude" or "inconsiderate." To the contrary, he was "gracious," "kindly," "decent." He was "a wonderful human being"; "such a joy to talk to"; "one of the nicest persons I ever met."[28] And just as he wrote letters of recommendations for his own clerks interested in teaching, he offered similar support to the clerks of other justices.

Along with these human qualities came a justice of high personal integrity, even in matters that might seem trivial. Justice Stevens recalls, for example, that Rutledge would never enlist his government-paid law clerks to help with personal projects, such as speeches or even formal lectures such as his series on the Commerce Clause at the University of Kansas.[29] Stevens also remembers that Rutledge would not even accept free books from legal publishers because that might appear to be favoring a publisher's point of view. And Rutledge almost never let his clerks hear negative comments from him about the other justices, aside from his visible anger—shared by his other colleagues—at the way Justice Frankfurter would go on and on and on at the Court's Saturday conferences.

Justice Rutledge and Justice Stevens

For the public at large, the most consequential Rutledge clerkship was that of John Paul Stevens. As if to underscore the point, the official Rutledge portrait has hung in Justice Stevens's chambers, not along the first floor corridor of the Court where portraits of the other 1940s justices can be found. That clerkship is the subject of outstanding essays on the influence of Justice Rutledge on the jurisprudence of Justice Stevens (particularly on the exercise of executive power during wartime and on interpretation of the First Amendment)[30] and on the Stevens work style (reviewing every cert petition in chambers rather than through the Court's "cert pool," writing his own first draft opinions, exhibiting an affection for footnotes, and frequently writing separate concurring opinions).[31]

The impact of Justice Rutledge on John Paul Stevens—indeed, on all the Rutledge clerks as we have seen—was personal as well as professional. It was positive, powerful, even profound. Surely Justice Stevens spoke for all these clerks in saying: "I did feel quite close to him. . . . He had a great influence on me; I think about him a great deal."

Notes

1. *Hamdan v. Rumsfeld,* 548 U.S. 557 (2006); *Rasul v. Bush,* 542 U.S. 466 (2004); see Laura Krugman Ray, "Clerk and Justice: The Ties That Bind John Paul Stevens and Wiley B. Rutledge," *Connecticut Law Review* 41, no. 1 (2008): 243–46, 258–59; Craig Green, "Wiley Rutledge, Executive Detention, and Judicial Conscience at War," 84 *Washington University Law Review* 99 (2006): 115–23, 156–58; Joseph T. Thai, "The Law Clerk Who Wrote *Rasul v. Bush:* John Paul Stevens's Influence from World War II to the War on Terror," 92 *Virginia Law Review* 501 (2006).

2. All the information in this essay about Wiley Rutledge, including quotations, is drawn from my biography of Justice Rutledge unless otherwise footnoted. John M. Ferren, *Salt of the Earth, Conscience of the Court: The Story of Justice Wiley Rutledge* (Chapel Hill: University of North Carolina Press, 2004).

3. That honor belongs to Justice Douglas, who hired Lucile Lomen for the 1944 term.

4. Wiley Rutledge to Virginia Morsey, March 3, 1943, Box 89, U.S. Court of Appeals, Applications, Law Clerks 1942–43, Wiley Blount Rutledge Jr. Papers, Manuscript

Division, Library of Congress, Washington, D.C. All other correspondence cited can be found in this collection under the name of the Rutledge correspondent.

5. Virginia Morsey to Wiley Rutledge, March 8, 1943, Box 89, Rutledge Papers. Morsey soon embarked on a career with the World Bank. For a brief biography of Morsey see http://law.wustl.edu/alumni/index.asp?ID=757.

6. Ferren, *Salt of the Earth*, 227, 472n13 (quoting Wiley Rutledge to Philip Mechem, April 6, 1949, Rutledge Papers).

7. Ibid., 227–28, quoting author's interview with Victor Brudney, October 3, 1995. Later quotations from Professor Brudney are taken from this interview.

8. See Case Memoranda, Box 119, Rutledge Papers.

9. Harry L. Shniderman, interview with author, November 29, 1995. Later quotations from Shniderman are taken from this interview.

10. John Paul Stevens, interview with author, September 28, 1995. Later quotations from Stevens are taken from this interview.

11. Stanley L. Temko, interview with author, September 27, 1995. Later quotations from Temko are taken from this interview.

12. *Wolf v. Colorado*, 338 U.S. 25 (1949).

13. *Ahrens v. Clark*, 335 U.S. 188, 193 (1948)(Rutledge, J., dissenting); see Thai, "Law Clerk," 510–13.

14. *Rasul v. Bush*, 542 U.S. 466 (2004); see Thai, "Law Clerk," 521–30.

15. *Marino v. Ragen*, 332 U.S. 561, 563, 570 (1947)(Rutledge, J., concurring); see Diane Marie Amann, "John Paul Stevens, Human Rights Judge," *Fordham Law Review* 74 (2006): 1569, 1589–92 (referencing Box 158, *Marino v. Ragen*, Rutledge Papers).

16. Philip W. Tone, interview with author, October 29, 1996. Later quotations from Tone are taken from this interview; see Todd C. Peppers, *Courtiers of the Marble Palace: The Rise and Influence of the Supreme Court Law Clerk* (Stanford, Calif.: Stanford University Press, 2006), 130.

17. See Thai, "Law Clerk," 510–13.

18. Louis H. Pollak, interview with author, July 13, 2009. See Rutledge's handwritten record of conference vote on back of first page of Pollak's bench memo dated "10/23/48," Box 172, *U.S. v. Kansas City Life Ins. Co.*, Rutledge Papers. Rutledge wrote a long opinion that incorporated Pollak's analysis. Before issuance, however, the case was reargued—after Justices Murphy and Rutledge died and were replaced, respectively, by Justices Tom Clark and Sherman Minton. With this change of Court personnel, the original disposition was preserved 5–4, and Justice Douglas, in dissent, wrote of his indebtedness "to the late Mr. Justice Rutledge for much of the phraseology and content of this dissent." *United States v. Kansas City Life Ins. Co.*, 339 U.S. 799, 812, 814 (1950) (Douglas, J., dissenting). As Justice Douglas's file reveals, however, his dissent was composed of paragraphs taken virtually word for word from Rutledge's earlier draft opinion. Box 194, *U.S. v. Kansas City Life Ins. Co.*, William O. Douglas Papers, Manuscript Division, Library of Congress, Washington, D.C.

19. See *Korematsu v. United States*, 323 U.S. 214 (1944). Shniderman recommended

denial of certiorari in *Korematsu*. See cert memorandum, Case No. 22, Box 119, Supreme Court File, Oct. Term 1944, Case Memos 1–50, Rutledge Papers. Rutledge, however, joined all his colleagues except Justice Black in voting to hear the case. For reasons why Rutledge voted to join the 6–3 majority in *Korematsu* see Ferren, *Salt of the Earth*, 255–59.

20. *Hirabayashi v. United States*, 320 U.S. 81 (1943).

21. Victor Brudney and Richard F. Wolfson, "Mr. Justice Rutledge: Law Clerks' Reflections," *Indiana Law Journal* 25 (1950): 455, and *Iowa Law Review* 35 (1950): 578, 583.

22. Ibid.

23. More specifically, Stevens and his classmate, Arthur R. Seder, both of whom wanted to clerk as soon as possible, flipped the coin for a clerkship during the October term 1947 with Justice Rutledge while the one who lost the toss would receive a clerkship in the 1948 term with Chief Justice Vinson—arrangements made by Northwestern professors W. Willard Wirtz for Rutledge and Willard Pedrick for Vinson. See John Paul Stevens, "A Personal History of the Law Review," *Northwestern University Law Review* 100 (2006): 25–26.

24. Sheridan L. Hill-Ellis, Secretary, Curator's Office, Supreme Court of the United States, to author, September 20 and October 26, 1995.

25. Louis H. Pollak, interview with author, December 21, 1995. Later quotations from Pollak are taken from this interview.

26. *In re Yamashita*, 327 U.S. 1, 41 (1946) (Rutledge, J., dissenting). Working at the side of his boss off and on, Wolfson supplied several memoranda and marshaled material for the footnotes. See *In re Yamashita*, Boxes 137 and 138, Rutledge Papers.

27. Francis A. Allen, interview with author, April 8, 1996.

28. Quoted from interviews noted in Ferren, *Salt of the Earth*, 343–44.

29. See Wiley Rutledge, *A Declaration of Legal Faith* (Lawrence: University of Kansas Press, 1947).

30. See Ray, "Clerk and Justice," 243–46, 258–59; Green, "Wiley Rutledge," 115–23, 156–58; Thai, "Law Clerk."

31. See Ray, "Clerk and Justice," 237–43, 249–50, 263; Artemus Ward and David L. Weiden, *Sorcerers' Apprentices: 100 Years of Law Clerks at the United States Supreme Court* (New York: New York University Press, 2006); John Paul Stevens, "How a Mundane Assignment Affected My Re-examination of *Miranda*," *Chicago Bar Association Record*, October 2000, 34, 37.

CRAIG ALAN SMITH

Strained Relations

Justice Charles Evans Whittaker and His Law Clerks

C harles Evans Whittaker served on the Supreme Court exactly five years (from March 1957 to March 1962), during what could arguably be considered a transitional period of the so-called Warren Court (a phrase that did not attain any real significance until after Whittaker left the Court). This transitional period saw few remarkable or "landmark" decisions, and Whittaker's contributions involved primarily economic or business-related opinions. While he was on the Court, Whittaker was disappointed with his appointment, was nervous and overwhelmed much of the time, and endured recurrent bouts of anxiety and depression that ultimately led to a near complete nervous breakdown. Thus, historians have alternately dismissed Whittaker as an inconsequential justice or, worse, relegated him to the status of a failure despite recent efforts to resuscitate his reputation.[1]

Notwithstanding his undistinguished service at the Supreme Court, Whittaker achieved a few distinctions. He continues to be the only native Kansan to serve on the Court and also the only justice to date from Missouri, where he spent his entire adult life (save his five years at the Court).[2] He was also the second justice in history to serve at all three levels of the federal judiciary. The first to do this, Justice Samuel Blatchford, took fifteen years and three presidents to move from the Southern District Court of New York through the Second Circuit Court of Appeals and onto the Supreme Court. Whittaker, on the other hand, advanced so quickly through the federal judiciary that each of his commissions was signed by President Eisenhower. Whittaker left the Western District Court of Missouri after two years and spent only nine months serving on the Eighth Circuit Court of Appeals.[3] So brief was his service as a lower federal court judge that Justice Felix Frankfurter reportedly joked, "We can get a judge from the district court quicker than we can get a case from that court."[4]

What was remarkable about Charles Whittaker was his upbringing and education, factors that would greatly influence his choices for law clerks. He grew up on a remote farm in northeast Kansas, where he received what amounted to a ninth-grade education at a one-room schoolhouse located a quarter mile from his home. He never finished high school due, in part, to the anguish he felt at the death of his mother on his sixteenth birthday. Instead, he worked tirelessly at farming and trapping to raise enough money to attend a part-time law school with no college affiliation in Kansas City, Missouri. Without the equivalent of a high school diploma, though, his admission was doubtful. Determined to become a lawyer, Whittaker convinced the president of the law school that he could finish high school at the same time as law school. To accomplish this, he worked full-time as an office boy at one of the local law firms.

Once he graduated law school, having passed the Missouri bar exam eight months earlier, Whittaker joined the same Kansas City law firm where he worked as an office boy. He practiced corporate law there for thirty years, becoming a senior partner after six years and adding his name to the firm's title two years later.

This provincial life, venturing no more than seventy miles from the place of his birth, meant that Whittaker felt most comfortable remaining in the Midwest. Unlike his one-time classmate at law school, future president Harry S. Truman, Whittaker never served in uniform or ran for elected office (other than as a member of the Missouri Bar). When he started law school he began calling himself Charles "Evans" Whittaker (his given middle name was Ernest) because his identity was singularly focused on becoming and sounding like a great lawyer.[5] This myopic view of himself and his surroundings caused Whittaker to seek out in law clerks what he missed most as a justice—people with whom he could identify.

Clerk Backgrounds and the Appointment Process

Whittaker had no formal application process for his law clerks; in fact, what was most striking about each of their appointments was the haphazardness of the process. Due to his relatively short tenure as a justice, Whittaker selected only nine clerks. Each term he chose two new clerks except for his last term, when he chose only one new clerk and asked one of his clerks from the previous term to stay a second year. Quite possibly he was encouraged to do this because five of his colleagues on the Court had their clerks stay a second year.[6]

Whittaker's first clerk was Alan Kohn (October term 1957), who began with

Whittaker in April 1957 and stayed for eighteen months. Kohn's path to the Supreme Court is striking because he initially had no intention of clerking at the Court. Like Whittaker, Kohn's educational background was parochial; he attended public schools around St. Louis, Missouri, and then went to college and law school at Washington University in St. Louis, where he became the editor-in-chief of the school's law review. Kohn participated in ROTC training through law school; afterward he volunteered for the Army Security Agency, where he was trained in code breaking and data collection of electronic intelligence. Anticipating that he might be stationed in Washington, D.C., Kohn's wife, Joanne, applied for graduate school at Catholic University. When Kohn was sent to Germany instead, Joanne received a two-year deferment on her admission.

Kohn intended to return to St. Louis to practice law when his Army enlistment ended in spring 1957, but his wife wanted to pursue her studies in D.C. She persuaded him to apply to clerk at the Supreme Court, reminding him that his constitutional law professor, Charles Fairman, had recommended it. In fall 1956 Kohn applied to both Justice Tom Clark (who was assigned the Eighth Circuit) and Chief Justice Earl Warren (who had three law clerks instead of two), hoping to increase his chances. Clark declined Kohn's application in early February, but Kohn heard nothing from Warren. Then, near the end of March 1957, Kohn received an invitation from the Court's newest member, Charles Whittaker, to come in for an interview. As Kohn remembered it, he was shocked—he did not know Whittaker had been appointed to the Court or even that Whittaker had his application.[7]

According to Kohn, Warren "remembered" his application and gave it to Whittaker. Warren probably knew of Justice Stanley Reed's plans for retirement before they were announced on January 31, 1957, since Reed had been considering retirement for over a year.[8] Whittaker's Republican ties, Midwest origins, prior judicial experience, and relative youth made him a leading candidate to replace Reed. Waiting to see if Whittaker would be the pick, Warren held on to Kohn's application. After the announcement of Whittaker's nomination, Warren asked him, "Do you have a clerk yet?" Whittaker replied, "I don't even have a place to stay yet." "I've got one for you from Missouri," Warren told him.[9]

Kohn appeared at his interview just a few days after returning from overseas; to prepare himself he studied a book on constitutional law, but Whittaker was more interested in discussing mutual acquaintances. With nothing more than geographic and social familiarity, Whittaker hired Kohn. "Thus, with lightening-like suddenness," Kohn remembered, "I became the beneficiary of an incredible chain of serendipitous coincidences."[10] In some respects, though, Kohn's experience was not unique. Whittaker had no established procedure for selecting clerks, and because he chose so few the process evolved incidentally.

What mattered most to Whittaker was a Midwest connection, but hiring clerks with similar backgrounds and experience did not distinguish him in the eyes of the Court. The first few months they served together, Whittaker and Kohn were assisted by one of Justice Reed's former clerks, Manley Hudson (October term 1956), who was a Harvard law graduate. Hudson served as a kind of mentor for both the newest justice and his clerk, but like other clerks at the Court, Hudson was "stiff" with the new arrivals. Whittaker's legal training was continually a source of embarrassment for him, and Kohn frankly conceded that Washington University was a "second-tier" law school. Undeniably, their background and education set them far apart from other justices and their clerks.[11]

The next term Whittaker needed a second clerk to join Kohn, and he chose Kenneth Dam (October term 1957), a Kansas farm boy like himself who went to Kansas University and the University of Chicago Law School. Dam knew he wanted to apply for a clerkship as soon as Whittaker was appointed to the Court. His interview with Whittaker was actually his second trip to Washington; he, too, had been turned down by Justice Clark.[12]

For his second term Whittaker hired Heywood "Woody" Davis (October term 1958), another midwesterner who grew up in Kansas City. As an undergraduate Davis studied history at Kansas University, where his grandfather, Frank Heywood Hodder, headed the history department and served as president of the Kansas State Historical Society. Afterward Davis became an ensign in the navy and three years later returned to Kansas University for a law degree. Although he was editor-in-chief of the *Kansas Law Review,* Davis had not considered applying for a clerk's position until he was reminded that Whittaker preferred clerks from the Midwest. This time Whittaker held the interview at his home in Kansas City, and he offered Davis the job on the spot, saying, "Woody, if you'll take a chance on me, I'll take a chance on you."[13]

The narrowness of Whittaker's vision in selecting law clerks extended to his one clerk on the district and appeals courts, Clyde Rayburn (1954–57), who attended law school at Whittaker's alma mater.[14] Rayburn acknowledged that several other candidates had applied for the position, but his law school affiliation got him the job. Whittaker may also have been sensitive to Rayburn's status for military conscription. Rayburn's student deferment expired at graduation, and in his interview he admitted that he was "draft bait." Whittaker offered him the job anyway. Rayburn stayed with Whittaker for two years at the district court and then followed him to the court of appeals.[15]

Sympathy for his clerks' military potential may have influenced *Judge* Whittaker, but *Justice* Whittaker was not so magnanimous. For his second term Whittaker chose a University of Minnesota Law School graduate, William Canby (October term 1958), who had completed his undergraduate work at Yale. Canby served in the ROTC during law school and afterward went into the air force in the judge advocate's office. When his law school dean, Bill Lockhart, recommended Canby for a clerkship, Whittaker called him for an interview. At the end of the interview Whittaker told Canby he could have the job if he could get an early release from the air force (new clerks were expected in July but Canby's tour of duty ended in September). Canby could tell the air force about the job, but Whittaker would not assist in his release from duty.[16]

During his third term, however, Whittaker had to intervene to prevent the military from drafting one of his clerks, Patrick McCartan (October term 1959), a Notre Dame Law School graduate. Whittaker's letter to the draft board received a less than gracious reply. Two years later another clerk, James Adler (October term 1961), a University of Michigan graduate, took it upon himself to ask for a military deferment, but since no one knew exactly what it meant to be a clerk at the Supreme Court, Whittaker still had to write an explanation. This time Whittaker's reply was ambiguous; he wrote, "I hired this man to do this job, but if he is needed elsewhere there are plenty of others who could do it also."[17]

Possibly the most unconventional hire of Whittaker's law clerks was Adler, who served during Whittaker's last term. Adler certainly possessed several compelling qualifications for the job: he attended Princeton before going to the University of Michigan Law School, where he was first in his class and editor-in-chief of the law review. More important, though, to someone like Whittaker, Adler was raised in Kansas City, where his parents owned a prominent department store. Whittaker's son, Kent, was studying law at Michigan one year ahead of Adler, and it was there that they met and became friends. Although both of them grew up in Kansas City (Kent attended Rockhurst High School and Adler went to what is now Pembroke Hill School), Kent had never heard of Adler's department store and Adler had no idea that Whittaker was on the Supreme Court. When Kent first explained that his father was a Supreme Court justice, Adler thought it was a joke.

Adler first met Charles Whittaker when Kent got married in Ann Arbor during his senior year. It was during this initial meeting that Whittaker asked Adler to be his law clerk—no application or interview required.[18] Two years earlier Whittaker had hired another Michigan Law School graduate, Jerome Libin (October term 1959), who was one year ahead of Kent at law school. Raised in Chicago and a graduate of Northwestern University, Libin fulfilled Whittaker's preference for clerks with Midwest backgrounds. James Adler believed it was Whittaker's positive experience with Libin, in part, that compelled Whittaker to accept another Michigan law student. No doubt it was also due to the recommendation of E. Blythe Stason, dean of Michigan Law School.[19]

Recommendations carried some weight in Whittaker's two remaining clerk selections, but the outcomes varied considerably. In his fourth term he chose James Edwards (October term 1960), a University of Illinois and Yale Law School graduate. In part, Whittaker made the selection because of strong recommendations from Yale Law School faculty. Whittaker may not have been as comfortable with this choice as others because, as one of his previous clerks stated, "Those bright boys from Harvard and Yale had considerable egos; they thought they could solve the world's problems." Another clerk admitted confidentially that had Whittaker stayed on the Court, he would not hire another Yale law graduate.

For his part, Edwards was candid in his appraisal of Whittaker: "It was evident he had trouble; he had little experience on constitutional questions, and this could be taxing. A Yale graduate had more perception of constitutional questions than his forty years as a trial lawyer."[20] The other clerk Whittaker hired based on a strong recommendation was Lawrence Gunnels, the only clerk to stay with Whittaker more than one term (October terms 1960 and 1961). Gunnels grew up in Kansas and was a graduate of Washington University Law School, the same school attended by Whittaker's first clerk, Alan Kohn. Moreover, it was Kohn who recommended Gunnels to Whittaker.[21] When Whittaker retired in the middle of his fifth term, Gunnels went to work for Whittaker's replacement, Justice Byron White.

Law Clerk Duties

In each term of Whittaker's service eighteen clerks were hired for the Court (each justice except Douglas had two, and the chief justice had three). Whittaker hired nine men for clerkships, and the consensus among them was that they were free to share their views with other clerks about cases before the

Court. All of the clerks ate lunch together in a room separated from the public cafeteria, and as one of them observed, "there was no one else to talk to." On occasion there were invited guests at the clerks' lunches, officials from the Justice Department or other government agencies, and each of the nine justices took their turn dining with the clerks; but for most of these lunches clerks exchanged their views with each other, discussed the merits of cases, how their justice had voted, and generally argued among themselves.[22]

Communication with other chambers outside the cafeteria setting, however, rarely happened. The justices communicated principally by written memoranda, and because of the configuration of Whittaker's chambers—his two clerks had desks positioned near a window and could not see into the outer office where the secretary greeted visitors—his clerks were unaware even if another justice came into the office.[23] The only time one of Whittaker's clerks recalled going to visit another justice was when Whittaker had to be out of Washington over the weekend and asked his clerk, Jerome Libin, to see Justice Frankfurter about a draft opinion. Whittaker believed he had Frankfurter's support, but he wanted his clerk to confirm it. The most memorable part of the encounter was when Frankfurter, well known for his intellect and his ego, asked unexpectedly, "What's your favorite coerced confession case?" Dissatisfied with Libin's reply, Frankfurter proceeded at length to explain his favorite.[24]

One of the principal responsibilities that Whittaker's clerks shared was doing an inordinate amount of research, often on obscure points of law. At times, though, his clerks were hampered in their assignment because Whittaker preferred to do his own research. Whittaker's clerk on the district and appeals courts, Clyde Rayburn, remembered how other clerks occasionally got to draft opinions, but his duties were confined almost exclusively to the library. To make matters worse, Whittaker often gave Rayburn an assignment without fully informing him of the facts of the case, and Rayburn had to request the case file to know how to proceed. If Whittaker became impatient he would join his clerk in the library—as his clerk set a book down Whittaker picked it up and began reading. The one time in two and a half years Rayburn remembered drafting an opinion, Whittaker rewrote it entirely.[25]

This became the pattern for Whittaker's clerks at the Supreme Court, at least in the beginning. Over time his clerks' duties changed as Whittaker himself evolved and overcame his own difficulties. During Whittaker's first full term his two clerks, Alan Kohn and Ken Dam, performed duties familiar to most law clerks from that time: they read petitions for certiorari and summarized them for the justice, and they wrote bench memoranda on the cases accepted for oral argument. Kohn aptly summarized these duties, writing, "Essentially, my life became reading and typing, reading and typing, reading and typing."[26] Whittaker's two clerks took several petitions home every evening, "which we grabbed willy-nilly from a pile," and prepared a two-page summary of the facts of the case, the applicable law, the decision below, and a recommendation whether or not to accept the case for review.[27] These recommendations, however, were not determinative of how Whittaker voted. One of his second-term clerks recalled: "We researched law for him—advice is too strong a word. Our analysis of petitions was more important to him than our recommendation. He talked to us about bench memos, too, but it was not our place to advise him. He was the justice."[28]

Whittaker's predilection for doing his own work, for depending more on himself than his clerks (especially when it came to drafting Court opinions), was the by-product of thirty years as a corporate lawyer where he gained the reputation of a "lone wolf." Once on the Supreme Court his self-reliance did not subside. His clerks were aware that their responsibilities for drafting opinions were severely limited compared to other justices' clerks. One of Whittaker's first-term clerks admitted candidly: "We did not have the same role as other clerks (we knew this because it was discussed at lunch). The other justices, except for Douglas, had their clerks work on first drafts. Whittaker drafted his own, and we made comments."[29]

Clerks from Whittaker's last two terms had similar experiences: rarely, if ever, did they get to draft an opinion, and if they did it was regarded as the one customary draft for the term.[30] One of Whittaker's last clerks, James Adler, believed that other clerks embraced the responsibility of drafting opinions because they harbored ambitions to be the justice: "That made Whittaker uncomfortable. He either liked to do it himself, or felt he should do it himself, or felt uncomfortable if he was not doing it himself."[31] Adler further observed that it would be a mistake to find fault with Whittaker for drafting his own opinions, writing, "Many people would find fault with a justice who did not."[32]

Whittaker accepted, some might say imposed, the responsibility to write his own opinions, in part, because of the turmoil surrounding the Court at the time of his appointment and the implication that law clerks exerted undue influence on the justices. In June 1957, just a few months after Whittaker's swearing-in, the Court was embroiled in a controversy with Congress and the public over several national security decisions involving suspected communists.[33] This led to an editorial in *U.S. News and World Report* suggesting that law clerks were behind the controversial decisions. To some extent this article influenced Whittaker to draft his own opinions rather than share that responsibility with his clerks.[34] In fact, the few times that his clerks remembered drafting opinions, they invariably remarked how the final opinion bore little resemblance to their drafts. "On occasion, he would have us draft opinions," Heywood Davis recalled. "If there was any similarity between any draft that we might have submitted and the final one that came out from him, it was because it had the word 'a' or 'the' in it."[35] In another example, Alan Kohn remembered drafting the majority opinion in *Lawn v. United States*,[36] but the final Court decision contained none of his original language.[37]

The only exception to Whittaker's reluctance to assigning draft opinions to his clerks came in his third term when his clerks' persistence compelled him to relinquish some of the opinion writing duties. At conference the justices had no difficulty disposing of a relatively insignificant case involving a question of federal jurisdiction on a 7–2 vote. After Justice Frankfurter's majority opinion circulated, Whittaker's clerks were convinced that his conference vote was correct and encouraged him to write a dissent. Whittaker was reluctant to take on the erudite Frankfurter, who used any means to control Whittaker's vote. Nevertheless, he told his clerk, Jerome Libin, who remembered hearing from previous clerks that Whittaker drafted his own opinions, to go ahead with a draft if he wished.

When the draft was finished, Whittaker apparently liked it enough to send it to the other justices, who responded favorably. Now the vote was 7–2 the other way, and Frankfurter found himself in the minority. Whittaker then made some adjustments to Libin's draft, but essentially the final opinion was Libin's work.[38] As a result, Whittaker gained more confidence as a justice; he dissented more often, and he permitted his clerks to draft more of his dissents.

This turnaround during Whittaker's third term was short-lived, and by his fifth term Whittaker returned to completing his own assignments—which undoubtedly played a part in leading to the depression that caused him to suffer a nervous breakdown. The mental instability Whittaker suffered periodically throughout his life caused him to be dismissive with subordinates, even disdainful. He once told an interviewer: "You must realize that these are just youngsters, bright boys but [they have] no experience practicing law [and are] necessarily quite immature and not very adequate as a sounding board. Besides, I don't think justices of the Supreme Court need a sounding board. He knows what sounds right to him."[39]

His two first-term clerks were aware that Whittaker used medication to control his anxiety, and they realized how fragile his emotional health had become. "He was sometimes curt, that was his style," one of them commented. "I learned then to know ahead of time what I was going to say before I said it."[40]

Once during his first term Whittaker lost control of his temper, and one of his law clerks bore the brunt of his fury. After completing the draft of his separate opinion in a relatively insignificant workmen's compensation case, Whittaker left it for his clerks to review.[41] They both agreed that it was insufficient for a Court opinion—the sentences were exceedingly long, and more important, it lacked a clearly stated rationale.

Concerned that other clerks would ridicule the opinion and its author, one of Whittaker's clerks, Alan Kohn, approached him about it. "With some trepidation I went past the secretary and into his office," Kohn recalled, "'How do you like it?' he asked proudly from behind his huge desk. I said, 'It's great, but there are some things we ought to change.' He became upset, so upset that he picked up the decision and threw it at me and said, 'If you can do better, you take a crack at it!' I was mortified; this was so uncharacteristic."[42] Kohn had until the next morning to make the revisions, and after working all night he managed to cut down the length of some sentences and added a final paragraph explaining the rationale. The next day, following a stern reprimand from his secretary over the previous day's tantrum, Whittaker announced that the revised draft was ready for the printer. "He obviously felt badly about his outburst," Kohn remarked, "and he was too embarrassed to change the opinion. Accepting my changes was his way of apologizing." As a result, Alan Kohn had one paragraph published in a Supreme Court opinion.[43]

Law Clerk Relations with the Justice

The instance recounted above was an aberration, and by all accounts Whittaker was a gentle, considerate man. This does not mean, however, that he was easily approachable or personable with his clerks. To the contrary, his relationship with his clerks was characterized as dignified and businesslike. Few of his clerks remembered socializing with Whittaker outside of the office, and one could not remember even going into the justice's office. Several years after his clerkship, William Canby heard one of Justice Douglas's clerks describe wearing blue jeans to lunch with the justice. Although this occurred several years after Whittaker resigned, Canby remarked, "I was shocked to hear a later Douglas clerk talk about being at work in blue jeans, because in my time we *all* wore suits and ties—in every chamber."[44]

Other justices were known for socializing more with their clerks, but

Whittaker remained detached with his. On Saturdays he might have lunch with his clerks at a nearby cafeteria, but even then the conversation typically concerned Court business. "We'd chit-chat," recalled Heywood Davis. "He was just pretty much his own man and very professional and not a back-slapper or gossiper."[45] Whittaker shared conference votes with his clerks, but not conference discussions. In fact, he apparently kept a detailed record of conference discussions (which he destroyed after his resignation), and his clerk, Alan Kohn, relied on the secretary to get it out of the safe so he could secretly examine it.[46] Otherwise, Whittaker was circumspect with his clerks, maintaining his privacy and revealing himself only when circumstances warranted.

Once while Whittaker was still a judge on the Eighth Circuit Court of Appeals he was asked to assist some of the district courts with their caseloads, and he took his clerk, Clyde Rayburn, with him. While riding together for long stretches in Whittaker's car, Whittaker became contemplative, revealing a personal side few of his clerks ever saw. "I learned then that he liked to ballroom dance when he was young," Rayburn remembered. "He said to me, 'This is the first time in my life when I don't feel like I'm scratching to get ahead. . . . All my sons are adults now. I missed their growing up.'"[47] Rayburn's devotion to Whittaker led him to serve as Whittaker's clerk for two and a half years. Whittaker's secretary, Celia Barrett, possessed a similar devotion, starting in the secretarial pool at Whittaker's law firm, accompanying him to the district and appeals courts, and staying with him for two years at the Supreme Court. She left Whittaker's service when she got married, and he performed the wedding ceremony for her.[48]

Developing personal bonds with his subordinates was not typical for Whittaker at the Supreme Court. There were two notable exceptions, though; one occurred during the anxiety and disappointment of his first term, and the other was during his relaxed, more optimistic third term. Each time Whittaker developed a rapport with his clerks and took them into his confidence. His first term clerk, Alan Kohn, remembered once attending a cocktail party for all the justices at Whittaker's home, and Kohn spent time together with Whittaker outside the Court. Every day after work Whittaker drove Kohn to a D.C. bus stop, a habit Whittaker developed as a lawyer in Kansas City when he drove younger associates home.

One time a tire valve snapped off at the curb, and the tire became instantly flat. "For some reason the valves on the tires were very long," Kohn stated, "This was in rush hour; I suggested we call a service station, but he said, 'We can fix this ourselves.' It was hot that summer, and he took off his jacket and worked as hard as I did."[49] No one on the street that day realized they were passing a Supreme Court justice and his law clerk changing a flat tire together. As they worked side by side, Whittaker admitted to his clerk that coming to the Supreme Court had been a big mistake: "He seemed ready to quit right then and there."[50]

Two years later Whittaker found a new confidant in another clerk, Jerome Libin, who admitted that he enjoyed a warm relationship with the justice. This was due, no doubt, to the role Libin played in restoring some of Whittaker's confidence by encouraging him to dissent more often. The two of them continued to correspond with each other after Whittaker left the Court; in fact, letters from Libin were the only ones from former clerks found among Whittaker's personal papers.[51] Because Libin had known Whittaker's son Kent at law school, he was invited to the Whittaker's home for dinner whenever Kent visited Washington. The year he clerked, Libin also met the woman who would become his wife, and Whittaker took an uncharacteristic interest in his clerk's courtship. In the years following, Libin continued to update Whittaker on the relationship, and Whittaker encouraged Libin to marry.[52]

The most significant testament to their relationship, however, occurred six months after Libin's clerkship ended. Following his military basic training, Libin returned to Washington in time for the inauguration of John Kennedy. During his visit to the Court the day before the inauguration, Whittaker asked him about his plans for the event. Libin admitted that his plans were to watch it on television, but Whittaker told him, "No, you'll ride with us, and while I'm seated on the podium with the other justices, you'll be seated with Mrs. Whittaker."[53]

This type of social interaction with his law clerks was rare; in the five years he served on the Court, only during his third term did Whittaker develop any kind of camaraderie with his clerks. Sometimes he read his letters to them, letters he had written to his friends in Kansas City. In his first two terms he wrote his friends that he was "serving out a five-year sentence," but by his third term he began to confide to his clerks that "maybe he could make it ten years."[54] Whittaker maintained his relationship with his third-term clerk, Jerome Libin, after their term together ended, and his other clerk that year, Patrick McCartan, visited him in his office in Kansas City. "We always ended up in the library discussing cases," McCartan recalled. "He just couldn't keep out of the books."[55]

Other clerks, however, admitted they never saw Whittaker again following their clerkship. Certainly they were grateful for the opportunity he gave them, but they had their own lives and their own challenges once they left the

Court. Whittaker understood this. He did not delude himself with the notion that clerking for him—or for anyone at the Court—should be the pinnacle of a lawyer's career. In fact, when one of his second-term clerks, William Canby, attempted to express his gratitude at the end of their term together, saying how the experience "would be the highlight of his life," Whittaker responded by asking, "Why would you say that?"[56] Whittaker believed his clerks were destined to accomplish much more than serving with him.

The Law Clerks and the Legacy of Charles Evans Whittaker

Since Whittaker's death there have been few occasions to commemorate Whittaker's service to the federal courts. One occurred in October 1998 at the naming of the new Kansas City federal courthouse, the Charles Evans Whittaker United States Courthouse, where at least one former clerk, Ken Dam, was on hand, and Justice Clarence Thomas spoke at the dedication. Nine years later, September 2007, the University of Missouri–Kansas City Law School, which claims Whittaker as an alumnus although he graduated thirty-nine years before the school became part of the state system, sponsored a program commemorating fifty years since Whittaker's elevation to the Supreme Court. This time Kenneth Starr, former clerk to Chief Justice Warren Burger, former appeals court judge (D.C.), and solicitor general (1989–93), was the keynote speaker. Three of Whittaker's clerks, Heywood Davis, Jerome Libin, and Alan Kohn, were also present.[57] In his own remarks, Kohn extolled Whittaker's perseverance and adherence to stare decisis, relying to some extent on his own recollections but also on this author's biography of Whittaker.

To his credit, Alan Kohn has been the most active of Whittaker's former clerks in writing about and responding to criticism of Whittaker as a justice. This began in 1995 with the publication of a collection of judicial biographies for the Supreme Court Historical Society. When it came time to choose someone to write Whittaker's short biography, Maggie Bryan, former secretary for Chief Justice Warren, suggested that Kohn write it.[58] Three years later Kohn described for the Supreme Court Historical Society his eighteen months working for Whittaker.[59] Kohn considers himself the "self-appointed chronicler" of Charles Whittaker, and other clerks recognize his proclivity in this.[60]

Thus much of Charles Evans Whittaker's legacy has been shaped by the common perception that he was a failed justice and by his clerks' public reactions to the judgment of historians and scholars. When asked specifically about this rating, each of his clerks agreed that it was unreasonable. In a 2002 article in the *Supreme Court Historical Society Quarterly* that addressed Justice Whittaker's lowly judicial rating, Kohn proposed his own criteria for evaluation that made Whittaker "hardly worthy of such a low ranking."[61] Based on this new criteria, which included Whittaker's ability to "overcome the obstacle of unremitting, severe depression," Kohn concluded that the raters "apparently chose to give little or no weight to these additional factors." Kohn similarly responded to a 1970s ranking, this one establishing five categories of Supreme Court "greatness" where Whittaker occupied the bottom realm of "failure," by arguing to a friend who participated in the survey that the ranking was "palpably unfair" due to Whittaker's poor health.[62] In Kohn's opinion, viewing Whittaker with a broader perspective places him a bit better than last.

Other law clerks have expressed similar dissatisfaction with the label of "failure" that historians have affixed to Whittaker's tenure on the Supreme Court. Jerome Libin stated that "I think 'failure' is too strong; it was used to incite a reaction. Whittaker could not 'fail' to influence his brethren because he had not intended to influence them."[63] Patrick McCartan remembered reading the survey and remarked, "I was incensed when I read it. Before anyone can have any kind of an impact they need to serve for a longer term. I thought it was terribly unfair to him."[64]

If ratings and surveys have distorted the public's impression of Charles Whittaker as a justice, what would be a fair evaluation? James Adler, who was the last clerk Whittaker hired, offered this assessment: "When I was there he was probably the best lawyer on the Court. If you needed a lawyer and your choices were the nine justices, he was the best."[65]

Notes

1. For a discussion of this transitional period of the Court and an analysis of Whittaker's failure rating, see Craig Alan Smith, *Failing Justice: Charles Evans Whittaker on the Supreme Court* (Jefferson, N.C.: McFarland, 2005), 82, 118–19, 125 especially n. 152, and 177–93. Two notable decisions in which Whittaker participated but for which he did not write an opinion were *Cooper v. Aaron*, 358 U.S. 1 (1958), and *Mapp v. Ohio*, 367 U.S. 643 (1961).

2. Justice David J. Brewer is noted as being from Kansas, where he practiced law and served both on the federal district court and state supreme court, but he was born in what is now Izmir, Turkey.

3. Andrew Johnson first appointed Blatchford to the district court in 1867, Rutherford Hayes sent him to the circuit court in 1872, and, finally, Chester Arthur named him to the Supreme Court in 1882.

4. William O. Douglas, *The Court Years, 1939–1975: The Autobiography of William O. Douglas* (New York: Random House, 1980): 250. Whittaker did, in fact, arrive at the Court *before* his one district court opinion was appealed there, but four of his appeals court opinions arrived for consideration *after* him; two of those were denied certiorari and the other two were affirmed. See Smith, *Failing Justice*, 80n152.

5. Smith, *Failing Justice*, chapter 1.

6. According to one of Whittaker's last clerks, James Adler, it was not at all unusual then for clerks to stay a second term: "[Justice Potter] Stewart had most of his clerks stay for two years. [Justice Hugo] Black never did except for one [George Saunders] during the time I was there." James Adler, interview with author, June 26, 1995. The year Whittaker arrived at the Court, three different clerks were finishing their second term: Roderick Hills (Reed), Andrew Kaufman (Frankfurter), and Jerome Cohen (first Warren, then Frankfurter); and Robert Girard (Black) began the first of two terms. Court records confirm that Justice Stewart had a clerk stay two terms each year he served with Whittaker, beginning with John Lloyd Evans (October terms 1958 and 1959), Jerold Israel (October terms 1959 and 1960), Thomas Kauper (October terms 1960 and 1961), and Robert Hudec (October terms 1961 and 1962). Justice William J. Brennan Jr. had Dennis Lyons stay two terms (October terms 1958 and 1959), and Chief Justice Earl Warren kept Murray Bring two terms (October terms 1959 and 1960).

7. Alan Kohn, "Supreme Court Law Clerk, 1957–1958: A Reminiscence," *Journal of Supreme Court History* 2 (1998): 41–42.

8. For an analysis of Reed's retirement and the influences behind that decision, see Smith, *Failing Justice*, 83–84.

9. Alan Kohn, interview with author, June 13, 1996. See also Smith, *Failing Justice*, 84–85, especially n. 12 where Smith doubts Warren "remembered" Kohn's application but suggests he instead held on to it intending to give it to Whittaker.

10. Kohn, "Supreme Court," 42.

11. Kohn, interview, 1996.

12. Kenneth Dam, interview with author, July 19, 1996.

13. Heywood Davis, interview with author, June 11, 1996. Davis was so fond of this anecdote that he regularly repeated it; see Mindie Paget, "School's First Supreme Court Clerk Recalls Experience Fondly," *Kansas University Law Magazine*, Fall 2008, 7. Davis became the first of five (to date) Kansas University law graduates to clerk at the Supreme Court.

14. Strictly speaking, Whittaker attended the Kansas City School of Law; in 1938, fourteen years after Whittaker graduated, the school merged with the University of Kansas City, a small private college, and the law school became its first professional program.

15. Clyde Rayburn Jr., interview with author, June 19, 1996. Rayburn was especially grateful to Whittaker for assisting him in finding employment after Whittaker left for the Supreme Court, remarking, "Next to my parents, he was the most important

person in my life. He gave me my start, which led to my next position that continued to retirement."

16. William Canby, interview with author, July 17, 1996.

17. Adler, interview, 1996.

18. Ibid.; and James Adler, interview with author, February 26, 2009.

19. Jerome Libin, interview with author, February 6, 2009.

20. James Edwards, interview with author, June 17, 1996.

21. Alan Kohn, interview with author, February 2, 2009. Kohn was quick to point out that another former clerk, Paul Freund, who clerked for Justice Louis Brandeis, also attended Washington University as an undergraduate, but Freund did not attend the law school; he earned his law degrees at Harvard, where he later taught. Therefore, Washington University Law School produced only two Supreme Court clerks (to date), both Whittaker's.

22. William Canby, interview with author, January 28, 2009; Libin and Adler interviews, 2009; and Edwards interview, 1996.

23. Canby interview, 2009; and Heywood Davis, interview with author, February 2, 2009.

24. Libin, interview, 2009.

25. Rayburn, interview.

26. Kohn, "Supreme Court," 42.

27. Davis and Canby, interviews, 2009.

28. Canby, interview, 1996.

29. Dam, interview, 1996.

30. Edwards and Adler, interviews, 1996; see also Smith, *Failing Justice*, 129.

31. Adler, interview, 1996.

32. Adler, correspondence with author, July 23, 2009.

33. Smith, *Failing Justice*, 122–24.

34. Ibid., 129–30, especially n. 9, which considers whether a more likely candidate was "The Bright Young Men behind the Bench," *U.S. News and World Report*, July 12, 1957, 45–48, or "Who Writes the Decisions of the Supreme Court?" *U.S. News and World Report*, December 13, 1957, 74.

35. Davis quoted in Paget, "School's First Clerk," 7; twelve years earlier Davis made a similar remark, interview, 1996.

36. *Lawn v. United States*, 355 U.S. 339 (1958).

37. Kohn, interview, 2009; see *Lawn v. United States*, 355 U.S. 339 (1958). Kohn donated his original draft to Washington University's Law School. For a description of *Lawn*'s significance as a federal precedent, see Smith, *Failing Justice*, 171.

38. Libin, interview, 2009. The case was *Florida Lime & Avocado Growers v. Jacobsen*, 362 U.S. 73 (1960). Libin was less forthcoming in his first interview (1996), claiming he had encouraged Whittaker to dissent, not that he drafted it himself; see Smith, *Failing Justice*, 165.

39. Quoted in Judith Cole, "Mr. Justice Charles Whittaker: A Case Study in Judicial Recruitment and Behavior" (M.A. thesis, University of Missouri–Kansas City, 1972), 128.

40. Dam, interview, 1996. The other clerk, Alan Kohn, stated: "He was taking medication—maybe valium. He was nervous and could not concentrate. I remember our secretary, Celia Barrett, told me about a previous nervous breakdown. I don't think he had good medical care. It was typical in those days to overmedicate." Kohn, interview, 1996.

41. *Byrd v. Blue Ridge Rural Electric Cooperative*, 356 U.S. 525 (1958).

42. Kohn, interview, 1996; see also Kohn, "Supreme Court," 52, and Smith, *Failing Justice*, 131–32.

43. Kohn, interviews, 1996 and 2009.

44. Canby, Davis, and Adler, interviews, 2009, and Kenneth Dam, interview with author, February 2, 2009. Although Whittaker's clerks have never held reunions with each other, some of them have attended reunions at the Court for all the clerks from their term. Clerks in the 1957 term were close personally and held reunions at the Court every ten years with Justice William Brennan serving as host; Kohn, interview, 1996. Canby and Davis both attended Court reunions, and in 2008 they went to the fiftieth anniversary reunion for the clerks from their term.

45. Davis quoted in Paget, "School's First Clerk," 7, and Davis interviews, 1996 and 2009.

46. Kohn, interview, 1996.

47. Rayburn, interview.

48. Celia Barrett, interview with author, June 8, 1996. Barrett's father was a schoolmate and close friend of Whittaker and no doubt helped her secure her job with him. On her first day of work she made the mistake of addressing him as "Uncle Charlie."

49. Kohn, interview, 1996.

50. Kohn, "Supreme Court," 47. Kohn related the same incident in this article as in his interview (1996), but the theme of the incident in the article was Whittaker's disappointment, whereas the theme of the interview was more comical—a Supreme Court justice changing a tire in D.C. completely unnoticed; see Smith, *Failing Justice*, 95–96.

51. Charles Whittaker's personal papers are in the possession of his son, Kent Whittaker, a lawyer in Kansas City, Missouri.

52. Jerome Libin, interview with author, June 29, 1996, and Libin, interview, 2009.

53. Libin, interview, 2009.

54. Libin, interview, 1996.

55. Patrick McCartan, interview with author, June 27, 1996.

56. Davis, interviews, 1996 and 2009; Canby also recollected this incident in his 1996 interview.

57. Heywood Davis, message to author, January 27, 2009; Alan Kohn, message to author, January 15, 2009; and Libin, interview, 2009.

58. See "Charles E. Whittaker, 1957–1962," in *The Supreme Court Justices: Illustrated Biographies, 1789–1995*, ed. Clare Cushman, 2nd ed. (Washington, D.C.: Congressional Quarterly, 1995), 451–55.

59. See Kohn, "Supreme Court," 41–52.

60. Kohn, interview, 2009. When asked about his own contributions, another clerk, Jerome Libin, responded, "Alan Kohn does most of the writing."

61. Alan Kohn, "Evaluating Justice Whittaker," *Supreme Court Historical Society Quarterly* 23, no. 3 (2002).

62. In his article, Kohn mentioned a "1978 ranking by sixty-five academicians," referring to the publication of Albert Blaustein and Roy Mersky's book, *The First One Hundred Justices: Statistical Studies on the Supreme Court of the United States* (Hamden, Conn.: Archon Books, 1978), but the 1970 survey by Blaustein and Mersky first appeared in "The Twelve Great Justices of All Time," *Life,* October 15, 1971, 53–59, and was later expanded in "Rating Supreme Court Justices," *American Bar Association Journal* 58 (November 1972): 1183–89.

63. Libin, interview, 1996.

64. McCartan, interview, 1996.

65. Adler, interview, 1996. Thirteen years later Adler had not changed his opinion; without prompting, he stated again: "He was the best lawyer on the Court. If you had a difficult legal problem, of the nine justices he was the one you would want." Adler, interview, 2009.

III The Modern Clerkship Institution

Clerking for Chief Justice Earl Warren

I met Chief Justice Earl Warren more than a month after starting as one of his law clerks. I arrived at the Court on July 1, 1960, a few days after taking the D.C. bar exam. The Chief was traveling abroad during that summer (as he often did), and Murray Bring, who had clerked during the previous term, introduced me and Joseph Bartlett, the other new law clerk, to the job. We began by reviewing the accumulated cert petitions and writing memos about them in preparation for the Court's first conference in late September.

Although I had not yet met the Chief, I certainly knew a great deal about him. As governor of California, he was a popular national political figure when he first entered the race for president in 1948. Four years later, my radio broadcasted the 1952 Republican National Convention, where Warren, the third-term governor, was a serious candidate for the nomination in the event of a deadlock between the World War II hero, General Dwight D. Eisenhower, and "Mr. Republican," Senator Robert A. Taft of Ohio. The Chief's stature in the American political landscape was so great that when he welcomed us upon his return to the Court in August, I was surprised to find that we were about the same height. Beyond that, however, there was no mistaking him. The John Birch Society had made his face famous with its "Impeach Earl Warren" billboards in many parts of the country, mainly in reaction to the school segregation cases and to a series of decisions protecting the rights of alleged Communists.

The way Supreme Court justices selected their clerks was a good deal different in the 1950s than it is today. During my third year at the University of Pennsylvania Law School, in 1959, I went on the law school teaching market. At the same time, a committee of professors decided to propose two of my classmates and me for Supreme Court clerkships; they applied to the Chief on my behalf, to Justice Black for another of us, and for the third to Justice Frankfurter, who only took Harvard Law School graduates, and Justice Harlan. My recollection is that my professors told me about this opportunity rather than asking me about it. Word came in March that the Chief had hired me, with no interview. This was not atypical—he often selected candidates based solely on their records and recommendations.

Many of the Chief's clerks had some connection to California, and the Chief always hired at least one clerk from a law school in his home state. That term, Joe Bartlett was the California clerk. He was from Boston and went to Harvard, but he had graduated from Stanford Law School. The Chief's other clerk, Murray Bring, was a Los Angeles native who attended the University of Southern California and New York University Law School. We also occasionally worked with Mark Ball, clerk for Justices Reed and Burton, who had retired but maintained an office at the Court.

About a day or so after the Chief returned to the Court that summer, he called the three of us down to his office. (Unlike the other clerks, who occupied a room immediately adjacent to their justice's office, the Chief's clerks had their own set of offices on the second floor.) He welcomed us and put us at ease immediately. He was a very regular guy—no airs or pretense about him whatsoever. He had been a hero of mine, and his affable way only made me admire him more.

After chatting for a short time, the Chief gave us a single instruction: "I don't want you ever to talk to the press." Confidentiality was, of course, a major concern at the Court—no one outside the building knew when a particular decision was coming down or anything about the opinions until the morning the Court delivered them. But I don't think secrecy alone prompted this warning from the Chief. Rather, it reflected his caution about the media, his understanding that they stand at a distance and that they can be adversaries. It likely came from a life in politics and seemed to me quite reasonable, never imagining it would cause me to alter my behavior in any way. But one evening quite soon thereafter, a clerk from another office invited me to a small dinner party at his home along with Anthony Lewis, who was then the Supreme Court reporter for the *New York Times*. This made me extremely uncomfortable —socializing with Lewis might well violate the Chief's clear instructions. I wondered if it would be best to simply leave the gathering. But doing so seemed ungracious, and likely not what the Chief would have wanted. Plus, I did not want to leave—Lewis was a fascinating figure. I stayed but was very careful not to say anything that would indicate what was happening in our office. Indeed, I hardly spoke very much at all.

Mrs. Margaret McHugh ran the Chief's office. She was a long-time Washington bureaucrat with a quite serious demeanor who had been Chief Justice Vinson's secretary at the Court and before that, when he was secretary of the Treasury. When Warren arrived, Mrs. McHugh continued to run the office while the Chief's longtime secretary from California, Maggie Bryant, handled his personal work. Maggie Bryant was "Maggie" to us, but Mrs. McHugh was always "Mrs. McHugh," even to the Chief.

Mrs. McHugh was extremely businesslike. While we revered the Chief from the beginning, Mrs. McHugh was the tough guy in the office. In retrospect, the Chief probably liked the fact that Mrs. McHugh kept us in line. For example, the Chief used to work at home in the mornings, and we knew for sure he would not come in before 10:00 a.m. or so. (At that time oral argument did not begin until noon.) As time wore on, we began arriving a little late. After all, we were working six days a week, not infrequently late into the evenings. Mrs. McHugh soon corrected this habit, informing us that the office opened at 9 a.m. We always arrived by that time thereafter. That is not to say we had a bad relationship with Mrs. McHugh. After a while we all loosened up, and if she was championing a particularly rigid rule, we might get away with a little tease, saying, "Oh, come on, Mrs. McHugh."

Job Duties of the Warren Clerks

The Court received some 2,200 cert petitions during the 1960 term, and more than half were in forma pauperis ("i.f.p.") cases brought by people—almost all prisoners—who could not afford a lawyer. The Chief's chambers initially handled these cases, and the extra work they created entitled the Chief to three law clerks instead of the two that each of the other justices had—except for Justice William O. Douglas, who filled one of his law clerk allocations with a second secretary. We also had our own secretary/typist because of the need to prepare for all the justices more than ten carbon copies (or "flimsies," we called them) of the memos we wrote in the i.f.p. cases. I was not much of a typist, and our secretary transformed my longhand drafts into typed pages for the Chief.

Our duties as clerks divided into three general tasks. First, we wrote a short memo to the Chief on each cert petition—some might be very brief, just a few pages; others could run to more than twenty pages. Second, we wrote considerably longer bench memos discussing the briefs in cases scheduled for oral argument. (We made a recommendation to the Chief in both sets of memos.) Third, we ordinarily composed a first draft of an opinion, almost always assigned by the Chief to the clerk who had written the bench memo in the case.

We divided most of the certs according to our areas of interest. I chose federal income tax, church and state, labor, civil rights, race, freedom of speech (including all the Communist cases), and Commerce Clause problems. I worked on 3 of the 110 cases in which the Court published opinions during our term. (Today the Court files opinions in fewer than 100 cases.)

We tried to go to oral argument when we could, especially to hear some of the renowned advocates of the time: Solicitor General Archibald Cox and two of his senior deputies, Oscar Davis and Philip Elman; Leonard Boudin; Hugh Cox; Frederick Bernays Wiener; and Edward Bennett Williams. We also had a special interest if we had written the bench memo, though very often time constraints prevented us from leaving our work in the office. If we were assigned to draft an opinion in a case in which we had missed the argument, we would listen to it on phonograph recordings.

Criminal procedure, Communism, and race were the major constitutional issues that term. The criminal procedure rulings dealt mainly with search and seizure, confessions, and the privilege against self-incrimination.[1] The Court decided almost all of the cases involving rights of the accused in favor of the individual, a result that did not come easily given that the Court's five conservative-leaning justices outnumbered its four liberals. In order of seniority, the conservatives were Justices Frankfurter, Clark, Harlan, Whittaker, and Stewart, and the liberals were Justices Black, Douglas, Warren, and Brennan. While the liberals overcame this division in the criminal procedure area, they could not do so in most of the cases involving Communist and other internal security issues. There the Court rejected broad challenges to statutes, including those that outlawed Communist Party membership or required the party to register and disclose information.[2] And the race cases, which had enjoyed unanimity in the early years of the Warren Court, began to draw concurrences and dissents during the 1960 term.[3]

The Court also decided several major cases dealing with statutory interpretation.[4] In one of the most watched rulings of the term, the Court held that the Clayton Act required DuPont to sell its 23 percent share of General Motors to cure their anticompetitive relationship.[5]

We did our work in a small, quiet office, a setting that has remained familiar to me during my years in academia. But it was foreign to the Chief when he arrived in Washington. Before being governor of California for ten years, he had been attorney general for four years and district attorney of Alameda County for fourteen years prior to that—jobs that suited him as a man of action. The Chief felt quite constrained at the Court. As a judge he could only react, with limited power to improve peoples' lives and a very small staff to match. Yet the skills that made him a natural politician—intuition, decisiveness, keen practical sense, and life experience—contributed to his great prominence on the Court.

The Other Law Clerks at the Supreme Court

Nineteen clerks worked at the Court that year, all of them white men. Although the Chief never hired a woman law clerk, that was a different era, and I am confident that would not have been his practice in later years. Indeed, in 1967, the Chief appointed Tyrone Brown, only the second African American law clerk in the Court's history to that time.

All of the clerks on the Court that year went on to notable legal careers. A number engaged in successful law practices, usually in large firms in metropolitan areas throughout the country. Taking a less conventional path, Justice Harlan's clerks, Charles Fried and Philip Heymann, taught at Harvard Law School and worked in government. Heymann was deputy attorney general in the Clinton administration, and Fried was President Reagan's solicitor general. Fried also served as associate justice on the Supreme Judicial Court of Massachusetts.

Justice Stewart's clerks, Tom Kauper and Jerry Israel, both taught law at the University of Michigan. Kauper was also assistant attorney general in charge of the Antitrust Division during the Nixon and Ford administrations. Larry Wallace, who clerked for Justice Black and was briefly on the faculty at Duke Law School, went on to spend some thirty-five years as deputy solicitor general, arguing more than 150 cases before the Supreme Court—a record for a government lawyer. Bernard Jacob and Malachy Mahan, clerks for Justices Douglas and Clark, respectively, became law professors at Hofstra University.

Justice Frankfurter's clerk, Tony Amsterdam, was a law professor at the University of Pennsylvania, Stanford, and New York University and became the lead strategist and advocate in the NAACP Legal Defense Fund's challenge to capital punishment. One of Justice Brennan's clerks, Richard Arnold, spent more than twenty years on the U.S. Court of Appeals for the Eighth Circuit and was one of the most respected federal judges in the nation. The other, Dan Rezneck, became senior corporation counsel for the District of Columbia after a long career in practice.

My co-clerks also went on to similarly illustrious positions. Murray Bring became vice chairman of Phillip Morris after several significant government positions and a notable career as a senior partner at a great Washington law firm. After a stint in the Johnson administration, Joe Bartlett pursued a lifetime in law practice with a series of firms in Boston and New York.

Most days, the clerks ate lunch together in a private room adjacent to the Court's basement cafeteria. The cafeteria was open to the public, and we stood in line to select our food along with everyone else. Security was best preserved, however, if we took our trays into another room. Once there, we often had lively discussions about cases before the Court. For example, one clerk was particularly disappointed with a draft opinion of the Chief's. He thought the statutes at issue should be overturned, and he let me know it. But we invariably maintained allegiance to the justices for whom we worked. No one ever revealed information that was not already known. We did not speculate as to how a given justice would vote. And apart from an occasional casual conversation, it would have been highly unusual if a clerk had tried to find out the views of another justice through that justice's clerk.

A number of times during the year, we asked notable guests to our lunch. Murray Bring, who was our "chief clerk" given his prior year at the Court, arranged the invitations. Each justice came, as did some high-powered political figures such as Dean Acheson, who had served as secretary of state in the Truman administration, newly appointed secretary of state in the Kennedy administration Dean Rusk, McGeorge Bundy, who was Kennedy's national security adviser, and Senator Eugene McCarthy from Minnesota. We could ask any question we wanted, but for the most part the clerks were quite deferential. Luckily, one of us was particularly forthright and asked the questions most of us were afraid to ask. (Fifty years ago, young people were more inhibited than they are today.)

Although we all saw each other most days at lunch, the clerks did not associate outside of work with any frequency. Occasionally a clerk from another office would invite me to a dinner party, or Murray and Joe and I would socialize. But for the most part, the time we spent together was at the Court.

The Chief's Political Instincts and His Style as a Boss and Mentor

The Chief's writing was concise and attracted attention. He wrote clearly—his hand-drafted opinion in *Brown v. Board of Education,* plain speaking and eloquent, is perhaps the best example.[6] He also had a skillful notion of how his statements would be perceived outside legal circles. An illustration may be found in the Sunday Closing Laws cases.[7] At that time, few places of business were allowed to open on Sunday in some parts of the country, and four cases from Maryland, Massachusetts, and Pennsylvania raised two major issues. The first was whether Sunday Closing Laws were impermissible religious legislation in violation of the Establishment Clause. The second was whether they abridged the Free Exercise Clause by placing Orthodox Jews (or other Sabbatarians) at a significant disadvantage because their religion forbade them to work on Saturday, their day of rest. The Court rejected both challenges, reasoning that the closing laws derived from religion but had taken on a secular purpose. And while the Orthodox Jews raised a sympathetic claim, the Court concluded that finding for them would open the door to analogous pleas for exemptions from various laws by the nation's many religious groups. The Chief assigned himself the opinions, and I prepared drafts.

A short time after I sent them down to him, Mrs. McHugh summoned me to the Chief's office. He told me he had two points to make regarding the Sunday Closing Laws opinions. First: "I don't use the words 'albeit' or 'arguendo.'" Then he said, "You know, Jesse, these opinions are going to be read from many church pulpits across the country. I think we ought to add something like this." He handed me a piece of paper containing a handwritten paragraph. I looked it over. It was a brief, straightforward summation of the opinions, which ran over one hundred pages. He asked me if the paragraph troubled me in any way, which it did not. I included the Chief's language in the final drafts, deleted any reference to "arguendo" or "albeit," and sent the opinions back to him.

When the Sunday Closing Laws cases came down, they were widely reported. Laws in virtually all states had been placed at risk. Of the two major newspapers covering the opinions that I read, only one quoted from the opinions, and that was just a single paragraph—the Chief's.

The Chief relied on his political instincts again in *James v. United States*.[8] This was a tax case, and as an accounting major who had several tax courses in law school, I took the cases dealing with that subject. A man had challenged his conviction for willfully failing to pay income tax on embezzled funds, which he argued were not "income." An earlier Supreme Court decision agreed with him, but a more recent case had held that extorted funds were taxable income.[9] My bench memo stated that there was no principled distinction between funds obtained by extortion and money generated by embezzlement. Because the extortion case came later, I suggested that embezzled funds should also be treated as income for federal tax purposes.

The justices took an initial vote at their Friday conference after the case had been argued. After every conference, the clerk of the Court came to the

Chief's office, and the Chief read him the list of orders to be announced the following Monday.[10] Usually the three of us also attended. After the clerk left, the Chief answered any questions we had about the conference—mainly how the justices had voted, and why. We always looked forward to this meeting because it was our primary means of finding out the fate of various cases on which we had worked. On this Friday afternoon, I asked about *James,* and the Chief said, "We're all over the lot on that case." He wanted to overrule the old case and hold that embezzled funds are taxable income, but because the rule was otherwise when James prepared his tax return, the Chief also wanted to overturn the conviction. Other justices favored overruling *Wilcox* but did not want to disturb the conviction. Still others felt that *Wilcox* should stand and James's conviction should be reversed.

The Chief asked me to try my hand at drafting a per curiam opinion. I was at a loss at first, but in the end my short draft of about ten pages overruled *Wilcox* by declaring embezzled funds to be income, yet reversed James's conviction because he could not have "willfully" evaded taxes in light of the then-existing Supreme Court precedent. After reviewing the draft, the Chief circulated it to the other justices. They responded with about forty pages of concurring and dissenting opinions. Only Justices Brennan and Stewart joined the draft, which now had the Chief's name on it. Another three justices agreed with us to overrule *Wilcox,* but not to overturn the conviction. And three other justices would reverse the conviction, but not overrule *Wilcox.*

My draft had certainly not persuaded a majority, and the other justices' opinions made many arguments worthy of response. I urged the Chief to permit me to draft a defense of our analysis, saying something like, "They are really ripping us up on this thing." "No, we're just going to stand firm," he said. "We've got the votes." He was right. We had six votes on each of the positions he wanted to take. So, I wrote a paragraph to that effect at the end of the opinion and sent it back down to the Chief.

A few days later Mrs. McHugh called saying the Chief would like to see me. I went down to his office and sat in one of the two chairs in front of his massive desk. He asked Mrs. McHugh to also come in, and she took the other chair. "Mrs. McHugh disagrees with what you have proposed about the *James* case," the Chief said, somewhat tongue in cheek. He explained that she did not think we could cobble together the votes to reach a result like this, and he asked me to reply. I agreed that what we had done was unusual, but said we had two distinct issues, each had six votes, and that made a majority for the Chief's views. Mrs. McHugh remained silent. As if presiding over an oral argument, the Chief solemnly looked at Mrs. McHugh, waiting for a response. She sort of shrugged. The Chief looked back at me and gave his ruling in my favor.

The Chief was subtle in his dealings with his clerks when he believed we had made a mistake. I was responsible for creating two problems in the course of working on a single case, *Times Film Corp. v. City of Chicago*.[11] It was the first movie censorship ruling that tested the system of censorship itself rather than whether the film had been censored properly. The majority held that the First Amendment allowed cities to require that all films be submitted to a reviewing agency before they could be shown. My draft of the Chief's dissent inventoried the kinds of films that had been censored by the city of Chicago. For example, it had banned newsreels of Chicago policemen shooting at labor picketers and a Disney film depicting the birth of a buffalo.[12] A similar system in Memphis rejected a movie that showed scenes of white and black children in school together.[13] The list went on, and it was quite damning.

The briefs in the case gave me many of these examples, and one of them cited materials at a library in Chicago. One Friday afternoon after the conference, the Chief told me that *Times Film* would likely come down a week from the following Monday. I still needed to check the citations in the draft against the materials in Chicago. The Court's library arranged for the sources to be sent to Washington that week. When they arrived, I checked the citations, which were correct.

In the meantime, a Chicago newspaper reported over the weekend that the Court's decision in *Times Film* would be released on Monday. This was a major breach of security. When the Chief learned about it on Monday morning, he stopped the opinion from being handed down as planned. I immediately suspected myself as the source of the leak—we had made our deadline too clear to the library in Chicago. I asked to see the Chief and told him what happened. "No problem," he said, to my great relief. He seemed to feel that my actions were reasonable.

Not so with my second misstep. The Chief's dissent in *Times Film* relied heavily on *Near v. Minnesota,* the landmark decision on the First Amendment bar to censorship and prior restraints.[14] The Chief's opinion noted that "even the lone dissenter" in *Near,* who sought to uphold the censorship statute in that case, would object to the kind of program at issue in *Times Film.* Given the media's major interest in the censorship issue, the newspapers widely reported the Court's judgment. As would be expected, they gave the Chief's dissent substantial praise. Overall, the Chief said some nice things to me about my effort.

Not much time had passed, however, when the Chief called me down to his office. He showed me a letter someone had sent concerning my citation of *Near*. It pointed out that there was no "lone dissenter"; in fact, *Near* had four dissenters. I was mortified. It did not take long to figure out what had happened—in the days of *Near*, opinions often noted the names of joining justices at the end, not the beginning, and I had obviously missed this in reading *Near*. (Of course, my mistake was corrected in the court reporter's next printing of *Times Film*.) I explained the cause of my error to the Chief. He was clearly displeased, but he just looked at me and did not say anything. He had a way of communicating that he was not happy, as he rightfully was in this situation, but he did so through subtle facial and body language.

Such moments were rare, but they demonstrate the ways in which the Chief treated his clerks like family. He was also generally very protective of his staff. During the term, an incident occurred between Justice Clark and Joe Bartlett stemming from a Texas death penalty case. Clark, a Texan, objected to the way Joe had presented the case in the cert flimsy that Joe had prepared. Justice Clark circulated his own memo, which was quite hard on Joe, who explained to the Chief why he thought Clark's complaint was not justified. Several days later Justice Clark phoned Joe and apologized. Clearly, the Chief had communicated his concern to Clark.

The Chief was unusually thoughtful and generous. Late one afternoon we came down to the Chief's office and found him dressed in a dinner jacket. We asked him where he was going, and he named the embassy of a little known nation. We inquired whether he went to many of these events, and he said no, very few. Why was he going to this one? "It's a small country," he said. "They feel really good when the Chief Justice or other high ranking official appears." This graciousness likely led the Chief and Mrs. Warren to accept an invitation early in the term to attend a dinner party with his clerks at Joe Bartlett's home in Georgetown.

The Chief was also very kind to me personally. Early in the term, I met and began dating a young woman who had recently divorced and had an infant son. She came as my date to dinner at Joe's house, and the Chief took an interest in our relationship. He went out of his way to tell me that Mrs. Warren had been widowed with a young son when they met, and that he had adopted the son and made him a full part of what became a wonderful marriage and family. It meant a lot to me that the Chief would identify his experience with mine, especially given that divorce was much less frequent in those days.

The day before the young woman and I got married, at the end of term, the

Chief sought me out to wish me well. He sensed that I was apprehensive. It was not marriage that troubled me, but the ring was not yet back from the jeweler and might not be ready in time to reach the wedding site, which was 120 miles away in Pennsylvania. "Don't worry about it," the Chief said. He offered to have his driver, Gene, pick it up the next day and drive it to Pennsylvania. Fortunately, the jeweler came through, but the Chief's gesture was most touching.

While the Chief was fully aware of his status as chief justice, he could also be humorously self-deprecating. During the term, he hosted a black-tie dinner for the entire office staff and our spouses or dates. We sat at a long table with the Chief at one end and Mrs. Warren at the other. I was close to the center and could hear the conversations at both sides. Mrs. Warren was telling a story to someone near her, saying the chief justice had said this, or the chief justice did that. The Chief called from the other end of the table: "Nina, are you dropping names again?"

Our main bonding experience with the Chief was Saturday lunch, a highlight of our work at the Court. We came to the office six days a week, and on Saturdays when the Chief was in town he would usually come up to our office to take us to lunch. These sessions were extraordinary, often lasting four or more hours, and the Chief talked about anything we asked. He was very open with us—ordinarily we talked about matters other than what was going on at the Court at the time, but no topic was off limits. We rotated among a few restaurants—the University Club, the restaurant in Union Station, which was a short walk from the Court, and the cafeteria in the Methodist Building just across the street.

During one Saturday lunch, the Chief listed three rulings that he now wished he had not supported. First, he regretted dismissing the original interracial-marriage case, which came before the Court just after *Brown*.[15] Second, he thought he should have voted to exclude evidence gleaned from a microphone illegally installed in a gambler's bedroom. At that time, the exclusionary rule did not apply to the states, and in his first term on the Court, the Chief joined an opinion by Justice Jackson reaffirming the existing rule.[16] His third regret, also from his first months on the bench, was not following his instinct to subject Major League Baseball to the antitrust laws. A 1920s decision granted baseball an exemption, and the Chief, who was a great baseball fan, declined to overrule it when it reached the Court again.[17] "[Justice] Shay Minton told me this would be the end of baseball," he said. "I couldn't do that."

At lunch, the Chief told many stories about his career in California. One of

[handwritten margin note: '55 cf. Loving '67]

his favorites was when, as district attorney of Alameda County, he commanded a launch to raid gambling ships offshore. He personally tried many cases and argued several times before the U.S. Supreme Court. He was especially proud of the integrity of the office he ran as district attorney.

The Chief also talked at length about the Japanese Exclusion Order. He was not without reservations about his support for the internment as attorney general. Although he later wrote that he "deeply regretted" the action as "not in keeping with our American concept of freedom," he also defended the relocation at our lunches. He explained that at that time, Japanese immigrants, even those who had become citizens, were treated extremely poorly. They lived in segregated neighborhoods and suffered various discriminations, and when the war broke out, they were largely out of the mainstream. He heard many threatening reports—for example, Japanese submarines off the coast of Santa Barbara and elsewhere, people communicating from shore via Morse code using their the window shades during blackouts. When the internment began, an old friend of the Chief's wrote to say that what was going on was indefensible. The Chief wrote back with a fable, which he relayed to us. Suppose we decided to leave the United States for a better life in Japan, he said to his friend. We took our young families with us and were full of hope when we set off. When we got there, we found that there were many places we could not live. Many schools, certainly the better schools, were closed to our children. When our wives left the house, they were subjected to antagonistic comments. We were lawyers back home, but the only jobs open to us were menial labor. Suppose after we lived there a while, war broke out between Japan and the United States. "Whom would you support?" he asked.

It was sometimes dusk by the time these lunches ended. The Chief's home was about a twenty-minute walk from the University Club, and often he would say he was going to walk home. He was very visible and recognizable. We used to tell him to be more careful, that he was too controversial a figure to walk around by himself. The Chief would not hear it. He had no security whatsoever. Nearly the same was true for the Supreme Court Building. A few older men served as the principal security for the courtroom itself, and they seemed more concerned about whispering in the visitors' section than someone getting through the readily opened double doors that separated the public area from the justices' chambers. The most robust security in the building was the police outpost in the basement, which contained a parking lot for the justices and other staff. Their main duty seemed to be making sure people did not park illegally. Fortunately, no one tested what little precautions there were.

Planning a Reunion of the Warren Clerks

During the term, we decided to organize a reunion of the Chief's clerks to mark his seventieth birthday in March 1961. This subsequently became an annual event. The Chief had been on the Court for seven years, and about fifteen clerks came to Washington for the party, which we held at the Metropolitan Club. The only nonclerk present was President John F. Kennedy, who had recently been inaugurated. Joe Bartlett arranged it—he came from a prominent Boston family, knew the Kennedys from Boston politics, and dined at Bobby's house in McLean, Virginia, while we clerked. Joe knew a member of the president's staff well enough to invite Kennedy for cocktails before dinner. The president had been in office only a few months, but he and the Chief had developed a cordial relationship. We were delighted when he agreed to attend our small gathering. The Chief knew about the party, but Kennedy was a total surprise.

The night of the event, at around 7:00 p.m., Joe got a call from the White House that the president was en route. Joe told Murray and me to go downstairs and greet him at the door. We went down, and minutes later a large black limousine pulled up. All the doors flew open, and Secret Service officers jumped out. Kennedy bolted out of the back seat and walked quickly in front of the Secret Service agents toward us. One of us, either Murray or I, greeted the president and introduced ourselves as two of the Chief's clerks. We all went inside the club to the tiny elevator, and when it opened, the president stepped inside. Murray and I hung back, assuming that the agents would go with the president. They said no, you go on up, so we got in, shoulder to shoulder because it was such a small space. The president asked us where we went to law school. Murray said NYU and I said Penn. "What happened to Harvard?" he asked with a smile.

When the elevator door opened and the Chief caught sight of the president, he was taken aback. "Mr. President," the Chief said. "What a surprise." Kennedy said: "Happy birthday, Mr. Chief Justice. You know I've had more constitutional problems than you this week." He was referring to a political issue involving aid to parochial schools, which was a big deal because of the president being Catholic. The Chief asked the president what he would like to drink, and Kennedy asked for a beer. The small private bar had no beer. The club's waiters hustled off to get one, and the president stayed for about half an hour.

The Chief's Judicial Approach: Activism and Principle

The Chief cared deeply about doing the right thing in each case. During oral argument, when counsel defended a challenged practice by relying on precedent or statutory language, the Chief was known to ask, "Yes, but is it fair?" His commitment to fairness earned him the reputation as an activist, which was accurate in some instances. *Boynton v. Virginia,* the first "sit-in" case to reach the Supreme Court protesting racial discrimination by restaurants, was one of those cases.[18]

Bruce Boynton was an African American law student at Howard University traveling by bus from Washington, D.C., to Montgomery, Alabama, his hometown. The trip had a 10:40 p.m. stopover at the bus terminal in Richmond, Virginia, where Boynton tried to get something to eat at the terminal's restaurant. The restaurant had a "white" and a "colored" section, and Boynton sat on a stool in the white section. When he refused to move, he was arrested and fined $10 for trespass. Boynton challenged his conviction all the way to the Supreme Court, with Thurgood Marshall arguing his case during the first week of term.

Boynton alleged violations of the Fourteenth Amendment and the Commerce Clause. The major obstacle to reversing Boynton's conviction was whether the terminal restaurant's racial discrimination involved state action, which is required to find a violation of the Fourteenth Amendment, and probably the Commerce Clause as well.

The solicitor general had filed an amicus brief revealing that two heavily regulated interstate bus companies owned the bus terminal and leased space to the restaurant that refused to serve Boynton. This was extremely helpful because it provided a basis for turning an incident of private discrimination into one that was the responsibility of government. However, this fact was not in the record, and after carefully researching Virginia's evidence rules, it did not appear to me that Virginia courts could take judicial notice of the documents showing who owned the terminal. Without this information, Boynton's constitutional claim seemed extremely difficult to sustain. Reluctantly, my bench memo recommended that the Court dismiss the case as improvidently granted. Boynton would pay a small fine, and future victims of the restaurant's race-based conduct would be on notice to put a fact like this in the record.

The Chief called me to his office. He was not happy with my suggestion in the bench memo. He made two points. First, Boynton's fine was hardly the worst that could come of his conviction. He could be denied admission to the bar, particularly if he sought to practice in the South, which was his home.

Second, the Chief said that he might not be on the Court the next time a case like this came up, and therefore waiting for a better one was not a desirable option. "I want you to go upstairs and search that record with a fine-tooth comb to see if you can't find more," the Chief said.

I restudied the record as carefully as possible, but it simply did not contain the facts we needed. Oral argument held some hope for me—perhaps the historic civil rights advocate, Thurgood Marshall, could find a way. But after just a few minutes of argument, it appeared that he would not provide the missing ingredient. Marshall knew the case was not a strong platform—it had not been planned as a test case—to pursue one of the great constitutional issues of the day: the extent to which private discrimination might violate the Fourteenth Amendment. Each time the Court threw out a theory meant to limit the holding and let Marshall win on narrow grounds, he took it. Although Marshall's course of action was clearly in the best interest of his client, my strong desire to salvage the constitutional claim made it disappointing.

Counsel for Virginia was a distinguished member of the Virginia bar who had been specially retained by the state for oral argument. Soon after he came to the podium, the Chief leaned forward and asked gently, "Counsel, who owns the terminal?" The lawyer, with marked southern gentility, responded, "That's not part of the record, Your Honor." He was obviously prepared for the question. The Chief followed up: "I didn't ask if it was in the record, I asked who owned it." They went back and forth several more times, and finally the lawyer said, "Mr. Chief Justice, do you want me to testify here?" Everyone involved knew who owned the terminal. The Chief pushed the lawyer awfully hard but could not get him to provide the needed information.

In the end, Justice Black wrote the Court's opinion, reversing Boynton's conviction without reaching the constitutional issue. Black told the conference that he had helped draft the Interstate Commerce Act as a senator. In what I thought was a masterful opinion, he argued that the facts in the record demonstrated illegal discrimination against interstate passengers in violation of the act, and six justices joined him.

As *Boynton* illustrates, the Chief made his own decisions and never hesitated to go against his clerks' recommendations when he disagreed with the outcome we suggested. On a number of occasions, he looked past legal analysis to the real-world impact of a decision, something for which he had a keen sense based upon a lifetime of experience off the bench. For example, in an income tax case, my bench memo proposed that the Chief follow a theory that I had developed in a Student Note in the *University of Pennsylvania Law Review*. He voted against the recommendation. He told me that my analysis would make it much more difficult to collect taxes in a timely fashion—a point that I had never considered. My theory worked in the abstract, but he understood the reality of tax enforcement. He and the other justices in my term had such rich pre-judicial backgrounds, persuading me to believe in the desirability of appointing justices from varied walks of life, especially from other branches and levels of government as well as law practice and the legal academy, and not only after long service on the federal courts of appeal.

Another example of the Chief following his own instincts arose in connection with one of the many Communist cases that year. After several losses, my recommendation was to deny certiorari in the latest Communist case scheduled for conference.[19] He was just going to lose this one too, my cert memo said. When the Chief returned from conference and read the orders to the clerk, he indicated that he had voted to grant cert in the case. When I asked why, he answered, "I'm going to keep voting to take them. If the Court continues to make bad law, it will sooner or later fall of its own weight." In fact, as a result, he ended up prevailing in a few of the Communist cases on very narrow grounds. In one, for example, the Court's four liberals were joined by Justice Stewart in reversing a person's contempt conviction for refusing to answer questions from a subcommittee of the House Un-American Activities Committee about alleged Communist affiliations of people other than himself, reasoning that the questions were not pertinent to the Committee's inquiry.[20]

The Chief interpreted the specific provisions of the Constitution broadly in light of contemporary problems. However, principle limited his desire to do the right thing in each case. He was wary of unbounded judicial discretion leading to ad hoc decision making. In all, the Chief's approach might be described as a principled activism.

Poe v. Ullman, a pre-*Griswold* challenge to Connecticut's anticontraceptive law, affords a case in point.[21] Justice Frankfurter circulated an opinion that avoided the merits by using a nonjusticiability doctrine, arguing that the law forbidding use of birth control devices had never effectively been enforced in Connecticut. The Chief called me to his office to discuss the issue and, when asked, I recommended that the Chief join Frankfurter. The Chief said he was uncomfortable about subscribing to Frankfurter's opinion because he was inclined against technical arguments such as lack of standing. On the other hand, he disapproved of the statute as a policy matter. In the end, he decided to go along with Frankfurter. "I just don't believe in striking down a law, even one that I think is wrong, that was passed in the name of the public interest," he said.

cf 'but is it fair?' p. 276

My understanding was that he did not subscribe to the use of substantive due process to reach results simply because he would have supported them as a legislator. Four years later, I was surprised when he joined the majority in *Griswold v. Connecticut,* which realistically grounded its rationale in substantive due process.

Torcaso v. Watkins also reflected the Chief's pragmatic and principled approach.[22] An aspiring notary public challenged the denial of his notary commission, which resulted from his refusal to take an oath to God as required by a Maryland statute. My bench memo urged the Chief to find this a violation of the Religion Clauses. He asked to discuss it in his office. He said he agreed, but he could not hold the Maryland law unconstitutional while induction to the Supreme Court bar, which the Chief himself administered at the beginning of each day that the Court was in session, ended with the line "So help me God." I replied by asking him what he would do if someone refused to repeat that phrase. The Chief thought a moment and smiled. He could ask them to say it, but he would never deny membership in the Supreme Court bar simply because they did not believe in God.

Staying in Touch with the Chief and Honoring Him after His Death

After my clerkship, I still saw the Chief at least once a year at the reunion dinner and sometimes when he came to the Bay Area, which was quite often. The reunion was a black-tie dinner on a Saturday night after the end of term. Thurgood Marshall often came for cocktails, a tradition that started when he was solicitor general. Once we had trouble getting him to leave before dinner, great raconteur that he was.

After dinner, the Chief talked for a short time and opened the floor to questions from all of us. It was like our old Saturday lunches, though the setting was somewhat more formal. The Chief was very frank about what was going on at the Court. During the years before he retired, the Chief sometimes took criticism. For example, one of the clerks had become a United States Attorney and was very unhappy with some of the Court's decisions. The Chief was good humored about it and explained his point of view. While he was unquestionably disappointed with the conservative direction of many decisions after his retirement, he seemed to accept them, without bitterness, as the inevitable product of the way our democracy works.

I always enjoyed visiting with other Warren clerks. A number of them became law teachers, and we sometimes found ourselves on the same campus. Three—Mike Heyman, Phil Johnson, and Mike Smith—joined me in spending our careers at Berkeley and teaching at Boalt Hall, the Chief's alma mater. Jerry Cohen also taught there for a short time before moving on to Harvard and New York University. I came to Berkeley by way of the University of Minnesota, and later served as dean of Boalt Hall. Mike Heyman became chancellor of the University of California at Berkeley. During my second semester as a visiting professor at Harvard, John Ely, who clerked for the Chief several years after me, came as a visitor from Yale.

Our shared connection with Boalt Hall cemented my bond with the Chief. This likely led the Chief to ask me to help select his California clerk the year Adrian Kragen, a Boalt professor who worked for Warren when he was attorney general, and who typically performed the task, was away on sabbatical. Four California law school faculties—Boalt, Stanford, University of California at Los Angeles, and University of Southern California—recommended clerkship candidates, which helped to winnow the pool. As an interviewer, I traveled to Southern California and talked with Scott Bice, a USC graduate, who got the job. Henry Steinman, a former Warren clerk in private practice in Los Angeles, also participated. One of our important criteria was someone who would get along well with the Chief, although this was not a narrow standard.

Bice went on to join the USC law faculty after his clerkship and became the dean in 1980, a job he held for twenty years. Several of the Chief's former clerks took a similar path. During one period, three of us were California law school deans at the same time. In addition to Bice and me, John Ely, a leading constitutional scholar at Yale and Harvard, moved to Stanford to become its dean. (At that same time, Mike Heyman was chancellor at Berkeley and Jim Gaither was president of the Stanford Board of Trustees.) Several of the Chief's former clerks took similar administrative paths. Dallin Oaks, now a member of the Quorum of the Twelve Apostles of the Church of Jesus Christ of Latter-day Saints, was a law professor at the University of Chicago, president of Brigham Young University, and a justice on the Supreme Court of Utah. Benno Schmidt served as dean of Columbia University Law School and president of Yale University and is now chairman of the board of trustees of the City University of New York (CUNY). Other of the Chief's clerks who became law professors are Frank Beytagh (Notre Dame), George Cochran (Mississippi), Earl Dudley (Virginia), Ted Eisenberg (Cornell), Marc Franklin (Columbia and Stanford), Gerry Gunther (Columbia and Stanford), Peter Low (Virginia), Bill Oliver (Indiana), Curt Reitz (Pennsylvania), Art Rosett (UCLA), Larry Simon (USC), and Ted White (Virginia).

Many of the Chief's clerks also spent time in government. Among these,

Joe Bartlett was undersecretary of commerce. Tyrone Brown was a Federal Communications Commission commissioner, and C. Boyden Gray was White House counsel under President George H. W. Bush. Four of the Chief's clerks became judges. Dallin Oaks has moved on from the Utah Supreme Court, but Ted Boehm sits on the Indiana Supreme Court, Jon Newman on the Court of Appeals for the Second Circuit, and Stuart Pollak on the California Court of Appeals in San Francisco.

The Chief surprised us all when he announced his retirement in 1968. He was seventy-eight years old but sharp as ever. We knew that he worried about overstaying his effectiveness on the Court. At his seventieth birthday party during my term, he told us about his role model in California politics, Hiram Johnson, a former governor and U.S. senator. "I saw Hiram Johnson die on the vine," the Chief said. He made it clear that he relied on his clerks to tell him if we thought he was heading in the same direction. To my knowledge, no one told the Chief anything of the kind, but he retired anyway. My belief was that he had hoped President Johnson would appoint his successor, but the stalled nomination of Abe Fortas made that impossible. To the Chief's great credit, he stood firm in his decision to retire even though that meant President Nixon would appoint his successor.

I had lunch with the Chief in advance of the first reunion dinner after he announced his retirement. At his office before lunch, I asked him why he had stepped down when he was still fully engaged. He said the assassinations of Robert Kennedy and Martin Luther King Jr. had affected him intensely. He thought it was time for change, for new blood in government. I asked the Chief who he thought his successor would be. He opened his desk drawer and pulled out a slip of paper. On it he had written "Warren Burger," then chief judge of the U.S. Court of Appeals for the D.C. Circuit, an outspoken critic of the Warren Court, and one of at least a half-dozen names floated as the Chief's successor. The Chief had it pegged, uncannily savvy as always.

After the Chief died, in 1974, I undertook several efforts, particularly during my time as dean, to commemorate the clerkship relationship, and twice a large contingency of the Chief's former clerks gathered for lunch. The first was during a two-day event I helped organize celebrating the screening of the film about Warren called *Super Chief.* Justices Brennan and Marshall came to San Francisco for the event. The second event was when the Berkeley Law School honored the Chief's one hundredth birthday with a gala attended by over four hundred people. Clearly mine was not the only life the Chief—a towering American statesman—had enhanced.

Notes

Special thanks to Sarah Ruby, class of 2010, for exceptionally skillful assistance in preparation of this essay.

1. See, e.g., *Mapp v. Ohio*, 367 U.S. 643 (1961) (extending the exclusionary rule to illegal searches conducted by state officials); *Culombe v. Connecticut*, 367 U.S. 568 (1961) (reversing a state court decision holding a confession to be admissible evidence where the defendant was not beaten but was held for five days, denied counsel, and not advised of his rights); *Rogers v. Richmond*, 365 U.S. 534 (1961) (holding that where law enforcement officials solicit a confession by overcoming a defendant's will to resist, the confession, true or not, is involuntary and inadmissible under the Due Process Clause of the Fourteenth Amendment); *Silverman v. United States*, 365 U.S. 505 (1961) (holding that electronic eavesdropping violated the Fourth Amendment).

2. *Scales v. United States*, 367 U.S. 203 (1961) (holding Congress could criminalize Communist Party membership); *Communist Party of the United States v. Subversive Activities Control Bd.*, 367 U.S. 1 (1961) (upholding an order against the Communist Party to register and disclose membership and other information). See also *Cafeteria Workers v. McElroy*, 367 U.S. 886 (1961) (holding a military commander could deny civilian employee access to a weapons facility for security reasons without affording a hearing or advising the employee of the specific reasons for exclusion); *In re Anastaplo*, 366 U.S. 82 (1961) (upholding a court-made rule denying bar admission to candidates refusing to answer questions about Communist Party affiliation and finding the applicant challenging the rule was adequately warned of the consequences of silence); *Konigsberg v. State Bar*, 366 U.S. 36 (1961) (holding states could condition membership in state bar associations upon candidate's willingness to answer ethics questions, including questions about Communist Party membership); *Wilkinson v. United States*, 365 U.S. 399 (1961) (upholding contempt conviction for failing to answer questions from the subcommittee of the House Committee on Un-American Activities); *McPhaul v. United States*, 364 U.S. 372 (1960) (upholding contempt conviction and confirming defendants' duty to speak at congressional subcommittee hearings). The liberals won a few cases on narrow grounds, such as *Deutch v. United States*, 367 U.S. 456 (1961) (reversing contempt conviction where government failed to show questions asked were relevant to the committee's investigation); *Noto v. United States*, 367 U.S. 290 (1961) (reversing a conviction citing insufficient evidence that defendant advocated action against the United States beyond general Communist doctrine); *Shelton v. Tucker*, 364 U.S. 479 (1960) (striking down, on freedom of association grounds, an Arkansas statute requiring public school teachers to disclose all organizations to which they had belonged or made donations because it was overbroad, reaching affiliations that had no bearing on a teacher's competence).

3. See, e.g., *Burton v. Wilmington Parking Auth.*, 365 U.S. 715 (1961) (extending Fourteenth Amendment state action to a private restaurant leasing space from a public agency) (Frankfurter, Harlan, and Whittaker, JJ., dissenting); *Monroe v. Pape*, 365 U.S.

167 (1961) (holding in 42 U.S.C. § 1983 cases that state action under color of state law includes action contrary to state law) (Frankfurter, J., dissenting in part); *Boynton v. Virginia*, 364 U.S. 454 (1960) (reversing a trespass conviction because a restaurant's refusal to serve a black patron violated the Interstate Commerce Act) (Clark and Whittaker, JJ., dissenting). But see *Gomillion v. Lightfoot*, 364 U.S. 339 (1960) (striking down redistricting plan that excluded all but a few black voters) (unanimous).

4. *Int'l Ass'n of Machinists v. Street*, 367 U.S. 740 (1961) (interpreting labor laws to prohibit unions from spending dues to fund political activities opposed by members, avoiding whether such expenditures violated the First Amendment); *E.R.R. Presidents Conference v. Noerr Motor Freight, Inc.*, 365 U.S. 127 (1961) (construing the Sherman Act to not outlaw a deceptive publicity campaign aimed at harming the interests of competitors, avoiding whether such a prohibition would violate the First Amendment).

5. *United States v. E. I. du Pont de Nemours & Co.*, 366 U.S. 316 (1961).

6. *Brown v. Board of Education*, 347 U.S. 483 (1954); the handwritten opinion can be found at http://www.npr.org/news/specials/brown50/gallery1/warren1.html.

7. *McGowan v. Maryland*, 366 U.S. 420 (1961); *Two Guys From Harrison-Allentown, Inc. v. McGinley*, 366 U.S. 582 (1961); *Braunfeld v. Brown*, 366 U.S. 599 (1961); *Gallagher v. Crown Kosher Super Market of Mass., Inc.*, 366 U.S. 617 (1961).

8. *James v. United States*, 366 U.S. 213 (1961).

9. *Comm'r of Internal Revenue v. Wilcox*, 327 U.S. 404 (1946); *Rutkin v. United States*, 343 U.S. 130 (1952).

10. The clerk during my term was James R. Browning, now senior chief judge of the U.S. Court of Appeals for the Ninth Circuit.

11. *Times Film Corp. v. City of Chicago*, 365 U.S. 43 (1961).

12. Ibid., 69.

13. Ibid., 70.

14. *Near v. Minnesota*, 283 U.S. 697 (1931).

15. *Naim v. Naim*, 350 U.S. 891 (1955). cf *Loving v VA 1967*

16. *Irvine v. California*, 347 U.S. 128 (1954). In a paragraph joined only by the chief justice, Justice Jackson directed the clerk of the Court "to forward a copy of the record in this case, together with a copy of this opinion, for attention of the Attorney General" for possible prosecution of the police for violating a federal civil rights law (138).

17. *Federal Baseball Club of Baltimore v. National League of Professional Baseball Clubs*, 259 U.S. 200 (1922); *Toolson v. New York Yankees*, 346 U.S. 356 (1953).

18. *Boynton v. Virginia*, 364 U.S. 454 (1960).

19. See the cases discussed in note 2.

20. *Deutch v. United States*, 367 U.S. 456 (1961).

21. *Poe v. Ullman*, 367 U.S. 497 (1961); *Griswold v. Connecticut*, 381 U.S. 479 (1965).

22. *Torcaso v. Watkins*, 367 U.S. 488 (1961).

Charting Civil Liberties and Protecting Free Expression

Learning from and Working
with Justice William J. Brennan

At what turned out to be the last gathering of Justice William J. Brennan's clerks in which the justice could participate meaningfully, we witnessed an extraordinary performance. By that time there had been 113 clerks, most of whom were present at a gala dinner in a downtown Washington hotel. When the tables had been cleared, the justice scanned the audience and, without a single note, went around the room, identifying each clerk by name and term and summarizing one case in which that person had been deeply involved during his or her year at the Court. Not only was no former clerk overlooked; most remarkably, each felt suitably honored—as well as dazzled—by the justice's recall.

Such a recitation attested not only to the justice's extraordinary powers of recall—even in his late eighties—but to the inviolable connection he had made and maintained with every young lawyer who ever served him in this role. Remarkably, some of the clerks later noted that the justice had recited that evening certain aspects of their collaboration of which their own recollection had dimmed or muted through the intervening years. Yet it was not simply the depth and accuracy of his recall, but equally the affection with which he evoked such memories.

Of course, some terms and some cases had been far more significant than others. For that matter, some clerks were more highly acclaimed by the justice than others—and they learned privately of such esteem. But when the entire group gathered for this remarkable occasion, there were no favorites. Each person who had served the justice from 1956 through the mid-1990s received momentary recognition and left the evening with a sense that his or her contributions to the Brennan legacy mattered as much as did those who might elsewhere have been seen as stars or leaders.

At such times we recalled the justice's own struggle for acceptance on a Court dominated by his onetime administrative law professor, Felix Frankfurter, who upon hearing President Eisenhower's nomination phoned a friend in Cambridge to learn what grade he had given this still relatively unknown New Jersey judge who had undoubtedly once been his student. Among the Brennan clerks, there would be no such differentiation—at least not when we were all gathered for such a festive event. Behind the closed doors in his chambers, each of us knew just where we stood, but that was for private consumption.

Not all of the clerks' reunions were nearly so festive. During what for the justice were the darkest days of the Burger Court—dark not only because of an unwelcome judicial turn, but also because the first Mrs. Brennan was terminally ill and suffering terribly—we gathered for a rather somber Saturday dinner. What occurred that evening was a startling experience that illustrated a quite different dimension of our relationship with the justice and his with us. We could tell the justice was dispirited, and we all knew of his wife's despair, but we were hardly prepared for his remarks. After a few words of welcome, he suddenly declared: "I've had it with this Court. I'm out of here. I've had enough of this place." We were startled, but as always we were pledged to secrecy on such matters. We were even more startled to find on the front page of Sunday's *Washington Post* a box headed "Brennan to Quit High Court?" quite accurately summarizing the justice's lament.

Of course, we all rallied and through every available means told him that he must stay on the Court for a host of reasons we knew were crucial to him. Within a week or ten days, he assured us he would heed our counsel and would remain, despite the gloomy prospects he faced both personally and professionally. How had the news reached the *Post*, we wondered. Could there have been a leak within a totally trustworthy group? Then one of us learned that when the justice began his remarks a single waiter was still in the room—visible only to the justice, because we were all facing him. Thus we came to suspect that the actual scenario was precisely the one envisioned by the brilliant strategist whom we had served and revered. Yet each of us felt we had a crucial role to play in guiding and supporting him in his hour of need, in the very best spirit of what Paul Freund so aptly termed "Judge and Company." He would serve for nearly two decades thereafter, and each time he achieved another judicial triumph, we thought back to that gloomy evening and its providential outcome.

The Selection Process: Becoming Brennan Clerks

The first two of Justice Brennan's clerks joined him by a process illustrative of his caring and compassion. Justice Sherman Minton had chosen two clerks for the 1956 term without informing them of his already well-formed intention to retire from the Court upon completion, late that summer, of two decades of judicial service that would vest his full federal pension. Justice Brennan would, upon his nomination to succeed Minton, have been completely free to disregard these appointments and either bring former clerks from New Jersey or select two new clerks of his own. Yet without hesitation, he invited the Minton clerks-designate to remain and serve him during that initial term. Despite such a serendipitous journey to the Court, they were ever after treated as full-fledged members of the group—just as were the last several clerks who joined after the justice's retirement in 1990 and, since they served at least one other retired judge, could have been relegated to less than equal status.

The retention of the Minton appointees involved a special irony. It was his predecessor's self-serving delay in retirement that placed Brennan in the untenable position of a recess appointee—a status that subjected him to merciless questioning by a still dangerous Senator Joseph McCarthy during days of testimony before a Judiciary Committee whose approval was needed for confirmation. McCarthy repeatedly demanded to know, after the October 1956 term had begun, how Brennan voted in several highly sensitive national security cases. The justice demurred, politely but firmly, citing the sanctity of the judicial process. Eventually a now weakened and even unstable McCarthy abandoned his unconscionable quest, and Brennan was confirmed. Throughout the next three and a half decades, he vowed he would spare his successor such peril, and for that reason announced his own retirement early in the summer of 1990 so that Justice David Souter could be comfortably confirmed before the next term began. When Justice Souter's own departure time came in the spring of 2009, there is reason to believe his own alacrity in declaring his intention drew upon a keen awareness of the Minton-Brennan transition and his resolve never to place a successor at such risk. Meanwhile, a generation and a half of Brennan clerks had come to share deep resentment of Minton's delayed departure while accepting the Minton holdover clerks as full and equal partners.

After the initial term, Justice Brennan turned to his law school classmate Professor Paul Freund for nomination of successor clerks. For nearly a decade the eminent Harvard constitutional scholar was empowered to make the selection and, upon acceptance, inform the justice—though it would have seemed unlikely that some informal consultation did not precede the extension of what in Cambridge seemed like a decision made entirely within Langdell Hall. By the mid-1960s the justice felt the time had come to broaden the field from which clerks were drawn. That expansion reflected two quite different forces. On one hand, he declared a felt need to reflect more directly his own close ties with the Third Circuit (Pennsylvania, New Jersey, and Delaware) by looking to that region's major law schools (mainly the University of Pennsylvania, where he himself had been an undergraduate). He also felt the time had come to involve those of his early clerks who had gone into law teaching and might now be able to recommend students of their own to follow well-marked footsteps. In later years the process would become more complex, though the justice retained full control of the critical selections.

The relationship between the justice and clerks-designate became firm and cordial from the moment of selection. It also became occasionally a source of compassion and counseling—as in one notable case of a clerk-designate who had not even yet met the justice when he felt compelled to call and explain that he and his wife had just separated and would be in the process of divorce by the time he reported for duty. Quite apart from a felt duty to alert the justice to so momentous and imminent a change, the clerk-to-be had surely come to the right place. The justice dropped everything else and spent the next half hour consoling the young man, getting him to place his marital woes in perspective, and inviting happy thoughts about what would surely be a lively year in the capital. Mention of Saturday lunches at the Senate cafeteria (the only reputable nearby dining spot in those days)—just the justice and the clerks—enhanced the prospect. The divorce did indeed occur, but the clerk-designate's equanimity upon arrival in Washington was immeasurably enhanced by his early and quite unexpected encounter with his prospective mentor.

So it was with myriad other (and usually less momentous) personal needs—where to find a doctor or dentist, or a florist or a good restaurant, and for the substantial number of Catholics among the clerks, where to worship. Only once was the justice known to have failed in this regard. Early clerks needed to know whether, as short-term D.C. residents, they were subject to District of Columbia income tax. The justice blithely assured one pair of clerks (both of whom rented houses on Capitol Hill) that they were exempt. That advice turned out to be erroneous, if well intentioned. But the taxes were eventually paid, and the legal careers of both innocently misguided clerks survived the encounter.

A Brennan clerkship might occasionally entail more than legal research and drafting. The Brennans owned a single car, a result of years on the New Jersey courts at salaries that were a tiny fraction of what Newark's largest firm paid its partners. The Court provided a car only for the chief justice. Thus the justice was often dependent on the kindness of friends to get to and from his Georgetown home. Any clerk who lived in Northwest D.C. and had a car was a prime prospect. Not surprisingly, clerks' cars were not always dependable and occasionally broke down. More than once pedestrians on Pennsylvania Avenue or M Street would have been startled to observe—had he been more readily recognizable than his modesty ensured—a justice of the nation's highest court pushing a derelict vehicle while its owner, the deeply embarrassed clerk, steered toward the nearest service station. Such service finds no recognition in the *United States Reports*.

The Education of the Brennan Clerks—and of the Justice

One favorite vignette illustrates a very different dimension of the Brennan clerkship. Midway through the 1962 term, my co-clerk Dick Posner was asked to draft an opinion in a moderately important but not earth-shaking criminal procedure case. After the justice had reviewed the text—which he invariably did within twenty-four hours of its receipt—he gave us his assessment. "Dick," he said, "that's a really fine draft. There's only one problem. We voted decisively the other way." But then he added, "I'm convinced you're right, and I'll ask the Chief for permission to circulate your draft as a prospective majority opinion." The chief justice acquiesced, and a Court that had voted by 7–2 to affirm ended up reversing by exactly the same margin. While this experience was singular and unlikely to be replicated, it provides clear evidence of Justice Brennan's readiness to learn from, and even follow the guidance of, his clerks when he felt they understood better—or just differently—a crucial facet of a case in which he had reached a contrary conclusion.

We might add to that experience another from the same term. A new colleague on the Court had just circulated his very first opinion when a lapse in the final paragraph drew attention and concern. The new justice circulated a memo noting that "my law clerk erroneously included material that had been deleted." Upon reading this disclaimer, Justice Brennan leaped from his chair and ran next door to advise his colleague that though he was entirely free to berate the errant clerk within the privacy of his chambers, as far as the rest of the world knew—even within the building—"only the justice can make a mistake." Moments later a corrective memo appeared, conceding that "I erroneously included material that had been deleted."

The wise counsel thus conveyed to his colleague reflected precisely the way in which Justice Brennan related to his own clerks. Whatever leaves our chambers, he would caution each incoming group of clerks, is my responsibility, adding that he counted heavily upon the clerks for meticulous standards of accuracy and integrity. Such guidance was strikingly concordant with an experience related by Dean Acheson (October term 1919) of his clerkship with Justice Louis Brandeis. Early in that term, Acheson awaited the delivery of an opinion on which he had labored, and when it was bypassed he anxiously sought out the justice, who was clearly not happy. Brandeis told the future secretary of state that a case on which the opinion relied heavily could not be read to support the summary, as the justice happened to discover by checking that source moments before entering the courtroom. "Acheson," he declared, "the law clerk's job is to catch the justice's mistakes, not to make new ones of his own." Justice Brennan would have put it a bit more gently, but would have conveyed the same idea. Every one of the 115 men and women who served Brennan through four decades realized that awesome responsibility. Behind that genial demeanor and heartening manner lurked extremely high expectations that no Brennan clerk ever wished to fail or disappoint.

The "only the justice makes mistakes" rule evokes one striking example of a very different sort. When Justice Brennan met with all the clerks for lunch—as did each justice back in the days when the group was a manageably small number—he invited (indeed welcomed) questions. A slightly irreverent clerk for a fellow justice inquired about an obscure footnote in a rather technical public utility case. I was terrified, since I had drafted the footnote and could not imagine Brennan had read it carefully, much less that he could recall its content. I should have known better. The justice smiled, faced the questioner, and calmly replied, "Dick, if you'd read the next sentence in that footnote, you'd understand exactly why we did what we did there." The irreverent clerk was crushed; whether he had planned on embarrassing the justice we never knew. What we did know—and should have realized as soon as the colloquy occurred—was that every word that appeared in every opinion Brennan authored bore not only his imprimatur but his keen understanding as well. It was not only the major issues or the great constitutional imperatives with which he was intimately familiar, but the details of a natural gas case that by that time I had forgotten—but not the justice.

Curiously, however, the role that clerks played in drafting Brennan opinions seems to have varied substantially by term. A few months before I began my year with the justice, I met for dinner with one of my predecessors to seek guidance and insight. When I asked whether he had any regrets about his clerkship, or anything he might wish to change, his only lament was that during his term the justice relied less heavily upon him and his co-clerk than he would have wished in the drafting of opinions. Thus I was prepared for a comparably muted role. To my surprise and delight, the dynamics of the ensuing term proved quite different. After reviewing initial drafts of the first two cases assigned to him that year, he declared with feigned frustration that he had "spent the whole weekend going over them and couldn't change but a few words here and there." The experience gleaned through informal conversation about later terms seems consistent with this early contrast. Some Brennan clerks seem to have been more deeply involved in the drafting process than others—and for reasons that do not clearly reflect differences either in literary skill or in knowledge of the subject matter. One suspects that the justice's own inclination to control the drafting process may have varied from one term to the next, or that early experience with each successive group of clerks may have guided in differing ways the actual practice that prevailed during the balance of the year of collaboration. It is also possible that some incoming clerks were more familiar with the justice's style, and his penchant for using particular words and phrases, and that such familiarity evoked greater comfort and confidence. Whatever the cause, it seems clear that the Brennan clerks' experience in the drafting of opinions was not entirely consistent.

What was wholly consistent, however, was the collegiality of the Brennan chambers in the discussion and resolution of major issues facing the Court. The clerks and the justices seem to have gathered regularly for coffee or tea nearly every morning and at that time reviewed the challenges that lay ahead, not merely for the next twenty-four hours but usually well beyond. As the number of clerks grew from two to three, and then quickly to four per term, some of the intimacy of the early years may have been lost, though apparently never compromised was a sense of collegiality and collaboration that pervaded such discussions. These sessions were, moreover, quintessentially educational. It was through such discussions that every clerk appreciated the justice's insistence, for example, that "incorporation" was not the proper way to describe the gradual application to state and local action of Bill of Rights constraints that directly constrained only the U.S. Congress. Instead, and for reasons that afforded greater latitude in addressing historical anomalies, the justice consistently described this process as "absorption," even as his opinions from the early and mid-1960s expanded dramatically the reach of these rights and liberties below the federal level.

Many other lessons could be noted within the legacy of a Brennan clerkship. One that seems oddly out of character concerned federal preemption of state regulatory authority. When it came to matters such as racial equality, free expression, and religious liberty, few judges were more deeply committed than he to the supremacy of the national government and its protective powers. Yet on slightly less august matters, clerks who became overly brash about the primacy of national power were occasionally stopped short by the justice's question—"What makes you think we know better the needs and interests of the state of ___ than do its own lawmakers?" The conclusion that inexorably followed, and imposed a healthy humility upon young lawyers not often so constrained, was that the Supreme Court had no business ranking or prioritizing state regulatory interests for this purpose. Justice Brennan's view on this issue doubtless reflected his years as a state supreme court judge—indeed for much of his service the only person who had come to the high Court with such experience. Despite the justice's esteem for the eminent constitutional law teachers of the late twentieth century, Professor Brennan's course conveyed the final word, and that word would not always confirm precisely to what one may have learned from such luminaries as Professor Freund or Professor Tribe.

Brief note should also be taken of the justice's embrace of former clerks who not only did not fully share his views but who actively espoused contrary principles. He continued with pride to claim Judge Richard Posner as a protégé, despite growing divergence on basic constitutional premises. And when he chose the group that would advise the Thomas Jefferson Center for the Protection of Free Expression on those to be honored by the William J. Brennan, Jr. Award, he insisted on including then professor (later judge and now professor again) Michael McConnell (October term 1980)—not despite their differences in fundamental matters, but indeed because of those differences. Time and again the more liberal members of that group would defer to McConnell's concerns about a potential recipient—not only because of our esteem for a colleague with whom we often profoundly disagreed but because we knew the justice wanted him there to keep the rest of us honest.

A Brennan clerkship taught caution as well as humility in important matters. Even in areas where his own views and values might have called for intervention, he was loath to provide a fifth vote to review a lower court ruling if the inevitable result of doing so would have been to entrench at a higher level an already unwelcome precedent. There were also important areas of

such as ?

constitutional law in which he would insist on biding his and the Court's time. The increasingly anomalous denial of any First Amendment protection for commercial speech or advertising offered a prime example. By the late 1950s Justice William O. Douglas, at least, was ready to extend partial protection to commercial messages and had signaled that readiness quite publicly. More than one clerk in the 1960s importuned Justice Brennan to join Justice Douglas and thus accelerate this seemingly inevitable process. Yet he consistently rebuffed such pleas, apparently feeling the time was not ripe, and it was not until the mid-1970s that he would eventually join a majority to give commercial advertising a modicum of respectability. Indeed, the justice often counseled patience among his clerks even where matters of principle were potentially at risk, feeling that haste should yield to deliberation, and confident that later times would better afford an optimal occasion. Far better than any of his clerks, he knew when the time would be right. He also knew when a premature salvo could be counterproductive. And most of all, he understood how impatient his clerks could be, and how difficult it could be to restrain their eagerness to remedy a perceived injustice or enhance due process.

Justice Brennan, His Clerks, and the Other Justices

From the outset, Justice Brennan not only encouraged his clerks to get to know (and respect) the other justices—even those for whom their legal education might have inspired less than admiration—but also valued his ties with congenial clerks from other chambers. New York University professor Norman Dorsen (October term 1957), long-time president of the American Civil Liberties Union, actually clerked for Justice John Harlan, but both he and Justice Brennan recalled a relationship so close and cordial than the official affiliation nearly yielded to the informal affinity that developed during that year and persisted until the justice's death. Much the same could be said of many other legal scholars, such as the late professor Gerald Gunther (October term 1954), actually a Frankfurter clerk though unofficially like so many others an adopted member of the Brennan team. Indeed, some of the credit for Justice Brennan's extraordinary success in forging improbable coalitions for everything from equity in legislative apportionment in 1962 to constitutional protection for flag desecration (1990) should be attributed in part not only to these relationships with his colleagues but as much to the admiration of so many of his colleagues' clerks.

Ties with fellow justices also occasionally involved judicious use of Brennan's own clerks. A personal example may be useful. The first argued case of the October term 1962 involved the location of a suspect at a Chinese laundry in San Francisco (*Wong Sun v. United States*, 371 U.S. 471 [1963]). Justice Brennan was assigned to write the majority opinion reversing a conviction that involved evidence tainted as "fruit of the poisonous tree." Justice Tom Clark vigorously dissented. The initial draft that he circulated began, "Anyone familiar with San Francisco's Chinatown" and then argued that locating the laundry should have been easy. Since I had spent the previous summer teaching in San Francisco, I had a city street map, on which I showed Justice Brennan that the site in question was actually on the back side of Russian Hill, some distance from Chinatown. I assumed he would call Justice Clark, which he did at once. But I was unprepared for what followed—that the justice was sending his clerk down the hall with a street map because he had some relevant information.

With much trepidation I set forth, clutching my map. When I clarified the geography for Justice Clark, he was grateful, and I left promptly with a sense of relief. Only minutes passed before we received a revised dissent, which now began, "Anyone familiar with San Francisco's Chinese community." Nothing else had changed, including, of course, the result of the case. But a law clerk's intervention had been arranged in a way that reflected Justice Brennan's view of a clerk's potential utility. Obviously if I had not had my Bay Area map close at hand that day, I would have been spared a memorable experience—and Justice Clark would not have received the geography lesson for which I could hardly have prepared in law school or anywhere else along the way. Yet in retrospect, that experience and countless similar journeys that Brennan clerks were invited to make in later terms illustrated not only his genius in relating to his colleagues but also a degree of trust of which his clerks were ever the beneficiaries.

Finally, it may be worth noting that the Brennan clerks have not gathered as such since the justice's death. Several events sponsored by the Brennan Center for Justice at NYU have sought to reconvene the group, though the most aggressive such effort yielded barely a quarter of the living clerks, with many even in the metropolitan area absent. Later, a splendid reception at a midtown Manhattan restaurant in the summer of 2008—with former Treasury secretary (and already Obama adviser) Robert Rubin as the speaker—produced *why?* only two clerks, even though all had been cordially invited, and many were surely close at hand.

The mission of the Brennan Justice Center itself admirably exemplifies the justice's relationship with his clerks. During negotiations that led to the center's founding, and led to an inaugural board comprising mostly former clerks, the one condition that was indispensable to the justice was the center's independence even on matters where his views had been clear and consistent. So it was that from the outset the center has espoused and advanced in court positions on campaign finance reform that could hardly diverge more dramatically from the justice's own well-known views. Some loyal Brennan clerks have even wondered whether the center has disowned or disavowed its legacy by departing so dramatically from the views and values of its namesake. Tempting though such concerns may be, they overlook the parting guidance each of us received upon leaving the Court, with a signed and very personally inscribed portrait of the justice in hand: "Though you will always be a member of the extended Brennan family, you must never feel constrained if your own convictions diverge, even dramatically, from mine." In the end, that is the most important lesson of all.

Justice Arthur Goldberg and His Law Clerks

Justice Arthur Goldberg was a man of action. Before being nominated at age fifty-four to the Supreme Court by President John F. Kennedy, Goldberg had accomplished an enormous amount. Unlike most of the current justices, he would have been in the history books even had he never served on the High Court. Arthur Goldberg helped establish the profession of labor law. He represented the most important labor unions in the country. He helped merge the American Federation of Labor (AFL) with the Congress of Industrial Organizations (CIO). He helped rid unions of Communist influence. He argued some of the most important and influential cases before the Supreme Court and other courts, including the Steel Seizure Case of 1951.[1] He was perhaps the most successful secretary of labor in history, settling one strike after another and being recognized as a legendary mediator.

The Supreme Court is not a place of action; it is an institution of reaction—to cases and controversies generated by others. It is a place of thoughtful, often solitary, meditation and research. Justice Goldberg was used to working with many people. He was accustomed to crisis. His phone always rang. When he arrived at the Supreme Court, as he once summarized the situation, "my phone never rings." The Supreme Court is the loneliest of institutions; as Justice Louis Brandeis once put it, "here we do our own work." The justices only rarely interact: on the bench; in the weekly, somewhat formal, conference; and in informal one-on-one meetings, which were rare then and even rarer today. It is fair to say that Justice Goldberg was somewhat lonely, often restless, and craved the active life he had left behind.

This is not to say that Justice Goldberg was not a serious intellectual. He was. He was also one of the smartest justices in history. He loved the Supreme Court. He loved the law. He loved having intense discussions with his law clerks about jurisprudence and the role of the Supreme Court. But he needed more than contemplation, deliberation, and discussion. The "passive virtues," as Professor Alexander Bickel once characterized the Supreme Court's role in *not* making decisions, was a vice to Arthur Goldberg. He wanted to get things done.

I will never forget my first meeting with my new boss when I came to work in the Supreme Court during the summer of 1963. He tossed a certiorari petition at me from across his desk and asked me to read it in his presence. It was only a few pages long and I did. He then asked me, "What do you see in it?" I said, "It's just another pro se cert petition in a capital case." He said, "No, what you're holding in your hand is the vehicle by which we can end capital punishment in the United States."

My initial assignment was to write a memorandum on the possible unconstitutionality of the death penalty. I set to work but found no suggestion in the case law that any court had ever considered the death penalty to be of questionable constitutionality. Just a few years earlier, Chief Justice Earl Warren had written in *Trop v. Dulles* that "whatever the arguments may be against capital punishment, both on moral grounds and in terms of accomplishing the purposes of punishment—and they are forceful—the death penalty has been employed throughout our history, and, in a day when it is still widely accepted it cannot be said to violate the constitutional concept of cruelty."[2]

I duly reported this to Justice Goldberg, suggesting that if even the liberal chief justice believed that the death penalty was constitutional, what chance did he have of getting a serious hearing for his view that the cruel and unusual punishment clause should now be construed to prohibit the imposition of capital punishment? Justice Goldberg asked me to talk to Justice William J. Brennan Jr. and see what his views were. Unless Justice Brennan agreed to join, the entire project would be scuttled, since Justice Goldberg, the Court's rookie, did not want to "be out there alone" against the chief justice and the rest of the Court.

I had previously met Justice Brennan several times over the preceding few years, since his son, Bill, was my classmate and moot-court partner at Yale Law School. I had also had lunch several times with the justice and his friend, federal circuit court judge David L. Bazelon, for whom I had clerked the previous year. But none of our discussions had been substantive, and I nervously anticipated the task of discussing an important issue with one of my judicial heroes.

I brought a rough draft of the memorandum on which I was working to the meeting, but Justice Brennan did not want to look at it then. He asked me to describe the results of my research to him, promising to read the memorandum later. I stated the nascent constitutional case against the death penalty as best I could. I told him that *Weems v. United States* could be read as recognizing the following tests for whether punishment was "cruel and unusual": (1) giving full weight to reasonable legislative findings, a punishment is cruel and unusual if a less severe one can as effectively achieve the permissible ends of punishment (that is, deterrence, isolation, rehabilitation, or whatever the contemporary society considers the permissible objectives of punishment); (2) regardless of its effectiveness in achieving the permissible ends of punishment, a punishment is cruel and unusual if it offends the contemporary sense of decency (for example, torture); (3) regardless of its effectiveness in achieving the permissible ends of punishment, a punishment is cruel and unusual if the evil it produces is disproportionally higher than the harm it seeks to prevent (for example, the death penalty for economic crimes).[3] In addition to these abstract formulations, I also told Justice Brennan that our research had disclosed a widespread pattern of unequal application of the death penalty on racial grounds. I cited national prison statistics showing that between 1937 and 1951, 233 blacks were executed for rape in the United States, while only 26 whites were executed for that crime.

Justice Brennan encouraged me to continue my research, without making any promise that he would join any action by Justice Goldberg. Several weeks later, Justice Goldberg told me that Justice Brennan had agreed to join a short dissent from the denial of certiorari in *Rudolph v. Alabama*—a case involving imposition of the death penalty on a black man who was convicted of raping a white woman.[4] Justice William O. Douglas signed on as well. The dissenters invited the bar to address the following questions, which they deemed "relevant and worthy of argument and consideration":

1. In light of the trend both in the country and throughout the world against punishing rape by death, does the imposition of the death penalty by those States which retain it for rape violate "evolving standards of decency that mark the progress of [our] maturing society," or "standards of decency more or less universally accepted"?

2. Is the taking of human life to protect a value other than human life consistent with the constitutional proscription against "punishments which by their excessive . . . severity are greatly disproportional to the offenses charged"?

3. Can the permissible aims of punishment (e.g., deterrence, isolation, rehabilitation) be achieved as effectively by punishing rape less severely than by death (e.g., by life imprisonment); if so, does the imposition of the death penalty for rape constitute "unnecessary cruelty"?

As soon as the dissent was published, there was an immediate reaction. Conservative journalists had a field day lambasting the very notion that a court could strike down as unconstitutional a long-standing punishment that is explicitly referred to in the Constitution. One extreme criticism appeared in the *New Hampshire Union Leader* under the banner headline "U.S. Supreme Court Trio Encourages Rape":

> In a decision handed down last week three U.S. Supreme Court justices, Goldberg, Brennan, Douglas, raised the question of whether it was proper to condemn a man to death for the crime of rape if there has been no endangering of the life of the victim. This incredible opinion, of course, can serve only to encourage would-be rapists. These fiends, freed from the fear of the death penalty for their foul deed, . . . will be inclined to take a chance.
>
> Thus, not content with forbidding our schoolchildren to pray in school, not content with banishing Bible reading from our schools, and not content letting every type of filthy book be published, at least three members of the Supreme Court are now out to encourage rape.

Several state courts went out of their way to announce their rejection of the principal inherent in the dissenting opinion. This is what the Georgia Supreme Court said:

> With all due respect to the dissenting Justices we would question the judicial right of any American judge to construe the American Constitution contrary to its apparent meaning, the American history of the clause, and its construction by American courts, simply because the numerous nations and States have abandoned capital punishment for rape. First we believe the history of no nation will show the high values of woman's virtue and purity that America has shown. We would regret to see the day when this freedom loving country would lower our respect for womanhood or lessen her legal protection for no better reason than that many or even all other countries have done so. She is entitled to every legal protection of her body, her decency, her purity and good name.

There was scholarly criticism as well. In the *Harvard Law Review*, Professor Herbert Packer of Stanford Law School wrote:

> In an interesting development, some members of the Supreme Court appear disposed to employ [recent constructions of the "cruel and unusual

punishments" clause] to regulate the appropriate relation between crime and punishment. Three justices recently noted in their dissent from a denial of certiorari in terms that invite speculation about the role of constitutional adjudication in solving the age-old problem of whether and how the punishment may be made to fit the crime.... [However,] [s]ympathy with the legislative goal of limiting or abolishing the death penalty should not be allowed to obscure the difficulties of taking a judicial step toward that goal on the theory outlined by Justice Goldberg in [*Rudolph v. Alabama*]. . . . if one may venture a guess, what Justice Goldberg may really be troubled about is not the death penalty for rape but the death penalty. The problem may not be one of proportionality but of mode of punishment, the problem that concerned the framers of the eighth amendment and to which its provisions still seem most relevant. The Supreme Court is obviously not about to declare that the death penalty *simpliciter* is so cruel and unusual as to be constitutionally intolerable. Other social forces will have to work us closer than we are now to the point at which a judicial *coup de grace* becomes more than mere fiat. Meanwhile, there may well be legitimate devices for judicial control of the administration of the death penalty. The burden of this Comment is simply that the device proposed by Justice Goldberg is not one of them.[5]

These were the short-term reactions. Far more important, however, was the long-term reaction of the bar, especially the American Civil Liberties Union and the NAACP, which combined forces to establish a death-penalty litigation project designed to take up the challenge of the dissenting opinion in *Rudolph*. The history of this project has been recounted brilliantly by Professor Michael Meltsner in his book *Cruel and Unusual,* and I could not possibly improve upon it here.[6]

But the results achieved were dramatic. Meltsner and the other members of the NAACP Legal Defense Fund, a group that included a number of talented and committed lawyers, litigated hundreds of cases on behalf of defendants sentenced to death and, in many of these cases, succeeded in holding the executioner at bay until the Supreme Court was ready to consider the constitutionality of the death penalty. The strategy was simple in outline: the Supreme Court should not be allowed the luxury of deciding the issue of capital punishment as an abstraction; instead, it must be confronted with the concrete responsibility of determining the immediate fates of many hundreds of condemned persons at the same time. In this way, the Court could not evade the issue or lightly refuse to decide it if the Court's refusal would result in the specter of mass executions of hundreds of convicts. However, the Court could decline to decide the ultimate issue—the constitutionality of capital punishment if in doing so it could find some other way of keeping alive those on death row. And the litigants always provided the Court with this other way—a narrower issue, usually in the form of an irregularity in the procedure by which the death penalty was imposed or administered.

Thus in the late 1960s the Supreme Court decided a number of cases involving the administration of the death penalty; in each of these cases the Court declined to consider the ultimate issue, but it always ruled in favor of the doomed, thereby sparing their lives—at least for the moment. With the passage of each year, the number of those on death row increased, and the stakes grew higher and higher. Then in 1971 the Court took its first turn toward the noose: in *McGautha v. California* it held that a condemned person's constitutional rights were not violated "by permitting the jury to impose the death penalty without any governing standards" or by permitting the imposition of the death penalty in "the same proceeding and verdict as determined the issue of guilt."[7] At that point it looked like the string might have been played out: there were no more "narrow" procedural grounds. The Court would have to confront the ultimate issue. But it was not the same Court that had been sitting when the strategy was originally devised; there were four new Nixon appointees, and it was clear that at least some of them believed the death penalty to be constitutional. The umpires—if not the rules—had been changed after the strategy of the game had been worked out and irretrievably put into action. Now there was no pulling back.

The drama intensified. The Court let it be known that finally it was ready to decide the ultimate issue. Knowledgeable lawyers—counting noses on the Court—were predicting that the death penalty would be sustained. Some thought that it might be struck down for rape but sustained for murder. Some predicted that the Court would once again find—or contrive—a reason for avoiding the ultimate issue. A few, of optimistic bent, kept the faith and expressed the belief that the Court—even this Court—would simply not send hundreds to their death. And then a major and unanticipated break occurred. The California Supreme Court—perhaps the most influential state court in the nation—ruled that its constitution (which had substantially similar wordings as the federal Constitution) forbade the death penalty. Then, on the last day of the United States Supreme Court's 1971 term, the decision was rendered: the death penalty, as administered in this country, was unconstitutional.

Before all this occurred, Justice Goldberg sent me to work on his "pet project." Justices are not, of course, supposed to come to the Court with "projects," but Justice Goldberg had several, most prominently the judicial abolition of the death penalty. Ultimately, after Justice Goldberg left the Court, the death penalty was restored, at least for certain crimes, though I am convinced that Justice Goldberg's "pet project" marked the beginning of what will be its ultimate demise in the United States.

Justice Goldberg's "pet project" and the way he might try to implement it tell us much about the man and his relationship to his law clerks, but it doesn't tell us everything. He regarded his "one-year clerks" as "law clerks for life." After I completed my clerkship, Justice Goldberg continued to give me assignments: ranging from helping him pick future clerks and assistants, to editing his speeches and articles, to helping him draft resolutions at the United Nations, to assisting in his campaign for governor of New York.

Even while he served on the Supreme Court he took an interest in his law clerks and their intellectual development. He included us in his weekly Friday afternoon lunches or teas with noteworthy people. When such people came to visit the justice, he always introduced us and encouraged us to sit in on part of the discussion. Knowing that I was interested in Israel, he invited me to meet the Israeli ambassador to the United States as well as visiting Israeli public officials. When I went to Israel in 1970 he asked me to smuggle a carton of Lucky Strike cigarettes to Israel's Prime Minister Golda Meir, whom he had known from their earliest Zionist days together in the Midwest.

Since Justice Goldberg had very few clerks—he served only three terms —he was able to remain close to all of us. He invited us to his famous Passover Seders, where he and his wife Dorothy sang labor and Zionist songs from their youth. When he moved to New York, he attended High Holiday services with my family in Brooklyn. He was close to each clerk in a different way, following our careers, advising us on life choices and encouraging us to "do great things."

I recall one incident in particular that was typical. During my first year of teaching at Harvard Law School, an alumnus wrote a critical letter to the *Harvard Law Record* about a course I was teaching on psychiatry and law. That wasn't "real" law, according to the alumnus. Goldberg, who was still a justice, fired back with a letter of his own, defending the course as important to the education of students. That was not the only time he defended me or his other clerks from criticism.

Another incident was revealing as well. In my second summer of law school, I applied at the law firm of Paul, Weiss, Rifkin and Garrison. I received an offer at $100 a week which I gladly accepted. When the senior litigating partner of the firm, Simon Rifkin, learned that I could not work on Saturday because I was Sabbath observant, he told me I had no future with the firm and that I would be better off working at Kaye Scholer, a firm that did hire Sabbath observant Jews. I spent the summer with that firm. So when Justice Goldberg offered me the job the following year, I asked him if my Sabbath observance would create a problem. He said, "of course not. You will work on Sunday, my Christian law clerk will work on Saturday. That way I'll be covered seven days a week." But that's not the end of the story. Several years later, when Goldberg was offered a named partnership at the Paul, Weiss firm, he remembered my experience with Simon Rifkin and insisted that the firm change its policies as a condition to him joining the firm. They did so, and the firm now has many Sabbath observant employees—and they are the better for it.

Justice Goldberg was also proud of our accomplishments. I only regret that he didn't live to see one of his law clerks, Stephen Breyer, take his very seat on the High Court thirty years after he left the Supreme Court to serve as United States Ambassador to the United Nations.

Notes

1. *Youngstown Sheet & Tube Co. v Sawyer,* 343 U.S. 579 (1952).

2. *Trop v. Dullas,* 356 U.S. 86 (1958).

3. *Weems v. United States,* 217 U.S. 349 (1910).

4. *Rudolph v. Alabama,* 375 U.S. 889 (1963).

5. Herbert L. Packer, "Making the Punishment Fit the Crime," *Harvard Law Review* 77, no. 6 (April 1964): 1071–1072, 1081–1082.

6. Michael Meltsner, *Cruel and Unusual: The Supreme Court and Capital Punishment* (New York: W. Morrow, 1974).

7. *McGautha v. California,* 402 U.S. 183 (1971).

Shirt-Tales

Clerking for Byron White

In honor of Byron White's twenty-fifth anniversary as a Supreme Court justice, his current and former clerks presented him with a T-shirt. Emblazoned on the shirt were short, mainly one-line statements expressing the clerks' thoughts about the justice, his career, and their experiences as his clerks. The melange of brief messages conveys much about the relationship between Justice White and those who were privileged to work as his clerks. It also provides meaningful insights into the clerkship experience, as well as into the nature of the man who defined the experience by the force of his personality.

No slogan-laden T-shirt can fully capture the flavor of a White clerkship, which differs from year to year and from clerk to clerk. Nor can any brief law review essay or book chapter. Nonetheless, an examination of some of the messages found on the T-shirt presented to Justice White in 1987 provides a generalized portrait of that experience, as well as of the character of the individual who made that experience so rewarding for his clerks.

"Here's to another 2nd quarter century of being 'often in doubt'"

"I said it all in my memos and you didn't listen"

(I have refrained from identifying the authors of the various statements on the T-shirt, in particular because of this second, audacious statement. Anonymity in this respect serves two purposes: it protects those who may not want to be identified with the lines they penned, and at the same time it allows those who wish they had said something like that to claim they did.)

These two quotes somewhat cryptically summarize the way in which judicial decisions were made in the White chambers. The first refers to Justice White's oft-repeated statement that the clerks were "rarely in doubt and often in error," while the justices "were often in doubt and rarely in error." The second statement indicates the freedom clerks felt to express their opinions and their continual doubt as to whether those opinions changed the justice's mind.

Even though Justice White may have often been in doubt as to how a particular case was resolved, there was rarely any doubt about who would make the final decision.[1] One former clerk recalls that he once wrote "we have previously held" when referring to a previous Supreme Court decision in a memorandum to the justice.[2] Justice White's response to the memo characteristically reminded the clerk of the nature of the relationship: "I didn't know you were on the Court then, Bill." (This same clerk once described how he had "negotiated" with Justice White concerning the position the justice should take in a particular case, prompting his co-clerk to respond with a loud laugh, "Negotiate?") While Justice White would occasionally refer to his clerks as "the big brains," there was little question as to who the big brain really was.

That is not to say that the justice did not listen to his clerks or was not interested in hearing what they thought on a subject. Quite the contrary. Justice White wanted to hear all that the clerks had to say. Clerks were used as sounding boards, to make sure that the justice fully considered all possible arguments and points of view. This required that the clerks feel free to say it all, in their memos and in informal discussions. Most clerks did so, and the justice listened carefully. The clerks' task became difficult when they tried to guess what the justice was really thinking before a vote. As one former clerk explained: "[Justice White] would take a particular position on one of the cases that was going to be argued, and that was our clue to take the opposite view. And the position he took (in the discussion with the clerks) . . . was only about half the time the position he took when it came time to vote."[3]

Sometimes, the uncertainty continued even after the justices had voted on the case and the assignment to write the draft opinion was made. The first time Justice White was assigned to write an opinion for the Court in the October 1983 term, my co-clerk, who had been assigned to work on the first draft, began to pepper the justice with questions about what course the draft should take. The justice quickly ended the questioning, and at the same time indicated to us the role he expected his clerks to play, when he remarked, "If I had wanted someone to write down my thoughts, I would have hired a scrivener."

At times, this leeway in drafting opinions and expressing views about a case could be heady for the clerks. As clerks worked on draft opinions, they could entertain thoughts of shaping the course of the law, of penning words that would live on in Supreme Court decisions to be studied with awe by succeeding generations. But the euphoric dreams were generally short-lived—terminating with the return of the draft bleeding with red ink from the justice's pen, or more recently with the sound of the justice's word processor as he worked on revisions to the draft. Sometimes the justice would not even wait for the clerk's draft to arrive on his desk. Many clerks have had the experience of working furiously to finish a draft opinion within the ten-day deadline imposed by the justice, only to find the justice in their office on day nine with a set of papers in his large hands and the "suggestion" that "we work with this [his own version] as a draft" on his lips.[4]

This does not mean the justice was closed-minded. Again, quite the contrary. One former clerk observed that Justice White "wasn't invested in an argument; (if) you could hit him back with a chair, intellectually speaking, he could be convinced."[5] For Justice White, the judicial decision-making process was a two-step process: first, make sure the problem had been fully considered, and second, decide. The primary role of the clerks was to assist with the consideration, not the decision. The justice did the deciding on his own, perhaps beginning with doubt, but rarely ending in error.

The role of sounding board or debate opponent was for many the most gratifying aspect of their clerkships. To be able to engage in free-flowing debate on important legal issues—knowing that the justice really wanted to know what you thought, not what you thought he thought—was an unforgettable and, for many White clerks, a never-again-to-be paralleled experience. We truly felt we could, and should, say it all in our memos and discussions. Whether we ever really convinced the justice was always somewhat unclear, but it was also beside the point. The clerks would perhaps raise doubts in those often-spirited discussions, but it was the justice who, mindful of those doubts, would ultimately make the final decision.

"To the Justice with the Sharpest Elbows on the Court": "Happy Putting"

Much has been written, and almost as much surmised, about Justice White's incredible athletic ability and his penchant for engaging in competition with his clerks. Contrary to popular belief, the justice did not choose his clerks based on athletic ability—anyone who has seen the basketball games played by the clerks at reunions can testify to that. Still, competition was a central part of a White clerkship. In the words of one former clerk: "You can't understand Justice White if you don't understand competition. He values it. He relishes it."[6]

But some have misunderstood the purpose of the competition. I believe Justice White valued competition not because it gave him a chance to show off his magnificent abilities, but because it was a way of bringing out the best in those who competed. If that did not happen, the competition ended. For example, during the first month of my clerkship, Justice White engaged in an in-chambers putting contest with his clerks on an almost daily basis. In order to be successful, the putt would have to travel from one office, across another office, into the justice's office, under the side of his couch, and out under the front two legs. Neither I nor my co-clerks proved particularly proficient at the task, and the justice consistently won. As this pattern became apparent, the competition soon ended—not because the justice couldn't win, but because he didn't feel challenged to do his best. If the competition was not accomplishing that, it was not worth engaging in.

The purpose of the justice's challenging and competitive style soon became apparent in other activities, including discussions of the cases. On one occasion early in the term, I wrote a bench memo noting that the briefs of one party had not adequately responded to what I thought was the determinative argument. Several days after I had turned in the memo, but before conference on the case, the justice and I were discussing the case. When I raised what for me was the dispositive argument, the justice countered in quite a loud voice, "Don't you think (the party opposing the argument) rebutted that argument in their brief?" I said, somewhat hesitantly, "No." Then, even more challengingly, he said, "You really don't think they did?" I said, somewhat more assertively, "No." He then smiled and said, "I guess you're right." A string of similar encounters soon made it clear that the challenges came not because Justice White wanted to unnerve me (though early on they certainly had that effect), but because he wanted to make sure I had thought deeply enough about my position to be confident of it.

Competition did characterize a White clerkship, but a kind of competition that left those who engaged in it better for the experience, win or lose. In the words of one former clerk: "Clerking for Justice White was a thrilling and wonderful exercise in combat, from intellectual to basketball. Every day was like the Athenian youth going with Socrates and Socrates won 38 to 0 on a daily basis."[7]

"Dissents from Denial: Breakfast of Champions"

A Supreme Court clerk's daily regimen includes several different writing assignments such as cert memos, bench memos, and draft opinions. Some of these—draft opinions, for example—are more interesting and "prestigious" than others. Work on draft opinions, after all, might actually be published in a somewhat recognizable form for the world to see. Bench memos, on the other hand, are generally read only by the justice and then relegated to the case file, never again to see the light of day.[8] Dissents from denial fit somewhere in between. They are written for two purposes (ranked in order of importance): (1) to persuade enough other justices to change their votes and grant certiorari or, failing that, (2) to explain to the rest of the world why those other justices had made a mistake in not doing so. Ironically, those dissents from denial that were most successful (by persuading the other justices to grant cert) did not achieve more widespread publication.[9]

To me the significance of the quote "Dissents from Denial: Breakfast of Champions" is twofold. First, it reminds me of the judicious way in which Justice White assigned work to his clerks. At least at the time I clerked, clerks wrote nearly as many dissents from denial as they did bench memos. Make-work projects such as summarizing the contents of a brief, suggesting questions to be asked at oral argument, and checking cites—a regular staple for clerks from some other chambers—were simply not assigned. Work that was assigned— even the less glamorous work—was meaningful.

Second, it reminds me that a certain amount of work had to be done even before the justice made the decision to write a dissent from denial. When a conflict among lower courts (one of the most overlooked reasons for granting cert in Justice White's opinion, and thus one of the oft-repeated bases for White's dissents from denial) was alleged, clerks were not allowed to rely on the parties' assertion that the conflict existed. They were not even permitted to take the word of clerks from other chambers who may have prepared the cert memo. Clerks had to read the cases themselves and certify whether the conflict was real. And while the research and writing may not have been quite as thorough as that of a full opinion, care was demanded to make sure the facts and reasoning were in order—all for a work product that might never see the light of day.

When these dissents from denial were assigned to clerks after the Friday conference, few clerks rejoiced. It was an often unanticipated addition to the voluminous work for which the clerk was already responsible. Yet few complaints were heard—both because the work was meaningful (if not glamorous) and because it was hard to complain about too much work to a justice who even in his seventies arrived at work at 7:00 a.m. (long before most clerks had arrived) and who regularly frequented chambers on weekends.[10] Hard, meaningful work, even if not of the flashiest variety, often was the regular diet of the White clerks. Willingness to perform such work at a high level of quality made the head of the chambers a champion.[11] Most clerks sensed a similar menu might do the same for them.

"To Justice White—The Man Who Taught Me When to Get Off the Trolley"

Clerks would frequently assert during in-chambers discussion of cases that taking a position in the case before the Court would require that a future hypothetical case would have to be resolved in a seemingly uncomfortable way, seeking to persuade the justice that he should adopt the general rule that would best resolve a variety of cases. A common rejoinder from Justice White was, "I'm not afraid to get off the trolley half way down the hill." The justice's intellect enabled him to see the complexities in each case, and the potential weaknesses in any position, including his own. This led to a cautious, skeptical approach to general rules. "The defining characteristic of Justice White is hesitation about or doubts about general propositions, simplifying propositions," opined one former clerk.[12]

On more than one occasion, I recall the clerks debating a legal issue for a considerable period of time, creating, defending, and attacking grand theories to explain the proper result in the case being discussed. The justice would then stride into the office, ascertain the content of the discussion, and in one or two sentences suggest a resolution of the issue that had not been raised at all and that seemed nearly impervious to attack. The justice's comments, while premised on some larger philosophical foundation, generally focused on the narrow legal issue and the particular fact situation involved in the case.

It was hard to predict when the justice might get off the trolley; however, his exit, while not always fully explained to his clerks or in his opinions, was not a precipitous act.[13] Justice White would carefully consider the merits of the various arguments, debate them with his clerks, study the issues on his own, and then reach a decision. Before getting off the trolley, Justice White would carefully study the map to make sure he knew exactly where the trolley was, a trait he apparently acquired before coming to the Court. His former partners described his work habits in private practice:

> His research was exhaustive and ironclad. His methods were somewhat unusual, however. Donald Stubbs refers to him as the only lawyer he ever knew who physically attacked a library. Richard Davis recalls that he gave

new meaning to the term "hit the books." Donald Graham describes his processes as those of a fierce worker who advanced on a problem, shredded it and put it together again. There was always something disproportionate about the way his massive energy extracted the truth from masses of cases, only to be expressed through the medium of a massive hand and forearm producing tiny, illegible scribbles.[14]

He used the same approach in chambers (though he was easier on the books than he apparently was in private practice). There was never any need to inform Justice White of the contents of the briefs or the nature of the arguments being made. He had read and analyzed them himself. The justice might then ask for further research on a particular point that at the time could appear mundane, but that, when placed in context, was often critical to the proper resolution of the case. His examination and analysis were thorough and exhaustive, often much more so than the end product evidenced.

Nor was the justice afraid to get off the trolley on his own. Requests from other justices that a White opinion be amended were considered solely on their merits, not on the probable impact such an amendment would have on securing additional votes for the opinion. If the other justices wanted to write something that differed from the White opinion, they were free to do so. Changing the opinion simply to keep them on board was not a standard practice. While this practice has been criticized as evidencing a lack of leadership, it reflected a well-thought-out view of the proper role of a Supreme Court justice, as well as the intellectual modesty of a mind able to see that no argument is completely without flaw.

The trolley analogy aptly described the justice's jurisprudence. He was on a trolley with the other justices, but not to see the sights or travel as far as the car would take him. He had a duty to perform during the ride: to decide the particular case before him, with all the thoroughness and analysis possible. That required an exhaustive consideration of all he could see along the way, including what had happened in prior cases and what might arise in future ones. However, once the proper resolution appeared, it was time to act, regardless of where the trolley was or who else was headed for the exit.

"I'd Rather Be Wettin' a Line"

Fishing was one of the great loves of Justice White's life. But this quote from the T-shirt conveys more to me than just his fondness for angling. It reminds me that there was much more to Justice White and to a clerkship with him than just legal work. The justice's interests ranged far and deep. Pick any topic of conversation, and the justice was comfortable discussing it. He may have been as close to a true renaissance person as our modern complex times would allow.[15] Most striking to me, however, was that often Justice White's contribution to the conversation consisted largely of insightful questions, which allowed him and all present to learn even more about the subject. He was a person who was not content with knowing a lot about a lot—he always wanted to know more.

The justice's penchant for learning all he could was brought home to me one day when he called me into his office to discuss a draft opinion on which I was working. Shortly after I entered the room, the sound of a high-pitched whistle began to emanate from some unknown location near his desk. Justice White, who was sitting at his desk, began to look around for the source. When he couldn't identify it immediately, I walked around the desk to see if I could locate the source of the whistle. It was his dictaphone, which had reached the end of the tape. The justice pushed the eject button, and the tape popped out of the dictaphone. To my surprise it was not the generic tape that the justice used for dictating, but a cassette version of Michael Jackson's *Thriller,* which was one of the hottest selling albums of the time. As I sat back down the justice explained, somewhat sheepishly (or at least as sheepishly as I had ever seen him), that he and Mrs. White had been talking to one of the younger guards at the Court about music. The Whites mentioned that they had not heard the Michael Jackson album that was the subject of so much talk. The guard sent the tape up to chambers the next day, and the justice had listened to it. I asked him his impression of the tape. In typically cryptic White fashion, he said listening to it had prompted him to finally look at my draft opinion. I took the comment to mean that anything was better than listening to the tape, even reviewing the draft opinion I had written, so he apparently was not overly impressed with either the tape or the draft. The point, though, was that he wanted to listen to the tape so he could know what other people were talking about.

Conversations about the America's Cup races, which were taking place during the term, also revealed a similar thirst for knowledge and a great capacity to assimilate and analyze information. In the early conversations, the justice would ask one of my co-clerks some fairly basic information about yachting and then proceed to discuss what was happening in the early races. Eventually, the questions were about the racing strategy being employed, often in the form of analysis about what the competing skippers were hoping to accomplish with different moves: "Do you think he did that to gain this advantage, or was it to accomplish this end?" The questions led to informative discussions, not only for the justice and the clerks who knew about yachting, but for the less informed of us as well. I'm sure the conversations in other terms were equally diverse and equally enlightening.

"Of the 25, I still think OT 63 was the best"

"OT 83 was a wonderful experience"

"With gratitude for an unforgettable year"

"The best job I ever had was working for you"

The most common theme in the messages on the T-shirt is gratitude for the clerkship experience. All the White clerks, many of whom have gone on to distinguished careers, were clearly affected in a fundamental and positive way by their year at the justice's side.[16] The impact was not solely on the intellectual process. The standard Thanksgiving dinner at the Whites' home (complete with a session of the English board game Skittles), field trips to buildings in Washington, afternoon basketball games, and similar activities created a bond between justice and clerk that went much deeper than that of intellectual mentor and pupil. Although reserved in demeanor, the justice managed to convey to his clerks the genuine warmth he felt for them.

When President John F. Kennedy nominated Byron White to the Supreme Court, he noted that White had "excelled in everything he had attempted."[17] He continued to excel in many ways after he joined the Court, but in none more successfully than as a role model, mentor, and friend to those who clerked for him.

Notes

This essay has been adapted with permission from Kevin J Worthen, "Shirt-Tales: Clerking for Byron White," *Brigham Young University Law Review* 1994, no. 2 (1994): 349–61.

1. This independence apparently extended beyond the confines of the immediate chambers and into the conference room. According to one account, Justice Thurgood Marshall once informed his clerks that "Byron White listened to Byron White and to no one else." Bob Woodward and Scott Armstrong, *The Brethren: Inside the Supreme Court* (New York: Simon & Schuster, 1970), 180.

2. Several of the quotes in this essay, come from conversations that took place at reunions or in chambers and are reproduced from the author's memory.

3. Fred Barbash, "From Case to Case, Justice White the Loner Defied Labeling," *Washington Post,* March 20, 1993, A12 (quoting Rex Lee). Many of Justice White's former clerks have gone on to accomplish such great things in their own lives that reporters from the best papers called them for comments about the justice when he retired and quoted them by name in the ensuing article. See, e.g., Barbash, "From Case to Case" (quoting Rex Lee, former U.S. solicitor general and former president of Brigham Young University); Tony Mauro, "Another View of White: A Caring Person," *Legal Times,* March 29, 1993, 12 (referring to James Loken of the U.S. Court of Appeals for the Eighth Circuit, David Ebel of the Tenth Circuit, Rhesa Barksdale of the Fifth Circuit, and the Federal Circuit's Raymond Clevenger III). Other clerks toiled away in relative anonymity and are generally referred to, if at all, as "one former clerk." See, e.g., Stuart Taylor Jr., "Justice Byron White: The Consistent Curmudgeon," *Legal Times,* March 22, 1993, 1, 30 (quoting "a former clerk").

4. To those who characterize Justice White as gruff, competitive, and insensitive, I point out that when the wedding of my friend in Charlottesville, Virginia, fell in the middle of the first drafting assignment that I received, the justice suggested I spend the entire weekend seeing Charlottesville and the surroundings, indicating that he would grant an "extension" for that period of time. For the cynics who might be tempted to think that he did it so that he could finish his own draft first, see Jeffrey Rosen, "The Next Justice: How Not to Replace Byron White," *New Republic,* April 12, 1993, 21, 24 (asserting that Justice White would "race his clerks to see who could finish drafting an opinion more quickly"), I note that Justice White made no effort to produce the first draft on his own while I was gone.

5. Barbash, "From Case to Case" (quoting David Kendall).

6. Linda P. Campbell, "Justice White: The Democrat Who Often Votes with Court Conservatives," *Chicago Tribune,* March 21, 1993, section 1, 18 (quoting David Ebel).

7. Barbash, "From Case to Case" (quoting Robert B. Barnett). Barnett is also a partner at Williams & Connolly.

8. Or at least that's what I thought when I wrote them. Maybe I should not have been so sure. See Neil A. Lewis, "Rare Glimpses of Judicial Chess and Poker," *New York Times,* May 25, 1993, A1 (quoting from clerk memos in Justice Thurgood Marshall's now-public papers).

9. Not that there was much loss. The notoriety or prestige gained by even the most brilliant dissent from denial can easily be overstated. After all, how many lawyers, law students, or even law professors can name even one published dissent from denial? Indeed, when was the last time that they even read one? Probably in a case in which they represented one of the parties. While most law clerks who drafted them may recall the general thrust of a published dissent from denial, even they would be hard pressed to cite them by name.

10. One former clerk observed, "I tried beating him into work in the morning, but I finally figured it was like trying to open the refrigerator door . . . before the light comes on. It can't be done." David G. Savage, *Turning Right: The Making of the Rehnquist Supreme Court* (New York: John Wiley & Sons, 1992), 93.

11. The justice's penchant for hard work apparently had its roots in his early life. When asked what he had learned growing up in his small hometown of Wellington, Colorado—where he first began topping sugar beets at age six and later helped his father unload lumber and shovel coal from railroad cars—Justice White responded simply: "Work hard and don't be late for dinner." Gannett News Service, "Justice White Never Forgot His Rural Roots," March 20, 1993.

12. *All Things Considered*, NPR radio broadcast, March 19, 1993 (quoting Lance Leibman).

13. A classic example is Justice White's short concurring opinion in *Pennsylvania v. Union Gas Co.* (491 U.S. 1 [1989])in which he supplied the fifth vote for the proposition that Congress has the authority under the Commerce Clause to abrogate the Eleventh Amendment immunity of the states. That issue had sparked extensive debate among the justices in three separate opinions. Justice White's contribution to the written discussion consisted of a single sentence: "I agree with the conclusion reached by Justice Brennan in Part III of his opinion, that Congress has the authority under Article I to abrogate the Eleventh Amendment immunity of the States, although I do not agree with much of his reasoning." The absence of an explanation should not, however, be attributed to lack of thought or rationale for the decision. In Justice White's case, it was generally the result of having a mind that sees things at a higher level where difficult concepts are so clear that they need no explanation. As one former clerk observed, "You have to remember, he's three steps ahead of everybody else." Taylor, "Justice Byron White," 30 (quoting a former clerk).

14. Donald W. Hoagland, "Byron White as a Practicing Lawyer in Colorado," *University of Colorado Law Review* 58 (1987): 365, 366.

15. Justice White's ability to learn and master a variety of talents was one of his most well-known attributes. As one reporter put it: "Some people get 15 minutes of fame. Whizzer White is one of those men famous in several different phases of his life—for totally different reasons. Before he was a famous jurist, he was a famous presidential friend. Before that he was a famous lawyer. Before that a famous military man. Before that a famous athlete. Before that a famous scholar." Gannett News Service, "White's Life Marked with Many Successes," March 19, 1993.

16. As of 1994 when this essay was written, among White clerks were four federal courts of appeals judges, a former United States solicitor general, a member of Congress, a former state attorney general, the president of a university, and the dean of an Ivy League law school. There were also, of course, numerous law professors. (Not even Justice White could redeem all his clerks.)

17. "Statement by the President upon Appointing Byron White to the Supreme Court," Pub. Papers 283, 283 (March 30, 1962).

DEBORAH L. RHODE

Thurgood Marshall and His Clerks

Above the Supreme Court's door is the inscription "Equal Justice Under Law." At the memorial service for Thurgood Marshall in 1993, Chief Justice William Rehnquist noted: "Surely no one individual did more to make that a reality."[1]

Nor were any individuals more aware of that legacy than his law clerks. Our relationship with the justice carried a special honor, responsibility, and challenge. It also offered a unique window on the legal world. During his tenure, Marshall was the only member of the Court who had not "led a life of privilege."[2] Not only did that set him apart from his colleagues, but it also drew him closer to his clerks. The qualities that made him a great lawyer also made him a great teacher and a model of how to live a life of public service.

In attempting to capture those qualities for this essay, I reviewed not only published biographies and articles. I also contacted all the clerks whom I could locate, and asked for insights about their experience.[3] Over 40 percent responded, and the warmth of their accounts is further evidence of Marshall's special gifts as a mentor as well as a justice. What emerges from all of this research is Marshall's close, and in some ways distinctive, relationship with his clerks. To understand that relationship, it is necessary also to understand the justice's unique background and role on the Court.

Marshall's Background and Role on the Court

Thurgood Marshall was the grandson of slaves. He grew up in segregated Baltimore and attended a "separate but equal" Colored High and Training School with no library, cafeteria, or gymnasium. He studied law at Howard University because the University of Maryland would not admit blacks. When he graduated, he entered a profession that was 99 percent white.

Marshall never forgot, and never escaped, the legacy of racism. Nor did he want his clerks to forget the massive injustices and petty indignities that constituted race relations in America. Even once he became a Supreme Court justice, there were more than occasional reminders. His informal clothes during summer months invited confusion over his status. And he delighted in telling clerks how he was mistaken for a messenger or, once, for an elevator operator by tourists who demanded that he take them to the second floor.[4] One of his clerks, Harvard law professor Scott Brewer (October term 1990), put the point directly: "while [Marshall] was certainly *in* that august . . . building, he sure as hell was not *of* it."[5]

Not only race but also background, ideology, and temperament set Marshall apart from most of his colleagues. Although he was generally on cordial relations with other justices, he was not close to any except for William Brennan. Nor did Marshall have many shared interests that might have forged such bonds. His tastes were simple, and he had little patience for pompousness or pretence. Kevin Baine (October term 1975), a partner at Williams & Connolly, writes: "He was as down to earth and humble as a man could be. He was not impressed with his . . . exalted position. He treated everyone exactly the same. That meant he had no less respect for us than he had for his fellow Justices and no more respect than he had for the lowest level employee in the building. Equality was not an abstract principle with him; it was a natural instinct."[6]

Elena Kagan (October term 1987), now a Supreme Court justice herself, recalls the same quality from her clerkship a decade later and offers a telling illustration. When drafting Kenya's constitution, Marshall had the chance to meet Prince Philip, who opened their conversation by asking: "Do you care to hear my opinion of lawyers?" To which Marshall responded, "Only if you care to hear my opinion of princes."[7]

Marshall's informality set him at odds with Chief Justice Warren Burger, who delighted in fine wine, British legal traditions, and all the trappings of office. As one clerk noted, Marshall had "no use for the pretence and mystification that surrounded the Court's processes."[8] Burger was intent on preserving them. Marshall's common greeting, "What's doing, Chiefy baby?" was not calculated to please, and the justices' clashes in style sometimes carried a substantive undertone.[9] An example occurred in the year of the bicentennial of the United States Constitution. Burger was in charge of various celebrations, including a historical pageant in which members of the Court would reenact the original signing of the document. Marshall was offended by the unqualifiedly celebratory tone. As he noted, when the founding fathers spoke of "we the people," they were not, in fact, using the term generically. Nor did they "have in mind the majority of America's citizens."[10] Under the Constitution as originally drafted, only white landowners had the right to vote. Racial minorities and women of all colors were originally excluded from the Constitution's protections, uninvited in its formulation, denied a voice in its ratification, and, until the late twentieth century, largely absent in its interpretation. Marshall told the chief justice he was willing to participate in the ceremony, but only on terms that would be faithful to the nation's racial history; he would appear in livery and knee britches, carrying trays.[11] The reenactment never happened.

Such clashes with the chief justice affected the kind of opinions that Marshall was assigned to write, his interest in the drafting process, and the corresponding role of his clerks. Under the Court's assignment system, the most senior justice who was in the majority had the authority to determine who would write the opinion for the Court, and the most senior justice in the minority would determine who wrote the dissent. Marshall was at odds with a majority of his colleagues on most of the important controversies that came before the Court during his tenure.[12] In the cases where he had the greatest interest, he generally sided with Justice Brennan, who had the right to assign those opinions. Brennan kept most for himself, leaving Marshall to write separately if he felt strongly.[13] On matters where Marshall was in the majority and Chief Justice Burger assigned the opinion, Marshall often joked that he would get the case "Least likely to be cited by any person for any purpose under any circumstances."

He was also likely to get any case in which he did not take the conventional liberal position or voted against sympathetic litigants, particularly if they were persons of color. In some instances, such assignments made sense because they increased the likelihood that Marshall would write a narrow decision that would attract broad consensus. But Marshall and his clerks also experienced punitive dimensions to the assignments; these opinions were the ones we least enjoyed writing and we received a disproportionate share. In some years, the clerks ran an informal wager. Before each conference we ranked our least favorite cases, and the justice would stride off with the promise: "I'll do my best to get them for you." Depressingly often, he succeeded.

On the Inside with an Outsider: The Clerking Relationship

As the Court moved increasingly to the right during Marshall's tenure, the frustrations of being an outsider, both personally and ideologically, took a toll. Cass Sunstein (October term 1979), now a professor at University of Chicago

Law School and member of the Obama administration, recalled that when he effusively accepted Marshall's offer of a clerkship, the justice growled, "I don't know what you're so excited about—you're just going to be working on dissents."[14] In both published accounts and responses to my questionnaire, some clerks recalled the justice's dark moods, while others stressed his persistence in the face of reversals. Scott Brewer recalled Marshall as "always sober, never sullen."[15] Never did he lose his sense of humor. In my term, he would return from Conference to recount his defeats with an ironic undertone: "Well, I was in the majority on one issue—breaking for lunch."

Yale Law School professor Steven Carter (October term 1980) noted: "It would have been easy for the Chambers to develop a bunker mentality. But the Justice would have none of that. He was far too good-humored." One of the qualities that Carter respected most was Marshall's "ability to maintain his warmth even as his [civil rights] edifice began to crumble."[16]

Marshall's outsider status on the Court affected his relationships with his clerks along several dimensions. Most important, it made him more dependent on their support, both personally and substantively. Although the closeness of the ties varied, depending partly on the justice's health and spirits during their term, many clerks reported feeling part of Marshall's extended family. He invited them to his home, spent many hours sharing personal stories, and was delighted to see them after their clerkships ended. The affection came through in nicknames. Clerks were "knucklehead," "girl," "boy," or "shorty."[17] He was "Boss," "Judge," or "TM," never "Justice." Particularly during periods when Marshall felt embattled or frustrated with the Court's conservative direction, clerks provided crucial emotional support, respect, and affirmation of his values.

These close relationships also allowed discussion about what his values demanded in particular cases. Georgetown law professor Mark Tushnet (October term 1972), one of the justice's biographers, noted that "his deepest views were sometimes different from the more traditional ones he initially expressed, and he relied on his clerks to remind him when he went astray."[18]

Marshall also depended heavily on his clerks for substantive recommendations and drafting. He chose not to join the "cert pool," in which a single clerk wrote a memo for all the participating justices on every petition for certiorari. Marshall preferred having one of his own clerks review each of the hundred or so petitions that came in every week.[19] For most of his tenure, Marshall required bench memos for all of the cases accepted for review. Clerks also had major responsibility for drafting opinions, subject to Marshall's instructions and review. And they sometimes provided an interface with other chambers. That level of responsibility imposed corresponding obligations. The hours were long, and the internal editing process was grueling. Every draft was extensively revised and checked before it ever reached the justice. He expected a high quality of performance, and his clerks expected it of themselves.

The demanding nature of the clerkship made Marshall extremely careful in his selection process. He relied largely on conventional criteria: top grades and law review experience at leading schools, along with recommendations from a few particularly well-respected judges. As a result, his clerks were highly regarded in Court circles, and many went on to teach at elite law schools or to occupy prominent leadership positions.[20] Biographer Juan Williams notes that despite Marshall's strong support for affirmative action in his judicial rulings, it was not much reflected in his own employment practices. Of the twenty-eight clerks over his first ten years, only one was African American (his god-daughter). In the 1980s, about 15 percent were minorities, but almost all were from the top of their class at elite law schools. None came from Howard, his own alma mater, or other predominantly black institutions.[21] Yet if Marshall was reluctant to give special preferences to underrepresented groups, he was equally careful not to perpetuate their disadvantages. His chambers was the first to have two women clerks, when some other justices had still never hired even one.

The extensive responsibility that Marshall gave his clerks led to an occasional testing of the boundaries. New York University law professor Rick Pildes (October term 1984) described the "tension between the fact that we all genuinely revered TM and the fact that from time to time we all thought he was taking some stubborn and unreasonable position . . . and would be oh-so-better off if he would only listen to his law clerks."[22] Several clerks recalled Marshall's icy rejoinder when told that he "had" to join or oppose a particular opinion. "There are only two things I *have* to do; stay black and die."[23] Another common response was typified in an experience of Georgetown University professor Susan Loh Bloch (October term 1976): "Once when I suggested a change in the draft of an opinion we were working on, he commented: 'A pretty good idea, but you're missing two things. . . . Nomination by the President and confirmation by the Senate.'"[24] Looking back on these examples, and on other cases in which Marshall had made crucial editorial changes, many clerks came to realize that "there was a reason he had the commission on the wall and I didn't."[25]

Occasionally, however, a clerk felt strongly enough on a matter to engage in passive resistance. One recalls the arrogance that led him to tell the justice that he "could do what he wanted" in a particular case, "but I'd be damned if I'd write the opinion for him. Amazingly enough, he didn't fire me on the spot." He just took out a legal pad and wrote a quite "serviceable" opinion. Marshall showed similar tolerance for the antiwar clerk who would not work on a decision refusing to halt the bombing of Cambodia. Without even expressing a cross word, Marshall simply drafted the ruling himself.[26]

Once, during my own clerkship, I tested the limits of my role, although I felt then, as now, that it had been in a worthy cause. Marshall had grown up in an era in which "Negro" was the term of choice; "Black" was a racial slur. As common usage changed, and Marshall's language did not, a series of clerks attempted to persuade him to stop using "Negro." Having received advice from my predecessors to make such an effort, I wrote a draft of a 1978 voting rights opinion describing parties as "Black." It was the first opinion on which I had worked, and when Marshall summoned me into his chambers, I was more than a little uneasy. He handed me the draft, laced with large red Xs, and then rolled up his sleeve. Pointing to his arm, he asked: "Does that look black to you?" It was a rhetorical question. Marshall was not interested in my attempted explanation of the draft language. "Just change it," he barked. But he held no grudges, and I dutifully passed on the traditional instruction to my successor. Eventually, his clerks' persistence helped win him over, and he began using the term "Afro-American."[27]

Marshall was also open to persuasion on whether to write a separate opinion. Many clerks encouraged this option, in part because it offered their only chance to work on the term's more important cases, which were generally assigned to other justices. But sometimes clerks flagged matters that others on the Court refused to consider important. An example from my term was *Hollenbaugh v. Carnegie Free Library*. It involved a librarian and custodian who had been fired from their positions at a state-subsidized library in rural Pennsylvania. After the librarian became pregnant with his child, the custodian left his wife and moved in with the librarian. When some members of the community complained, the library's board of trustees urged them to stop living together. When they refused, they lost their positions and subsequently brought suit claiming a violation of constitutionally protected rights of privacy. Neither adultery nor fornication was then illegal in Pennsylvania. However, the board contended that the librarian's "open adultery" interfered with her job performance. The lower courts accepted this justification on the theory that her position involved "direct and frequent contacts with the community, and the community was well aware of [petitioners'] living arrangement."[28]

The petition failed to gain sufficient votes for review. My co-clerks and I were appalled, and Marshall agreed to write a dissent from the denial of certiorari. He had seen more than enough of such moralism during his civil rights work, particularly when the couple was multiracial. As his dissent noted, board members "apparently did not object to furtive adultery, but only to petitioners' refusal to hide their relationship. In essence, respondents sought to force a standard of hypocrisy on their employees and fired those who declined to abide by it."[29] No evidence suggested that the relationship affected the public's use of the library or "diminished [the librarian's] ability to discharge her duties."[30] Nor was there any indication that the custodian's job called for contacts with the community or that his performance was affected in any way by his extramarital relationship. Marshall closed his dissent with the claim that "individuals' choices concerning their private lives deserve more than token protection from this Court."[31] Those of us who clerked for him that term were especially proud to see that principle affirmed.

Marshall as Mentor

Cases like *Hollenbaugh* held a number of lessons about law and life that shaped the clerkship experience. In both their responses to my questionnaire and their published accounts, clerks made clear how much they learned from Marshall, and not just about constitutional jurisprudence. As Baine put it, "TM gave his clerks a great gift by letting us into his world. We learned a little bit about how to live and a little bit about how to [litigate]."[32] In clerks' descriptions of Marshall as mentor, several common themes emerged.

The first involved priorities. Harvard law professor Martha Minow (October term 1980) explained: "Marshal taught his clerks to pick their battles carefully.... Known as the champion of the rights of the excluded and oppressed, Justice Marshall nonetheless taught his clerks that we—and he—would be worn out by trying to fight for every conceivable claim.... Fighting every battle would not leave time to fight any of them successfully and to work effectively with colleagues on the Court."[33]

A second important lesson concerned empathy. In choosing his struggles, Marshall was guided by an understanding of "human nature and human suffering" and the impact of legal doctrine on daily lives.[34] "He was a realist," observed Harvard law professor William Fisher. "He didn't have much patience for . . . formal arguments that ignored. . . . how the law affected real people."[35] "Litigants can sometimes get lost in the shuffle of legal arguments and precedents," Baine noted. Marshall had a unique capacity "for bringing the argument back to earth and reminding everyone of what was at stake for those who were affected by the Court's decisions."[36] Marshall also had what Minow described as an "unparalleled" ability "to put himself in the position of people quite unlike himself": prisoners, minors seeking abortions, the elderly and disabled.[37]

Yet at the same time, the justice remained ever mindful that empathy for some could carry costs for others, and that there were reasons why the symbol of Justice was blind. For example, although he categorically opposed capital punishment, which he believed could not be impartially administered, Marshall never lost sight of the horrific nature of the crimes at issue. Rick Pildes recalled the justice's response to one particularly grisly description in a case seeking a stay of execution: "You mean there are people out there doing things like this and I'm against the death penalty?"[38]

For many clerks, TM's perspective offered a window on an unfamiliar world. He reminded the "haves" what passed for justice among the "have-nots." His early litigation experience kept him sensitive to the gap between formal rights and social practices. He had been appellate counsel after robbery trials that observed the formalities but lasted less than fifteen minutes; the proof was presented so swiftly no one ever even learned what was stolen. All three stages of a southern court proceeding—arraignment, trial, and sentencing—could sometimes be completed in less than a half hour.[39] As colleagues as well as clerks noted, Marshall "would tell us things that we knew but would rather forget; and he told us much that we did not know due to the limitations of our own experiences."[40]

An often cited example was Marshall's 1973 dissent in *United States v. Kras,* in which the Court declined to strike down a $50 bankruptcy filing fee for impoverished litigants.[41] What angered Marshall about the majority's approach was the cavalier assertion that the amount, about $250 in 2011 dollars, was a relatively trivial sum even for those in poverty: "It is perfectly proper for judges to disagree about what the Constitution requires, but it is disgraceful for an interpretation of the Constitution to be premised upon unfounded assumptions about how people live. . . . No one who has had close contact with poor people can fail to understand how close to the margin of survival many of them are."[42]

A third important lesson involved respect for the rule of law. In a tribute to Marshall's commitment to procedure, Harvard law professors Randall Kennedy (October term 1983) and Martha Minow characterize the justice as a "lawyer's lawyer," who recognized the value of "agreement about how to disagree," and a neutral "framework for the fight."[43] In his civil rights battles in hostile southern courtrooms, Marshall found that procedural rules were a crucial tactical weapon. They were worth defending "even when they ran counter to a perceived substantive goal in a given case. Homage to the guardrail is necessary even when your side does not need it, if you want it to be around when you do.... Invigorating the ideal of the Rule of Law ... enables the powerless to call upon the powerful to play by their own rules."[44]

For that reason, Marshall demanded strict observance of formalities, however inconvenient. So, for example, when requests for a stay of execution came in, the justice insisted that his clerks call him at home, whatever the hour. Because Marshall opposed the death penalty, his position on stays was a foregone conclusion, and he could have simply left standing instructions about drafting an order. But instead he demanded that clerks rouse him, even after midnight, and read the petition over the phone. He would listen groggily then announce, "I *always* vote to grant," and slam down the phone.[45]

A fourth lesson was the importance of stories. Harvard law professor David Wilkins summarized a common view: "stories were such an integral part of who he was and why he was such a great man. He had such an eye for ... understanding the humanity of people."[46] The anecdotes would always "evoke a laugh [but also] ... make a point."[47]

When workload pressures became intense, clerks occasionally were ambivalent about extended recollections. As Jon Weinberg noted, "stories are what now I cherish most," but at the time he experienced some tension. "This was the experience of a lifetime ... but I [knew there was] work I need[ed] to be doing."[48] For the most part, however, clerks recognized that stories were one of the best parts of the job, and that much of what they were learning was not about doctrine. As Elena Kagan put it:

> The stories were something more than diversions ... They were a way of showing us that, bright young legal whippersnappers though we were, we did not know everything; indeed, we knew, when it came to matters of real importance, nothing. ... And they reminded us, as Justice Marshall thought all lawyers ... should be reminded, that behind the law there are stories—stories of people's lives as shaped by law, stories of people's lives as might be changed by law. ... his stories kept us focused on law as a source of human well-being.[49]

Sandra Day O'Connor made much the same point in her tribute to Marshall as a "raconteur." Part of his great contribution to the Court was "his life experiences constantly pushing and prodding us to respond not only to the persuasiveness of legal argument but also to the power of moral truth." He was "a man who knew the anguish of the silenced, and gave it a voice."[50]

A final lesson from a Marshall clerkship was the importance of giving back. Those fortunate enough to have the experience were also likely to have many other professional opportunities. With those opportunities came obligations, and Marshall was not hesitant to remind clerks that whatever career path they chose would have room for public service. Glen Darbyshire (October term 1986) recalls such a conversation years after his clerkship. He was planning to leave large-firm practice, and Marshall reminded him both to volunteer for pro bono cases and to "come by and see me, *boy*."[51] And when someone did, the same advice was forthcoming, along with a few stories that made it clear what constituted a life well-lived.

Asked how he wished to be remembered, Thurgood Marshall was fond of saying: "He did what he could with what he had."[52] And, by his example, he inspired his clerks to do the same.

Notes

1. Juan Williams, *Thurgood Marshall: American Revolutionary* (New York: Crown, 1998): 397–98 (quoting William Rehnquist).

2. Michael D. Davis and Hunter R. Clark, *Thurgood Marshall: Warrior at the Bar, Rebel on the Bench* (Bridgewater, N.J.: Replica Books, 2001): 14, 15 (quoting Lawrence Tribe).

3. The questionnaire, sent by email and hard copy in October 2008, asked former clerks about matters including the nature of their work; the relationship that they had with other justices' chambers; their relationship with the justice; any distinctive aspects about their relationship in comparison to the relationship that other law clerks had with their justices; and any interesting anecdotes or other information that they would like to share. Those who responded had the option of remaining anonymous, and the few who did so are quoted without attribution in the discussion that follows.

4. For the messenger story, see Janet Cooper Alexander, "A Tribute to Justice Thurgood Marshall: 'TM,'" *Stanford Law Review* 44 (June 1992): 1231, 1234. For the elevator operator experience, see Susan Low Bloch, "Remembering Justice Thurgood Marshall: Thoughts from His Clerks," *Georgetown Journal on Poverty Law and Policy* 1 (1993): 9.

5. Scott Brewer, "In Memoriam: Justice Marshall's Justice Martial," *Texas Law Review* 71 (May 1993): 1121, 1122.

6. Kevin Baine, email correspondence, October 2008.

7. Elena Kagan, "In Memoriam: For Justice Marshall," *Texas Law Review* 71 (May 1993): 1125, 1126.

8. Howard Ball, *A Defiant Life: Thurgood Marshall and the Persistence of Racism in America* (New York: Crown, 1999): 202n12 (quoting clerk).

9. Mark Tushnet, *Making Constitutional Law: Thurgood Marshall and the Supreme Court* (New York: Oxford University Press, 1997): 64n29; Ball, *Defiant Life,* 202 (discussing references to colleagues as "baby").

10. Thurgood Marshall, "Reflections on the Bicentennial of the United States Constitution," *Harvard Law Review* 101 (November 1987): 1, 2.

11. Glen M. Darbyshire, "Clerking for Justice Marshall," *American Bar Association Journal* 77 (September 1991): 48; Deborah L. Rhode, "A Tribute to Justice Thurgood Marshall: Letting the Law Catch Up," *Stanford Law Review* 44 (Summer 1992): 1259, 1264.

12. Ball, *Defiant Life,* 202.

13. Tushnet, "Making Constitutional Law," 64.

14. Cass Sunstein, email correspondence, November 3, 2008.

15. Bloch, "Remembering Thurgood Marshall" (quoting Scott Brewer).

16. Stephen L. Carter, "Living without the Judge," *Yale Law Journal* 101 (October 1991): 1, 3.

17. Kagan, "In Memoriam," 1125, 1126; Susan Low Bloch, email correspondence, November 2008.

18. Tushnet, "Making Constitutional Law," 59.

19. Darbyshire, "Clerking for Justice Marshall," 50.

20. Tushnet, "Making Constitutional Law," 57, 209; Bloch, "Remembering Justice Thurgood Marshall," 9.

21. Williams, *Thurgood Marshall,* 377.

22. Rick Pildes, email correspondence, November 21, 2008.

23. Kagan, " In Memoriam," 1127.

24. Bloch, email; Ball, *Defiant Life,* 216n64.

25. Jon Weinberg, professor of law, Wayne State, email correspondence, October 2008.

26. Bob Woodward and Scott Armstrong, *The Brethren: Inside the Supreme Court* (New York: Simon and Schuster, 1979): 278.

27. Williams, *Thurgood Marshall,* 387.

28. *Hollenbaugh v. Carnegie Free Library,* 436 F. Supp. 1328, 1332–33 (W.D.PA, 1977).

29. *Hollenbaugh v. Carnegie Free Library,* at 1054.

30. Ibid., 1057.

31. Ibid., 1058.

32. Baine, email correspondence.

33. Bloch, "Remembering Thurgood Marshall" (quoting Martha Minow), 23.

34. Baine, "Wit, Wisdom and Compassion of Justice Thurgood Marshall," *Hastings Constitutional Law Quarterly* 20 (Spring 1993): 497, 499.

35. Kevin Cullin, "Former Clerks Recall Raconteur Who Played Devil's Advocate," *Boston Globe,* June 28, 1991 (quoting William Fisher).

36. Baine, "Wit, Wisdom and Compassion," 500.

37. Bloch, "Remembering Thurgood Marshall" (quoting Minow).

38. Rick Pildes, email correspondence, November 20, 2008.

39. Rhode, "Tribute to Justice Thurgood Marshall," 1260.

40. Byron R. White, "A Tribute to Justice Thurgood Marshall," *Stanford Law Review* 44 (Summer 1992): 1215, 1216.

41. *United States v. Kras,* 409 U.S. 434, 460 (1973) (Marshall, J., dissenting). See Susan Low Bloch, "Do What You Can," *Oklahoma Law Review* 47 (1994): 12.

42. *United States v. Kras,* at 460.

43. Randall Kennedy and Martha Minow, "Thurgood Marshall and Procedural Law: Lawyer's Lawyer, Judge's Judge," *Harvard BlackLetter Journal* 6 (1989): 95, 99.

44. Ibid., 100.

45. Rosemary Herbert, email correspondence, November 3, 2008.

46. Bloch, "Remembering Thurgood Marshall" (quoting David Wilkins).

47. Baine, "Wit, Wisdom and Compassion," 497, 499.

48. Weinberg, email correspondence, November 2008.

49. Kagan, "In Memoriam," 1125.

50. Sandra Day O'Connor, "Thurgood Marshall: The Influence of a Raconteur," *Stanford Law Review* 44 (June 1992): 1217.

51. Darbyshire, "Clerking for Justice Marshall," 48.

52. Ruth Marcus, "Plain-Spoken Marshall Spars with Reporters," *Washington Post,* June 29, 1991, A1, A10.

RANDALL P. BEZANSON

Good Old Number Three

Harry Blackmun and His Clerks

A justice's relationship with his or her law clerks is wider ranging and more complex than most people realize. It is professional and personal, intellectual and avocational (baseball!), individual and familial. The relationship shapes the justice and the clerks alike. It relies upon shared intellectual values, not shared ideology, and on a shared commitment to the goals a Supreme Court justice seeks to achieve through his or her office. Mostly, though, it is the clerks and their personal and professional futures that are shaped.

Each year Justice Blackmun invited three, and later four, young people, equipped with the very best educations, full of imagination and enthusiasm, to join him for a year in his chambers in the Marble Palace that is the Supreme Court. The young clerks enter the building a bit naïve, idealistic, and impatient. If all goes well, they leave a year later more experienced in the world, still idealistic, but more tempered in it, more patient, and, most importantly, much wiser. That, at least, was the case with those fortunate enough to spend a year with Justice Harry Blackmun, a kind, wise, demanding, but forgiving mentor.

A relationship so intimate and personal cannot be described even for one clerk, much less for a group of ninety-four clerks. I attempt to sketch it indirectly through various prisms. Who were the clerks Justice Blackmun selected; where did they come from; how did he select them; who have they become today? What were the working patterns and clerking responsibilities in the chambers? How were the clerks' days filled, how did work change over the term, and what patterns and practices marked the justice's working relationships with the clerks? Finally, what can be said, by example only, about the working and personal relationships Justice Blackmun had with his clerks?

The Clerks

Who were the clerks that worked with Justice Blackmun?[1] Over the course of his tenure on the Court from 1970 to 1994, and his five years as a retired justice before his death in 1999, Justice Blackmun had ninety-four law clerks. During his first full term and the next five terms he had three clerks;[2] thereafter, beginning with October term 1976, he had four clerks; and in the five years after his retirement he had one clerk each year. They were trained at forty-five undergraduate colleges and universities located throughout the country, east to west, north to south, thirteen public and thirty-two private. Those most represented were Yale (thirteen), Harvard (eight), Princeton (four), and Brown and Berkeley (three each). Just over twenty of the clerks had also completed nonlaw graduate work. Five were Rhodes Scholars; five had PhDs; two were Marshall Scholars and one a Fulbright Scholar.

The clerks attended twenty-three different law schools, again from all over the country, public and private. The law schools most represented were Yale (twenty-one), Harvard (Justice Blackmun's alma mater, twenty), Stanford, Columbia, and Virginia (five each), and the University of Chicago (four). Seven of the law schools were public: Texas, Iowa, Michigan, Virginia, Georgia, Berkeley, and North Carolina. Virtually all of the clerks had clerked for another judge on a lower court before joining Justice Blackmun's chambers. The previous clerkships were almost all federal (only two in state courts) and dominantly appellate courts. The most represented courts were the D.C. Circuit, the Second Circuit, and the U.S. District Court for the Southern District of New York, perhaps the most distinguished federal district court during much of the justice's tenure.

The clerks were a talented and diverse group. They came from all over the country. Thirty-two of the ninety-four clerks were women, a quite remarkable number for the time. After serving their year clerking with Justice Blackmun, the clerks went on to successful, interesting, and influential careers. Thirty-four former clerks went into private practice and most are now partners and leaders in many of the most respected firms in the United States. Thirty-five of the clerks went into teaching, mostly on the faculty of the nation's best law schools. Many hold distinguished chairs, and some have served as deans, vice presidents, and presidents at their academic institutions. Fourteen clerks hold government positions, most often in the Department of Justice. Five are federal and state judges. Five work in nonprofit and public interest fields, two are corporate CEOs, and one is a writer and filmmaker.

I recall helping Justice Blackmun review the many applications for clerk-ships in the late fall of 1972. He was always the last justice to select his clerks. My most distinct memory is wondering how I ever got there.

Starting Out: A Personal Account

I don't remember much about my clerkship interview with Justice Blackmun in the winter of 1971. Like many of the clerks, I was too apprehensive to remember much afterward. But thanks to Ann Alpers (October term 1990), an occasion important to all of his clerks can be reconstructed, at least in spirit:

> HAB[3] was still late (the last usually) in hiring clerks. He used to say be-cause he hired so late, he got the dumbest clerks. He interviewed me in January, I think. I was clerking for Judge William Norris on the 9th Cir-cuit at the time.
>
> I remember meeting Wanda Syverson Martinson [Justice Blackmun's able and devoted secretary] and Dooley Stephanos [Justice Blackmun's assistant secretary, who had been preceded by Wannett Smith], the cur-rent clerks (one of whom was a former Norris clerk, the wonderful Vik Amar), and HAB. When Justice Blackmun took me into his office, I was terrified. He looked sternly at me and held up Judge Norris' recom-mendation letter. Judge Norris wrote extremely long, gossipy letters of recommendation. HAB said, "I have a letter from Judge Norris that is three pages long. Single spaced." I didn't know what to say, so I stam-mered, "Did Judge Norris have a lot to complain about?" I thought, "I am such a fool. I can kiss this clerkship goodbye." But I ended up get-ting the phone call from Justice Blackmun the following week. He called Judge Norris' chambers and the judge's secretary was out so I answered the phone. HAB asked to speak to the judge (it was HAB himself, not Wanda, on the phone) because it was his practice to first tell the judge that he was going to make an offer to the clerk. The judge was on the bench so I replied that he wasn't there and HAB then asked to speak to his law clerk, Ann. I gulped and said, "I'm Ann" and HAB laughed and said, "Oh you poor thing," and offered me the job. I was shocked, de-lighted and overwhelmed.

I remember being quite apprehensive—scared, really—when I first walked in to work through the tall, majestic marble halls of the Supreme Court

Building. I was a young boy from the farm state of Iowa. Justice Blackmun's suite of offices, or chambers, consisted of one very large room where the clerks and the messenger worked, a secretary's office, and finally the justice's office at the corner of the building looking south to the Library of Congress and west to the Capitol Building. Justice Blackmun and two of his clerks from the previous term, George Frampton and John Rich, made me comfortable—Justice Blackmun did so by phone from northern Wisconsin, where he and Dottie rented a lakeside cabin for the latter part of the summer. True to his nature, Justice Blackmun spent much of his Wisconsin days doing certs, conducting business, and reading, producing a constant flow of work for the clerks and staff back at the Court.[4] Mrs. Blackmun, whom the clerks all came to know as Dottie, enjoyed herself by swimming, seeing friends, reading, and soaking in the seclusion.

George and John familiarized me with the job and the stages through which it would pass over the term. The first order of business for me and my fellow clerks, Jim Ziglar and Ralph Miller, was, of course, cert petitions and jurisdictional statements. Each week the clerk's office brought library carts with the briefs and responses, and the three of us then divvied up the cases. We spent our days reading and, as we got better at it, simultaneously writing the highly structured memos the justice wanted: facts, jurisdiction, issues, discussion of the importance of the case/issue(s), and recommendation (grant certiorari, deny certiorari, affirm, dismiss, summarily dispose of, grant probable jurisdiction for hearing, etc.). Our memos were then forwarded to Justice Blackmun.

For the first half of October term 1972, we three clerks did memos for all of the certs and jurisdictional statements. Starting in early 1973 the cert pool began, with five of the justices participating (except for Justices William O. Douglas, Thurgood Marshall, William J. Brennan Jr., and Potter Stewart). The cert pool was an arrangement by which a number of chambers shared the duty of doing cert memos for multiple justices, rather than each chamber doing its own. This significantly cut down the number of cert memos that law clerks had to do, and it proved also to improve the quality of the cert memos. In each of the chambers in the pool, the particular justice's clerks would usually review the briefs and the pool memo, add to the memo if needed, and attach their own recommendation and reasoning.

The cert pool was controversial because of the danger that one clerk preparing the pool memo could, inadvertently or not, have too much influence on the Court's decision to accept a case for review. Many clerks felt that it was important that at least a few chambers not participate in the cert pool in order to serve as a check on the process by having at least one or two other clerks look at all of the petitions independently. Justice Blackmun seemed to share some concern about the cert pool as well, at least as reflected in Bill Murphy's (October term 1979) account:

> In our day, HAB would mark up the pool memos with strange hieroglyphs —indicating some secret coded commentary about the court or specific judges who authored the opinions below, and sometimes—we theorized —on the author of the pool memo from another Chambers, as in "this law clerk is not to be trusted on this sort of issue." We never really cracked the code.

As the late summer progressed and we clerks became very efficient at the certs, we began work on the second major part of our job: bench memos. In Justice Blackmun's chambers, a bench memo was prepared by a clerk (the clerks tended to divvy up the memos, too) for each case to be argued during the term. The only exceptions were tax cases, which the justice took on himself without a clerk's memo, or with only a brief memo. Tax law had been a large part of his practice, and he was rightly respected by his fellow justices as the tax expert on the Court. Our memos followed a general form but varied in length and content depending on the complexity of the case or its importance. The memos included a summary of the arguments made by the parties and then an independent analysis based on research conducted by the clerk, pointing out weaknesses in the case, problems that might arise because the facts did not present the issue well, and the forms of reasoning or doctrine that would need to be applied to decide the case and the implications of such reasoning in light of prior and, as important, future cases.[5] A clerk would often offer his or her own recommendation in a separate section of the memo.

All of the memos and certs were typed on the new Smith Corona electric typewriters that the Court had just purchased. The paper used had one or two carbon copy sheets behind the front page so that there was always a copy for the file. Justice Blackmun called the copies "flimsies." Typing errors would be corrected with whiteout, but the flimsies were always pretty messy. If a sentence needed to be changed, it would often be X'd out and replaced with another in the margin. The Smith Coronas were very loud typewriters, and even more so because of the flimsies attached to each sheet. When all of the clerks were typing, it sounded like being trapped in the middle of enemy crossfire. Since the justice's clerks all worked in one room in my term, the capacity to concentrate amid the noise was a finely honed skill that we quickly learned.

Some years later computers were acquired for the chambers. But the Court's turn to computer technology wasn't all that important to Justice Blackmun. He was a write-it-in-longhand person. Ann Alpers (October term 1990) reports the change with a characteristic bit of the justice's often dry humor:

Technology changed during our term. Larry Lessig was clerking for Justice Scalia and he was already a technology fan. The Court's old ATEX computer system was quite antiquated and Larry urged Justices Scalia and O'Connor (and maybe Kennedy) to get PCs for all the clerks, secretaries and Justices. The Court did so and we switched over to PCs and Word halfway through the term. This gave us a much more user-friendly e-mail system and Internet access, as well. I remember Wanda showing HAB the new system. He was thoroughly disgusted and already on a campaign to keep all his Shepherds volumes in his library. Wanda showed him how spell check worked and he lifted an eyebrow and asked, "Then why do I need you?" while glaring at Wanda and me. We clerks certainly used the on-line citation checking to check the opinions and bench memos, but HAB always used the books.

The justice would read the certs before conference, make notes on the memos, ask questions of us if needed, and then report back to us on the petitions and jurisdictional statements that were granted for oral argument after the conference. Most of the communication between the justice and the clerks about certs or bench memos occurred at breakfast. As described by Danny Ertel (October term 1987), near the end of breakfast, HAB would "take out a small index card with some notes, usually about which of us owed him a memo or draft or something else. Breakfast was also when he would usually tell us whether he agreed with our recommendations in a bench memo, or whether he was going to 'disappoint us.' We all hated having something on that index card." But if Justice Blackmun wanted something more to be done on a memo or case, he strongly preferred having our response in writing.

Clerks always attended oral argument in the cases on which they were working, and occasionally in other, often big, cases. I recall especially the oral argument for *Roe v. Wade* and its companion case, *Doe v. Bolton*. The courtroom was full. Many clerks attended. Clerks sat in an open hallway on the south side of the courtroom, watching from between the columns running along the hallway. The press was on the opposite side of the courtroom. The excitement was palpable, and the oral arguments were quite good. They weren't always so.

One of the highlights of our work occurred when we all gathered in Justice

Blackmun's office after the Court's Friday conferences to hear about the Court's action on certs and jurisdictional statements and on the votes cast by the justices after oral argument in accepted cases. Justice Blackmun would report to us on the discussion among the justices, the tentative vote, the reasoning, the likely opinion assignment, and whether the justice would likely write the opinion (assignments were formally announced the next Monday, as a rule) or would otherwise want to write a dissent if the conference vote held. These Friday meetings gave the clerks a true glimpse into the judgment-formation process of the Court and the intellectual preferences and habits of all the justices. But more than anything else, they gave us a sense of Justice Blackmun's values and judgments. As we sat with him in his office, we could see two framed documents that hung above his writing desk. The first was a certificate of sale. It noted that "on February 21, 1853, S. E. Cotterliss of South Carolina had bought a twelve year-old boy named Titus for the sum of $625.00." The other was a quotation entitled "Duty as seen by Lincoln": "If I were to try to read, much less answer, all the attacks made on me, this shop might as well be closed for any other business. I do the very best I know how—the very best I can; and I mean to keep doing so until the end. If the end brings me out all right, what is said against me won't amount to anything. If the end brings me out wrong, ten angels swearing I was right would make no difference."[6]

The clerk who worked on the bench memo in a case would, almost without exception, assist in the justice's preparation of an opinion (majority, concurring, or dissenting). If a clerk had a special interest in working on a case, he or she usually asked to prepare the bench memo, and the other clerks would oblige, or perhaps the justice would agree and assign the case to that clerk. In the October 1972 term there were a large number of very interesting and important cases, so working on such a case was rarely a problem for any of the three of us. The cases included *Roe v. Wade; Miller v. California,* an important obscenity case; *Keyes v. Denver School District No. 1,* the Denver desegregation case; *Richmond School Board v. Board of Education,* the Richmond metropolitan desegregation case, which washed out four-to-four; *Pittsburg Press Co. v. Pittsburgh Commission on Human Relations,* a major free press case; *Sugarman v. Dougall,* involving discrimination against aliens in public employment; *San Antonio v. Rodriguez,* which challenged unequal school funding at the K-12 level; and *Frontiero v. Richardson,* the first case to address the standard for sex discrimination under the Equal Protection Clause.

Justice Blackmun's opinions were very much his own. He would write them surrounded by books in the justices' library on the second floor, to which he might disappear for days. Clerks would often prepare a draft of the statement of facts, which HAB would often change. Clerks would review and edit his opinions after the first draft, occasionally seeing with satisfaction that something they had written in the bench memo had found its way into an opinion (although this was often wishful thinking in a strictly textual sense, as HAB had his own style and form of writing opinions). Occasionally a clerk would be asked to offer a draft opinion, and some of it might be reflected in the final opinion after Justice Blackmun had added and subtracted. Justice Blackmun also, at least in October term 1972, did his own citation checking, not as a separate exercise but instead as part of his very thorough manner of writing with all of the material before him. The effort HAB put into opinions may well be one reason that he tended to take a great deal of time and, thus, be very late in circulating his opinions. He was, after all, educated as a mathematician at Harvard, with all of the insight and attention to detail that such training requires. His reliance on clerks was limited when it came to the chosen words of his opinions.

Harold Koh (October term 1981) put the point as nicely as anyone could:

Clerks rarely appreciate until much later in life just how much a Justice really set the tone for his or her chambers. The clerks operate within that atmosphere, and adopt that tone, and therefore every law clerk's work product strongly takes on the Justice's voice. To me, the best image is the School of Michelangelo. As we all know, the myriad students in Michelangelo's school of painting produced marvelous works of Renaissance art, many of which can barely be distinguished from the master's own work. Michelangelo himself did not personally put paintbrush to canvas on all of these works, but they nevertheless all look like the work of Michelangelo for the simple reason that he set the tone; he was the guiding intelligence behind the work of the entire school.

In the same way, I look now at opinions published in the *U.S. Reports* where I can remember typing many of the words myself, but now they do not seem like my words at all. They were ideas that I got from Justice Blackmun, the result of conversations we had within the chambers. For a year, I was under the influence of Justice Blackmun, I was doing what I was directed to do, and so what I produced was much more a part of his jurisprudence than it was any part of mine. I was not a free agent; I worked as a student in his School, and like the many students of Michelangelo, there is now no meaningful way for me to extricate my own contribution from Justice Blackmun's pervasive influence.

On this score, Professor David Garrow's recent overblown claim that the law clerks were really "the brains behind Blackmun" operates under quite a significant and serious misunderstanding. What Professor Garrow simply misses is that Justice Blackmun always communicated with his clerks orally, while the clerks always replied in writing. In going through a tiny portion of the Blackmun papers, Professor Garrow read only what the clerks wrote and erroneously assumed that he was seeing the entire conversation, rather than only half of it. In fact, however, he never heard all of the instructions, all of the oral messages from Justice Blackmun, all of the ways in which he guided his law clerks and inspired their responses. At the end of the day, in virtually every case, Justice Blackmun wrote notes to himself, or came to pivotal decisions without any help from the clerks at all.[7]

The final stage of the work during the year was the gathering of votes for opinions, obtaining "a Court" if possible, the preparation of dissenting and concurring opinions, and ultimately the issuance of opinions. All of the justices' law clerks were involved in this process, though in limited and indirect ways. As opinions were being written in a case, a justice's law clerks often served as a source of information to other clerks about the progress and reasoning of an opinion, and problems that a justice was encountering in making the opinion "write." These kinds of communications took place on an individual level as well as by discussions that took place among all of the law clerks over lunch in the clerks' dining room next to the Supreme Court cafeteria. The law clerks were a known and important part of the interchambers communication process. Confidences were not disclosed, but shared information was essential to the functioning of a collegial decision-making process in which at least five justices would join in the same opinion. It was important, too, to those chambers planning to join an opinion, to write a separate concurring opinion, or to write a dissent.

The justices' communications among themselves were, in the 1970s, pretty formalized—they rarely visited each other's chambers, and only limited opportunities existed for informal conversation when the Court gathered for hearings. The formal Friday conference meetings were the only regularized time for exchange, and the justices seemed not to be as comfortable with interchange and debate at the conferences as some prior Courts had been. As a result, the informational and consultative role of the clerks became very important.

In Justice Blackmun's chambers, and many others, the clerks would serve this role by writing or speaking to the justice about important pending matters. After drafts of opinions circulated, the clerks would often speak or write to Justice Blackmun about changes in the opinion suggested by another justice who might, with a slight change in wording, join one of Justice Blackmun's circulating opinions. This process was far from horse-trading. It was instead an effort to improve draft opinions, craft approaches that would gather enough votes, or clarify the meaning of a decision so that other government and private actors, and especially lower courts, would have sufficient guidance for the future. Indeed, often a dissenting justice or his or her clerks would provide the same sort of constructive advice to the author of the majority opinion.

The Personal and the Professional

Breakfast with Justice Blackmun and his clerks happened every day of the work week, at eight o'clock sharp, when he walked into the law clerks' office and announced that it was time to head to the Court's cafeteria for breakfast. The justice and the clerks would usually have done an hour or two of work before breakfast. On Saturday, breakfast would take place later. When everyone was in on Sunday, work might begin in the late morning, followed after a few hours of work by brunch with the justice (who usually treated).

At breakfast in the Supreme Court cafeteria we would sit together at the same table virtually every day. Justice Blackmun was a man of habits. Other justices would occasionally join us, as would former clerks, though there weren't many in the early 1970s. Talk would occasionally be about Court business, often about baseball, always about our families, and often about politics, as it was the time of Watergate. Justice Blackmun would not make any remarks that even appeared partisan. He wasn't a partisan person: never had been, and never would be. But that didn't mean that he had no feelings or thoughts about what was going on about us. Indeed, he once gave a speech at a prayer breakfast that showed his feelings about what was going on in and around the Watergate episode. As Jim Knicely (October term 1973) tells the story:

> On August 5, 1973, the Justice spoke at the Prayer Breakfast of the American Bar Association meeting in Washington. I had only been [clerking] for about a month, but the Justice had given me the text of the speech to review a few days before the event. It was very well done and accurately portrayed the story of Nehemiah's rebuilding of the Walls of Jerusalem,

which included reference to the "Water Gate," and included some limited commentary making the passage relevant to today. I reviewed it and made a few marks and suggestions, which the Justice seemed to appreciate, though I don't know that he altered the text. I did not consider it to be a particularly political document.

However, the day after the event, a front page story appeared in the *New York Times,* with the very prominent headline: "Blackmun Decries 'Pall' of Watergate." The Justice was shocked to read it. Having previewed the speech, I was likewise surprised. He told me it had been an extraordinary experience. He said when he delivered it—and I can imagine him doing so with his low, steady, sometimes grave, delivery—that an extraordinary hush fell over the assembled gathering. As he looked out in the middle of the speech, he saw Mrs. Powell (Justice Powell's wife) with tears streaming down her face. The audience, he said, was spellbound. It had been a very moving event, as the report from the *Times* confirms. The bulk of the speech was the Nehemiah story, and the Justice was simply tying it in limited form to recent revelations of official wrongdoing and their impact on the rule of law. I am certain he had no idea that the speech would be published, nor did he intend it to be a political statement, but in hindsight, it was a moral commentary presaging the inevitability of what was later to unfold. Senator Talmadge (a member of the Senate Watergate panel) was [at that time] saying that "there was no evidence that would now justify impeaching President Nixon and the public would not support such a move." I saw Justice Blackmun as troubled about what he had read and heard and felt his concern that lawyers and public officials should adhere to a higher moral standard.

Much of the breakfast conversation was personal. Justice Blackmun was interested in our experiences, our families, and especially our spouses and children. He got to know them all and would inquire about them regularly. It was really the first order of business each day.

Jim Knicely again tells a particularly revealing story about the justice:

Midway through the 1973–74 Term, my mother fell severely ill and was hospitalized in Cheyenne, Wyoming, with a brain condition. The Justice became aware of her condition and called me in to ask about her. He volunteered that he could get her admitted to the Mayo Clinic. He said he knew all the staff there and would make a call. I called my parents and told them of his offer. They were very grateful, but decided it would be too difficult to travel and because the surgery was urgently needed, thought it best to go ahead with the neurosurgeon in Cheyenne. When it looked like my mother might not recover after brain surgery, I asked to take a few days to go out. Without hesitation, he generously encouraged me to go. (As I recall, the Justice's mother was alive at the time and he often spoke fondly of his relationship with her.) I visited a few days, and came back, but shortly thereafter, my mother encountered an unexpected hepatitis infection and died. Again, I had to ask for more time off to go to the funeral. He immediately pulled out his checkbook and wrote me a check for $200 (as I recall) to help with expenses. I protested that he didn't have to do that, but he said he wanted to help. These actions reflected the compassionate nature exhibited every day in his relationships with employees of the court, whether it be the clerks, messengers or janitors.

We worked six days a week, with Saturday shortened so that we could have time for our families. On Sundays we worked when absolutely necessary. Of course the clerks often worked at home as well, and Sundays were no exception to that rule for us. Many later clerks report an increasingly grueling schedule, amusingly described by Jim Brudney (October term 1980):

There was sometimes a sense of gallows humor about the hours we kept as law clerks. In OT 80, I recall taking three days off out of 365. At breakfast the Tuesday before Thanksgiving, the Justice looked around the table at his rather pallid and hollow-eyed quartet and said something like "I'm really worried about your health; I know you have been working very, very hard and there is a long tough road ahead. But I want to make one thing perfectly clear—I don't want to see any of you in this building on Christmas Day." Now this was long before the Court had come to venerate the canon of *expressio unius est exclusio alterius*,[8] but as we walked back to chambers after breakfast, my co-clerk Bruce Swartz assured me that we should understand our presence *was* anticipated on Thanksgiving morning. Two days later, I was in the shower around 8:30 a.m. when a call came from the Court—Bruce was on the phone, and the Justice wondered if I was available to discuss a draft concurrence with him. Within 30 minutes, I was walking into his office.

During the work week we would be in the chambers at 7:00 a.m. or so, and usually leave at 7:00 p.m.; Saturdays we worked from 9:00 a.m. to mid-afternoon. All three of us in the 1972 term had young children . . . and patient wives. Justice Blackmun met and knew them all very well, as of course did Dottie. I've always wondered whether Dottie simply ordered the justice to leave us alone with our families for one day each week. Maybe she even ganged up with Nancy, Sally, and Susie, the Blackmuns' daughters. He wouldn't have stood a chance.

In the 1972 term Justice Blackmun had three law clerks. All of us shared a large room (with Coleman, the justice's messenger, too) in the chambers. Justice Blackmun would leave the chambers to exercise in the exercise room on the ground floor every day at, as I recall, 5:00 p.m. He would return an hour later. He would always walk through our office as he left and when he returned. Sometimes he was grim or upset when he returned, which often meant that the chief justice had joined him and they had a frustrating conversation about a case. Justice Blackmun and Chief Justice Warren Burger, while good and longstanding friends, were never the "Minnesota twins" of popular accounts, but in the 1972 term they were separating even more—or, I think, Justice Blackmun was separating, and Chief Justice Burger didn't like it and handled the disagreements poorly.

Justice Blackmun was, famously, a wordsmith, grammarian, and a stickler for details. Bill Murphy (October term 1979) noted "the Justice's practice of correcting for the benefit of the official Reporter grammatical or spelling lapses in the Court's official reports, including the syllabus. HAB was also famous, of course, for refraining from [splitting infinitives or] what he construed to be a misuse of the mathematical term 'parameter,' and the medical term 'viable,' and lecturing others who sought to broaden their technical definitions."

We had a few dinners at the Blackmun apartment over the course of the year, and each of the clerks entertained the Blackmuns and the other clerks in our homes. At our apartment we played a game of charades after a cookout on the porch. We had a great time, none more, I think, than Justice Blackmun. One of his titles was a "little risqué," and he had a fun time acting it out, laughing at himself often afterward.

The relationship was very much one of family, including the relationship with Dottie. As described by Keith Ellison (October term 1977):

> The circle of support and affection that embraced each of us four lucky young lawyers was drawn not by the Justice alone. Mrs. Blackmun added fresh meaning to the concepts of caring and largeness of spirit. We were invited to their home for dinner shortly after the Blackmuns returned from Minnesota, and regularly through the year. Exquisite Christmas

presents were selected by Mrs. Blackmun and were presented at a special Christmas party that she arranged. In the spring, sensing that we needed some relief from the Prussian regimen of the Court, Mrs. Blackmun arranged for a private tour of the White House. Later, we had a delightful summer evening watching the Marine Corps Silent Drill Team. Remarkably, Mrs. Blackmun kept track of everyone's birthday [children, too] and departure dates and gave us the unmistakable sense that she shared completely our particular feelings of satisfaction, sorrow or loss. We loved her.

The decision in *Roe v. Wade* was surely the most important event in my clerkship. It also began the most challenging yet important period of Justice Blackmun's service on the Court. The weekend following the announcement of the decision in *Roe v. Wade*, Justice Blackmun accompanied me to my home town of Cedar Rapids, Iowa, to give a speech to a large public audience at an event sponsored by the Chamber of Commerce. Publicity about *Roe* was at its height nationally, but everything was respectful, even caring, in the Cedar Rapids newspapers. We were driven from the hotel to the large ballroom in city hall, and as we turned a corner to head for city hall Justice Blackmun noticed four or so people quietly standing with signs protesting *Roe*. He turned to me and said, quietly, that this was his first experience with a public protest directed at him—and, he feared, only the first of many. The speech was lovely, humorous in an unprepossessing way, and very well received. As all of the clerks know, Justice Blackmun was a very good speaker, always speaking in his own wonderful style and personality—that of Old Number Three.[9]

The next week the mail in reaction to *Roe* started flowing in. Some days nearly a full mail van was needed to bring it to an area in the Court where HAB could see it. And he did. He would occasionally spend time going through the letters, reading many (most letters were written from a form letter, many with the exact same text), and the terrible picture postcards. He was saddened by it, but I think in the end he was greatly strengthened in his confidence in his own views as a justice and in the way he wrote his opinions. Just like the statistician he was (especially regarding baseball), he searched for and detected trends in the mail: it started coming from dioceses in the Northeast, then moved inexorably through dioceses in New York, Pennsylvania, and west and south across the country. It kept up a very heavy daily pace (one or more bags per day) for months. He would say, regretfully yet stoically and proudly too, that he feared he would be remembered only as the author of *Roe v. Wade*. He would, in time, prove that wrong in many ways.

Roe, of course, was the big case of the term for Justice Blackmun. But he would write thirty-five opinions in addition to *Roe* and *Doe* in the 1972 term. Including *Roe* and *Doe v. Bolton,* he wrote sixteen opinions for the Court, including one in which he originally wrote a dissent and then, after its circulation and a vote switch, wrote the majority opinion for the Court. And over the next twenty or so terms, Justice Blackmun went on to write many important and memorable opinions for the Supreme Court. In those opinions we can hear his moral force and personal compassion. Harold Koh recalled:

> I later learned that when strangers asked what he did for a living, he would answer, "I'm a lawyer in Washington." . . . He worked constantly, arriving at seven, leaving at seven, and reading at home until midnight. . . . He read and pondered his mail, even the most vicious hate letters. . . . Justice matters, we learned, but doing justice exacts its price. To protect the privacy of others, he sacrificed his own. . . . "What drove him?" I often wondered. . . . Early on, he wondered whether he was worthy. . . . Would *Roe* have survived without him there to defend it, fighting for the "full emancipation of women"? Who else would have argued in *Bakke* that "[i]n order to get beyond racism, we must first take account of race"? Would another Justice have written a defense of privacy more powerful, more understandable to the average American, than Blackmun's dissent in *Bowers*? Without him, who would have spoken up for the Haitians or against the death penalty? *DeShaney* would be remembered as a technical case about municipal liability, not about the Joshuas of the world and how we treat them. . . . For years, he gave the Court its natural sympathy, its human face.[10]

He gave those things to us, his clerks, too.

Notes

1. The specific numbers provided here are based on a complete listing of the Blackmun clerks, but certain information was not available to the author for a small number (no more than five) of the clerks, and therefore the numbers and percentages, while likely representative, often reflect a total population of probably no less than 95 percent of the clerks.

2. During October term 1975, Justice Blackmun's clerks were supplemented for part of the year by the law clerk for retired Justice Stanley Reed.

3. HAB was the shorthand way the law clerks referred to Justice Blackmun among themselves.

4. I use the term "certs" to represent all of the petitions for review presented to the Court. Certs include petitions for certiorari in cases lying within the Court's discretionary jurisdiction, as well as jurisdictional statements, which are petitions for review of appeals that fall within the Court's appellate, and mandatory, jurisdiction. The task of reviewing the filings (in the form of short briefs) in the 7,500 cases was dubbed "doing certs."

5. Clerks would also briefly review the arguments made in amicus curiae (friend of the court) briefs, which were submitted by organizations or groups that were interested in the outcome of a case but were not a party to it.

6. Harold Hongju Koh, "A Tribute to Justice Harry A. Blackmun," *Harvard Law Review* 108 (November 1994): 21.

7. Harold Hongju Koh, "Unveiling Justice Blackmun," *Brooklyn Law Review* 72 (Fall 2006): 18–19.

8. A canon of statutory construction, the Latin phrase is translated as "the expression of one thing is the exclusion of another."

9. President Nixon had nominated two other judges for Justice Blackmun's seat on the Court before finally turning to him. They were Judges Haynsworth and Carswell, neither of whom made it through the confirmation process. So Justice Blackmun, baseball allusion in mind, referred to himself as "Old Number Three."

10. Koh, "Tribute," 21.

Justice Lewis F. Powell Jr.

A Personal View by a Former Clerk

My experience as a clerk may seem somewhat unusual, perhaps because I knew Justice Powell long before I became his clerk and because I sat with him as a colleague on the Fourth Circuit Court of Appeals long after my clerkship had ended. But as wonderful as the befores and afters were, I was in his eyes and my own his law clerk in the end. Once a clerk, always a clerk—that's how most of us would wish it to be.

Some of my memories of Justice Powell and my clerkship seem quite trivial and incidental, but then life's less consequential moments can be revelatory in their own way. At times, I find it difficult to believe that our lives—to my great good fortune—were so closely intertwined. Our relationship, however, was always characterized by a certain formality, which was not so much stiff but appropriate to our respective ages and stations and to the way we had been raised. For that reason, I refer to Justice Powell as "Justice" throughout, even when speaking of his precourt years.

When I say that Justice Powell had a profound impact on my life, that doesn't wholly capture it. His influence actually began well before I was born. He and my father were best friends. They went to McGuire's School in Richmond, Virginia, together and shared a reverence for its headmaster, John Peyton McGuire. They won the Jack Gordon medal in successive years. That medal was awarded to the outstanding student at the school, and it forged a bond between the two of them for life. It was Justice Powell who introduced my mother and father to each other. He encouraged my father, who needed no encouragement, to marry my mother. He is, quite literally, the reason I am able to write this today.

Justice Powell was not only like a second father to me, but he was also a constant school master in my childhood. Every Sunday night, he and Mrs. Powell would come over for dinner with my parents, and this practice continued without serious interruption for some ten or fifteen years. He and my father would gather in the family den for an hour or so before dinner, and the sense of hierarchy in that room was conveyed by the seating arrangements. I sat on a small stool at the foot of their chairs. My role was to be seen but not heard, and to learn the value of listening.

The discussions on those Sunday evenings were wide-ranging. I remember the justice talking about the terrible conditions in North Africa during World War II and how it took every sinew of American might to defeat the Nazi war machine. The justice became alarmed at the launching of the Russian satellite Sputnik. He thought the great threat to America was its own complacency, and he fretted about the absence of rigorous science and economics instruction in the public schools.

It was also clear to me in his discussions of the law that Felix Frankfurter and John Harlan were the justices he admired most in the 1950s and 1960s. He was deeply concerned during those years about violent tactics used in student protests and the antiwar movement, the extent of urban unrest, and the intransigent resistance in the South to the *Brown v. Board of Education* decision. Each of these things he thought was in itself a threat to the rule of law. And in combination, they threatened the very foundations of a stable society. The justice was a deeply pessimistic man in the 1960s. I remember my father asking him how he managed to devote so much time to organizations like the American Bar Association and the American College of Trial Lawyers on top of the demands of a busy law practice. The justice replied that he thought the rule of law was literally on the verge of collapse and that professional organizations represented the best hope that it could still be preserved.

The grave concerns expressed in some of these conversations about the rule of law led Justice Powell to reject the position of the Nixon administration in two landmark cases. He had come to the conclusion that government had no more right to break the law than campus protesters or urban rioters did. In *United States v. U.S. District Court* (407 U.S. 297 [1972]), he voted to require the Executive Branch to get a warrant even for those wiretaps involving alleged domestic threats to the national security. And, of course, in *United States v. Nixon* (418 U.S. 683 [1974]) he voted to reject claims of executive privilege and require the president to respond to the process of the courts. These decisions redeemed the rule of law in his own eyes and helped him, I think, to regain a sense of faith in legal institutions that grew stronger as the years went by.

Indeed, the last decade of his life found him a far more optimistic person than in those earlier years. Justice Powell felt that the country had survived the most serious external crises of World War II and the Cold War and the equally serious internal threats to the legitimacy of the legal order. It is fair to say that, at the end, he achieved greater serenity and peace of mind than in the storm-tossed middle decades of his professional life. In this sense, he was one of America's great patriots because his outlook depended on what was happening to the country and the profession that he so loved, even more so than on his own state of personal well-being and health.

Justice Powell was a very kind man with very high standards—his children and his Hunton & Williams partners and associates will all attest to it. I knew of this firsthand. The justice learned from my father precisely what my grades were each semester that I was in school. I had a bit of a sophomore slump at college with truly abominable marks in geology and astronomy, which I had to take to satisfy my physical sciences requirement. The first day of my summer vacation I received a call from Justice Powell. It was a chilling conversation, focused on the fact that one had to do best those things that one liked the least. There was nothing like that stern, measured, precise, but caring voice at the other end of the telephone to jolt me into improvement.

Given his knowledge of my undergraduate science grades, I am still surprised that he chose me as his law clerk. Justice Powell went on the Supreme Court for fifteen years at the age of sixty-four and spent another eight years sitting with the Fourth Circuit during his eighties. On both courts, he turned in high-energy performances. It was hard for any clerk to keep up with him. His work schedule at the Supreme Court was seven days a week. Seven days a week during the decade of his seventies. If we were gone on Sundays, there would be the products of his weekend efforts on our desks Monday morning.

I clerked for him the first two terms he sat on the Court. My co-clerks that first year were Larry Hammond and Pete Parnell, whom the justice inherited from his predecessor, Justice Hugo Black, and Phil Fox, who was on loan from retired Justice Stanley Reed. Soon enough we all settled in as the justice's Court family. This process was mightily assisted by his secretary, Sally Smith, who was as much a master of straight talk as the justice was of diplomacy. Sally had been with the justice at Hunton & Williams, and she was not about to move over for a bunch of green law clerks. Clerks occasionally come to appreciate a great secretary the way privates do a superb staff sergeant, and Sally was the best.

What a happy time my clerkship was. Each morning and evening I drove with Justice Powell and Sally to and from the Supreme Court. The conversations in the car were slightly different from those in the family den. The weight of his office made his words more measured. Judging never became quick or easy for him. He was astonished, I think, at the closeness of the cases before him and of their importance. When he cast a vote, he often said he could write a very strong opinion for the opposite side. During all our trips together, he never once snapped at me or raised his voice, even when I said something silly or when much was on his mind. Still, we had our moments. The law clerks often played basketball on the fourth floor of the Supreme Court Building toward the end of the day. I was in the habit of stuffing my sweaty clothes into a duffle bag, which I placed on the back seat of the car. One day Justice Powell decorously suggested that the bag go hereafter in the trunk.

Justice and Mrs. Powell would sometimes ask me to dinner at their Harbor Square apartment, even at the end of a long court day. Occasionally after dinner, the justice would close his eyes, and Mrs. Powell would read a mystery or even certiorari petitions to him in the living room. This was his idea of relaxation. On other occasions, we would sit on the balcony of the apartment watching the distant airplanes glide over the Potomac and into National Airport.

The apartment next to his was occupied by Senator Hubert Humphrey and his wife, Muriel. Tragically, Senator Humphrey was in the advanced stages of cancer at that time, but that did not slow him down. His knock would come on the door around 8:00 p.m. "Oh, that's Hubert," the justice would say, and Senator Humphrey would stride into the room in his long red bathrobe. Many times Senator Humphrey would stand and talk for a full hour without stopping. He did this in utter defiance of his wife and doctor's orders, but no one could slow him down. He talked a lot about his teaching experience after the 1968 presidential campaign, and what a professor he must have been—I doubt the students got out even when the bell rang.

In time, this unlikely pair of Justice Powell and Senator Humphrey became quite close friends. The justice admired the senator's magnanimity and benevolence, and the senator found great support in the justice's even demeanor and quiet assurances. For years after the senator's death, the justice could not pronounce the name "Hubert" without a little shake of the head and a smile.

Regarding Justice Powell's relationship with his law clerks, I think that we would all testify that Justice Powell was a gifted motivator. The way he went about this, however, bore little resemblance to the locker-room speech of a football coach at halftime. One of his favorite techniques was saying nice things about people out of their presence—when a compliment reached us indirectly, it made us want to work all the harder. Justice Powell was forever praising other clerks to me. He would speak, for example, of Larry Hammond's humanity, Bill Kelly's gift for cutting to the core, John Jeffries's brilliance and erudition, John Buckley's warmth and humor, and so on. It was his way of telling us we had as much to learn from each other as from him.

At first, he thought his law clerks might resemble the associates or even junior partners at Hunton & Williams, his old law firm. He was quickly disabused. One day he expressed surprise that we knew little of the mechanics of garnishment proceedings, the first of several rude awakenings for him. Over the years, he came to understand that practical experience was not the only way one measures law clerks, but at the time, we wondered if he wanted to trade us all in.

The justice did not hire clerks ideologically. Many—perhaps most—of his clerks were probably more liberal than he was, but he was so devoted to law as a profession that political leanings didn't seem to matter. He was as different from Judge David Bazelon of the D.C. Circuit as any two men could be, but one of his favorite clerks was a Bazelon protégée. He was so secure within himself that he often hired law clerks quite different from himself—he would focus on academic merit and likeability and be almost nonchalant about the rest. In fact, the justice preferred that his clerks be of different persuasions and stir "crosswinds," as he once put it, through his chambers. And perhaps because he was the father of three daughters, he hired women as clerks long before it became fashionable.

Justice Powell thought of his own career path as a desirable one—go back to the town where you grew up, go into practice there, remain with one firm, become a leader in the bar and the community—that way had been good to him and seemed a sure-fire formula for our success. Many of his clerks, however, remained in Washington, interspersing practice with government service. Others entered academia or pursued careers in business or the media. Few followed the justice's traditional course. If the law clerk system is supposed to expose justices to different ways upcoming generations act and think, that quality was on display in the justice's chambers. To his credit, what was eye-opening to the justice was never cause for censure.

We had reunions every June at the end of the Court term. On Saturday evening, we had a reception and dinner at the Court itself. Mrs. Powell always attended, and often so did the justice's children, Jo, Penny, Molly, and Lewis. In ways large and small, these gatherings had the feel of family about them. After dinner, John Buckley gave us his (gentle?) impersonation of Chief Justice Burger, and Justice Powell went over some of the highlights of the term. On Sunday morning we met for brunch at the Alibi Club, with its cartoonish sketches of Washington notables and its signature Triscuits topped with warm peanut butter and bacon bits. Tradition means everything in the family of clerkships; no one so much as mentioned a change in routine.

At the age of eighty, the justice retired from the Supreme Court and came to sit with the Fourth Circuit. He sat with us regularly for some seven or eight years. The Fourth Circuit has its special traditions, with which Justice Powell felt quite at home. One of those is that the judges come down from the bench and shake the hands of counsel after every oral argument. I think the Fourth Circuit may also be the only court of appeals in the country where all the judges do not address one another by their first name. At least I never, during my service with them, addressed Judge Haynsworth or Judge Russell as anything other than "Judge." That seemed entirely fitting because Judge Russell had been an assistant secretary of state before I was born. During the nearly fifty years I knew him, Justice Powell never once suggested that I call him by his first name. It is one of those small ironies in life that a few special relationships grow much closer, precisely because they are not on a first-name basis.

For some reason, Justice Powell never wished to be the presiding judge of our panels. Of course, he was given his choice of where to sit, and he always preferred the seat to the right of the presiding judge on our three-judge panels. This meant at conference that he would vote second. I never knew exactly why he preferred this arrangement; perhaps it was because it most closely paralleled his place on the seniority ladder at the Supreme Court. In all events, he was a pleasure to sit with. Even the smallest and most fact-intensive case commanded his conscientious attention, and he was a model of considerateness to his colleagues and the bar. He only asked questions to which he did not know the answer—always a refreshing quality in a judge. The Fourth Circuit judges meet frequently for dinner during court week, and the Justice and Mrs. Powell were our constant companions. One evening, I accidentally spilled a glass of water all over the justice and his nice suit. He was too dignified to say anything about it at the time, but henceforth I noticed that he managed to sit at least a seat away from me.

The last years of Justice Powell's life were spent at his Rothesay Road home in Richmond, where, as you might expect, a constant stream of visitors came to see him. Those years were marked by the tragedy of Mrs. Powell's death in 1996, but also by the solace of lifelong friends and the sweetness of reflection.

One story the justice always loved to tell during those years involved the fabled romance of Colonel Henry Watkins Anderson, a founding partner of Hunton & Williams, and Ellen Glasgow, a celebrated novelist. The justice had practiced briefly with Colonel Anderson, but this is not at all what he chose to recount. He was fascinated with Colonel Anderson's way with women and his adventurous life. During World War I, the justice would say, Colonel Anderson left Ellen Glasgow the day after their engagement and went to Romania as chairman of a Red Cross commission to aid in the war relief effort. During the winter of 1917–18, Glasgow heard from Romania about Colonel Anderson's growing friendship with Queen Marie. Perhaps because of that relationship, Anderson and Glasgow never married, and Glasgow wrote several novels in which the colonel was treated none too kindly and in which his identity was scarcely concealed. Why this story so fascinated Justice Powell always intrigued me. He was a splendid dancer and cosmopolitan traveler in his own right, but he was about as different from Colonel Anderson as two men could possibly have been. I am not sure that he ever unraveled the precise nature of the affections between the colonel and his various companions, but he remained fascinated by the relationships to the end.

The justice's kindness was much in evidence during these last years. He was adored by his nurses, and he would occasionally dance in the hallway with them to the tune of "Mack the Knife." When I would get up to leave after a visit, the justice would always rise, put on a floppy hat, accompany me to the front porch, and wave goodbye until my car had vanished from sight. He did this even in the most inclement weather.

Over thirty-five years have now passed since my clerkship and over a decade since Justice Powell's death. But his personal example has not faded with the passage of time. It is important to have different kinds of judges on an appellate court. Some judges are catalytic thinkers whose expressiveness and creativity help drive the terms of a debate. I admire them greatly, but when all is said and done, Justice Powell's qualities are the absolute best. He combined breadth of experience, firmness of conviction, and considerateness of manner to an extent that few other judges ever have or will have. During his long life, Justice Powell always sought to soothe feelings and bridge differences. America needs believers in the possibilities of compromise.

Watching him day upon day and year upon year led his clerks to understand that it was the appreciation of difference that made him a great man. Age, gender, outlook, and so much else were seamlessly subsumed in a mutual devotion to the law. It is said that no man is a hero to his valet, but when someone makes hard decisions and handles heartfelt disagreement in a manner you respect, proximity enhances rather than diminishes that person in your eyes.

Judicial clerkships may thus help to counter in their own small way the mistrust of American institutions that pervades modern times. That, I suspect, is what the justices most want—that those who see the Court at closest hand leave with the deepest respect for its mission and its work. Perhaps writing about clerkship experiences varies between kiss-and-tell and hagiography. If so, both forms have their value. The Supreme Court is an institution whose mystique is altogether real, and the conveyance of the awe and majesty surrounding it is important to its public acceptance. But the Court is also a secretive institution, prone to some pomposity, and periodic peeks behind the veil are both humbling and salutary. For those of us who clerked there, however, I suspect the experience was like no other. "It sounds too good to be true," a friend remarked after hearing me describe my clerkship. But it was true. Every last bit of it.

Note

Portions of this essay have been reprinted with permission from J. Harvie Wilkinson III, "Lewis F. Powell, Jr.—A Personal View," *Washington and Lee Law Review* 65 (Winter 2008): 3–8.

Making Work for Idle Hands

William H. Rehnquist and His Law Clerks

T he following portrait of William Rehnquist and his clerks details both the personal and the professional sides of the justice-clerk relationship. A former clerk to Justice Robert Jackson in the 1950s, Rehnquist was uniquely positioned to return to the Court in the 1970s with both an historical—and critical—perspective on law clerks as well as fresh ideas of how to handle the justice-clerk relationship. Indeed, no justice has shed more light—both directly and indirectly—on Supreme Court law clerks. The controversial memo on racial segregation that he wrote as a clerk and its role in his Supreme Court confirmation, his postclerkship magazine article on the potential influence of clerks, and his willingness to speak with journalists and write about clerks while serving as a justice make his Supreme Court years the ideal case study.

Lavishing Scorn: Jackson's Clerk

While attending Stanford Law School, Rehnquist was recommended for a clerkship with Justice Robert Jackson by one of Jackson's former clerks: Stanford law professor Philip C. Neal. On campus to dedicate a new Law School building, Jackson interviewed Rehnquist, and after the pro forma meeting Rehnquist recalled, "I walked out of the room sure that in the first minutes of our visit he had written me off as a total loss." Yet during fall 1951 Jackson found that he and his clerk—George Niebank—could use assistance. Jackson wrote Rehnquist, who agreed to serve during the second half of the 1951 term as well as the following 1952 term. Rehnquist's law school classmate Sandra Day O'Connor recalled: "Our class was very excited when Bill got a Supreme Court clerkship. . . . At that time not many Stanford law graduates were invited to clerk at the Court. He left for Washington in his dilapidated Studebaker for a life in our highest Court."[1]

Like all of the clerks with whom he served, Rehnquist reviewed petitions and drafted memos for cases petitioned to the Court. When Niebank informed him that he would have to make recommendations on whether the case should be granted or denied by the Court, he remembered: "I told George that this seemed like a lot of responsibility for a brand-new law clerk." Rehnquist had a similar reaction when he set to drafting his first certiorari memo: "Who are you, two months out of law school, to give such a patronizing evaluation of an opinion written by a judge of a United States court of appeals who was appointed to his office by the president of the United States and confirmed by the Senate?"[2]

Rehnquist's introduction to the clerkship institution contained further surprises as he recalled his first lunch around the clerks' dining table in the Supreme Court cafeteria:

> The conversation turned to a proposed opinion for the Court which Justice Jackson had authored and, unbeknownst to me, circulated to the other justices the preceding day. . . . The case about which the law clerks were now talking was entitled *Sacher v. United States.* . . . Judging from the discussion among the clerks, the Court had been sharply divided in voting on the case at conference, and Justice Jackson's opinion . . . was not very popular at this particular lunch table.
>
> George, who knew about the case and had apparently helped Justice Jackson with it, stoutly defended the result, but he seemed to have few supporters. There were dark predictions of stirring dissents from justices who disagreed with the majority of the Court, and I became quite uneasy about what would happen to Justice Jackson's opinion. Only later did I come to realize that it would be all but impossible to assemble a more hypercritical, not to say arrogant, audience than a group of law clerks criticizing an opinion circulated by one of their employers. Their scorn—and in due time it became my scorn too—was not reserved for Justice Jackson, but was lavished with considerable impartiality upon the products of all nine chambers of the Court.[3]

Rehnquist's introduction to the other clerks slowly made him aware of the informal "clerk network" where clerks routinely discuss cases and even the leanings or positions of their justices to aid in the coalition formation process.

Rehnquist recalled how the clerks reacted to the much-anticipated Steel Seizure Case *Youngstown Sheet & Tube Co. v. Sawyer*:

> Naturally George and I devoured the briefs, talking with one another about them, and debating the merits pro and con with law clerks from other chambers. . . . As I recall, in fact, during one lunch hour we even took a formal vote of the clerks on how the case should be decided. The result was an even division between eighteen law clerks, nine voting for the government and nine voting for the steel companies.
>
> George and I would of course have liked to know [Jackson's position], and so would all the other law clerks, just as we would have liked to know of any straws in the wind with respect to the inclinations of the justices for whom they worked. We had no straws in the wind from Justice Jackson, and I suspect that most, if not all of our colleagues were pretty much in the same position. Yet one did not like to admit this fact openly. . . . So our exchanges with one another were somewhat guarded when it came to what was going on in our respective chambers; I don't believe anyone claimed to be privy to his justice's thinking, but there were veiled references to "work being done" in the various chambers.[4]

Rehnquist also drafted the occasional memorandum for Justice Jackson. One memo in particular, analyzing the racial segregation issue, would prove controversial. At the end of his memo, entitled "A Random Thought on the Segregation Cases," Rehnquist concluded, "I realize that it is an unpopular and unhumanitarian position, for which I have been excoriated by 'liberal' colleagues but I think *Plessy v. Ferguson* was right and should be reaffirmed."[5]

While the memo was for internal consumption only, it became public nearly two decades later when Rehnquist was nominated to the Court by President Richard Nixon. Rehnquist responded to the controversy surrounding the memo in a letter to the chair of the Senate Judiciary Committee, James Eastland, who read the letter on the Senate floor:

> As best I can reconstruct the circumstances after some nineteen years, the memorandum was prepared by me at Justice Jackson's request; it was intended as a rough draft of a statement of *his* views . . . He expressed concern that the conference should have the benefit of all of the arguments in support of the constitutionality of the "separate but equal" doctrine, as well as those against its constitutionality.

I am satisfied that the memorandum was not designed to be a statement of *my* views on these cases. . . . I am fortified in this conclusion because the bald, simplistic conclusion that "*Plessy v. Ferguson* was right and should be re-affirmed" is not an accurate statement of my own views at the time.[6]

Rehnquist was ultimately confirmed, but the issue did not die. Journalists and authors sought to shed new light on the controversy by contacting those involved. One of the journalists making inquires was Anthony Lewis, then Supreme Court reporter for the *New York Times,* who at the end of 1975 contacted both Rehnquist and his October term 1952 Jackson co-clerk Donald Cronson. Cronson wrote Rehnquist: "The enclosed paper setting forth my best recollection of the episode has been prepared for you. You may, if you so wish, send it to Mr Lewis, or to any one else. Or, if you so request, I will send it to Mr. Lewis. I incline to the view that the best course would be to do nothing. Much as I enjoy having an excuse to write you, I hope that the basically trivial episode of the WHR Memorandum will soon be allowed to attain the obscurity that it deserves."[7] Cronson's four-page memo, which included an addendum, is reproduced in Appendix B. In short, Cronson explained that while Rehnquist had forcefully argued around the clerks' lunch table that *Plessy* should not be overturned, he often argued contrary positions for the sake of argument. Cronson further confirmed that it was Jackson who later requested Rehnquist draft the memo but that Cronson contributed substantially to it at the very least and was likely the memorandum's primary author. Rehnquist replied to Cronson:

I already wrote Lewis telling him that my recollection of the events have been hazy enough when called into question nineteen years afterwards, and it certainly has not improved in the intervening four years. I think you probably have a clearer recollection of the events than I do, judging from the memorandum which you enclose, but I am inclined to think it is a case where it is best to let sleeping dogs lie. . . .

I think there is a basic inconsistency in the way you recollect matters back in the chambers those days, and the way I do, and I think that whatever this inconsistency amounts to in fact, it probably results from your having a more orderly and retentive mind about the thing than I do. When it was first raised to me in 1971, during my confirmation hearings, it simply rang no bell whatever, as I think I told you at the time, and only when I was furnished a Xerox copy of the memorandum—and identified from that typewriting with which one gets all to familiar during a year of clerkship—was I satisfied that I had ever written anything at all on the subject.

It was good of you to take the trouble to do this, Don. I suggest that it is best to send nothing to Lewis for the present time.[8]

The issue was once again raised during Rehnquist's confirmation for chief justice in 1986. A study of the memos he wrote for Jackson during his clerkship year showed "no evidence that Rehnquist used his cert or appeals memos to further his conservative goals, and only occasionally did he employ his bench memos for this purpose." The study concluded that he instead largely acted as Jackson's surrogate, tending to "anticipate the views" of Jackson when writing memos.[9] While the views of both Cronson and Rehnquist on the *Plessy* memo may still leave questions unanswered, the episode serves to highlight the important role clerks played as early as the 1950s.

Rehnquist also drafted the occasional opinion for Justice Jackson at a time when many justices were still doing most of their own writing. In response to articles published in *U.S. News and World Report* and the *New York Times* about the role of clerks, now-former-clerk Rehnquist entered the discussion in a 1957 article for *U.S. News and World Report:*

> On a couple of occasions each term, Justice Jackson would ask each clerk to draft an opinion for him along lines which he suggested. If the clerk was reasonably diligent in his work, the Justice would be quite charitable with his black pencil and paste pot. The result reached in these opinions was no less the product of Justice Jackson than those he drafted himself; in literary style, these opinions generally suffered by comparison with those which he had drafted.

Rehnquist's article was controversial. While he made the point that "[t]he specter of the law clerk as a legal Rasputin, exerting an important influence on the cases actually decided by the Court, may be discarded at once," he also suggested that the justices were delegating too much authority to clerks and that there was some "unconscious slanting of material by clerks."[10] He recommended that the power to select clerks should not be left in the hands of the justices alone. Rehnquist's charge of clerk influence was covered by both the Associated Press and the *New York Times*.[11] A former clerk to Justice Stanley Reed during the 1952 term, William D. Rogers, responded to the Rehnquist piece two months later in his own *U.S. News and World Report* article. Rogers said that during his term, no justice changed his vote because of clerk influence and that Rehnquist's allegation of clerk slanting would provide further ammunition for Court critics who felt that law clerk appointments should have congressional approval.[12]

Sensing a brewing storm, Justice Felix Frankfurter prodded his former clerk from the 1952 term, Alexander Bickel, to take on Rehnquist's claims. In April 1958, Bickel's article appeared in the *New York Times*. In it, he downplayed clerk influence: "The law clerks are in no respect any kind of kitchen cabinet. [They] generally assist their respective justices in researching the law books and other sources for materials relevant to the decision of cases before the Court."[13]

A month later, Senator John Stennis of Mississippi, who was a critic of the Warren Court, raised the issue on the Senate floor. He quoted at length from Rehnquist's article, advocated a return to career appointments for clerks, for minimum qualifications to be set via legislative statue, and for Congress to "determine whether or not Senate confirmation should be required for these positions of ever-increasing importance and influence."[14] He argued that clerks were more influential than many executive branch undersecretaries and assistant secretaries: "To the extent that they participate in shaping the work of the Court they are deciding vital questions of national effect. Within the judicial branch, these are equivalent to policy-level decisions in the executive branch."[15] As with Rehnquist and Rogers, Stennis's remarks were reprinted in *U.S. News and World Report* as well as the *New York Times*. Though Rehnquist's article prompted a spurt of speculation about clerks, the issue died, and clerks faded from their brief moment in the spotlight.

After his clerkship ended, Rehnquist went into private practice. He wrote Jackson:

> I have occasionally reflected on the experience which I got while working for you; I think there is a tendency when one first leaves a job like that, and turns to the details of a general law practice, to feel "why, hell, that didn't teach me anything about practicing law." In a sense it didn't, and in that regard I am sure you would be the first to agree that there is no substitute for actually practicing. But I can't help feel that, in addition to the enjoyment from the personal contacts, one does pick up from a clerkship some sort of intuition about the nature of the judicial process. It is so intangible I will not attempt to describe it further, but I think it is valuable especially in appellate brief-writing.[16]

Years later, Rehnquist reflected on his postclerkship years and how he lost touch with the institution for which he once worked: "After I finished my clerking in 1953, I would in practice pick up a copy [of *U.S. Law Week*] to follow the

Court's 'trends,' but found myself doing so less and less frequently. I think now that probably one reason for my partial loss of interest was Justice Jackson's death the year after I had clerked for him, and the resulting fact that there were no clerk reunions to attend."[17]

Yet the author of the early critique of law clerks did return to the Court as a justice in 1971, and soon thereafter clerks were once again in the national spotlight. The publication of *The Brethren* in 1979 by Bob Woodward and Scott Armstrong renewed allegations of excessive law clerk influence and also raised questions regarding confidentiality of justice-clerk communications. The authors spoke with 170 former clerks and five justices: Potter Stewart, Lewis Powell, Harry Blackmun, Byron White, and Rehnquist.[18] Once again, Rehnquist was at the center of law clerk controversy.

Given his concerns over law clerk influence, and willingness to discuss the issue with Court outsiders, one might think that Rehnquist selected, utilized, and otherwise interacted with his clerks in ways different from his colleagues. Yet as the rest of this essay shows, Rehnquist's chambers functioned much like the chambers of his colleagues. And while he did much to improve the personal and social lives of clerks, he took few if any steps to stem their growing influence. Indeed, he was a willing participant in reforms that served to bolster clerk responsibility.

Working for a Living: Clerk Selection

Former clerk R. Ted Cruz (October term 1996) recalled Rehnquist's humor even with the selection of his law clerks: "Once, when a law clerk asked him how he went about choosing law clerks, the Chief replied, 'Well, I obviously wasn't looking for the best and the brightest, or I wouldn't have chosen you guys.'" In all, Rehnquist selected 105 clerks during his tenure on the Supreme Court. He always hired three clerks per term though he could have increased his annual hires to four and later five when he served as chief justice. It was rumored that Rehnquist limited his number to three so that he would have an even number for doubles tennis matches. As a new justice he was assisted—in addition to his own clerks—by the clerks to retired Justices Stanley Reed and Tom Clark, who still had offices at the Court and whose clerks routinely helped with the cert process and other tasks as needed. However, during his second term Rehnquist wrote his colleagues: "My present feeling is that I will not be needing the services of the law clerks to Justices Reed and Clark."[19]

In this 1973 response to an inquiry from Associate Dean Edward A. Potts of the George Washington University, Rehnquist outlined his selection process: "I screen written applications in the early part of the fall in order to come up with about eight or ten applicants for clerkships whom I wish to interview personally. I make the final selection later in the fall. I put some emphasis on class standing, less on law review participation, and give some weight in selecting at least one of my three clerks to the fact that I am Circuit Justice for the Seventh Circuit. I do not normally select law clerks from any one particular school."[20]

Like his colleagues, Rehnquist received annual letters from law schools attempting to place their best students at the Supreme Court. For example, Louisiana State University wrote: "We hope that receiving this packet will allow you, or the other members of your court, to give early consideration to these seniors. If you have already made your selection, or for any other reason are unable to consider these applicants, please circulate their resumes to the other members of your court." Similarly, Columbia law professor Benno Schmidt wrote Rehnquist in 1973: "I am writing to supplement the letter . . . from our Clerkship Committee. . . . I might say that as a member of that committee with a particular interest in candidates for your clerkship, I am very largely responsible for, and fully support, the three recommendations which the committee has forwarded to you. However, I do have some personal evaluations of the three candidates which may be of some use to you in considering their applications."[21]

When Professor Abraham D. Sofaer took over the clerk-screening process from Benno Schmidt at Columbia, Sofaer asked Rehnquist whether he preferred to continue with the school's screening committee or whether he wanted to screen his own applicants. Sofaer explained the school's process:

> If you think you might want our help, here is what we do. We tell all students interested in your clerkship to apply to the Committee. We collect all pertinent information on all the applicants, and forward the "best" ones for your consideration. In determining who is best, we try to rely exclusively on objective criteria, except that we will consider any criterion you might want us to consider. Usually, we sent a Justice no more than four applications (narrowed down from 10–15); we narrow the field even further when a judge asks us to do so. We have also made it a practice of recommending to the Supreme Court only those graduates who have clerked one year for an excellent federal or state court judge.[22]

Rehnquist replied:

> I have a feeling that [law school] screening may be more useful for a Justice who relies upon a Clerkship Committee to make his decisions than for a Justice who relies on his own personal interviews. I do the latter. I would be glad to get recommendations from your committee; I would think four or even five would not be too many. I have a feeling that some of my criteria are very subjective, but they also seem very difficult to articulate. I want someone with a first rate professional ability, who is easy to get along with, and who has generally had at least some accomplishments other than good academic performance. Other things being equal, I think a clerkship for a federal or state court judge before coming here is useful, but I do not regard it as a prerequisite. What I do regard as a prerequisite is at least one year's working for a living, whether in a clerkship or some other position. I realize that these criteria probably seem vague, and are vague, but they are about the best I can do.[23]

When Rehnquist's cousin Alden suggested a potential clerk, the justice wrote him: "I have today written him, telling him that I have made it a pretty firm policy not to hire anyone as a law clerk who has not had one full year of working experience of some sort over and above his years in school. I don't necessarily require that it be experience after graduation from law school, but I do think working for someone else is a lot different from going to school, and I don't want my clerks to learn this for the first time from me." Rehnquist further explained his preference for post–law school experience in a letter to Dean John E. Cribbet of the University of Illinois College of Law: "I do feel quite strongly a preference for hiring a law clerk who has spent at least a full year doing something besides going to school—whether it be clerking for another judge, working in a law firm, serving in the Army, or selling municipal bonds. I think this sort of experience gives a recent graduate some sort of feel for how the world's work is done, and bridges the transition between the rather unstructured life of school and the rather structured life of working for someone else."[24]

Rehnquist's secretary Janet Barnes wrote a prospective applicant in 1996 about the chief's criteria: "The Chief Justice would like to see a fairly comprehensive resume including how you spent your time during the summers between your years at law school. We would like to see a writing sample, preferably one that is not too lengthy as well as three to four recommendations.

... A law clerk applying for a clerkship position must spend a year clerking for a lower court judge after graduating from law school."[25]

Former clerks also lobbied on behalf of others, another common practice at the Supreme Court. For example, in 1979 former clerk Robert W. Wild (October term 1972) recommended Tom Mayo: "While I of course don't know how Tom's qualifications stack up against the other applicants', I do think it would be worth your while to interview with him." Rehnquist always gave these suggestions a standard reply: "You may be sure that his application will receive every consideration." When former Blackmun clerk Randall P. Bezanson made a recommendation, Rehnquist replied: "I was gratified ... to see you have risen from the ranks of Law Professor to that of Vice President for Finance and University Services! This just shows the advantage of having clerked for a Justice of the Supreme Court. In the light of your own experience in that capacity, I will certainly take into consideration your recommendation."[26]

Recommendations can come in other forms as well. For example, one prospective clerk wrote to Donald Rumsfeld—then assistant to President Gerald Ford. The prospective clerk reminded Rumsfeld that he had worked on Rumsfeld's 1966 and 1968 congressional campaigns and asked for a letter of recommendation. Rehnquist replied: "Don Rumsfeld has forwarded to me a copy of your resume, along with a note that you wish to be considered as a law clerk.... I regret to say that I have already chosen my law clerks for next year."[27]

Initially, prospective clerks were relatively selective in choosing which justices to apply to. But over time they applied to a greater number of justices until it became routine for each applicant to apply to all nine active justices and even the retired justices who also receive law clerks. For example, after his interview with a prospective clerk, Justice Powell noted that the applicant "has interviewed [with] Justice Rehnquist and applied to all other Justices."[28] Given this increasing competition among the justices for what they perceived as the best talent, factors such as the law school the applicants attended and the judge for whom they worked during their lower-court clerkship took on greater significance.

LAW SCHOOL

Historically, three out of four Supreme Court clerks have come from only seven law schools: Harvard, Yale, Chicago, Columbia, Stanford, Virginia, and Michigan.[29] While these schools were also the top schools from which Rehnquist chose his clerks, his selections were somewhat more diverse than the norm.

Only 52 percent of his clerks (55 of 105) came from the "top seven." The top feeder schools for Rehnquist clerks include Virginia (14 clerks, or 13 percent); Chicago (11 clerks/10 percent); Harvard (10 clerks/10 percent); Yale (7 clerks/ 7 percent); Stanford (5 clerks/5 percent); Columbia, Duke, George Washington, Michigan, and Texas (4 clerks/4 percent each); and Arizona, Northwestern, and Pennsylvania (3 clerks/3 percent each). His list of schools also includes many that historically place few clerks at the Supreme Court such as Arizona State, Indiana, Kentucky, Miami, Minnesota, Missouri, North Carolina, Temple, UCLA, USC, Utah, and Washington. Furthermore, a number of Rehnquist clerks came from outside the Ivy League—particularly Harvard and Yale—which dominate the clerking ranks.

Indeed, early on Rehnquist exhorted his non–Ivy League track record in a 1973 letter to Dean John E. Cribbet of the University of Illinois College of Law: "I do give some weight in choosing at least one of my law clerks to the fact that he may have graduated from a law school in the Seventh Circuit. . . . My present law clerks are from Stanford, Kentucky, and Arizona State Universities, and so I don't believe that I can be accused of having a pro–Ivy League bias."[30]

PRIOR CLERKSHIP EXPERIENCE

It has become increasingly common over time for clerks to spend one year working on a lower court—particularly the United States Courts of Appeals—before joining the Supreme Court. For example, during the Burger Court (1969–85) 85 percent of Supreme Court clerks came from the courts of appeals, 12 percent from the United States district courts, and 3 percent from state courts. During the Rehnquist Court (1986–2005) the trend continued: 92 percent from the courts of appeals, 7 percent from U.S. district courts, and less than 1 percent (0.3) from state courts.[31] Rehnquist's own practices generally mirrored these developments. All of his clerks had prior clerking experience except for eight clerks who worked for him during his first five years on the bench and who largely came from positions in the Department of Justice, where Rehnquist himself worked before joining the Supreme Court. Of those with prior clerking experience, 91 percent (88 of 97) came from the courts of appeals, 6 percent (6 of 97) from the U.S. district courts, and 3 percent (3 of 97) from state supreme courts. But the trend is even more pronounced when one considers that the last district court clerk was selected in 1993 and the last state court clerk was chosen by Rehnquist in 1979. For the last decade of Rehnquist's tenure all of his clerks came from the courts of appeals.

FEEDER JUDGES AND IDEOLOGY

From which courts of appeals, and more specifically from which courts of appeals judges, did Rehnquist choose his clerks? Rehnquist selected clerks from all the federal circuits except the Sixth Circuit—which historically has the lowest rate of clerk placements—with the most (nineteen) coming from the D.C. Circuit, which historically has by far the highest placement rate.[32] The top "feeder" judges for Rehnquist clerks were J. Clifford Wallace of the Ninth Circuit Court of Appeals, who placed four clerks with Rehnquist, and Deanell Reece Tacha of the Tenth Circuit, James Hunter III of the Third Circuit, J. Harvie Wilkinson III of the Fourth Circuit, Frank J. Magill of the Eighth Circuit, Joseph T. Sneed of the Ninth Circuit, and David B. Sentelle of the D.C. Circuit who each placed three clerks with Rehnquist. Feeder judges have repeat success with placing their clerks for a number of reasons including the personal ties they may have with a justice, their reputations in the legal profession, and the quality of training that they provide their clerks.

Yet it is the ideological cue that lower-court judges provide that is perhaps most determinative—particularly when one considers that prospective Supreme Court clerks apply to all of the justices. Previous research has shown an ideological congruence between top feeder judges and placements with Supreme Court justices. Rehnquist's clerks also reflect this relationship, as all of his top feeder judges were appointed to the federal bench by Republican presidents. For all of the Rehnquist clerks who came from a clerkship in a lower federal court, 79 percent (74 of 94) served with judges appointed by Republican presidents. Furthermore, recent studies also confirm that clerks in general —and Rehnquist's clerks in particular—have a high degree of ideological compatibility, which in turn has an effect on the decisions their justices make. In one example of how ideology is important in clerk selection, former clerk David G. Leitch (October term 1986) recalled his interview with Rehnquist: "Our conversation included the obligatory review of Justice Rehnquist's well-worn and handy road atlas to identify the exact location of my hometown of Wallingford, Pennsylvania; perhaps the one and only known discussion of my *Law Review* note; and his advice that if I agreed with Justice Brennan more often than I agreed with him I was not likely to enjoy a clerkship in the Rehnquist chambers."[33]

Still, clerks—whether ideologically compatible or not—can and do disagree with each other, and it is ultimately the justice who makes the decisions. For example, when former clerk Craig Bradley (October term 1975) sent him a recent law review article that Bradley had published, Rehnquist responded: "It is interesting to see two of my former law clerks, serving one right after the other, writing articles which are in such disagreement with one another. . . . I do think you make some cogent points, given the current state of constitutional law, but I think the matter would be best left to the fifty states to work out as they choose—either in the manner you suggest or in the manner that Don [Ayer, October term 1976] apparently suggests."[34]

DIVERSITY

While the rate of gender and racial diversity in the Supreme Court clerking corps has slowly increased over time, there is considerable variation among individual justices. For his part, Rehnquist had similar rates to many of his colleagues yet considerably less diversity than others. In terms of gender diversity, of Rehnquist's 105 clerks, only 17 percent (18) were female. While this rate was comparable to some of his conservative colleagues such as Justices Antonin Scalia and Anthony Kennedy—who have hired female clerks 15 percent of the time—it pales in comparison to others such as Justices Stephen Breyer, Sandra Day O'Connor, and Ruth Bader Ginsburg, who have hired as many female clerks as male clerks.[35] Furthermore, of the three clerks Rehnquist selected each term, there was never more than one female clerk in a given term. Rehnquist's first female clerk was Fredericka Paff, who clerked for him 1973. He selected Maureen Mahoney for the 1979 term. He chose three female clerks during the 1980s and eight during the 1990s. From 2000 to 2005, he had a female clerk each term except 2004.

In terms of racial diversity, Rehnquist and his colleagues came under fire for what many charged was a dearth of minority law clerks. In a 1998 article, journalist Tony Mauro reported that Rehnquist, Scalia, Kennedy, and David Souter had never hired an African American law clerk, while O'Connor, Thomas, Ginsburg, and Breyer had each hired only a single African American clerk. John Paul Stevens had the "best" record hiring three African American clerks since he started serving in 1975. Furthermore, Mauro noted that Rehnquist and Scalia had never hired an Asian law clerk, while Stevens, Scalia, Thomas, and Ginsburg had never hired a Hispanic clerk. Critics seized on the fact that at the time there were 24,000 minority law students (19 percent of all law students in ABA-accredited law schools). The NAACP led a protest outside the Supreme Court building, and some of the justices were questioned about the matter after public lectures, in interviews with journalists, and by congressional subcommittees. In an interview Rehnquist explained that he selected clerks on the basis of "superior professional achievement in law school, together with an appraisal as to how well we would work together. I have never excluded consideration of anyone because of that person's race or nationality."[36] Congressional and bar association representatives asked to meet with Rehnquist, and on November 17, 1998, the chief justice formally spoke on behalf of his colleagues:

> We agree that the statistics set forth in your letter identify concerns which all of us share, but you must realize that many factors entirely unrelated to the hiring of law clerks are responsible for this situation. We select as clerks those who have very strong academic backgrounds, and have had previously successful law clerk experience, most often in the federal courts. As the demographic makeup of this pool changes, it seems entirely likely that the underrepresentation of minorities to which you refer in your letter will also change.[37]

While there is some evidence that in the years since the controversy the justices have made modest strides toward increasing their minority hires, the data also show that clerks continue to be overwhelmingly white. One study found that from 1986 to 2004, Asian Americans comprised 7 percent of all Supreme Court law clerks, African Americans 3 percent, and Hispanics 2 percent.[38] Of Rehnquist's 105 clerks, he hired only 6 Asians, 2 Hispanics, and no African Americans. In sum, both the racial and gender makeup of Rehnquist's clerks—though not as diverse as some of his colleagues—mirrored that of many of the other justices with whom he served and of the Court generally during his tenure.

Does a diverse clerking corps make a difference? There is some evidence to suggest that it does. For example, during the coalition-formation stage of *Rosen v. California* Rehnquist wrote Justice Blackmun:

> Please add my name to your dissenting opinion in this case. One of my law clerks, Fredericka Paff, has persuaded me that the sentence beginning on the last line of page 2 would be more consistent with present day views of women if it were to read as follows: "I believe that the state has a legitimate interest in protecting children and females, who have by tradition and custom had less exposure to it, from such personal abuse." I agree with her, but my joining you is not in any way conditional upon making the change.[39]

Though Blackmun ultimately withdrew his dissent in the case, Paff's proposed change and Rehnquist's willingness to bring it to Blackmun's attention suggests that diversity can matter.

Clerk Duties: Beyond Pinochle, Wafer Cookies, and Apple Juice

Working in close quarters, Rehnquist clerks, like nearly all Court clerks, developed intimate working relationships. A chambers functions like a team trying to stay on top of the endless amount of work that continually floods in. Landis Cox Best (October term 1993), wrote Rehnquist in 1996 reflecting on her year at the Court: "I like most of the work I've had here at Cahill Gordon, but I miss the comradery of clerking. I've seen Jim Ryan [October term 1993] and Katie quite a bit—they are doing well. I haven't seen Brian [Morris, October term 1993]—he is in Montana, waiting to see if he can get a job in Washington (at the Justice Department, I think)."[40]

As was almost universally true of all other clerks, Rehnquist's clerks worked at the Court for a single year before moving on to other positions. Dean Colson (October term 1980) wrote his former boss at the start of the 1981 term: "As fond as my memories are of the past year, I think it would be very difficult to gather up the physical and mental energy to begin anew the whole process so quickly. I am beginning to understand why you look forward so much to leaving for Vermont every summer." Rehnquist replied: "I see from your letter that you realize now what I realized when I clerked for Justice Jackson: that about one year of clerking at full pace is all you can wring out of a person, however able and highly motivated he may be."[41]

Michael J. Meehan (October term 1971) wrote Rehnquist in 1980: "I very much enjoyed your speech yesterday. The TV station that covered it broadcast only your statement that in the 1880's, when there were no law clerks, the Court did some 100 more cases on the merits than currently. Thus I am now obliged to confess that, when I worked for you, we did nothing but play pinochle, eat wafer cookies, and drink apple juice."[42]

Beyond the snacks and card games, Rehnquist clerks participated in the review of cert petitions, in the process of coalition formation, and in drafting opinions. At each stage of the process, clerks were expected to make their views plain. A Rehnquist clerk from the 1990s told me, "I would offer my view of the law in every case." Another Rehnquist clerk from the same decade said, "My role was to offer my view as to the correct legal view, identifying counterarguments to and/or weaknesses with that view." Unlike the role that Rehnquist played when he clerked for Jackson or the role that other clerks in other chambers have undertaken, Rehnquist did not want his clerks to anticipate his views by acting as surrogates. One of his clerks from the 1970s explained to me, "We were encouraged to say what we thought." Of course, this did not mean that Rehnquist blindly followed his clerks' recommendations. A Rehnquist clerk from the 1970s told me, "Justice Rehnquist always makes up his own mind—but he wants his clerks to tell him what they think before he does—he doesn't expect you to tell him what you think he wants to hear." Similarly, another Rehnquist clerk from the same decade explained to me, "I told him what I thought—and then he decided."

AGENDA SETTING

During his first year on the bench Rehnquist and his clerks were solely responsible for reviewing every case petitioned to the Court. Rehnquist received a brief memo from one of his own clerks that outlined the lower-court decision, listed facts and issues in the case, and provided a recommendation. For example, in *Kleindienst v. Mandel* Allen Snyder (October term 1971) noted at the top of his memo that the appeal was from the Eastern District of New York with an opinion by Judge Dooling, joined by Judge Feinberg, with Judge Bartels dissenting. Snyder's two-page memo advised:

> The Court has previously indicated that the first amendment does extend to the right to receive information. Given that premise I think the court below was correct that this provision is certainly overbroad, even assuming the legitimacy of all the governmental interests argued by the S.G. I would therefore conclude that this decision should be affirmed. Nevertheless, I am somewhat troubled by the prospect of a per curiam affirmance of a lower court opinion which declares unconstitutional a significant piece of Congressional action. Accordingly, even assuming the correctness of the decision below, I think the more appropriate resolution of this case *at this early stage* would be to note probable jurisdiction in order to give the S.G. the opportunity for full briefing and oral argument on the merits. RECOMMENDATION: NOTE[43]

Rehnquist was a founding member of the cert pool, which began during the 1972 term. Participating justices pooled their clerks in order to divide up the voluminous cert petitions that endlessly streamed into each chambers. Rehnquist was an enthusiastic supporter of the scheme, which freed up his and the other pool members' clerks from having to review and write memos on each petition. Instead, only one clerk from the pool would review the case. At the end of its first year of operation Powell trumpeted what he saw as a great success. Rehnquist agreed and wrote him back:

I unqualifiedly concur in your favorable appraisal of the pool's performance during the Term. My clerks too, by their participation in the pool
have had more time to devote to other work which is more important to
me and more interesting to them. I have followed your practice of asking
my own law clerks for their recommendation in those cases where they
had not prepared the pool memorandum, and have similarly benefited
from what you describe as the "double review." I am 100% in favor of the
continuation of the pool next Term.[44]

The pool continued the following year. Yet the pool only functioned during the term and was "off" over the summer months, forcing each chambers
to return to doing their own work. At the end of the 1973 term, Chief Justice
Burger suggested that the pool operate year-round, and Justice Powell agreed.
Yet Justices Blackmun and White thought there was some merit in going off
the pool over the summer. Rehnquist weighed in:

I agree with Harry and Byron that there should be some interlude in the
summer during which the law clerks are not pooled . . . but I think rapid
exposure to a wide variety of cases is a good indoctrination for the clerks;
writing individual cert memos on a greater number of cases, I believe,
gives them this to a greater extent than doing pool memoranda. I also
think that the greater feeling of personal responsibility that comes from
a memorandum the clerk has done himself, and the interchange that is
stimulated by the boss' reaction to the memorandum, makes the individual system one which more quickly acquaints all parties in the chambers
with the propensities and idiosyncrasies of one another.[45]

In the end, the justices agreed to operate the pool year-round. Rehnquist
wrote: "I am sure that no proposal with respect to the operation of the cert pool
during the summer months will completely please any of us; Lewis' suggested
resolution of the question . . . is fine with me."[46]

Like all pool clerks, Rehnquist's clerks were randomly assigned cases, reviewed the cert petitions, and drafted memos containing a recommendation
on whether or not the cases merited review by the Supreme Court. Pool clerks
recommend denial for nearly every petition. For example, in one of his pool
memos, Rehnquist clerk John E. O'Neill (October term 1974) concluded, "Both
issues are simply too narrow to be certworthy." In another example, Blackmun
clerk Robert Richter (October term 1973) concluded in one of his pool memos:
"I am convinced that petr [petitioner] received a fair trial and was convicted

on substantial evidence. I am still not 100% sure of some of the details in this record; however, there do not appear to be any certworthy issues. This case would be more trouble than it is worth. Deny."[47] Rehnquist also had his clerks "mark up" pool memos written in other chambers, with his clerks writing their own comments, recommendations, and sometimes even grades (A to D) as to certworthiness on the top of the pool memos. Rehnquist explained how his chambers operated: "As soon as I am confident that my new law clerks are reliable, I take their word and that of the pool memo writer as to the underlying facts and contentions of the parties in the various petitions, and with a large majority of the petitions it is not necessary to go any further than the pool memo. In cases that seem from the memo perhaps to warrant a vote to grant certiorari, I may ask my law clerk to further check out one of the issues, and may review the lower court opinion, the petition, and the response myself."[48]

Over time, an increasing number of justices joined the pool, and the pool memos became a crucial part of the agenda-setting process. In 1989 Rehnquist explained to the pool clerks, "The theory behind the cert pool is that the pool memos will save the time of the Justices because in many cases the Justices, after reading the pool memo, will not find it necessary to read the underlying petition and response." Yet the pool also created concerns that Rehnquist, as chief justice, addressed such as in the following "Memorandum to All Cert Pool Law Clerks":

> Pool memos are assigned to the various chambers participating in the pool on a random basis, partly because that is the easiest way to do it, and partly to avoid any temptation on the part of law clerks to select for themselves pool memos in cases with respect to which they might not be as neutral and detached as is desirable. There may be perfectly good reasons why a particular law clerk should not write a pool memo in a given case; the most obvious one would be if the clerk had worked on the case as a clerk in a court of appeals before coming here. But this sort of problem can, except in the rarest of circumstances, be handled by swaps within a chambers.
>
> It has been brought to my attention that not only this kind of swap, but swaps between chambers have on occasion occurred. This sort of trade has the potential for undermining the policy of random assignment of memos, and is, to put it mildly, "not favored." In the future, there are to be no trades of pool memos between chambers without my express permission, for good cause shown.[49]

BENCH MEMORANDA AND ORAL ARGUMENT

Clerks have long drafted memoranda on cases and issues when so instructed by their justices. These memoranda can take many forms. For example, in 1972 Chief Justice Burger wrote his colleagues: "I enclose a copy of a memo I have had some of my Clerks work up as a 'book review' on the memo Potter Stewart circulated.... I confess I have not come to rest on which of the two memos I think correct but it occurred to me that it might be useful if we exchanged such reactions as may develop."[50]

After the cert memo, the most common memo form is the bench memorandum that occurs after the case is scheduled for oral argument but before argument takes place. In the early years, Rehnquist did on occasion have his clerks draft bench memoranda on cases to be argued. A more detailed analysis of the cert memo, bench memos also contained possible questions for oral argument. For example, in *Milton v. Wainwright* (1972) Rehnquist clerk Michael Meehan wrote his boss: "Having read the briefs, I present the following thoughts on (1) applying retroactivity to *Massiah*, and (2) A more general disposition of the case.... (3) Suggested questions for argument: ... Ask petitioner whether the admission of this confession did not indeed constitute harmless error."[51]

Still, in most cases Rehnquist clerks did not draft bench memos. Instead, the Rehnquist papers contain brief, one-paragraph "Summaries of Cases to be Argued" taken from *U.S. Law Week*. In 1973 Rehnquist explained why he did not have his clerks draft bench memos:

> The method of operation which I have come to favor during my short tenure does not rely heavily on bench memos. For reasons doubtless peculiar to my own way of working, I have tended to concentrate my time heavily in the area of reviewing records and briefs in the argued cases, feeling that the time of the law clerks could be more usefully employed in working on the certs and in the drafting of opinions when assignments begin coming around.[52]

Maureen Mahoney (October term 1979) explained how in-person discussions substituted for bench memos: "Instead of sending us off to the library to draft long bench memos that he could read alone at his desk, he would take each of us for walks on Capitol Hill to discuss our assigned cases. He asked probing questions, listened attentively to our views, and carefully explained why he agreed or disagreed. He never asked, or cared, what the *New York Times* might have to say on the topic." Similarly, Richard Garnett (October term 1996) explained, "To prepare for oral arguments, the chief preferred not to read long, heavily footnoted memos, opting instead for talking through problems with his clerks, while walking around the block outside the Supreme Court building —sometimes twice, for a particularly tricky case. It was surprising, and always funny, that so few of the gawking tourists around the court recognized the chief justice as he ambled around Capitol Hill, doing his work. (He didn't mind at all)."[53]

Rehnquist clerks did attend oral argument and were standing by when needed. And while Rehnquist's requests to his clerks were usually case related, on more than one occasion his humor got the best of him. David G. Leitch recalled one episode: "While exhibiting a stern visage on the bench, he was occasionally penning notes to his law clerks asking trivia questions. One memorable day my co-clerks and I received a note from the bench listing the first lines of five college fight songs and asking us to identify the colleges to which they belonged. Our lame answers were returned graded: '2 out of 5—40%.'" Similarly, Richard Garnett remembered, "Chief Justice Rehnquist liked to put together friendly brackets and pools for the NCAA tournament, the Kentucky Derby, and the bowl games. One day, just after the 1996 election, he passed down to me a note from the bench. I assumed he wanted a law book or a memo, but instead he asked me to find out what was happening in one of the not-yet-called House races that was integral to our inter-chambers contest."[54]

COALITION FORMATION

Clerks act as informal emissaries on behalf of their justices in the process of negotiation and compromise that is routinely a part of forming coalitions. Clerks from different chambers regularly interact with each other, both formally and informally, providing ongoing opportunities to discuss cases. Rehnquist's clerks were not unusual in their routine participation in the "clerk network." For example, Justice Blackmun received the following memorandum from his 1991 clerk Molly McUsic concerning *Kraft General Foods v. Iowa Dept. of Revenue,* which highlights the participation of both Chief Justice Rehnquist's clerks and clerks from other chambers:

> You voted with the Chief in dissent on this case. Justice O'Connor has circulated a memo saying that she will wait for the dissent. The Chief's clerk sent me a message stating that the Chief was interested in knowing whether you were interested in writing. I think a dissent is important, because I am not convinced that the Court is correct. . . . I do think a dissent by us has a better chance of collecting SOC's vote than a quick job by the Chief. . . . What should I tell the Chief's clerk about *Kraft?*[55]

Richard Garnett explained how the clerks kept Rehnquist apprised of what was going on in other chambers: "For me, maybe the best part of the job was the daily 9:30 a.m. meeting. We'd drink our coffee, talk a bit about football, movies, and weather, and check up on pending cases and opinions. Sometimes he'd wonder aloud why one colleague or another still hadn't circulated a draft. (He was always, though, unfailingly fair and genial about and toward his colleagues; he would never have tolerated from any clerk a snide remark about a justice.)"[56]

When draft opinions were circulated, Rehnquist clerks reviewed them and made recommendations. For example, following the circulations of both Potter Stewart's majority opinion and Byron White's dissent in *Brennan v. Arnheim and Neely*, Rehnquist clerk Robert Wild (October term 1972) wrote his boss: "I remain persuaded by Mr. Justice Stewart's opinion for the majority in this case and still recommend that you join it. However, since you voted with Mr. Justice White's position in Conference you may feel differently." Rehnquist did indeed switch and joined the majority opinion the next day.[57] Similarly, Rehnquist clerk Allen Snyder advised in another case: "Attached is BRW's opinion concurring in the judgment in *Peters v. Kiff.* Justice White would rely on the statutory proscription, emphasizing its application to race (cf. Our opinion in *Weber*), thus reaching the same result but on somewhat narrower grounds than the majority. If you decide to join the majority in this case, BRW's opinion might be a good compromise."[58]

Another example followed Justice White's "Memorandum" circulation in *Frank Johnson v. Louisiana* and *Apodaca v. Oregon*. Snyder reviewed the drafts for Rehnquist: "Attached are BRW's opinions in *Johnson* & *Apodaca*. They are just as expected from his earlier drafts. He rejects due process claim in *Johnson,* and the 6th amendment claim in *Apodaca.* I see no objection from your standpoint to either draft, except as we discussed before that BRW assumes in *Apodaca* that the 6th amendment is incorporated by the 14th."[59] Rehnquist joined White's opinions.

A final example of clerk review, analysis, and recommendation of draft opinions involved Justice Thurgood Marshall's suggestion that the case of *Gilligan v. Morgan* was moot. Rehnquist clerk L. Gordon Harriss (October term 1972) drafted a lengthy memorandum on Marshall's argument and weighed in on the matter: "These are jurisdictional issues which the court can decide without a remand. If the quid pro quo for going along with Justice Marshall's suggestion is that such a decision might cut back on class actions, I do not see how that will, in a practical sense, result."[60]

After the clerks reviewed circulations and consulted with Rehnquist, they communicated changes to the other chambers. Sometimes, minor points could be communicated through the clerk network without memos being written. For example, in *Miller v. California*, Rehnquist told his clerk: "On p. 3 of Douglas, J. dissent Ralph Ginsburg's name is misspelled. You might let one of his clerk's know."[61] However nearly all of the major substantive changes to opinions as well as voting decisions were drafted in memo form by the clerks. For example, Michael Meehan wrote Rehnquist: "This is *Brunette v. Kockum*, the alien patent venue case. Since its distribution yesterday, all but you and the Chief have already joined it. The vote to affirm was unanimous in conference, and this opinion by TM well treats all the issues on its way to doing so. I have taken the liberty of getting a join letter ready for you to sign."[62]

If warranted, Rehnquist would edit the memos before they went out. For example, in *Pipefitters Union v. United States,* a Rehnquist memo to Justice Brennan was originally drafted by the clerk to say "I think, however, that the last sentence . . . does not significantly illuminate the general question which precedes it. . . . I would, therefore, prefer to have the last sentence deleted." Rehnquist changed the language to "I draw back a little at the rather unqualified intimation of approval . . . which seems to flow from your last sentence. Would you have any objection to rewording it to read . . . "[63]

The clerk network is particularly vital when one considers that not all written communications between a given set of justices is circulated to all the members of the Court. Consider this 1972 memo from Rehnquist to Burger:

> With the help of my secretaries and law clerks, I feel that I am at least staying even and perhaps moving slightly ahead in the unceasing battle to keep myself informed about what is going on within the Court. One modest change which would help the paper processing system in my chambers would be for join letters to be sent in duplicate to each chambers, just the way circulations now are. This is obviously not a matter of any great import, but I am wondering if some or all of the rest of you might also find it helpful.[64]

OPINION WRITING

Like many newly appointed justices, Rehnquist drafted a number of his own opinions when he first joined the Court because, as one former clerk told me, "he was new." But soon Rehnquist followed the institutional norm of delegating opinion writing to his clerks. However, Rehnquist made plain that while his clerks were drafting his opinions, "the law clerk is not simply turned loose on an important legal question to draft an opinion embodying the reasoning and the result favored by the clerk." Instead, Rehnquist said that his clerks were engaged in a "highly structured task" that they were expected to complete in ten days to two weeks. Dean Colson (October term 1980) commented: "This is a guy you didn't get anything by. The chief would say: 'Here's the way I want it outlined. Here's the way I want it written.' And then he'd edit heavily."[65]

David G. Leitch recalled his initiation into the opinion-writing process under Rehnquist:

> When I began to work in the Rehnquist chambers, I was soon advised of the Chief's 'ten day rule,' requiring that law clerks provide him drafts of opinions within ten days of being assigned the task. A little more than a year out of law school, we were being told—in the interest of keeping the trains running on time (and to keep hand-wringing law clerks from gumming up the works)—to prepare a draft opinion for the Supreme Court of the United States in ten days (weekends included). The first opinion I worked on involved what I thought was a particularly knotty issue, and the better part of my ten days of drafting involved working through four or five paragraphs of detailed explanation of that issue. When my draft was returned with the Chief's edits, the topic sentences of those paragraphs had been kept and condensed into one, with all my verbose and confusing discursus removed. It was, of course, a far better product, less prone to create confusion in the future. And, importantly, it was brief and efficient.[66]

Hence, in almost all cases, the clerks composed drafts of opinions, and Rehnquist edited them—almost always in a relatively minor way. A typical example is the draft concurrence in *United States v. Little Lake Misere Land Company,* which included the following original passage: "where a Minnesota statute extended the period of time in which the mortgagor might redeem his equity following foreclosure in the face of vigorous arguments that the statute impaired a valid contract. Were there no other ground..." Rehnquist made the following minor edits: "in which a Minnesota statute extending the period of time in which the mortgagor might redeem his equity following foreclosure was upheld in the face of vigorous arguments that the statute impaired a valid contract. Were there no simpler ground..."[67]

Another example is Rehnquist clerk Allen Snyder's draft majority opinion in *Socialist Labor Party v. Gilligan.* Not only did Rehnquist edit the draft but also a memo titled "Some Notes on WHR Opinion" written by Justice Potter Stewart's clerk Bill Jeffress, as well as a marked-up printed copy of the Rehnquist opinion with the heading "Stewart, J. Copy" written in pencil at the top, appears in the case file. Jeffress's memo was a biting critique of the opinion explaining how "there are problems with the standing analysis. But I think there are more serious problems with the *Rescue Army* analysis."[68] After extensive revisions and multiple drafts, Rehnquist was able to secure not only Stewart's vote but a Court majority.

In addition to the Court's work product, clerks draft speeches and articles for their justices. For example, following her term on the Court, Rehnquist wrote former clerk Maureen Mahoney (October term 1979): "This is to thank you, as well as Tom [McGough] and Jim [Asperger], for the bound volume of the opinions that the four of us worked on last year together. As far as opinions go, I think the *Kissinger-Forsham* ones probably were the most interesting of the ones that you helped me with, but the Edward Douglass White Lecture may well live longer in people's minds, thanks to the reporter who covers the Court for the *Washington Post.* Someone sent me a copy of an article he had done on me, quoting at length from that Lecture—only the language he quoted, as I recall ('be bounced out of the courtroom and back into the living room') was yours, not mine!"[69]

Fun with Bill: Chairman, Christmas Party Committee

There are many perks to being a law clerk, such as professionally taken photographs with your justice and the other law clerks from your term, use of the Court's unique facilities such as basketball games on the "highest court in the land" and regular lunches with the justices and other clerks. For example, the 1991 Stevens clerks wrote: "Dear Chief Justice Rehnquist, We would be honored if you would be our guest at lunch, at your convenience and at a restaurant of your choice. We hope that your schedule permits you to accept our invitation. Yours truly, Kathleen Moriarty, Nancy Marder, Robert Schapiro, and Peter Yu."[70]

From the beginning Rehnquist and his first three clerks enjoyed a spirited social life at the Court such as the following challenge to Justice White and his clerks regarding "Minimum Standards for a Meaningful Soccer Tournament":

Rather casual, almost bantering, conversation has been exchanged by various members of the above chambers as to who might prevail over whom in the event a match or series of matches were played on the soccer board now lodging in the White chambers. We are firmly of the view that issue ought to be joined, the questions for disposition sharpened, and a meaningful adjudication be had. . . . We propose . . . a series of matches between two teams consisting of two persons each, chosen from among the Justice and his law clerks. . . . The losers of the total match point score shall take the winners to the Monocle for lunch.[71]

Rehnquist undoubtedly brought a playful spirit to the Court. No doubt his experience as a former clerk sparked an interest in cultivating the social side of the institution—not only for the clerks but also for the justices and other Court personnel. At the start of the 1973 term he outlined some of his ideas in a memo to Chief Justice Burger:

1. *Coffee hour after oral argument.* I think that the practice which each of us appears to follow at the close of a day of oral argument—plodding back to his own individual salt mine—is bad for morale. While I know there is work to be done, I am wondering if there would be any substantial sentiment in the Conference in favor of opening either the Justices' Dining Room, or one of the Conference Rooms, to all Justices and law clerks who desire it, for a half hour of coffee or tea at 3:00 p.m. on at least some afternoons following oral argument. It would give law clerks a chance to get acquainted with the Justices for whom they don't work, and vice versa.

2. *Justices' Dining Room.* Seeing the dining facilities at your old court, and at the Court of Claims, convinces me that ours combines, to a degree that might be thought impossible, baronial elegance with dreariness. Might there be some possibility of using the new Chippendale table for those Justices who want to eat with other Justices, but also placing two or three other tables in the same room, in addition to the table in the next room, so that one of us who wanted to have a couple of friends over to lunch could come up and eat in the same dining room, and still not disturb those of the Brethren who wish to eat with one another?

I also wonder if there might be any possibility of our being allowed to use the Senate dining room. Your old court has at least partially catered food for its judges; Cabinet officers and the agency heads in the executive branch generally have the same. I would guess that we are the highest ranking members of the bureaucracy who are condemned to GSI food when we eat in the building.

3. *Mini-Gridiron show.* I would enjoy seeing what each annual crop of law clerks, together with such help from the Justices that they might wish, could do in the way of a gridiron show or other parody or satire on the Court. If we passed this along to the law clerks in the fall, and told them that we would expect a performance some time in the spring, I should think we could have a very enjoyable evening out of it when it occurred.

4. Please don't get the impression that I am not working hard in preparation for the first Conference.[72]

Rehnquist took responsibility for the incoming "Party for Law Clerks" each fall. He wrote Chief Justice Burger: "I do hope that the Justices will sponsor their annual informal get together for the law clerks sometime late next week, and I would be more than happy to assume all of the responsibility for the planning of the event, or share it with one or more of our colleagues." Burger was happy to delegate to Rehnquist, and following the event Rehnquist informed his colleagues: "I spent $35.54 in purchasing supplies for the reception for new law clerks. . . . I have several bottles of sherry left over, which I will hold in trust until the party next year."[73]

Rehnquist organized an annual Christmas party. He signed his memos on the subject "Chairman, Christmas Party Committee" and was even formally designated by Chief Justice Warren Burger, who wrote in 1977: "By popular acclaim you have been unanimously drafted to be architect, engineer and general contractor for the Annual Christmas Party for the Supreme Court household. Such popularity must be deserved." The relatively small affair soon grew to formal invitations for hundreds of attendees including clerks' spouses and guests all drinking punch spiked with Vodka and singing with the choir to "O Come All Ye Faithful," "Joy to the World," "Hark, the Herald Angels Sing," "America the Beautiful," "Jingle Bells," and many others. Rehnquist regularly laid out the program as in this 1975 memoranda: "Refreshments will be served. . . . We hope to have a strolling minstrel . . . playing Christmas music. . . . The first part of the program will consist of a skit. . . . a chorus of Court employees . . . will sing a few Christmas carols. . . . there will be a general sing-a-long . . . of the more familiar Christmas songs.[74]

Rehnquist routinely enlisted the help of law clerks and other staff for the humorous skits that were to be performed. For example, the 1975 list of "Skit Participants" included Marshall clerk Kevin Baine, Burger clerk Candy Kovacic, Rehnquist clerks Jack Mason and Craig Bradley, Clark clerk Tom Corrigan,

Blackmun secretary Wanda Syverson, and Stewart clerk Jim Gardner. Were one of these staffers responsible for the following alternate lyrics that appear in the Rehnquist papers? "Pack the Court with hacks and cronies, fa la la la la, la la la la. Weed out all those liberal phonies, fa, etc."[75]

Tennis was Rehnquist's sport of choice, and his clerks were regular participants. R. Ted Cruz recalled: "Once a week, the Chief played tennis with his clerks. We would play on a public court, and no one ever recognized the older gentlemen playing doubles with three young lawyers." Richard W. Garnett remembered: "We played on the same day that the week's 'cert memos' . . . were due, so—more than a few times—clerks played without having slept. We took our turns driving and buying a new can of balls. I was the Chief's doubles partner that year, and I several times beaned him with my hopelessly chaotic serves. One day, I am ashamed to admit, after yet another double-fault, I slammed my racket to the ground and yelled an extremely unattractive expletive. My co-clerks looked across the net at me in horror. The Chief, though, didn't turn around. He just slowly bent over, put his hands on his knees, and started laughing." David G. Leitch recalled: "Our weekly chambers tennis game never yielded to circumstances. We headed to the Haines Point tennis bubble for an hour of fun and relaxation even in the midst of snowstorms. In fact, one of those trips coincided with another of the Chief's fun-filled passions—wagering. Before heading to the tennis bubble one day in January 1987, we had to pause on the front plaza of the Court to measure the snowfall so we could resolve multiple bets about the amount of snow that would be on that plaza at 10 a.m. (Meteorology was another passion.) A picture of our escapade appeared the next day in the *Washington Post,* and I soon received a copy signed with the inscription: 'Decision '87: The snow bets on the first January blizzard.'"[76]

Rehnquist's correspondence is filled with references to tennis matches: past and future. For example, when a reporter doing a profile on former Rehnquist clerk Dean Colson asked Rehnquist a series of questions, Rehnquist had no comment on any of them except on the matter of who was the better tennis player. Rehnquist wrote: "Unquestionably he is." Ronald Tenpas (October term 1991) wrote Rehnquist from his home in Tampa during the winter of 1996: "We continue to play a lot of tennis, especially this time of year (you need to find a speaking/teaching engagement for Florida in February)." Jack Mason (October term 1975) wrote him in 1995: "I am so pleased to hear that you are returning to the tennis court after a successful surgery. I will come down and have lunch again and catch up with you."[77]

Rehnquist's betting pools were extremely popular. So much so that former clerks even proposed wagers. On October 27, 1980, Donald B. Ayer (October term 1976) wrote him: "Given the present time of the present year, a proposal: $5, even money—I bet Reagan wins any two of California, Texas, and Pennsylvania." Rehnquist replied: "We have not had quite the round of betting here at the Court as we had in 1976 when you were here, on the presidential election, but based on the time of the receipt of the letter, I must with all respect decline your proposed bet." John Roberts (October term 1980) recalled that he "enjoyed small wagers on anything—athletic contests, presidential elections, the day of the first snowfall."[78]

R. Ted Cruz recalled another of Rehnquist's interests, which he shared with his clerks: "He would also have us over to his house to play charades. One of my favorite memories is his lying on his stomach on the floor, pantomiming firing a rifle and mouthing 'pow, pow,' as he acted out *All Quiet on the Western Front*." David G. Leitch remembered: "Not long ago, in a game of charades following a dinner at the home of another former clerk, I had to act out a particularly choice 'quote' that the former Mayor of Washington, D.C. had repeatedly uttered upon being arrested in a hotel room. The Chief loved watching me struggle with that one."[79]

Rehnquist routinely shared walks outside the Supreme Court building with his clerks. John Roberts recalled how the unassuming justice was rarely recognized on these outings: "He was completely unaffected in manner. When strolling outside the Supreme Court with a law clerk to discuss a case, Chief Justice Rehnquist would often be stopped by visiting tourists, and asked to take their picture as they posed on the courthouse steps. He looked like the sort of approachable fellow who would be happy to oblige, and he always did. Many families around the country have a photograph of themselves in front of the Supreme Court, not knowing it was taken by someone who sat on the Court longer than all but six Justices."[80]

In keeping with Court tradition, Rehnquist held annual reunions for his clerks and their families: a formal dinner on Saturday night and a more informal picnic at his house the next day. Maureen Mahoney recalled, "He loved to laugh at himself. Each year the law clerks presented a skit at the annual clerks' reunion in which they would mimic the Chief's voice and mannerisms, and mock his opinions. In the Chief's book, this was not blasphemy—it was rollicking good fun."[81]

Of course, the reunions grew in size each year, and inevitably some clerks sent their regrets when they were unable to attend. For example, in 1983 James

A. Strain (October term 1972), wrote his former boss: "For the first time since the first reunion was held in our apartment, Cheryl and I will not be able to come to the annual reunion. We both regret this because we look forward to seeing you and Nan, as well as our other friends who attend or who live in the D.C. area. A combination of professional commitments, puny children, and no acceptable baby sitting option is causing us to cancel. If you can see fit to forgive us for this year, I will do what I can to convince unreasonable clients that some things are more important than their problems for next year."[82]

The reunions allowed Rehnquist to keep in touch both professionally and personally with his clerks and their families. David G. Leitch remarked: "Although we never could or would claim to experience his devotion the way his children or grandchildren did, the Rehnquist law clerks—privileged to consider ourselves members of the extended family—saw his love of family extend to us as well. He was our professional father, always ready with a word or advice or guidance when we sought him out, as well as a sort of professional father-in-law and grandfather, knowing and taking an interest in our spouses and children, who were fortunate to visit with him at annual reunions of the 'family.' It would have been easy enough for him to conclude that there were too many law clerks, spouses, and children to keep track of. He never drew that conclusion."[83]

To show their gratitude for his ongoing personal interest in them, Rehnquist's clerks presented him with three gifts throughout his tenure on the bench—each meant to symbolize one aspect of his judicial career. The first gift was a Lone Ranger doll meant to symbolize his early years as an impassioned dissenter. The second was an elaborate Indian feather headdress to commemorate his elevation to chief justice in 1986. On this transition, David G. Leitch recalled, "When he was an Associate Justice, Rehnquist was called 'Boss' by his clerks. After his confirmation as Chief Justice during the Term of my clerkship, we sheepishly approached him and asked what he wanted to be called, and he responded with characteristic directness: 'I guess you can call me Chief.' He has been "the Chief" ever since." The Chief's final gift came in 1996 when his clerks presented him with a large ship's captain's wheel, which he displayed with the other gifts in his office at the Court.[84]

As chief justice, Rehnquist even made an exception to allow clerks of deceased justices to use the Court's facilities for their reunions. Terrence G. Perris wrote him in 2004: "I was a law clerk to Justice Potter Stewart during the October Term 1973 and was one of the attendees at this weekend's law clerk dinner in memory of the Justice. I understand that you were kind enough to personally intercede to waive the normal policy precluding such events at the Court unless a sitting or retired Justice is in attendance. I want to personally thank you for graciously taking such action and thus helping to make the weekend events even more special. Our get-together was a wonderful tribute to Justice Stewart and was very well-attended by his former clerks. We also enjoyed the opportunity to visit once again with Mrs. Stewart, who befriended all of us during our service to the Justice."[85]

Also, the clerks from each of the justices for a given term have held reunions from time to time. One humorous example came in the form of an "Application for Authorization to Utilize Court Facilities" sent to Rehnquist by his former clerk John M. Nannes (October term 1974):

> Petitioner John M. Nannes ("petitioner") respectfully requests authorization for the Supreme Court clerks from the October 1974 Term ("clerks") to use the Court's facilities for a reunion dinner. . . . In support of this application, petitioner respectfully states as follows: The clerks have never had a reunion. Petitioner and Larry Simms thought that having the reunion would be fun. . . . Petitioner and Mr. Simms wrote each of the 30 clerks to determine interest in such a reunion and availability for a dinner on May 18 ("survey"). Over twenty of the clerks indicated both interest and availability. A number of the clerks worked for justices who are no longer on the Court and therefore have not been to the Court for a social function in some time. . . . Reunion dinners have a tradition of dignity, warmth, and good humor. See, e.g., *Reunion Dinners of Law Clerks for Chief Justice William H. Rehnquist* (1971–1990). . . . if this Application is granted, petitioner will be spared the embarrassment of having to explain to 29 other clerks why the survey, which represented that there would be a dinner at the Court on May 18, was false and misleading.[86]

The Chief granted the request, and the reunion took place.

Placement: Advice, Suggestions, and Passing the Word

Former Rehnquist clerks, like those from other chambers, found employment in many areas including private practice, government service, and academia. Rehnquist's enthusiasm for public service was rarely lost on his former clerks. Maureen Mahoney recalled: "I saw a man who placed little value on material wealth and who honored public service. When I told him one day that I was not certain whether I was willing to defer the purchase of a home in Nantucket in order to work for the government, he just frowned, and I went off to serve in the Solicitor General's office."[87]

Former Rehnquist clerk Bruce R. Braun (October term 1990)—then working for the law firm Winston & Strawn—wrote him: "I just finished a two-week evidentiary hearing before a federal magistrate in a pro bono case. . . . I enjoyed putting on four expert witnesses and writing the post-trial briefs. The experience whetted my appetite for more trial and appellate experience, which are few and far between in an associate's life. I have thus been giving much thought into returning to government service in a year or two. Any ideas or suggestions that you have on such opportunities would be greatly appreciated." Rehnquist wrote back: "Your reaction to private practice—better paid but vaguely dissatisfied after public service—is very common. A number of my former law clerks have reacted in the same way, and several of them have gone back to working for the government after a stint in private practice."[88]

Former clerk Ronald Tenpas wrote Rehnquist in 1996: "I am thinking about making a move to the US Attorney's Office if they are willing to have me. I like the firm and the people pretty well but I still have a belief in 'public service' that private life does not quench. I figure I better go cure myself of it before Nathan's college tuition—or pre-school fees—kick in. . . . Thanks for writing a letter for me. I'll let you know how it turns out once I've heard something." Rehnquist's recommendation stated: "I highly recommend him for this position. A year of working closely with him convinced me that he has absolutely first rate legal skills, and also that he is quite an easy-going and enjoyable person who would fit well into any large office."[89]

Similarly, 1981 clerk David G. Campbell wrote Rehnquist in 1995: "I am coming to the conclusion that I do not want to practice law for the rest of my life. . . . Truth be told, I am most interested in the federal bench . . . and have often thought I am too apolitical to attain a judgeship. . . . I write to ask if you have any thoughts or suggestions about pursuing a federal judgeship. . . . Problem is, I'm not sure where to start or how to proceed." Rehnquist replied: "If you want to become a federal judge, all my experience and all the experience of others with whom I have discussed the subject over time indicates that you must identify yourself with a political party. I don't know that you need to have been terribly active in the affairs of the party, though that surely helps; but if you are not even affiliated with a party, I would think your chances of appointment are virtually nil. Once you affiliate with a party, your LDS connections should be useful in bringing your name forward for a judgeship. I would also recommend bar activities because frequently politicians who have something to say about judicial appointments will consult with lawyers whom they know; if you are known to these lawyers, it would help your case."[90]

Rehnquist was also willing to aid his clerks and other clerks in finding employment following their time at the Court. For example, Professor Robert W. Bennett of Northwestern Law School wrote Rehnquist: "I am writing again to solicit suggestions you might have for candidates for positions on the Northwestern faculty. . . . Any suggestion . . . you might have would be appreciated. . . . In addition, I wonder if you would be kind enough to ask one of your clerks at the Court to see if there is sufficient interest to warrant my coming out to conduct interviews. Last year, Justice Powell's clerk, Jack Owens, was kind enough to do this." Rehnquist replied: "I asked one of my present law clerks to find out from the clerks in the other chambers as to whether there were any of their number who would be sufficiently interested in teaching at Northwestern to warrant your coming out to conduct interviews. I will advise you of the results shortly."[91]

Former judge Simon H. Rifkind wrote on behalf of his law firm: "A number of our partners and associates have served as clerks to judges. We have found such postgraduate period of exposure to, and participation in, the work of the courts exceedingly productive in the making of a lawyer. We are interested in recruiting lawyers who have had such experience. If your appraisal of your present clerk is high, we should welcome an opportunity to interview him now for employment beginning at the conclusion of his clerkship, provided you have no objection." Rehnquist replied: "I shall pass the word along to them, and suggest that they contact you in the event that they would like an interview." Similarly, Arizona attorney Frederick Robertshaw wrote Rehnquist: "I know that you have more important things to do than recruit for our firm, but I thought that you might want to pass on to someone else what was passed on to you—young lawyer years in the sunshine. The job will be on the commercial law side of our firm . . . and there will be plenty of litigation in those fields so that he will not just be working as an office-solicitor with a green eye shade, but will be a vociferous advocate for the oppressed private sector economy." Rehnquist replied: "I will try to pass the word around informally, and if I find any interest I will certainly let you know."[92]

Former clerk Donald B. Ayer, who worked for Rehnquist in 1976, wrote his law firm colleague William French Smith: "Justice Rehnquist requested this morning that I relay to you his recommendation of a candidate for a position as Special Assistant to the Attorney General. The individual is Chuck Cooper. . . . The gist of the message that Justice Rehnquist asked me to relay is that he would give Chuck the highest recommendation based on his association with him during the 1978 Term."[93]

Finally, not only was Rehnquist able to help his former clerks professionally through their association with him and through his recommendations, but they also received direct appointments from him. For example, Maureen Mahoney wrote him in 1994: "I am very honored that you chose to appoint me to the Judicial Fellows Commission. I am concerned that I do not deserve a place among such a distinguished group of commissioners, but will do my best to make a valuable contribution to the organization!"[94]

Personal acquaintance between a justice and those recommending new clerks or hiring former clerks may also play a role in clerk selection and placement. For example, in his letter of inquiry regarding potential Northwestern faculty members, Robert Bennett wrote Rehnquist: "Let me assure you that I am keeping my tennis game in shape for your next visit to Chicago when you have some free time." Similarly, in responding to a job inquiry for his current clerks, Rehnquist closed his letter to Simon Rifkind: "It was, incidentally, a pleasure to make your acquaintance at the dinner honoring Bill Douglas earlier this month." In his 1975 recommendation letter to Rehnquist, Cornell Law School dean Roger C. Cramton included a handwritten "P.S. It was great to see you and Nan in Vermont & Montreal."[95]

Gaining Considerable Ground: Postclerkship Relationships

The postclerkship relationship between justice and former clerk is almost always a singularly personal one with letters, cards, and notes concerning family matters and health issues. Rehnquist's papers, like those of many of his colleagues, are filled with such intimate correspondence. However, some former clerks continue their active professional relationships by requesting career advice including recommendations, attending and suggesting speaking engagements and other law-related professional activities, weighing in—both formally and informally—on current cases and controversies, and regularly meeting with their former bosses. In all, the postclerkship experience of many former clerks can be described as an ongoing one with their justice and with the Court.

One intriguing aspect of the relationship between former clerk and justice is the candor with which former clerks continue to weigh in on the work of the Court, lobby, defend their justice, and criticize other justices. For example, in a 1983 letter to Rehnquist, William S. Eggeling (October term 1975) commented on the decision in *EEOC v. Wyoming:* "JPS's concurrence was extraordinarily depressing, indicating a simplistic view of the Constitution which seems difficult to square with any meaningful concept of a federal republic. I was glad to see that LFP felt it appropriate to challenge the entirely vapid arguments advanced by JPS for overruling *National League of Cities.*"[96] In another instance, Rehnquist wrote Eggeling: "I enclose a copy of an extremely obscure opinion which we handed down today, *Railroad Retirement Bd. v. Fritz,* in which I think we have gained considerable ground in the year-long fight over the Equal Protection Clause application that went on during the Term you were here in *Massachusetts v. Murgia.* It was a negotiated opinion, as you might imagine, but I think we have finally buried most of the 'fair and substantial relationship to a legitimate state' language from some of the earlier cases."[97]

Craig M. Bradley wrote Rehnquist in 1994: "I enclose a copy of my latest article, as well as of a letter to your colleagues. I really believe that you are on the verge of a major clarification of Fourth Amendment law, if only the Court will acknowledge that the search warrant requirement has been abandoned for outdoor searches." Gary Born (October term 1982) wrote Rehnquist in 1996: "I am enclosing the third edition of my book on *International Civil Litigation in the United States Courts.* . . . Although the book is designed for practitioners and law schools, I hope that you will also find it of value in the international cases that come before the Court."[98]

In 1996—twenty-three years after his clerkship ended—1972 clerk Lowell Gordon Harriss wrote his former boss: "I still read every Court decision. . . . Although I have not attempted any study, my strong sense is that the fewer number of decisions by the Court is more than made up for by the number of individual opinions multiplied by the number of pages. I hate to think what some of the paradigm decisions of the past in 'tame' fields might be in length if written today. One field in which I have become increasingly involved over the years is 'corporate trusts and estates', a/k/a bankruptcy. Its always a pleasure to read any decision in that area: usually short, direct and brief in analysis and decision, and rarely encumbered by the seemingly accepted practice of writing the analysis as a series of partial quotations from sentences from prior decisions." Rehnquist replied: "I think your observation is quite right: although we are taking far fewer cases to decide, we are still filling up the same number of pages in the U.S. Reports deciding them. It may be an example of the maxim that the devil makes work for idle hands."[99]

Some former clerks argue cases before the justices for whom they used to work. In this setting where clerks have "switched sides" from working for the justice to working for the client, clerks continue their personal relationship with their former bosses. For example, Maureen Mahoney recalled, "During my argument in the University of Michigan case, *Grutter v. Bollinger,* he called me 'Maureen' while asking a question."[100] In another example, 1978 clerk Mark R. Kravitz was scheduled to argue a case before the justices. He phoned Rehnquist's secretary Janet Barnes to set up a lunch with the chief justice. Barnes wrote Rehnquist: "Mark Kravitz called to say that he will be in town next week and here at the Court to sit in on argument—he will be arguing *Doctor's Associates v. Casarotto* on April 17th and thought he would come to see argument beforehand. Anyway, he wants to know if he can stop in and say hello, he will be here all day on Tuesday, February 20th and most of the day on Wednesday, February 21st." Rehnquist noted on the message: "Yes—after arg[ument] on Wed or lunch on Wed." Barnes phoned Kravitz and sent another note to her boss: "Mark said he would be delighted to have lunch with you on Wednesday, February 21st and will be here at noon after argument." Two days later Kravits wrote Barnes: "Thank you so much for arranging for lunch with the Chief Justice. It was great to spend some quiet time with him."[101]

The access that former clerks have to their former bosses, whether it is in correspondence or in-person meetings, is a unique perk that other lawyers do not enjoy. And while the extent of this access in terms of substantive influence has never been examined, the opportunity for ongoing influence plainly exists and is indeed cultivated by both clerk and justice.

Conclusion: The Fondest Recollection

Rehnquist's journey from clerk to associate justice to chief justice not only demonstrates the important and growing influence that law clerks have on the U.S. Supreme Court but also highlights the many ways in which the ongoing clerk-justice relationship develops. Law clerks are a crucial part of the efficient functioning of the Court, and their relationship to the institution continues long after they leave, including ongoing contacts with their former justices, discussions about their clerkship experiences, advocacy before the Court, and even appointment to the Court as justices themselves. Rehnquist was an important part of this process for the five decades at the end of the twentieth century, and his experiences help to illuminate both the personal and professional sides of the clerkship institution.

Informed of the death of George Niebank, with whom he had clerked for Justice Jackson over fifty years before, Rehnquist wrote his former co-clerk's daughter: "I still have the fondest recollections of the time he and I spent working for Justice Jackson back in 1952."[102] The former Supreme Court law clerk had come full circle. Rehnquist fell ill a few weeks after writing Niebank's daughter. The chief justice died on September 3, 2005, after spending his final term battling throat cancer. Indeed, it was not lost on the press that one of Rehnquist's own former clerks, John Roberts, was a pallbearer at Rehnquist's funeral and ultimately succeeded his former boss as chief justice of the United States.

Notes

1. William H. Rehnquist, *The Supreme Court: How It Was, How It Is* (New York: William Morrow, 1987), 20; Sandra Day O'Connor, "In Memoriam: William H. Rehnquist," *Harvard Law Review* 119, no. 1 (2005): 3–5.

2. Rehnquist, *Supreme Court*, 27, 29.

3. *Sacher v. United States*, 343 U.S. 1 (1952); Rehnquist, *Supreme Court*, 36–37.

4. *Youngstown Sheet & Tube Co. v. Sawyer*, 343 U.S. 579 (1952); Rehnquist, *Supreme Court*, 61–62.

5. *Plessy v. Ferguson*, 163 U.S. 537 (1896); "Supreme Court: Memo from Rehnquist," *Newsweek*, December 13, 1971, 32.

6. *Congressional Record—Senate*, December 8, 1971, 45440.

7. Donald Cronson to William H. Rehnquist, December 9, 1975, William H. Rehnquist Papers, box 107, Hoover Institution, Stanford University.

8. William H. Rehnquist to Donald Cronson, December 17, 1975, Rehnquist Papers, box 107.

9. Saul Brenner, "The Memos of Supreme Court Law Clerk William Rehnquist: Conservative Tracts, or Mirrors of His Justice's Mind?" *Judicature* 76, no. 2 (August/September 1992): 81, 77.

10. William Rehnquist, "Who Writes Decisions of the Supreme Court?" *U.S. News and World Report*, December 13, 1957, 74, 75.

11. "'Sway' of Clerks on Court Cited," *New York Times*, December 10, 1957, 23.

12. William D. Rogers, "Do Law Clerks Wield Power in Supreme Court Cases?" *U.S. News and World Report*, February 21, 1958, 114.

13. Alexander M. Bickel, "The Court: An Indictment Analyzed," *New York Times*, April 27, 1958, 6.

14. John C. Stennis, Speech on the Senate Floor (May 6, 1958), reprinted in "Investigate Supreme Court's 'Law Clerk' System?" *U.S. News and World Report*, May 16, 1958, 117.

15. "Stennis Is Wary of Court's Clerks," *New York Times*, May 7, 1958, 27.

16. William H. Rehnquist to Robert H. Jackson, undated, Robert H. Jackson Papers, box 165, Manuscript Division, Library of Congress.

17. William H. Rehnquist to William S. Eggeling, April 22, 1983, Rehnquist Papers, box 113.

18. David J. Garrow, "The Supreme Court and *The Brethren,*" *Constitutional Commentary* 18 (Summer 2001): 55.

19. R. Ted Cruz, "In Memoriam: William H. Rehnquist," *Harvard Law Review* 119, no. 1 (2005): 16; William H. Rehnquist to the Conference, November 9, 1972, Rehnquist Papers, box 5.

20. William H. Rehnquist to Edward A. Potts, May 29, 1973, Rehnquist Papers, box 8.

21. Dale E. Bennett and Joseph J. Baiamonte to William H. Rehnquist, October 2, 1974, Rehnquist Papers, box 8; Benno C. Schmidt Jr. to William H. Rehnquist, September 13, 1973, Rehnquist Papers, box 8.

22. Abraham D. Sofaer to William H. Rehnquist, December 17, 1973, Rehnquist Papers, box 8.

23. William H. Rehnquist to Abraham D. Sofaer, January 4, 1974, Rehnquist Papers, box 8.

24. William H. Rehnquist to Alden Rehnquist, August 30, 1974, Rehnquist Papers, box 8; William H. Rehnquist to John E. Cribbet, September 25, 1973, Rehnquist Papers, box 8.

25. Janet E. Barnes to Leonard G. Brown III, July 2, 1996, Rehnquist Papers, box 145.

26. Robert W. Wild to William H. Rehnquist, June 14, 1979, Rehnquist Papers, box 113; William H. Rehnquist to Robert W. Wild, June 29, 1979, Rehnquist Papers, box 113. Mayo did not secure a Supreme Court clerkship with Rehnquist nor any other justice. William H. Rehnquist to Randall P. Bezanson, September 12, 1980, Rehnquist Papers, box 113.

27. Louis B. Goldman to Donald Rumsfeld, September 27, 1974, Rehnquist Papers, box 8; William H. Rehnquist to Louis B. Goldman, November 8, 1974, Rehnquist Papers, box 8.

28. "Nancy J. Bregstein Memorandum on Interview," September 9, 1976, Lewis F. Powell, Jr. Papers, box 129a, Powell Archives, Washington and Lee University School of Law.

29. Artemus Ward and David L. Weiden, *Sorcerers' Apprentices: 100 Years of Law Clerks at the United States Supreme Court* (New York: New York University Press, 2006), 72–73.

30. William H. Rehnquist to John E. Cribbet, September 25, 1973, Rehnquist Papers, box 8.

31. Ward and Weiden, *Sorcerers' Apprentices,* 77.

32. Ibid., 81.

33. Todd C. Peppers and Christopher Zorn, "Law Clerk Influence on Supreme Court Decision Making: An Empirical Analysis," *DePaul University Law Review* 57 (2008): 51; Ward and Weiden, *Sorcerers' Apprentices,* 83–84, 104–5; Todd C. Peppers, *Courtiers of the Marble Palace: The Rise and Influence of the Supreme Court Law Clerk*

(Stanford, Calif.: Stanford University Press, 2006), 31–36; Corey A. Ditslear and Lawrence Baum, "Selection of Law Clerks and Polarization in the U.S. Supreme Court," *Journal of Politics* 63, no. 3 (2001): 869–85; David G. Leitch, "In Memoriam: William H. Rehnquist," Harvard Law Review 19, no. 1 (2005): 22.

34. William H. Rehnquist to Craig M. Bradley, October 26, 1981, Rehnquist Papers, box 113.

35. Ward and Weiden, *Sorcerers' Apprentices,* 92.

36. Tony Mauro, "Rehnquist Won't Discuss Minority Clerks," *USA Today,* June 10, 1998.

37. Tony Mauro, "Rehnquist: Diversity a Grad Pool Function," *USA Today,* December 8, 1998.

38. Peppers, *Courtiers of the Marble Palace,* 24.

39. *Rosen v. California,* 416 U.S. 924 (1974); William H. Rehnquist to Harry A. Blackmun, March 14, 1974, Rehnquist Papers, box 7.

40. Landis Cox Best to William H. Rehnquist, February 9, 1996, Rehnquist Papers, box 145.

41. Dean Colson to William H. Rehnquist, September 28, 1981, Rehnquist Papers, box 113; William H. Rehnquist to Dean Colson, October 1, 1981, Rehnquist Papers, box 113.

42. Michael J. Meehan to William H. Rehnquist, October 24, 1980, Rehnquist Papers, box 113.

43. *Kleindienst v. Mandel,* 408 U.S. 753 (1972); Allen Snyder to William H. Rehnquist, December 16, 1971, Rehnquist Papers, box 26.

44. William H. Rehnquist to Warren E. Burger, June 8, 1973, Blackmun Papers, box 1374.

45. William H. Rehnquist to Warren E. Burger, June 11, 1974, Rehnquist Papers, box 8.

46. William H. Rehnquist to Warren E. Burger, June 12, 1974, Rehnquist Papers, box 8.

47. "Preliminary Memo," *Gooch v. Skelly Oil Co.,* 73–221, October 21, 1974, Harry A. Blackmun Papers, box 822, Manuscript Division, Library of Congress; Robert I. Richter to the cert pool, October 31, 1973, Rehnquist Papers, box 7.

48. Rehnquist, *Supreme Court,* 264–65.

49. William H. Rehnquist to Pool Memo Law Clerks, February 17, 1989, Blackmun Papers, box 1374;. William H. Rehnquist to Cert Pool Law Clerks, February 13, 1996 Rehnquist Papers, box 145.

50. Warren E. Burger to the Conference, January 25, 1972. Rehnquist Papers, box 24.

51. *Milton v. Wainwright,* 407 U.S. 371 (1972); *Massiah v. United States,* 377 U.S. 201 (1964); Michael J. Meehan to William H. Rehnquist, January 12, 1972, Rehnquist Papers, box 24.

52. William H. Rehnquist to Lewis F. Powell, June 8, 1973, Blackmun Papers, box 1374.

53. Maureen E. Mahoney, "In Memoriam: William H. Rehnquist," *Harvard Law Review* 119, no. 1 (2005): 25; Richard W. Garnett, "Tennis and Top Buttons," *Slate,* September 4, 2005, http://www.slate.com/id/2125686/.

54. Leitch, "In Memoriam," 23; Garnett, "Tennis and Top Buttons."

55. *Kraft General Foods v. Iowa Dept. of Revenue,* 505 U.S. 71 (1992); Molly McUsic to Harry A. Blackmun, May 26, 1992, Blackmun Papers, box 1556.

56. Garnett, "Tennis and Top Buttons."

57. *Brennan v. Arnheim and Neely,* 410 U.S. 512 (1973); Robert W. Wild to William H. Rehnquist, February 21, 1973, Rehnquist Papers, box 41; William H. Rehnquist to Potter Stewart, February 22, 1973, Rehnquist Papers, box 41. Rehnquist had initially told Stewart: "I voted the other way at Conference, and will wait to see what else is written; I do not rule out the possibility of joining your quite persuasive opinion." William H. Rehnquist to Potter Stewart, February 2, 1973, Rehnquist Papers, box 41.

58. *Peters v. Kiff,* 407 U.S. 493 (1972); *Weber v. Aetna Cas. & Sur. Co.,* 406 U.S. 164 (1972); Allen R. Snyder to William H. Rehnquist, April 28, 1972, Rehnquist Papers. box 42.

59. *Frank Johnson v. Louisiana,* 406 U.S. 356 (1972); *Apodaca v. Oregon,* 406 U.S. 404 (1972); Allen R. Snyder to William H. Rehnquist, March 31, 1972, Rehnquist Papers, box 18.

60. *Gilligan v. Morgan,* 413 U.S. 1 (1973); L. Gordon Harriss to William H. Rehnquist, undated, Rehnquist Papers, box 41.

61. *Miller v. California,* 413 U.S. 15 (1973); Allen R. Snyder to William H. Rehnquist, May 22, 1972, Rehnquist Papers, box 20.

62. *Brunette Machine Works v. Kockum Industries,* 406 U.S. 706 (1972); Michael J. Meehan to William H. Rehnquist, May 30, 1972, Rehnquist Papers, box 24.

63. *Pipefitters Union No 562 v. United States,* 407 U.S. 385 (1972); "Re: No. 70–74 —*Pipefitters Union v. United States,*" February 22, 1972, Rehnquist Papers, box 20.

64. William H. Rehnquist to Warren E. Burger, November 27, 1972, Rehnquist Papers, box 5.

65. Rehnquist, *Supreme Court,* 300; Adam Liptak and Todd S. Purdum, "As Clerk for Rehnquist, Nominee Stood Out for Conservative Rigor," *New York Times,* July 31, 2005.

66. Leitch, "In Memoriam," 23.

67. *United States v. Little Lake Misere Land Company,* 412 U.S. 580 (1973); "United States v. Little Lake Misere Land Company," Draft Concurrence, June 12, 1973, Rehnquist Papers, box 41.

68. *Socialist Labor Party v. Gilligan,* 406 U.S. 583 (1972); *Rescue Army v. Municipal Court of Los Angeles,* 331 U.S. 549 (1947); William H. Jeffress Jr., "No 70–21 *Socialist Labor Party* Some Notes on WHR Opinion," March 28, 1972, Rehnquist Papers, box 18.

69. *Kissinger v. Reporters Committee for Freedom of the Press,* 445 U.S. 136 (1980); *Forsham v. Harris,* 445 U.S. 169 (1980); William H. Rehnquist to Maureen Mahoney, October 16, 1980, Rehnquist Papers, box 113.

70. Kathleen Moriarty, Nancy Marder, Robert Schapiro, and Peter Yu to William H. Rehnquist, September 12, 1991, Rehnquist Papers, box 135.

71. William H. Rehnquist, Allen R. Snyder, Frederick W. Lambert, and Michael J. Meehan to The White Chambers, February 16, 1972, Rehnquist Papers, box 5.

72. William H. Rehnquist to Warren E. Burger, September 24, 1973, Rehnquist Papers, box 5.

73. William H. Rehnquist to Warren E. Burger, September 24, 1976, Rehnquist Papers, box 106; William H. Rehnquist to the Conference, October 14, 1976, Rehnquist Papers, box 106.

74. Warren E. Burger to William H. Rehnquist, October 6, 1977, Rehnquist Papers, box 106; William H. Rehnquist to the Conference, December 3, 1975, Rehnquist Papers, box 106.

75. Song lyrics, undated, Rehnquist Papers, box 106.

76. Cruz, "In Memoriam," 16; Garnett, "Tennis and Top Buttons"; Leitch, "In Memoriam," 23–24.

77. Notation of fax from Karen Branch to William H. Rehnquist, January 13, 1995, Rehnquist Papers, box 144; Ronald Tenpas to William H. Rehnquist, February 18, 1996, Rehnquist Papers, box 145; Jack Mason to William H. Rehnquist, November 30, 1995, Rehnquist Papers, box 145.

78. Donald B. Ayer to William H. Rehnquist, October 27, 1980, Rehnquist Papers, box 113; William H. Rehnquist to Donald B. Ayer, October 30, 1980, Rehnquist Papers, box 113; John G. Roberts Jr., "In Memoriam: William Rehnquist," *Harvard Law Review* 119, no. 1 (2005): 1.

79. Cruz, "In Memoriam," 16; Leitch, "In Memoriam," 24.

80. Roberts, "In Memoriam," 2.

81. Mahoney, "In Memoriam," 27.

82. James A. Strain to William H. Rehnquist, May 31, 1983, Rehnquist Papers, box 113.

83. Leitch, "In Memoriam," 22.

84. Leitch, "In Memoriam," 22; Cruz, "In Memoriam," 16.

85. Terrence G. Perris to William H. Rehnquist, October 11, 2004, Rehnquist Papers, box 171.

86. John M. Nannes to William H. Rehnquist, March 28, 1991, Rehnquist Papers, box 135.

87. Mahoney, "In Memoriam," 26.

88. Bruce R. Braun to William H. Rehnquist, March 17, 1992, Rehnquist Papers, box 144; William H. Rehnquist to Bruce R. Braun, April 8, 1992, Rehnquist Papers, box 144.

89. Ronald Tenpas to William H. Rehnquist, February 18, 1996, Rehnquist Papers, box 145; William H. Rehnquist to Charles Wilson, February 28, 1996, Rehnquist Papers, box 145.

90. David G. Campbell to William H. Rehnquist, November 8, 1995, Rehnquist Papers, box 145; William H. Rehnquist to David G. Campbell, November 24, 1995, Rehnquist Papers, box 145.

91. Robert W. Bennett to William H. Rehnquist, September 24, 1974, Rehnquist Papers, box 8; William H. Rehnquist to Robert W. Bennett, October 1, 1974, Rehnquist Papers, box 8.

92. Simon H. Rifkind to William H. Rehnquist, November 7, 1973, Rehnquist Papers, box 8; William H. Rehnquist to Simon H. Rifkind, November 19, 1973, Rehnquist Papers, box 8; Frederick O. Robertshaw to William H. Rehnquist, November 15, 1974, Rehnquist Papers, box 8; William H. Rehnquist to Frederick O. Robertshaw, November 19, 1974, Rehnquist Papers, box 8.

93. Donald B. Ayer to William French Smith, December 4, 1980, Rehnquist Papers, box 113.

94. Maureen Mahoney to William H. Rehnquist, June 7, 1994, Rehnquist Papers, box 144.

95. Robert W. Bennett to William H. Rehnquist, September 24, 1974, Rehnquist Papers, box 8; William H. Rehnquist to Simon H. Rifkind, November 19, 1973, Rehnquist Papers, box 8; Roger C. Cramton to William H. Rehnquist, September 5, 1975, Rehnquist Papers, box 107.

96. *EEOC v. Wyoming,* 460 U.S. 226 (1983); *National League of Cities v. Usery,* 426 U.S. 833 (1976); William S. Eggeling to William H. Rehnquist, April 13, 1983, Rehnquist Papers, box 113.

97. *Railroad Retirement Bd. v. Fritz,* 449 U.S. 166 (1980); *Massachusetts v. Murgia,* 427 U.S. 307 (1976); William H. Rehnquist to William S. Eggeling, December 9, 1980, Rehnquist Papers, box 113.

98. Craig M. Bradley to William H. Rehnquist, August 23, 1994, Rehnquist Papers, box 144; Gary Born to William H. Rehnquist, May 22, 1996, Rehnquist Papers, box 145.

99. Lowell Gordon Harriss to William H. Rehnquist, May 17, 1996, Rehnquist Papers, box 145; William H. Rehnquist to Lowell Gordon Harriss, May 28, 1996, Rehnquist Papers, box 145.

100. *Grutter v. Bollinger,* 539 U.S. 306 (2003); Mahoney, "In Memoriam," 25.

101. *Doctor's Associates v. Casarotto,* 517 U.S. 681 (1996); Janet Barnes to William H. Rehnquist, February 15, 1996, Rehnquist Papers, box 145; handwritten notation on letter from Janet Barnes to William H. Rehnquist, February 15, 1996, Rehnquist Papers, box 145; Janet Barnes to William H. Rehnquist, February 16, 1996, Rehnquist Papers, box 145; Mark R. Kravitz to William H. Rehnquist, February 23, 1996, Rehnquist Papers, box 145.

102. William H. Rehnquist to Cecily Neibank Noelker, September 14, 2004, Rehnquist Papers, box 171.

TODD C. PEPPERS

The Modern Clerkship

Justice Ruth Bader Ginsburg and Her Law Clerks

I f read in order, the previous essays provide a series of snapshots of the slowly changing clerkship institution. As the decades passed and the number of law clerks rose, the justices began giving their clerks more substantive job duties. First, legal research and opinion editing. Then the review of cert petitions. Finally, the proverbial Rubicon was crossed, and the clerkship institution forever changed as law clerks began preparing the first draft of majority, concurring, and dissenting opinions.[1]

As the professional staffs of the justices grew into what Associate Justice Lewis F. Powell Jr. nicknamed "nine little law firms," the unique personal bonds and mentoring relationships between justices and clerks have faded. This is not to say that modern law clerks do not interact socially with their justices or remain in contact after their clerkships. A careful study of the history of the clerkship institution, however, suggests that there is no longer the blurring of the line between law clerk and surrogate family member as one found in the clerkship practices of a Felix Frankfurter or Hugo Black. Clerks no longer spend a year in the "noble nursery of humanity," and the devotion and absolute fidelity of past generations of law clerks appear to be relics of a distant and quaint age.

If there is a representative example of the "modern" Supreme Court clerkship, it can be found in the chambers of Justice Ruth Bader Ginsburg. The former law professor, women's rights activist, and federal appeals court judge has been on the Supreme Court bench since 1993. In August 2009, I had the unique privilege of spending one hour interviewing Justice Ginsburg on her clerkship employment practices. My understanding of her clerkship model has been supplemented by correspondence with a few former Ginsburg law clerks as well as various written accounts by other former Ginsburg clerks. The account that emerges below is one of a staff that is fully engaged in the work that

392 | TODO C. PEPPERS

passes through chambers, but carefully supervised and held to the justice's exacting standards.

The Selection of the Ginsburg Law Clerks

Like most current justices, Justice Ginsburg herself does not review the hundreds of applications of prospective law clerks. Instead, she relies upon the "good judgment" of Columbia Law School dean David Schizer, himself a former Ginsburg law clerk, to fill one of the clerkship slots. "He will not bother me with five or six applications, but he will recommend one person—usually someone who has completed a clerkship." Regarding her selection criteria, Justice Ginsburg stated that "I don't want the brightest person in the graduating class; I want someone who has had a year of a clerkship." Justice Ginsburg will then meet with Dean Schizer's recommended applicant before making a hiring decision.[2]

For the remaining clerkship slots, Justice Ginsburg states that she "relies mostly on certain Court of Appeals judges for giving me an appraisal [of applicants]." Justice Ginsburg conceded that recommendations are not always reliable since some judges "exaggerate" the abilities of their clerks, but she added that there are other federal appeals court judges—such as William A. Fletcher of the United States Court of Appeals for the Ninth Circuit and David S. Tatel of the United States Court of Appeals for the District of Columbia Circuit—in whose recommendations she is confident.[3] Relying upon "feeder court judges" for law clerks is a well-established practice followed by all members of the present Court, and studies have suggested that the justices depend on federal appeals court judges to guarantee both the competence and ideological compatibility of their clerks.[4]

Until his death in 2010, Justice Ginsburg had her "in-house reader" (namely, her late husband and Georgetown law professor Martin Ginsburg) review the finalists' writing samples. Professor Ginsburg was familiar with the writing style that Justice Ginsburg prefers, and he tried to select those candidates who would be "someone that would be easy for me to deal with," stated the justice. "Some young lawyers tend to be more elaborate, and my husband will spot them." According to an interview with Professor Ginsburg, he looked for applicants who evidenced "[c]lean writing and non-complexity. I do not look for obvious consistency with RBG's writing, but I do hope for a clue whether the student likely will absorb and reflect RBG's writing."

Since the late 1960s, a federal appeals court clerkship has become a de facto requirement for a Supreme Court clerkship—a practice Justice Ginsburg herself follows. When asked why she prefers applicants with prior clerkship experience, Justice Ginsburg replied that it provides her with an "an appraisal of the applicant. Explained the justice: "A number of law clerks look very good on paper, but they didn't work out—mainly because they are terrific issue spotters, but they are lacking in a certain judgment and common sense. [This is a deficient that you really can't spot] just from their performance in law school."

Justice Ginsburg interviews the finalists, but she neither has a standard set of questions to ask nor routinely poses substantive questions about the law. "I don't quiz them to see how well prepared they are," stated the justice. "Many of them are [well prepared], so they try to work in 'your opinion in such-and-such.'" For the justice, the interview is designed to get to know the applicant. "I interview so few that I will have certain questions in my own mind about the person's background."

Former Ginsburg law clerk Kate Andrias (October term 2006) keenly remembers her interview with the justice, which she describes as a "wonderful experience."

> Even if I hadn't been hired, however, I would have treasured the chance to speak with the Justice for an extended period of time. We discussed a range of topics, including our shared interest in France (where my husband grew up and where her daughter spends a significant amount of time); her experiences as a litigator and as a woman in the legal profession; articles I had published and work I had done as a researcher for a professor; and a few recent cases of the Court. She did not ask specific legal questions, but I do recall discussing substantive legal issues during the conversation.

When asked if there is a particular type of applicant personality toward which she gravitates, Justice Ginsburg stated, "number one, they have to show respect for my secretaries." She further explained:

> There was one law clerk applicant who came to interview with me—top rating at Harvard—who treated my secretaries with disdain. As if they were just minions. So that is one very important thing—how you deal with my secretaries. They are not hired help. As I tell my clerks, "if push came to shove, I could do your work—but I can't do without my secretaries."

Concluded Justice Ginsburg: "I try to avoid the arrogant type."

In recent years, the Supreme Court justices have been criticized for a lack of diversity in their clerkship hiring.[5] While Justice Ginsburg hires more female and minority candidates than other justices, she still selects her clerks from a small handful of elite law schools (the majority of her clerks come from Columbia, Yale, or Harvard). Justice Ginsburg conceded that she does not make "a deliberate attempt" to pick applicants from law schools not traditionally represented in the law clerk corps, but the justice made it equally clear that a degree from a lesser law school does not disqualify a candidate—a fact evident in a few of her law clerks' educational backgrounds.[6]

As noted above, social scientists and legal scholars have written about the ideological harmony between modern justices and their clerks—a consistent pattern that suggests that the justices are using an ideological litmus test to pick their clerks. I asked Justice Ginsburg if she prefers to have clerks from across the ideological spectrum. She replied that she doesn't try to get such a mixture of preferences, but that "it sometimes happens." Former law clerks dismiss the suggestion that the justice applies an ideological litmus test, and it does appear that she is not deterred when the applications of potential law clerks manifest evidence of more conservative preferences, such as membership in the Federalist Society. "One of my best clerks was a Federalist Society member," observed the justice.

Given the 2009 confirmation hearings of Justice Sonia Sotomayor, I asked Justice Ginsburg if she herself started thinking about how she would select and use her law clerks during her Supreme Court confirmation hearings. "There really wasn't a serious question about my getting confirmed, because there was a bipartisan spirit prevailing and I was the beneficiary of their [Congress's] rebounding from what happened to Justice Thomas," remarked the justice. "So my hearings were rather boring, and there wasn't much doubt that I was going to be confirmed. So I started—after I got done filing the endless paperwork and forms and Senate questionnaire—I did think about law clerks."

While some justices have a clerk serve a second year as a "senior" or supervisory clerk, Justice Ginsburg traditionally hires clerks for one term. "During my first year here I had somebody for two years," recalled the justice, "but it didn't work out and I decided I wasn't going to do that anymore." The firm, one-year rule has the practical effect of guaranteeing that poor personality matches are rectified yearly. "Sometimes you will have someone you love and wish that the person could stay forever, but sometimes you are happy [to see them go]." As for why permanent clerks haven't caught on at the Supreme Court (as they have in the lower federal courts), Justice Ginsburg replied that a Supreme Court clerkship is "very intense. It's like a treadmill that gets faster and faster, and I think that you reach a burnout point."

The Job Duties of the Ginsburg Law Clerks

The day-to-day clerkship practices adopted by Justice Ginsburg are based, at least in part, on the previous traditions of her predecessor, Associate Justice Byron White. "I had very good counsel," observed Justice Ginsburg. "It was Justice White who gave me his chambers manual, the operating procedures that he had written for his chambers early on and gave it over to his law clerks." The chambers manual was later revised by the Ginsburg clerks. The tradition of passing down the chambers manual to the newest member of the Court has been perpetuated by Justice Ginsburg. "The day that Sonia [Sotomayor] was sworn in, I was away . . . but I had delivered to her that chambers manual."

The job duties of the Ginsburg law clerks fall into three main categories: reviewing cert petitions, preparing bench memoranda, and writing opinion drafts. The "pooling" of cert petitions for review by the law clerks of the justices is a fairly new institutional practice,[7] and like all current justices save Samuel Alito, Justice Ginsburg is a member of the cert pool. Justice Ginsburg stated that—in the beginning of her tenure—it "certainly wasn't much of a decision" to become a member of the cert pool. "So much was new, and I didn't need one thing more."

Justice Ginsburg, however, also requires her law clerks to review the cert pool memos, either annotating them in the upper left-hand corner or preparing a new cover memo. When asked why she has adopted a second layer of review, the justice explained that the law clerks who write pool memoranda are writing for the entire Court, and that her law clerks—who are reviewing the cert pool memos—are writing *just* for her and her particular interests. In other words, "the trouble with some law clerks [in the cert pool] is that they don't appreciate that they are writing for the Court rather than for their justice."

The justice categorically rejected the argument that the cert pool results in the justices abdicating their responsibility of "deciding to decide." In an interview given shortly after her confirmation to the Court, Justice Ginsburg bluntly stated: "Some people outside the court seem to think the cert. pool makes it all a piece of cake—that the justices simply read and follow what the law clerks recommend . . . [b]ut, to quote Sportin' Life, 'It ain't necessarily so.'"[8]

When asked if she ever feared that law clerks in other chambers were playing fast and loose with the cert memoranda in order to achieve a certain result, Justice Ginsburg quickly replied, "Not for grants." A few former Ginsburg law clerks have suggested that their review of the cert pool memos does ferret out mediocrity as well as clumsy efforts at manipulation, adding that clerks who tried to use the cert pool process to improperly influence other chambers were quickly identified and their future memos more closely scrutinized.[9]

Justice Ginsburg's clerks prepare bench memoranda in some—but not all—cases. "The cases in the October sitting are one-issue cases and easy to grasp," the justice explained. "I don't need bench memos in those cases." Justice Ginsburg asks her clerks to prepare bench memoranda in the more complex cases. "Their job is to give me a road map through the case, and then I can read the briefs. They also tell me which of the green briefs [the amicus curiae briefs] I can skip." While it is not obligatory in the bench memos, the law clerks can also suggest questions to ask at oral argument. Finally, the clerks inevitably give a recommended disposition on the merits of the case. "They want to give it to me, and they always do, but it's not important."

Justice Ginsburg quickly dismissed my suggestion that the bench memoranda might provide a conduit through which law clerks exercise influence, pointing out that her memoranda are designed to merely provide guidance to the court file and to summarize facts. In sum, the bench memoranda are designed "to be a road map to everything that I have to read [in the case] and to bring the case to the front of my mind just before oral argument."

Former Ginsburg clerks are equally skeptical that, at least in the Ginsburg chambers, the bench memo holds much sway over the justice's decision making. Writes law clerk Jay Wexler (October term 1998): "Some Justices discuss the cases intensely with their clerks; RBG tended to do relatively little of that (clerks generally refer to the Justices by their initials). In fact, one of the great things about my job was that, being generally brilliant and having been on the bench for twenty years already, RBG basically knew everything already and could make up her mind about a case without much help from her clerks at all. This made the job fairly easy. Some Ginsburg clerks have been known to work sixteen hour days, but I honestly can't imagine what they spent their time doing."[10]

Of course, the most controversial aspect of the modern Supreme Court clerkship involves the role of law clerks in drafting opinions. Presently, all justices routinely have their clerks prepare the first drafts of majority, concurring, and dissenting opinions (recently retired justice John Paul Stevens was the only member of the Roberts Court who followed the now-outdated practice of preparing his own opinion drafts). Once Justice Ginsburg is assigned to write a majority opinion, she adheres to the following process:

> I read over everything . . . I start with the opinion below, I reread the briefs, the bench memo—if I had one—and then I write the opening.

It will be any where from one to three paragraphs. It's kind of a press release, and it will tell you what the issue was and how it was resolved. After the opening, I will make a detailed outline of how I think the opinion should go. I give that outline to the law clerk. Sometimes, to my delight, they will give me a draft that I can make my own version through heavy editing, but I don't have to redo it. I'd say it's a good year if I have two law clerks that have that skill. In most cases, what they do is always valuable to me—sometimes I see that my organization was not right and should be done another way. So their draft is always of use to me, but in most cases I can't simply take it over.

Softly laughing, Justice Ginsburg added that "mostly, I would like to do all of my own work so I could write all my opinions myself, but there is just not enough time to do that."

As the Ginsburg clerks begin the opinion-drafting process, they undoubtedly keep in mind what former Ginsburg law clerk David Schizer (October term 1994) calls the "chamber motto"—"Get it right and keep it tight." Getting an opinion "right" means not only a correct analysis of the law, but duly acknowledging and analyzing opposing points of view. Explains Schizer: law clerks are instructed to "[b]e scrupulously fair to counter-arguments—or, as the Justice puts it, 'don't sweep the other side's chess pieces off the table.'"[11]

Moreover, a "right and tight" opinion is one that Justice Ginsburg described as "spare" and plainly written, limited to "the essentials" and devoid of "decorations and deviations" as well as arcane Latin phrases. Justice Ginsburg joked that she has worked on her colleagues to stop using Latin phrases in their opinions. "We do not say 'collateral estoppel' or 'res judicata'; we say 'claim preclusion' and 'issue preclusion.' So if I've left a mark on the Court, it's the change [in opinion writing] to plain language."

When asked why she has pushed for plainer language, Justice Ginsburg spoke of the dangers of "jargon" used in articles across different disciplines (such as law or sociology) and the impact of said jargon on the reader. "I don't fool myself into thinking that I can write for a layman, but at least I can write for a Linda Greenhouse or for my dear friend Nina Totenberg, who is not a lawyer."

Former Ginsburg appeals court clerk David Post explains that, for the justice, "[l]anguage matters more than you can imagine . . . I've seen her agonize over individual words many times. Not terms of art, but adjectives." Adds Post: "It's very important to her to get every word to say exactly what she wants it to say, with all the connotations she wants."[12] His comments are echoed by former Supreme Court clerk Andrias, who observes: "Justice Ginsburg has a distinct writing style. As the year went on, we became increasingly familiar with it and tried to hew closely to it. She likes precise and direct writing; does not like lengthy introductory clauses; prefers some words to others; and does not like excessive footnotes. I recall that after another clerk and I completed our first writing assignment for her—a draft of an introduction to a book—she sat down with us and went over our draft line by line to explain her edits and her writing style."

The care and attention paid to the substance and style of a draft opinion does not end when the law clerk assigned to the case finishes the draft; after said clerk completes a draft, it is reviewed by the other clerks before it is given to Justice Ginsburg—a procedure suggested to her by Justice Sandra Day O'Connor after Justice Ginsburg had been on the Supreme Court bench for three years. "Every clerk will have a copy of my outline," stated Justice Ginsburg, "and they review each other's work" before submitting to the justice.

As with the bench memoranda, former Ginsburg law clerks reject the claims that law clerks wield influence over crafting constitutional law. Referring to the role of law clerks in drafting opinions as "not that big a deal," former clerk Wexler writes that "the boss would give us a detailed outline to work from and then, once we turned in our drafts, totally rewrite them. The best you could really hope for as a clerk is to get a little pet phrase or goofy word or other quirky something-or-other into the final opinion." As an example of a "quirky something-or-other," Wexler adds (tongue in cheek): "[T]here may or may not be one Ginsburg opinion from our term which, when read backwards, will summon the demon Beelzebub from the seventh level of hell to earth where he will horribly murder the entire human race."[13]

In discussing opinion writing with the justice, I shared former Hugo Black law clerk John P. Frank's lament that the color and distinctiveness of judicial opinions are drained away when law clerks get involved in the drafting pro-cess.[14] Justice Ginsburg agreed in part, with the caveat that "it depends on the justice. I can always tell a Scalia opinion, even if there is no name on it—he will make each opinion genuinely his own. His spicy style is not something that is a function of a clerk."[15]

The Work Habits of the Ginsburg Clerks

Justice Ginsburg said that her law clerks come into work on the weekend "when they need to," but added that "we are very flexible," and the clerks can leave work for weddings and religious holidays. An example of the justice's willingness to accommodate her law clerks' schedules is recounted by author Jeffrey Rosen:

> Soon after she joined the Court, I recalled, she had introduced herself, as new Justices traditionally do, by granting an interview to The Docket Sheet, a newsletter for Court employees. Toni House, the Court's public information officer, asked why she had agreed to a flexible schedule for one of her law clerks, David Post. Ginsburg replied that when Post applied for a [Court of Appeals] clerkship, he was caring for his two small children during the day, so that his wife could sustain a demanding job as an economist. "I thought, 'This is my dream of the way the world should be,'" Ginsburg enthused. 'When fathers take equal responsibility for the care of their children, that's when women will be truly liberated.'"[16]

The justice's flexibility in work hours extends to all of her clerks. "There's no such thing as "face time" in her chambers, explains former clerk Schizer, "and the hours are flexible for clerks. I got in early and went home early, while one of my co-clerks came in late and worked late."[17] The justice, however, has the reputation of being a night owl in regard to work. "She works through the night, she's there during the day. And it's just this bottomless energy," recalls Schizer. "It's quite remarkable."[18]

This flexibility extends to permitting clerks to observe events at the Court. Unlike the notorious Justice William O. Douglas, who punished his law clerks for watching oral argument (they responded by hiding behind a pillar in the courtroom), Justice Ginsburg stated that she "encourages" and "welcomes" her clerks to watch oral argument. In fact, the Ginsburg clerks divide up the cases in the different sittings, and the clerk assigned a specific case is required to watch oral argument.

The Personal Bonds between the Justice and Her Clerks

Former law clerks, journalists, and law professors often speak of Justice Ginsburg's reserved nature. According to former Ginsburg appeals court clerks Susan and David Williams, this quiet and dispassionate public face is but one aspect of a unique mentoring style: "As a mentor, she has exhibited two quite distinct qualities in great degree. First, she demands of herself and those around her adherence to a most exacting standard of analytical rigor. Second, she offers a depth of warmth and kindness grounded in a sensitive emotional awareness. It is her combination of these qualities that, to us, is the most striking aspect of her mentoring."[19]

The justice's law clerks can be initially thrown by her deliberate manner of thinking. "[U]nlike most people, she carefully ponders each sentence, and so she often pauses at length before responding to a question or comment," the authors explain. "For trepidatious new clerks, this conversational style can be initially unsettling, as they might read disapproval into her silence and wonder whether they have said the wrong thing." In point of fact, "her pausing is a sign not of disapproval but of respect, as she carefully considers the words of clerks, just as she carefully considers everything in life."[20]

Regarding the more hidden, emotional aspect of the justice's mentoring style, the former clerks add that "[b]ecause Justice Ginsburg is a private person, she does not wear her warmth on her sleeve, and yet the warmth is there, with a depth that is sometimes startling." As an example of how her affection can surprise her clerks, Susan Williams recounts an instance during the justice's Supreme Court confirmation hearings:

> During the preparation for Justice Ginsburg's confirmation hearings, I arrived early and waited in the hall outside the conference room. Shortly, the other participants—Important People from the executive department and the academy—also arrived. And then Justice Ginsburg arrived, and we waited her pleasure. Ignoring for the moment the others in the hallway, Justice Ginsburg came straight over to me, stood on tiptoe to reach me and kissed my cheek. That moment is frozen in tableau in my mind: this tiny woman, radiating simultaneously enormous warmth and power, filling the hallway with her presence, briefly ignoring Important People so as to make contact with a distinctly unimportant ex-clerk, so justly confident in her judicial stature that she could publicly display the human tenderness that deeply grounds her.[21]

Their comments are seconded by former clerk Andrias. "Justice Ginsburg has a reputation for being reserved. This is true," concedes Andrias. "But she is also warm and engaging once you get to know her and she has a wonderful and surprising sense of humor."

Asked to describe the relationship that she has with her clerks, Justice Ginsburg simply replied that "[t]hey are my family for the year that they are with me." During past terms, the law clerks and secretaries routinely celebrated birthdays and special anniversaries with the justice, where they drank tea and enjoyed homemade cakes made by Martin Ginsburg. And the justice's law clerks have accompanied her to the opera, to local productions of Gilbert and Sullivan, and to the Kennedy Center to see the Washington Opera's Young

Artists Performance series. It was a local high school performance of a Gilbert and Sullivan operetta that Wexler points to as proof that Justice Ginsburg is not as serious as Court outsiders maintain: "[She] played along with the director's invitation to come up to the stage during intermission to dance with some other cast and audience members. The sight of a Supreme Court Justice on stage twirling around with her hands in the air to a goofy song next to a spinning six year old girl is not one that I can soon forget."[22]

During the 2009 interview, Justice Ginsburg proudly pointed out that her husband was a "master chef." She stated that "one of the highpoints of the year is a dinner that he makes for the law clerks—usually at the end of the first setting." "We eat what looks good in the market that day," added Professor Ginsburg, "usually prepared in an Italian (or less often a French) manner." Former clerks David and Susan Williams, however, quickly correct any impression that this is a perfunctory and rote affair—"the clerks generally feel feted at these dinners in the way that a visiting dignitary would."[23]

The law clerks' contact with the late Martin Ginsburg was not limited to the annual dinners, and for former law clerk Heather Elliott (October term 2001), "perhaps my favorite thing about my clerkship year is the glimpse it gave of RBG's wonderful marriage to Marty." She explains as follows:

> I remember one time I came into her office quite late, after they had been to some event downstairs, and she was working while Marty sat reading. I started to talk to her about the research I had done, and while I was talking, Marty got up and walked toward us. I started freaking out in my mind—"is what I am saying that stupid? What is he coming over here for?!"—only to watch him come up to RBG, fix her collar (which had somehow fallen into disarray), and then go back to his book. The comfortable intimacy of that moment was something I will always remember.

Former law clerk Margo Schlanger (October terms 1993 and 1994) also spoke of the Ginsburg marriage, commenting that it provided a "model" for her law clerks. "Her relationship with Marty was a model to us all—a model of a marriage of equals who helped each other."[24]

The justice monitors both the professional and personal accomplishments of her law clerks, including additions to the extended law clerk family. "I have a supply of 'grand clerk' t-shirts for when they become parents," stated Ginsburg. The shirts bear the words "RBG Grand-clerk" and the seal of the United States Supreme Court. Former law clerks have publicly stated that the justice stays in touch with her clerks and their families through a stream of steady notes and in-chambers visits. Justice Ginsburg "is very lovely to her law clerks," comments Schlanger. "She cares about our families and knows what is going on in our lives." As an example, Schlanger recounts that both Justice Ginsburg and Schlanger's mother were diagnosed with colon cancer in the same month. "The justice was very kind to me. She helped me get my mother to see her (RGB's) personal doctor, which would not have happened without the justice's help." Schlanger added that during her mother's illness, the justice periodically wrote her notes to check on her.[25]

Moreover, the former clerks monitor the justice as well and are quick to offer support during health crises. "Some of us were angry with her [when the justice worked from her hospital bed while being treated for colorectal cancer], but we were wrong," recalls former clerk Schizer. "We kept telling her to slow down, we kept telling her to take it easy. I sent her a couple of fiction books to read, and she wouldn't have any of it. She just bore down and went through the treatment, treated it as part of her work."[26]

Historically, the justices have held annual or semi-annual reunions for their former clerks. In her first years on the Supreme Court, Justice Ginsburg and her clerks had annual reunions until the corps of former law clerks grew too large (Justice Ginsburg includes her clerks from the D.C. Circuit Court of Appeals in the reunions as well). Now the reunions are held every five years. Unlike the black-tie affairs held by earlier generations of Black, Frankfurter, and Holmes law clerks, the reunions for Ginsberg's clerks are decidedly more relaxed and inclusive. "The Ginsburg reunions have always been distinctive for welcoming family members and children," explains Merritt. "Rather than holding formal dinners, the reunions usually follow a buffet/dinner reception format, with foods appropriate for children as well as adults. This allows children to enjoy the event without their parents worrying too much about keeping them still."

Conclusion

Whether law clerks should be as involved in the substantive work of the Supreme Court is a debate best reserved for another day. Like it or not, the "modern" clerkship institution is a reality. That being said, a case can be made that Justice Ginsburg has crafted and honed a clerkship model that best placates those Court scholars who fear pernicious influence by a small cadre of unscrupulous clerks. The law clerks are carefully supervised by a justice who provides exacting instructions, careful editing, and a willingness to put aside the clerks' work product and start anew. Memoranda generated by the cert pool clerks is subjected to an additional round of review, and within chambers the clerks review the draft opinions crafted by their fellow Ginsburg clerks. The work performed by the clerks is done in an atmosphere where the demands of dispassionate intellectual rigor coexist with a mentor's respect and genuine warmth.

Notes

The information in this essay is primarily based on my August 14, 2009, interview with Associate Justice Ruth Bader Ginsburg. Additional information comes from written correspondence with Georgetown law professor Martin D. Ginsburg and former Ginsburg law clerks Kate Andrias, Heather Elliott, Goodwin Liu, and Deborah Merritt.

1. Of course, there are additional responsibilities assigned to law clerks, from emergency death penalty stays to working on a specific justice's circuit duties. In this essay, however, I focus on the three major tasks assigned to the "modern" law clerk.

2. Justice Ginsburg added that she had a similar arrangement with former Harvard Law School dean Elena Kagan.

3. Both Fletcher and Tatel were appointed to the federal bench by President Bill Clinton, with Judge Tatel replacing Justice Ginsburg upon her nomination to the Supreme Court.

4. William E. Nelson, Harvey Rishikof, I. Scott Messinger, and Michael Jo, "The Liberal Tradition of the Supreme Court Clerkship: Its Rise, Fall, and Reincarnation?" *Vanderbilt Law Review* 62, no. 6 (2009): 1749–1814; Corey A. Ditslear and Lawrence Baum, "Selection of Law Clerks and Polarization in the U.S. Supreme Court," *Journal of Politics* 63, no. 3 (2001): 869–85.

5. See Tony Mauro, "Corps of Clerks Lacking in Diversity," *USA Today,* March 13, 1998; Mauro, "Only 1 New High Court Clerk Is a Minority," *USA Today,* September 10, 1998.

6. At least one on occasion, the justice has demonstrated a willingness to look for diversity regarding the age of her clerks. Typically, the modern Supreme Court law clerk arrives at the Supreme Court only a year or two removed from law school. During October term 1996, however, one of the justice's law clerks was W. William Hodes, a law professor in his early fifties who had once taken a class from the justice when she taught at Rutgers Law School. See Laurie Asseo, "Former Ginsburg Student Becomes Her Law Clerk," *Salt Lake City Deseret News,* June 8, 1996.

7. For a thorough discussion on the creation of the cert pool, see Artemus Ward and David L. Weiden, *Sorcerers' Apprentices: 100 Years of Law Clerks at the United States Supreme Court* (New York: New York University Press, 2006), 117–24.

8. Associated Press, "Ginsburg: Court Agenda Not Determined by Clerks," January 3, 1994.

9. Todd C. Peppers, *Courtiers of the Marble Palace: The Rise and Influence of the Supreme Court Law Clerk* (Stanford, Calif.: Stanford University Press, 2006), 198–99.

10. Jay Wexler, "Clerkin' for RBG." http://holyhullabaloos.typepad.com/files/clerkin2.pdf.

11. David Schizer, "Former Law Clerks to Justice Ginsburg Reminisce," Columbia Law School website, n.d., http://www.law.columbia.edu/law_school/communications/reports/winter2004/clerks.

12. David Post, quoted in Jeffrey Rosen, "The New Look of Liberalism on the Court," *New York Times Magazine,* October 5, 1997.

13. Wexler, "Clerkin' for RBG."

14. In discussing the role of Chief Justice Fred Vinson's law clerks in drafting Supreme Court opinions, John Frank argued that the practical result was that said opinions suffered from a lack of judicial personality, such as "the Holmes epigram, the Black way with facts, the Frankfurter vocabulary, the Brandeis footnote, the Stone pragmatism." John P. Frank, "Fred Vinson and the Chief Justiceship," *University of Chicago Law Review* 21, no. 1 (Autumn 1954): 212–46, at 224.

15. For an interesting take on the effect that law clerks have on the language of Supreme Court opinions, see Paul J. Wahlbeck, James F. Spriggs II, and Lee Sigelman, "Ghostwriters on the Court? A Stylistic Analysis of U.S. Supreme Court Opinion Drafts," *American Politics Research* 30, no. 2 (2002): 166–92.

16. Rosen, "New Look of Liberalism."

17. Schizer, "Former Law Clerks."

18. David Schizer, "Justice Ginsburg's Cancer Surgery," CNN Transcript, February 5, 2009.

19. Susan H. and David C. Williams, "Sense and Sensibility: Justice Ruth Bader Ginsburg's Mentoring Style as a Blend of Rigor and Compassion," *University of Hawaii Law Review* 20 (Winter 1998): 589–593, at 589.

20. Ibid., 590.

21. Ibid., 592.

22. Wexler, "Clerkin' for RBG."

23. Williams and Williams, "Sense and Sensibility," 591–92.

24. Margo Schlanger, interview with author.

25. Schlanger, interview.

26. Schizer, CNN Transcript.

Afterword

As soon as Supreme Court nominees are confirmed and sworn in, they tend to recede from the headlines as they immerse themselves in the mainly private work of the nation's highest court. But soon after Justice Samuel Alito Jr. was sworn in early in 2006, he made news again with the law clerks he had hired. One in particular, Adam Ciongoli, drew attention because he had been a key counselor to former attorney general John Ashcroft. Beyond the specifics of whom Alito had hired, the attention paid to this once-unremarkable personnel decision was something of a milestone in the history of Supreme Court law clerks.

The clerks themselves had become news, yanking them from their preferred position in the shadows. After decades of debate over the role clerks play in the work of the justices, a seeming consensus had been reached, consciously or not. Supreme Court law clerks are undeniably important, important enough to make note of, either as a window into the justice's thinking or as an account of who will have the justice's ear for the next year. This is a breakthrough in telling the full story of the Supreme Court.

The book you are holding, a remarkable and revealing collection of profiles of the clerks hired by some of the Court's best-known justices, is also part of that breakthrough. (The separate books on the law clerks authored in 2006 by the editors of this collection were, likewise, important markers of this trend.)

Ever since I began covering the Supreme Court thirty-one years ago, it has seemed clear to me that law clerks either understate or exaggerate their significance to one degree or other. But the cumulative import of the essays in this book seems to get it just right; law clerks are crucial, if not downright indispensable, to the work of the nation's highest court. This book lays to rest the notion that law clerks are minor players in the Court's work, mere office helpmates or stenographers of the justices' articulated views. It reveals the many dimensions of the relationship between clerk and justice: emotional support, affirmation, error correction, sounding board, editing, intelligence gathering, to name just a few. Any one of these roles would be significant; to have all of them described in rich, personal detail as they are in this book fills out the picture of how important the law clerks really are.

Justice William O. Douglas, this book reminds us, once described law clerks as "the lowest form of human life," and it appears he often treated them that way. But in the 1950s and 1960s, as he grew restless and wrote books and made public appearances, the clerks took on important duties, writing draft majority opinions and dissents. He could not have carried on as long as he did without these "low lifes."

In Bob O'Neil's vivid remembrance, we learn that in the early 1980s, depressed by his wife's death and dispirited by the Burger Court's conservative turn, Justice William Brennan Jr. told his clerks at a reunion that "I've had enough of this place" and would soon resign. The clerks rallied to his side "in his hour of need," O'Neil reports, and Brennan served for two decades more. It is easy to imagine that Brennan would have quit years earlier if not for his clerks.

Bennett Boskey recounts how Chief Justice Harlan Fiske Stone discussed with him the assignment of opinions to other justices—surely one of the most important powers of a chief justice. Stone's clerks also helped smooth out his opinion writing, which, Boskey diplomatically states, started out as "long and unwieldy—sometimes almost Germanic in appearance." Stone is certainly not the only justice whose writing has benefited from the scrutiny of clerks.

The clerks of Justice Harry Blackmun also played a significant role in his opinion writing, though not as important as some have claimed, in Randall Bezanson's view. Bezanson says he can read opinions from his term working for Blackmun "where I can remember typing many of the words myself," but he insists they were the ideas of the justice. He quotes Harold Koh, another Blackmun clerk, who put what is probably the most heroic and poetic gloss on the role of clerks ever, hoping to downplay their importance. Koh likened Blackmun's clerks to the students in Michelangelo's studio. "Michelangelo himself did not personally put paintbrush to canvas on all of these works," Koh said, "but they nevertheless all look like the work of Michelangelo for the simple reason that he set the tone."

But law clerks clearly do much more than imitate the brushstrokes of their master. Like many other justices, Wiley Rutledge felt isolated, so he looked to his clerks "to bridge the gap between the Court and the outside world." They gave him insights into the thinking of a new generation and considered him as something of a father figure.

Justice Thurgood Marshall, increasingly isolated as the Court turned right, depended heavily on his clerks for support, Deborah Rhode writes. They gave him emotional affirmation and even, at times, "reminded him when he went astray" from his deeply held views. His clerks also gently persisted over several years in trying to persuade him to change his practice of using the word "Negro" long after it had gone out of fashion. He finally switched to "Afro-American."

Justice Charles Whittaker, on the other hand, wrote his own opinions during his lackluster five years on the Court. Clerks performed research and occasionally wrote a draft, but they rarely recognized their words in any decisions he issued. "If there was any similarity between any draft that we might have submitted and the final one that came out from him," said Heywood Davis, "it was because it had the word 'a' or 'the' in it." Yet in one case discussed in the book, a clerk who encouraged Whittaker to take on Felix Frankfurter actually wrote a draft of a dissent that ended up persuading the Court vote to change course and rule 7–2 against Frankfurter's view.

On a smaller scale, we also learn in this volume that a clerk saved Justice Louis Brandeis from an embarrassing error about the then-new technology of television. In a draft of his dissent in *U.S. v. Olmsted,* Brandeis raised alarms about the expanding reach of government snooping on its citizens. He warned that with the advent of television, government could look into people's homes. With difficulty, clerk Henry Friendly, the future appellate judge, talked Brandeis out of that assertion.

Then there is the vivid image of a law clerk carrying the aging Brandeis up five flights of stairs when the elevator at his home was broken. Apart from that, however, Brandeis established the modern model for law clerks as highly professional and confidential aides.

But the essay on Brandeis's clerks illuminates another way in which Supreme Court law clerks are important. After their service to the justice, they fan out across academia and the legal world. Brandeis wanted his clerks to teach at major law schools or, as Thurgood Marshall urged his clerks decades later, to work for the public good. In this sense, a justice's law clerks extend and expand the justice's legacy collectively by espousing or exemplifying his or her values.

When Justice David Souter retired in June 2009, it was noteworthy that roughly half of his seventy-two law clerks had gone on to teaching positions, while many others were in government or public interest law positions. "The way a justice lives on is in his clerk family," Harvey Rishikof, law professor at the National War College, told me for an article on Souter's law clerks.

In a recent law review article, Rishikof and three other scholars argue that this legacy is another reason for studying Supreme Court law clerks. "They exert considerable influence on the legal profession and the law after their clerkships have ended," the article states. "Upon leaving the Court, former clerks find themselves in positions of power in government, private practice, or the academy and use those positions to transmit to others what they learned at the Court. The legal profession and, to a lesser extent, the general public thereby share vicariously in the law clerks' experiences. Above all, law students acquire their formative knowledge of the Court from former clerks or from other professors who have read the scholarship of those clerks. Through processes such as these, the clerks play a key role in communicating how the Supreme Court and, indeed, the judiciary as a whole work."[1]

Rishikof makes an important point. The clerks who contributed to this book have, by shedding light on their justices' clerk family, told us more of what we need to know about the Supreme Court. Any assessment of the modern Court would be woefully incomplete without acknowledging how truly important the law clerks are.

Note

1. William E. Nelson, Harvey Rishikof, I. Scott Messinger, and Michael Jo, "The Liberal Tradition of the Supreme Court Clerkship: Its Rise, Fall, and Reincarnation?" *Vanderbilt Law Review* 62, no. 6 (2009): 1751–52.

Survey of Threshold Interest in Forming and Joining an Association of Supreme Court Law Clerks

August 8, 1994

TO: ATTENDEES AT COCKTAIL PARTY
ABA CONVENTION, NEW ORLEANS

FROM: AD HOC ORGANIZING COMMITTEE
JACK MASON (REHNQUIST, O.T. '75)
BILL D'ZURILLA (WHITE, O.T. '82)

This first-time gathering of former clerks presents us with an opportunity to give some thought to forming an ongoing association of clerks. The ad hoc organizing committee is very interested in whether and to what extent, and in what form, interest exists in such an association. To that end, what follows are some preliminary thoughts and a few "market survey" questions designed to give some shape and direction to this idea.

Please put this questionnaire in your pocket and save it for the plane ride home—do not squander your valuable time at this, our first cocktail party! Mail or FAX your answers—confidentially—to the address/number on the last page. Thanks.

The Concept

The proposal is the creation of a voluntary, non-profit association whose membership is open to anyone who has been appointed to serve as a law clerk to a sitting or retired justice of the US Supreme Court.

Modest annual dues (perhaps alternatively a flat lifetime membership payment) would sustain the costs of start-up, administrative expenses, and the association's activities. The association's mission, by-laws, policies, activities, and expenditures would be established by an elected board of governors with, perhaps, a smaller executive director/administrator (initially, a part-time, contract position). Office space & access to equipment in a law firm could probably be arranged on a reasonable, commercial basis. A formal organizing committee would be formed to get the association from its initial stages through to the election of a board of governors.

On the assumption there is sufficient interest: volunteers for the formal organizing committee are welcome, certainly including those who have practice experience counseling non-profit associations.

A modest target for sending out the first membership solicitation: January 1, 1995; and for actual start-up: in time for next year's ABA in Chicago.

The Association's Possible Activities

Beginning with the core notion of the somewhat special "bond" among us, each of you could no doubt come up with an excellent short list of things the association could do. In perhaps no particular order of importance (or collective interest), here are some modest possible activities and collective benefits:

1. To just have fun. An excuse to give yearly continuity at the ABA to this first-time cocktail party; expandable, perhaps, into an annual dinner (brawl?) featuring Justice Scalia's terrific after-dinner jokes.

2. A newsletter offering pithy, want-to-read articles, insights, news, and short-takes concerning who's who and what's what in the wacky world of Supreme Court life—justices and would-be justices (and retired ones), the SG's office, the cert. petitions and the argued cases and the arguers and the amici. Also concerning some of the technical "stuff" like Court rule changes, proposed legislation, Court operations; the nomination and hearing process; current and former clerks and their professions and avocations; and an occasional piece reaching back into dark clerkship history. Also: perhaps a "classified" section—beach/mountain houses for rent; search for special practice tips; employment openings.

The newsletter could also be placed "on line" on one of the PC computer networks.

3. A comprehensive directory of all living and deceased Supreme Court clerks, with short bios. A directory could easily spawn sub-listings by, e.g., geographic area; law firm, corporation, or law school affiliation; specialized practice area. The directory, in turn, could become a useful reference within and without the profession.

4. Under careful control, the association could offer education, insight, and editorial views in its newsletter and/or speak through a formal policy committee, in a non-partisan manner, on issues related to the Court, e.g., it could educate the public on the pros and cons of videotaping oral arguments either for immediate public dissemination or merely for preservation for posterity.

5. Co-ordination, in varying possible degrees, with the activities of the Supreme Court Historical Society.

Questions re Expressions of Interest [1]

1. Your identity or characteristics—name, city/state, tele/fax #s, justice clerked for & year, current occupation, and if firm, size of firm.

2. As for joining the association (as outlined above) and paying modest annual dues,[2] I would . . .

_____ definitely sign up right away

_____ probably try it for a year

_____ wait & see

_____ probably not be interested

_____ think it is a waste of time

3. In short, my interest in an association is . . .

_____ positive

_____ lukewarm or neutral

_____ negative

4. If you checked POSITIVE above, check which of the 5 proposed activities most attracts your interest:

_____ annual drinks and dinner

_____ newsletter

_____ directory

_____ educational and editorial efforts

_____ working with the Supreme Court Historical Society

5. If you were LUKEWARM/NEUTRAL, briefly explain why:

6. If you were NEGATIVE, what turns you off? The idea or a particular activity?

7. Interested in serving on . . .

—organizational committee   yes   no   maybe

—board of governors   yes   no   maybe

8. Feel free to pen a closing comment or suggestion, here, on the back, or by separate letter or memo, including a proposed NAME of the association.

Source: William H. Rehnquist Papers, Box 144.

Notes

1. Information provided will not be publically disseminated, and will be used by the organizing committee solely for the purpose of determining whether and how to go forward. All completed questionnaires, with or without identity, will be destroyed as of the date the first solicitation letter goes out; if none, destruction will occur on or before June 1, 1995.

2. Circle what you think is acceptably "modest": $25   50   75   100   150   200 other: _____

Donald Cronson to William H. Rehnquist, December 9, 1975
—A Short Note on an Unimportant Memorandum

I herein set forth my recollection of the circumstances surrounding the composition of a memorandum ('the WHR Memorandum') entitled "A Random Thought on the Segregation Cases", and bearing the initials 'WHR' which is to be found in the papers of Justice Jackson. I am prompted to do so by the discussion of that subject contained in "Simple Justice" by Richard Kluger.

During the October Term 1952 of the US Supreme Court, when William Rehnquist and I were law clerks for Mr Justice Jackson, I prepared a memorandum ('the DC Memorandum') for Justice Jackson which is described on page 605 of Kluger's book. That memorandum espoused the position that *Plessy* v *Ferguson* had been wrongly decided, but that because of the importance of the institutions that had grown as a result of that decision, the Supreme Court should confine itself to a reversal of its prior decision, but leave to Congress the task of undoing those institutions.

I recall having discussed the thesis proposed in the DC Memorandum with Justice Jackson, and I believe that at least one such conversation took place after I had prepared, and he had read, that memorandum. I also recall Justice Jackson remarking that he personally was convinced of the merit of the position therein advocated, but doubted if the other members of the Court could be persuaded to follow such a course. The WHR Memorandum was prepared at Justice Jackson's request as a result of our discussion of the DC Memorandum. I have a faint recollection that Rehnquist participated in the discussion of the DC Memorandum and was present at the time that Justice Jackson requested preparation of a subsequent memorandum.

I do not recall why Justice Jackson requested that the WHR Memorandum be prepared. But one factor which may have been involved in the request for its preparation, and which may explain some of its content, was the renowned advocacy of Bill Rehnquist at the Court of Clerks (as we called our animated lunchtime meetings of all the Law Clerks).

No one has ever accused William H. Rehnquist of being afraid to defend an unpopular position. His is the sort of mind which dotes on opposition and adversity. It was entirely normal that he should challenge any position held sacred by his fellow law clerks, even if he agreed with that position. Since the principal doctrine upon which all other law clerks were united during October Term 1952 was the proposition that *Plessy v Ferguson* was wrongly decided, Bill Rehnquist defended the contrary position with gusto and cogency. His virtuoso performance on the Court of Clerks on the subject of *Plessy* may have led to composition of the WHR Memorandum. Perhaps Justice Jackson had heard of that performance from his colleagues on the Court; more probably he heard about it from me, or the other law clerks, or from Bill Rehnquist himself. The discussion of the DC Memorandum would have provided a logical occasion for a request that the noon hour rhetoric be put in memorandum form.

I have a clear recollection of the production of the WHR Memorandum. I interjected myself into its composition, thereby causing my colleague some annoyance. The topic of judicial restraint, to which most of the memorandum was devoted, was a favorite topic of Justice Jackson and both of his law clerks. And quite a lot of the memorandum is the result of my suggestions. (My first reaction, on having extracts from the memorandum read to me over transatlantic telephone almost 20 years after its composition[,] that it was "more my work than yours" was an exaggeration, though an honest one. It was attributable to the fact that the paragraph that was read to me contained an expression that I could positively identify even 20 years later as containing my "purple prose"—as I remarked to the reporter who read me the extract. It was the paragraph which asserted that if the Fourteenth Amendment did not enact Herbert Spencer, neither did it enact Myrdahl's *American Dilemma*. But if I was not the principal author of the memorandum, I did make a substantial contribution to it).

I cannot be completely sure that the facts were as I recall them simply because at a distance of 20 years it is easy for the human mind to confuse what he recalls and what he deduces on the basis of presently known facts and recollections. And I believe that just such a confusion occurred in the mind of William Rehnquist when asked about the WHR Memorandum during the proceedings which led to his confirmation. Since he believed in 1971 that the *Brown* case had been properly decided, his logical conclusion on being confronted with the WHR Memorandum was that it propounded an argument that he had been directed by Justice Jackson to propound. And in fact this deduction was correct. If, as Kluger asserts, Rehnquist further concluded that the memorandum was designed to set forth Justice Jackson's views at the time, that further conclusion was in error. But it was a trivial error, and an entirely honest one.

Addendum

In the footnote on pages 606–8 of his book Kluger raises three questions which are posed by the DC Memorandum. My responses to those questions are:

(1) Rehnquist failed to mention the first memo in his letter to the Senate because he did not remember it.

(2)(a) Jackson did not request two memos reaching opposite conclusions.

(b) Rehnquist deduced, rather than claimed, that the WHR Memorandum set forth Jackson's views. On seeing the Memorandum nineteen years after its composition, he deduced—correctly—that it was not a document which he had prepared for the purpose of setting forth his views. From which he concluded—incorrectly—that it was designed to set forth a point of view which was not Jackson's, and which may or may not have been Rehnquist's, but which Jackson "might use in conference when cases were discussed".

(3)Rehnquist did not mention my collaboration because he did not remember it.

Source: Donald Cronson to William H. Rehnquist, December 9, 1975. Rehnquist Papers, box 107.

RANDALL P. BEZANSON clerked for Judge Roger Robb of the United States Court of Appeals for the D.C. Circuit and Associate Justice Harry A. Blackmun of the United States Supreme Court. From 1972 to 1988 he was on the faculty at the University of Iowa College of Law, and from 1988 to 1994 he served as Dean of the Washington and Lee University School of Law. He returned to the University of Iowa in 1996, where he is presently the David H. Vernon Professor of Law. He is the author of *Art and Freedom of Speech; How Free Can Religion Be?;* and *How Free Can the Press Be?*

BENNETT BOSKEY clerked first for Second Circuit Court of Appeals Judge Learned Hand after graduating from Harvard Law School in 1939 and then served as a law clerk for Associate Supreme Court Justice Stanley Reed (October term 1940) and Chief Justice Harlan Fiske Stone (October terms 1941 and 1942). After a tour of duty with the United States Army during World War II, Boskey served as Deputy General Counsel at the United States Atomic Energy Commission before becoming a partner at the law firm Volpe Boskey & Lyons. Boskey served as Treasurer of the American Law Institute for thirty-four years, and since May 2010 he has been the Institute's Treasurer Emeritus. He is currently a solo practitioner in Washington, D.C.

JENNIE BERRY CHANDRA holds three degrees from Stanford University: a J.D., an M.A. in sociology, and a B.A. in information economics and policy. Chandra presently is Senior Counsel for Federal Policy at Windstream Communications.

JESSE H. CHOPER earned his LL.B. from the University of Pennsylvania School of Law before clerking for Chief Justice Earl Warren during October term 1960. Choper is currently the Earl Warren Professor of Public Law at the University of California, Berkeley School of Law, where he teaches, lectures, and writes on the U.S. Constitution. His publications include *Judicial Review and the National Political Process: A Functional Reconsideration of the Role of the Supreme Court* and *Securing Religious Liberty: Principles for Judicial Interpretation of the Religion Clauses.*

CLARE CUSHMAN is Director of Publications at the Supreme Court Historical Society and Managing Editor of the *Journal of Supreme Court History.* She is the editor and principal writer of *Supreme Court Decisions and Women's Rights: Milestones to Equality* and *The Supreme Court Justices: Illustrated Biographies, 1789–1993* as well as the author of *Courtwatchers: Eyewitness Accounts of Life on the Supreme Court.*

ALAN M. DERSHOWITZ, a graduate of Yale Law School, clerked for Judge David Bazelon of the United States Court of Appeals for the District of Columbia Circuit and United States Supreme Court Justice Arthur Goldberg before joining the faculty at Harvard Law School. A prolific author and lecturer, Dershowitz is currently the Felix Frankfurter Professor of Law at Harvard Law School.

BETH SEE DRIVER, a graduate of Roanoke College, is presently a third-year law student at George Mason Law School.

JOHN M. FERREN was a partner at the law firm of Hogan & Hartson before being appointed to the District of Columbia Court of Appeals in 1977. He is the author of *Salt of the Earth, Conscience of the Court: The Story of Justice Wiley Rutledge.*

ANDREW L. KAUFMAN is a graduate of Harvard Law School and a former law clerk for Associate Justice Felix Frankfurter. After several years in private practice, he started teaching at Harvard Law School in 1965. He is presently the Charles Stebbins Fairchild Professor of Law at Harvard Law School and the author of *Cardozo.*

TONY MAURO is Supreme Court correspondent for the *National Law Journal,* American Lawyer Media, *The BLT: The Blog of Legal Times,* law.com, and a new subscription newsletter, *Supreme Court Insider.* He has covered the Supreme Court for more than thirty years, first for Gannett News Service and *USA Today* and then, since January 2000, for *Legal Times,* which merged with the *National Law Journal* in 2009. He is the author of *Illustrated Great Decisions of the Supreme Court.*

DANIEL J. MEADOR is the James Monroe Professor of Law Emeritus at the University of Virginia and the former Dean of the University of Alabama School of Law. He clerked for Associate Justice Hugo Black during October term 1954. He is the author of *Mr. Justice Black and His Books,* the author or coauthor of eight other law-related books, and the author of three novels.

I. SCOTT MESSINGER is a graduate of Syracuse University College of Law. He is Chief Operating Officer of The Constitution Project, a nonpartisan legal think tank in Washington, D.C.

BRUCE ALLEN MURPHY is the Fred Morgan Kirby Professor of Civil Rights at Lafayette College in Easton, Pennsylvania. He is the author of *The Brandeis/Frankfurter Connection: The Secret Political Activities of Two Supreme Court Justices; Fortas: The Rise and Ruin of a Supreme Court Justice;* and *Wild Bill: The Legend and Life of William O. Douglas.*

ROBERT M. O'NEIL, a former law clerk to Associate Justice William J. Brennan Jr., began his teaching career at the University of California, Berkeley, Boalt Hall School of Law. The former President of the University of Wisconsin System and the University of Virginia, as well as the former Director of the Thomas Jefferson Center for the Protection of Free Expression in Charlottesville, Virginia, he is a Professor of Law Emeritus at the University of Virginia. He presently serves as the General Counsel of the American Association of University Professors and is a Senior Fellow of the Association of Governing Boards of Colleges and Universities. He is the author or coauthor of over a dozen books, most dealing with issues involving free speech and civil liberties.

TODD C. PEPPERS, a graduate of the University of Virginia School of Law, Emory University's Graduate School of Arts and Science, and Washington and Lee University, is the Henry H. and Trudye H. Fowler Associate Professor of Public Affairs at Roanoke College and a Visiting Professor of Law at the Washington and Lee University School of Law. He is the author of *Courtiers of the Marble Palace: The Rise and Influence of the Supreme Court Law Clerk* and the coauthor of *Anatomy of an Execution: The Life and Death of Douglas Christopher Thomas*.

CHARLES A. REICH clerked for Associate Justice Hugo Black during October term 1953 after graduating from Yale Law School. A former Professor at Yale Law School, he is the author of *The Greening of America* and *The Sorcerer of Bolinas Reef*.

DEBORAH L. RHODE, a graduate of Yale Law School, clerked for Associate Justice Thurgood Marshall during October term 1978 before beginning her academic career. She is presently the Ernest W. McFarland Professor of Law at Stanford Law School and the Director of the Stanford Center on the Legal Profession. She is a former President of the Association of American Law Schools, a former Chair of the American Bar Association's Commission on Women in the Profession, and the author or coauthor of over twenty books on legal ethics, leadership, and gender issues.

CRAIG ALAN SMITH earned his Ph.D. in political science and history from the University of Missouri at Kansas City. He is an Assistant Professor of history and political science at California University of Pennsylvania. He is the author of *Failing Justice: Charles Evans Whittaker on the Supreme Court*.

ARTEMUS WARD earned his Ph.D. in political science from the Maxwell School of Citizenship at Syracuse University. An Associate Professor in the Department of Political Science at Northern Illinois University, he is the author of *Deciding to Leave: The Politics of Retirement from the Unites States Supreme Court* and the coauthor, with David L. Weiden, of *Sorcerers' Apprentices: 100 Years of Law Clerks at the United States Supreme Court*.

J. HARVIE WILKINSON III, a graduate of the University of Virginia School of Law, clerked for Justice Lewis F. Powell Jr. and presently sits on the United States Court of Appeals for the Fourth Circuit. He is the author of *Harry Byrd and the Changing Face of Virginia Politics, 1945–1966; Serving Justice: A Supreme Court Clerk's View; From Brown to Bakke: The Supreme Court and School Integration, 1954–1978;* and *One Nation Indivisible: How Ethnic Separatism Threatens America.*

KEVIN J WORTHERN, after graduating from the Brigham Young University Law School, clerked for Judge Malcolm R. Wilkey of the United States Court of Appeals for the District of Columbia Circuit and Justice Byron R. White. He is presently the Hugh W. Colton Professor of Law and Advancement Vice President at Brigham Young University.